ARTIFICIAL INTELLIGENCE WITH UNCERTAINTY

Deyi Li and Yi Du

Tsinghua University
Beijing. China

Chapman & Hall/CRC
Taylor & Francis Group

Boca Raton   London   New York

Chapman & Hall/CRC is an imprint of the
Taylor & Francis Group, an **informa** business

Chapman & Hall/CRC
Taylor & Francis Group
6000 Broken Sound Parkway NW, Suite 300
Boca Raton, FL 33487-2742

© 2008 by Taylor & Francis Group, LLC
Chapman & Hall/CRC is an imprint of Taylor & Francis Group, an Informa business

No claim to original U.S. Government works
Printed in the United States of America on acid-free paper
10 9 8 7 6 5 4 3 2

International Standard Book Number-13: 978-1-58488-998-4 (Hardcover)

Visit the Taylor & Francis Web site at
http://www.taylorandfrancis.com

and the CRC Press Web site at
http://www.crcpress.com

Contents

Chapter 1 The 50-Year History of Artificial Intelligence 1

1.1 Departure from the Dartmouth Symposium 1
    1.1.1 Communication between Different Disciplines 1
    1.1.2 Development and Growth 3
1.2 Expected Goals as Time Goes On 4
    1.2.1 Turing Test 4
    1.2.2 Machine Theorem Proof 5
    1.2.3 Rivalry between Kasparov and Deep Blue 5
    1.2.4 Thinking Machine 6
    1.2.5 Artificial Life 7
1.3 AI Achievements in 50 Years 8
    1.3.1 Pattern Recognition 8
    1.3.2 Knowledge Engineering 10
    1.3.3 Robotics 11
1.4 Major Development of AI in the Information Age 12
    1.4.1 Impacts of AI Technology on the Whole Society 12
    1.4.2 From the World Wide Web to the Intelligent Grid 13
    1.4.3 From Data to Knowledge 14
1.5 The Cross Trend between AI, Brain Science and Cognitive Science 15
    1.5.1 The Influence of Brain Science on AI 15
    1.5.2 The Influence of Cognitive Science on AI 17
    1.5.3 Coming Breakthroughs Caused by Interdisciplines 18
References 18

Chapter 2 Methodologies of AI 21

2.1 Symbolism Methodology 21
    2.1.1 Birth and Development of Symbolism 21
    2.1.2 Predicate Calculus and Resolution Principle 24
    2.1.3 Logic Programming Language 26
    2.1.4 Expert System 28
2.2 Connectionism Methodology 30
    2.2.1 Birth and Development of Connectionism 30
    2.2.2 Strategy and Technical Characteristics of Connectionism 30
    2.2.3 Hopfield Neural Network Model 33
    2.2.4 Back-Propagation Neural Network Model 34
2.3 Behaviorism Methodology 35
    2.3.1 Birth and Development of Behaviorism 35
    2.3.2 Robot Control 36
    2.3.3 Intelligent Control 37

2.4   Reflection on Methodologies..38
References...39

Chapter 3   On Uncertainties of Knowledge 43

3.1   On Randomness 43
    3.1.1   The Objectivity of Randomness 43
    3.1.2   The Beauty of Randomness..46
3.2   On Fuzziness...47
    3.2.1   The Objectivity of Fuzziness...48
    3.2.2   The Beauty of Fuzziness 49
3.3   Uncertainties in Natural Languages 51
    3.3.1   Languages as the Carrier of Human Knowledge 51
    3.3.2   Uncertainties in Languages..52
3.4   Uncertainties in Commonsense Knowledge...............................54
    3.4.1   Common Understanding about Common Sense 54
    3.4.2   Relativity of Commonsense Knowledge 55
3.5   Other Uncertainties of Knowledge 57
    3.5.1   Incompleteness of Knowledge..57
    3.5.2   Incoordination of Knowledge...58
    3.5.3   Impermanence of Knowledge...58
References...60

Chapter 4   Mathematical Foundation of AI with Uncertainty 61

4.1   Probability Theory 61
    4.1.1   Bayes' Theorem 62
        4.1.1.1   Relationship and Logical Operation
                of Random Event..62
        4.1.1.2   Axiomization Definition of Probability 63
        4.1.1.3   Conditional Probability and Bayes' Theorem....64
    4.1.2   Probability Distribution Function 65
    4.1.3   Normal Distribution 67
        4.1.3.1   The Definition and Properties
                of Normal Distribution 67
        4.1.3.2   Multidimensional Normal Distribution 69
    4.1.4   Laws of Large Numbers and Central Limit Theorem.......70
        4.1.4.1   Laws of Large Numbers.......................................70
        4.1.4.2   Central Limit Theorem 71
    4.1.5   Power Law Distribution...73
    4.1.6   Entropy 74
4.2   Fuzzy Set Theory 76
    4.2.1   Membership Degree and Membership Function 76
    4.2.2   Decomposition Theorem and Expanded Principle.............78
    4.2.3   Fuzzy Relation 79
    4.2.4   Possibility Measure 81

4.3 Rough Set Theory 81
    4.3.1 Imprecise Category and Rough Set 82
    4.3.2 Characteristics of Rough Sets 84
    4.3.3 Rough Relations 86
4.4 Chaos and Fractal 89
    4.4.1 Basic Characteristics of Chaos 90
    4.4.2 Strange Attractors of Chaos 92
    4.4.3 Geometric Characteristics of Chaos and Fractal 93
4.5 Kernel Functions and Principal Curves 94
    4.5.1 Kernel Functions 94
    4.5.2 Support Vector Machine 97
    4.5.3 Principal Curves 100
References 104

Chapter 5 Qualitative and Quantitative Transform
               Model — Cloud Model 107

5.1 Perspectives on the Study of AI with Uncertainty 107
    5.1.1 Multiple Perspectives on the Study
          of Human Intelligence 107
    5.1.2 The Importance of Concepts in Natural Languages 110
    5.1.3 The Relationship between Randomness and Fuzziness
          in a Concept 110
5.2 Representing Concepts Using Cloud Models 112
    5.2.1 Cloud and Cloud Drop 112
    5.2.2 Numerical Characteristics of Cloud 113
    5.2.3 Types of Cloud Model 115
5.3 Normal Cloud Generator 118
    5.3.1 Forward Cloud Generator 118
    5.3.2 Contributions of Cloud Drops to a Concept 123
    5.3.3 Understanding the Lunar Calendar's Solar Terms
          through Cloud Models 124
    5.3.4 Backward Cloud Generator 125
    5.3.5 Precision Analysis of Backward Cloud Generator 132
    5.3.6 More on Understanding Normal Cloud Model 133
5.4 Mathematical Properties of Normal Cloud 138
    5.4.1 Statistical Analysis of the Cloud Drops' Distribution 138
    5.4.2 Statistical Analysis of the Cloud Drops'
          Certainty Degree 140
    5.4.3 Expectation Curves of Normal Cloud 142
5.5 On the Pervasiveness of the Normal Cloud Model 144
    5.5.1 Pervasiveness of Normal Distribution 144
    5.5.2 Pervasiveness of Bell Membership Function 145
    5.5.3 Significance of Normal Cloud 148
References 150

Chapter 6 Discovering Knowledge with Uncertainty
through Methodologies in Physics 153

6.1 From Perception of Physical World to Perception of Human Self 153
    6.1.1 Expressing Concepts by Using Atom Models................................154
    6.1.2 Describing Interaction between Objects by Using Field 155
    6.1.3 Describing Hierarchical Structure of Knowledge
        by Using Granularity 156
6.2 Data Field..158
    6.2.1 From Physical Field to Data Field 158
    6.2.2 Potential Field and Force Field of Data..160
    6.2.3 Influence Coefficient Optimization of Field Function 172
    6.2.4 Data Field and Visual Thinking Simulation..................................178
6.3 Uncertainty in Concept Hierarchy..182
    6.3.1 Discretization of Continuous Data 183
    6.3.2 Virtual Pan Concept Tree...186
    6.3.3 Climbing-Up Strategy and Algorithms..188
6.4 Knowledge Discovery State Space 196
    6.4.1 Three Kinds of State Spaces..196
    6.4.2 State Space Transformation 197
    6.4.3 Major Operations in State Space Transformation..........................199
References..200

Chapter 7 Data Mining for Discovering Knowledge with Uncertainty...........201

7.1 Uncertainty in Data Mining...201
    7.1.1 Data Mining and Knowledge Discovery 201
    7.1.2 Uncertainty in Data Mining Process 202
    7.1.3 Uncertainty in Discovered Knowledge..204
7.2 Classification and Clustering with Uncertainty......................................205
    7.2.1 Cloud Classification 206
    7.2.2 Clustering Based on Data Field...213
    7.2.3 Outlier Detection and Discovery Based on Data Field..................238
7.3 Discovery of Association Rules with Uncertainty 244
    7.3.1 Reconsideration of the Traditional Association Rules 244
    7.3.2 Association Rule Mining and Forecasting 247
7.4 Time Series Data Mining and Forecasting...253
    7.4.1 Time Series Data Mining Based on Cloud Models 255
    7.4.2 Stock Data Forecasting 256
References..269

Chapter 8 Reasoning and Control of Qualitative Knowledge 273

8.1 Qualitative Rule Construction by Cloud 273
    8.1.1 Precondition Cloud Generator and Postcondition
        Cloud Generator...273

      8.1.2   Rule Generator 276

      8.1.3   From Cases to Rule Generation 279

8.2   Qualitative Control Mechanism 280

      8.2.1   Fuzzy, Probability, and Cloud Control Methods 280

      8.2.2   Theoretic Explanation of Mamdani Fuzzy Control Method 289

8.3   Inverted Pendulum — an Example of Intelligent Control
with Uncertainty 291

      8.3.1   Inverted Pendulum System and Its Control.................................... 291

      8.3.2   Inverted Pendulum Qualitative Control Mechanism 292

      8.3.3   Cloud Control Policy of Triple-Link Inverted Pendulum 294

      8.3.4   Balancing Patterns of an Inverted Pendulum 302

References 312

Chapter 9   A New Direction for AI with Uncertainty 315

9.1   Computing with Words 316

9.2   Study of Cognitive Physics 320

      9.2.1   Extension of Cloud Model 320

      9.2.2   Dynamic Data Field 323

9.3   Complex Networks with Small World and Scale-Free Models 328

      9.3.1   Regularity of Uncertainty in Complex Networks 329

      9.3.2   Scale-Free Networks Generation 332

      9.3.3   Applications of Data Field Theory to Networked Intelligence 339

9.4   Long Way to Go for AI with Uncertainty 340

      9.4.1   Limitations of Cognitive Physics Methodology 340

      9.4.2   Divergences from Daniel, the Nobel Economics Prize Winner 340

References 342

Research Foundation Support 345

Index 347

Preface

It is said that there are three hard scientific questions that have not yet been well answered: the original source of life, the original source of the world, and the working mechanism of the human brain. This book is related to the third question by studying and exploring uncertainties of knowledge and intelligence during the human being's cognitive process. The authors pay particular attention to setting up models and experimental computations to deal with such uncertainties as well.

Why do humans have intelligence? How does the human brain work in daily life? As a result of human evolution, which may have taken billions of years for biology and hundreds of millions of years for humankind, the brain runs well in dealing with all kinds of uncertainty in sensation, perception, learning, reasoning, thinking, understanding, and action. Mysteries of the brain are studied by brain science, having achieved great success on molecule-level and cell-level research. However, there is still a long way to go to understand the cognitive functions of a brain as a whole. How can we understand the nonlinear function of a brain? How does the left brain (with the priority of logic thinking) cooperate with the right brain (with the priority of visual thinking)? We know very little about the working principles and scientific mechanisms of a brain today. A new direction for cognitive science is the interdisciplinary study by a diverse group of scientists, including biologists, psychologists, mathematicians, physicists, and computer scientists.

Knowledge representation is a fundamental issue in artificial intelligence (AI) study. Over the 50-year history of AI, it seems that people paid more attention to using symbolic representation and problem solving for simulation of human thinking. However, natural language is an essential tool for thinking in a brain. Human civilization comes from the history of humankind. Only because of the written natural language can human beings record the accumulation or knowledge of human history. The most important difference in intelligence between human beings and other life forms might be language. One of the most influential scientists in the past century, the so-called "father of the modern electronic computer," Dr. Von Neumann, after an in-depth study on the differences and similarities between the electronic computer and the human brain, asserted in his posthumous book *The Computer and the Brain*, "the thinking language for human beings is not mathematic language-like at all." We emphasize that one of the important perspectives for AI study should be directed to natural language, which is the carrier of knowledge and intelligence. A language concept expressed by the cloud model in this book contains uncertainty, and in particular, randomness and fuzziness and the correlation between them. With such a perspective, we are going to explore the AI with uncertainty in detail.

In the twenty-first century, information is becoming the leading industry in the global economy, and fast-developing information technology is drastically changing the global world, including the working mode and lifestyle of human beings. It is claimed that the knowledge age dominated by information technology is coming. While enjoying the

Internet technology and World Wide Web culture, we are also suffering from an information deluge. It is a good wish to mine the trustful and required information from such huge data, and mine the knowledge at multi-scales we have not discovered. From this perspective, we concentrate on the physical methods for data mining by use of the tools of cloud model, data field, and knowledge discovery state space in this book. Reasoning and control with uncertain knowledge are also given in an inverted pendulum example. What we have done in our research seems to develop a satisfying framework to show how the uncertainty AI expands and generalizes the traditional AI.

"Seeking unknown knowledge" and "seeking beauty" are the natural desires of human beings. How to understand the cognitive process of human beings, and how to explain and simulate human thinking with a "beautiful" theory is a challenging topic indeed. Due to the limit of the authors' academic and practical capabilities, the book is an exploration that inevitably contains some flaws and your help in pointing these out will be sincerely appreciated.

Readers of this book could be scholar researchers in the fields of cognitive science, brain science, artificial intelligence, computer science, or control theory, in particular research and development (R&D) personnel for natural language understanding, intelligent searching, knowledge engineering, data mining, and intelligent control. The book can also be used as a textbook or reference book for graduate students of relevant majors in colleges and universities. We hope more and more people will join us in discovering AI with uncertainty.

It is obvious that the development of a book of this scope needs the support of many people. We appreciate the stimulating and fruitful discussions with professors Shoujue Wang, Deren Li, Jiaguang Sun, Ruqin Lu, Yixin Zhong, and Jianmin Wang. Special thanks go to the graduate students: Wenyan Gan, Changyu Liu, Guisheng Chen, Ning Zhou, Hui Chen, Baohua Cao, Mi Tian, Zhihao Zhang, who did a very good job related to this book under the supervision of the first author. We would like to express our gratitude to Huihuan Qian, Ka Keung Lee, Meng Chen, and Zhi Zhong at the Chinese University of Hong Kong who spent numerous hours reviewing the final manuscript and providing us with valuable comments and assistance. The first author would also like to take this opportunity to thank Professor Yangsheng Xu for his long-term support, encouragement, and friendship that made his time in the Chinese University of Hong Kong more interesting and meaningful. Thanks go to the readers of the Chinese version of this book published in China two years ago who offered helpful comments for the English version. We also wish to acknowledge all the reviewers and editors for their contributions.

This book could not have happened without the support from our funding sources. The research and development work described in this book is partially supported by grants from the National Nature Science Foundation, China (Projects No. 69272031, 69775016, 69975024, 60375016, and 60496323), and by national 973 and 863 programs (Projects No. G1998030508-4, 2004CB719401, and 863-306-ZT06-07-02).

We are grateful to all who have extended care and support to us during the production of this book.

Deyi Li

Yi Du

About the Authors

Deyi Li, Ph.D., was born in 1944 in Jiangsu, China. He earned his Ph.D. in computer science at Heriot-Watt University in Edinburgh, United Kingdom in 1983. He was elected a member of the Chinese Academy of Engineering in 1999 and a member of the Eurasian Academy of Sciences in 2004. At present, he is a professor at Tsinghua University and director of the Department of Information Science at the National Natural Science Foundation of China, and vice president of the Chinese Institute of Electronics and the Chinese Association of Artificial Intelligence. He has published more than 100 papers on a wide range of topics in artificial intelligence. His other books include: *A Prolog Database System*, and *A Fuzzy Prolog Database System*.

Yi Du, Ph.D., was born in 1971 in Shan'xi, China. He earned his Ph.D. in computer science at PLA University of Science and Technology in Nanjing, China in 2000. He received his undergraduate degree from Nanjing Institute of Communications Engineering in 1993. At present, he is a senior engineer in a network management center in Beijing.

1 The 50-year History of Artificial Intelligence

During the Industrial Revolution in the nineteenth century, machines were employed to take over or reduce the routine functions of human physical labor, which consequently pushed forward science and technology greatly. The information technology in the twentieth century, especially with the advent of the computer, gave birth to and spurred the development of artificial intelligence (AI), and thus machines are able to take over or diminish the routine uses of human mental labor.

By AI we mean a variety of intelligent behaviors and various kinds of mental labor, known as mental activities, can be realized artificially with some sort of real machines.[1] These intelligent activities include perception, memory, emotion, judgment, reasoning, proving, identification, understanding, communication, designing, thinking and learning, etc.

Since ancient times, humans have been dreaming of intelligence by artificial means to explore and invent tools to free themselves from physical and mental labor. Evidence of AI folklore can be traced back to ancient Egypt in the 200s BC. There lived a man named Hero in the city of Alexandria. He invented a number of automatic machines to ease people's toil. His inventions were then used to demonstrate the power of God in sacrifice. When the sacrificial fire was lit, the gate opened automatically, and then two bronze priests standing on the sacrificial altar raised their sacrificial pots to pour holy water onto the fire. The worshippers were able to obtain the needed holy water automatically by inserting coins into the slit.[2]

If this kind of automation was regarded as intelligence, its connotation and denotation have been extended considerably ever since. If we trace back to the time when AI was first introduced academically, we cannot help mentioning the Dartmouth Symposium.

1.1 DEPARTURE FROM THE DARTMOUTH SYMPOSIUM

1.1.1 COMMUNICATION BETWEEN DIFFERENT DISCIPLINES

In June 1956, at Dartmouth, New Hampshire, four young scholars: John McCarthy (Figure 1.1), Marvin Minsky, Nathaniel Rochester, and Claude Shannon jointly initiated and organized the Dartmouth Symposium, which lasted for two months, on simulating human intelligence using a machine. Ten scholars from various fields such as mathematics, neurophysiology, psychiatry, psychology, information theory, and computer science were invited to the symposium. From their own interdisciplinary perspectives and backgrounds, they presented different arguments and gave rise to violent clashes of ideas.

1

FIGURE 1.1 John McCarthy (1927—).

Three events were highlighted in the Dartmouth Symposium: the neural network simulator demonstrated by Marvin Minsky, the searching method proposed by John McCarthy, and the "Logic Theorist" presented by Herbert Simon and Allen Newell. They discussed how to go through a maze, how to do search reasoning and how to prove a mathematic theorem, respectively.[3]

While working on the psychological process of proving a mathematic theorem by humans, Herbert Simon and his colleagues found a common law. First, the entire problem is broken down into several subproblems, then these subproblems are solved using substitution and replacement methods in accordance with the stored axioms and proven theorems. Based on this, they established the "heuristic search" technique for machines to prove mathematic theorems. And they did prove a number of theorems from chapter 2 of *Principia Mathematica*, a masterpiece in mathematics cowritten by B. Russell and A. N. Whitehead, using the program "Logic Theorist." Their work was highly appraised and regarded as a major breakthrough in computer simulation of human intelligence.[4,5]

Although the scientists had different perspectives, all of them converged on the study of the representative form and cognitive law governing human intelligence. Making full use of the accomplishments in symbolic logic and computer, they provided the theory of the formalization of computation and processing, simulated a number of basic ways and techniques of human intelligent behaviors, and created a few artificial systems with some sort of intelligence, which enable the computer to do a job that could be accomplished only by human intelligence.

At the Dartmouth Symposium, John McCarthy proposed the term "artificial intelligence" (AI) as the name of the cross-discipline. This conference of great historic significance was the first symposium on AI in human history, marking the birth of AI as a new discipline. Therefore, John McCarthy was referred to as the "Father of AI."[3]

Evidence shows that decades after the Dartmouth Symposium, many of its participants became experts in this field and stood in the vanguard of AI progress. John McCarthy, Allen Newell and Herbert Simon all are recipients of Turing Awards. Simon was also awarded a Nobel Prize in Economics.[3] The Dartmouth Symposium was the first significant event in the history of AI.

1.1.2 DEVELOPMENT AND GROWTH

Since its birth, AI has aroused fantastic imaginations and great expectations among people and has served as a brilliant goal in the development of discipline crossing.

In 1969, the first session of the International Joint Conference on AI (IJCAI) was convened. Since then, IJCAI has been held every two years and has become a top academic conference on AI. In 1970, the first issue of the *International Journal of AI* was published, and it has since ranked first among all the academic journals on AI. The American Association for Artificial Intelligence (AAAI) was founded in 1976. Up to 2006, twenty-one national conferences on AI had been convened. The association is very active, releasing its AI magazines periodically and holding various kinds of symposiums annually. All these events have played a guiding role for academic activities and worldwide exchanges, and they have enhanced research and development (R&D) of AI. In China, the Chinese Association for Artificial Intelligence (CAAI) was established in 1981 and ten conferences were held. In 1989, the China Joint Conference on Artificial Intelligence (CJCAI) took place, and up till now, seven conferences have been held. In 2006, CAAI had a set of activities for AI's 50-year anniversary.

Today, AI is increasingly popular. Intelligent economy, intelligent machines, intelligent communities, intelligent networks, and intelligent buildings are seen everywhere. In almost every university, there are colleges and disciplines conducting related research on AI. However, the development of AI has not shaped up smoothly, and collision, controversy, and misunderstanding still exist from time to time.

In the early 1980s, mathematic logic and symbolic reasoning became mainstream in the field of AI and logic programming languages such as Lisp and Prolog were a big hit throughout the world. At the beginning of the Japanese Fifth Generation Computer Systems, some knowledge information processing systems pushed the AI research to a new stage. However, the much-expected "Fifth Generation Computer" ended up in failure. It did not go beyond the structural framework of the Von Neumann system and still worked by means of program and data. As a result, it was unable to realize human–machine interaction through image, sound, and language in a natural way, not to mention simulating human thinking processes.

Research on neural networks (NNs) had also boosted AI development to a new high level. In the early 1940s, the method of NN was proposed, later rejected, and then proposed again. In 1982, John J. Hopfield suggested using hardware to realize the artificial neural network (ANN) (Hopfield Neural Network).[6] In 1986, David E. Rumelhart and others put forward the back propagation (BP) algorithm of multilayered networks, which became a milestone in AI development.[7] At that time, machines were expected to process information in the form of "thinking in images," and they were as well expected to simulate human visualization, instinct and common sense through biology NN model, artificial neuron model, typical training algorithm and excitation function. Nevertheless, the achievements were far from expectation, although the research passion on ANNs remained high.

In the 1970s, AI, space technology, and energy technology were regarded as the three top technologies in the world. In the new century, with information technology (IT) extensively penetrating into economy, society, and everyday life, there is an increasingly urgent demand for machine to simulate human intelligence. Now, people begin to question the simulation of the human brain by the Von Neumann computer as the "electric brain," and search for new structures like quantum computers. They put the study of AI in a broader scope of disciplines such as cognition science, brain science, information theory, bionics, psychology, linguistics, and philosophy.

1.2   EXPECTED GOALS AS TIME GOES ON

Looking back at the 50-year AI development and growth, the academic society has held various views on what goals AI research is going to achieve.

1.2.1 TURING TEST

In 1950, Alan Turing (Figure 1.2), a British mathematician, proposed a test standard called "Turing Test," with the aim to determine whether a machine had human intelligence.[3,5] It has been acknowledged by most people. The standard states that, if the action, reaction, and interaction of a machine are the same as a human being with consciousness, then it should be regarded as having consciousness and intelligence. In order to eliminate bias in the test, Turing uses an imitation method. A human interrogator, who was separated from other humans, asked various questions to two other parties, one human and the other a machine. In a given period of time, the interrogator had to guess which is the human and which is the machine based on the answers to his questions. A series of such tests were designed to test the level of AI of the machine.

People differed in their views as to whether the test standard has been met within the past 50 years.

At the beginning, the test subject was an electrograph. It gave answers in the form of typewritten words so that it was hard to tell whether the answers had come from the human or the machine. In this sense, the machine could be said to possess AI.

But some scholars argued that the intelligence of the machine was still a far cry from that of a human being. Let's imagine a machine engaged in a natural language conversation. No matter how smart it is, the machine cannot have the same

FIGURE 1.2 Alan Turing (1912–1954).

commonsense knowledge as a person, nor can it have correct pronunciation, intonation, and emotion. It is also not resourceful enough to cope with situations arising in the process of the conversation. In this sense, the machine can hardly be said to have any human intelligence, even that of a child.

Others have reproached the test standard, saying that there are too many uncertainties in the description and the constraint conditions cannot be well defined, that people should not be confined to the test standard, and that essential intelligence should be everywhere and should serve the people without their ever knowing it. Essential intelligence should be in harmony with the people and be human oriented. AI requirements on a machine may vary and grow as time goes on.

1.2.2 MACHINE THEOREM PROOF

Mathematics has long been crowned as the queen of science. As the basis for the most extensive disciplines, it mainly emphasizes number and shape. As a typical kind of mental labor, mathematics is characterized by preciseness in expression and convenience to be formalized. Therefore, theorem proof by machine became the first target of scientists in pursuit of AI. In the field of mathematics, while seeking proof for a known theorem, a mathematician is not only required to have the ability of deducing a hypothesis, but is also required to have intuition. In theorem proof, a mathematician will adroitly exploit the rich professional knowledge, guess which lemma to prove first, decide precisely which theorems to utilize, divide the main problem into several subproblems, and finally solve them one by one. If you can turn these tricky and difficult behaviors into sophisticated but easy mechanical calculations on a computer, you have already mechanized mental labor. Much progress has been made in this aspect.[1,8,9]

Generally speaking, the hypothesis and the conclusion of a theorem will be transferred into a system of polynomial equations and a polynomial equation, respectively. So it will become a pure algebraic calculus, i.c., how to get the result polynomial from the hypothesis polynomials. In particular, a mention should be made to the outstanding contributions made by the two Chinese scholars Professor Hao Wang and Professor Wenjun Wu in this direction.[8]

Deep research in theorem proof has led to the predicate logic language, expert systems, and knowledge engineering to help people solve problems in specific knowledge domains such as chemical and mineral analysis, medical diagnosis, and information retrieving. The authors themselves have conducted research on the equivalence between relational database querying and predicate logic proof.[10]

1.2.3 RIVALRY BETWEEN KASPAROV AND DEEP BLUE

Playing chess is considered a typical mental activity. In the year after the Dartmouth Symposium, research on chess played by computer against humans was carried out throughout the world. The history of chess playing (human vs. machine), to some extent, is the history of AI development and growth.

In 1956, Arthur Samuel of the IBM Corp. wrote a self-learning, adaptive checker program. Just like any other checker player, the computer checker player can not only see several moves ahead, but also learn from checker manuals. The computer

FIGURE 1.3 Garry Kasparov (1963—).

analyzed about 175,000 possible processes before it made a move. In 1958, an IBM704 became the first computer to play against humans, with a speed of 200 moves per second. In 1988, the Deep Thought computer defeated the Danish master player Bent Larsen, with an average speed of two million moves per second. In 1997, Deep Blue, a chess-playing computer, shocked the world with the results of two wins, three draws, and one defeat in matches against the reigning World Chess Champion Garry Kasparov (Figure 1.3) by using the "heuristic search" technique. Its speed then was two million moves per second. In 2001, the German "Deep Fritz" chess-playing computer defeated nine of the ten top chess players in the world, with a record-breaking speed of six million moves per second. Faced with successive victories made by the computer, people could not help asking: now that the world's chess champions are defeated, who can say that the computer is not intelligent?

From the perspective of AI, machine vs. human is in essence a way for scientists to demonstrate AI. In problems with similar property and complexity as chess playing, computers can be considered intelligent. When playing against humans, computers take advantage of reasoning and speed and focus more on logical thinking, while human brains may rely more on intuition, imagination, and brand new tactics and strategies, focusing more on thinking in images. The nature of machine vs. human is "human plus machine vs. machine plus human," i.e., the computer is acting onstage while humans are backstage or vice versa. A team of experts in their specific fields store in advance huge numbers of setups and strategies before the computer onstage can examine and evaluate moves or decide the appropriate response by means of complicated calculation and analysis. On the other side, top human players can enhance their techniques by interacting with computer players and find the weakness of intelligent computers. In some sense, the rivalry between human and machine is an endless process. Statistically speaking, the result may be a draw, fifty–fifty somewhat.

1.2.4 THINKING MACHINE

At the beginning, people called a computer an "electric brain," expecting that it would become a thinking machine. However, all existing computers differ considerably from the human brain in internal structure. The computer has experienced tremendous development from electric tube, transistor, and integrated circuit (IC) to very large-scale integrated circuit, making great progress in many aspects, e.g., performance and craftsmanship, central processing unit (CPU) speed, storage capacity, IC density and bandwidth for communication. Although, in every respect above, the development speed obeys the Moore's law or even faster, there is still no breakthrough in the Turing machine principle at all. And the computer is still constructed within the framework of the Von Neumann architecture. On the other hand, large numbers of intelligent software enable small-sized and miniaturized computers, even the embedded computers, to acquire more intelligent behaviors akin to humans, such as cognition, recognition, and automatic processing. With speedy advances made in pattern recognition, including image recognition, speech recognition, and character recognition, the computer has obtained some extremely intelligent behavior to a certain point. Such behaviors include self-learning, self-adaptation, self-optimizing, self-organizing, and self-repairing, etc.

To enrich the thinking ability of the machine, people have developed many kinds of perceptive machines, recognizing machines, and behavioral machines. Through perception, learning and understanding characters, images, voices, speeches, behaviors, and through information exchange with humans, the machines have raised their intellectual level. These machines include engineering sensors, intelligent instruments, character readers, manipulators, intelligent robots, natural language composers, and intelligent controllers, etc.

To sum up, the objective of research on the thinking machine is to enable a computer to think as a human being and to interact in harmony with humans.

1.2.5 ARTIFICIAL LIFE

Life is the foundation of intelligence. A long time ago, there was no life at all on Earth. It took billions of years for life to appear, and once it did it evolved slowly — from single cells to multicellular organisms, from simple life forms to complex animals, eventually giving birth to humankind. However, it has not been clear what the original source of human beings is. Is it possible to create a life from dead material? Can an artificial material make an essential life? Many scientists tried to work out this puzzle.

In the middle of the twentieth century, Alan Turing and Von Neumann tried to describe the logical specification of self-reproducing life. In the 1970s, Chris Langton discovered the fact that life or intelligence may come from the edge of chaos. His idea is to set up a group of rules for the edge of chaos. This kind of life is quite different from the life based on carbohydrates and was named artificial life since then, such as computer virus, cell automation, etc.

In 1987, at the Los Alamos National Laboratory, the first symposium on artificial life was held. Among the 160 participants were life scientists, physiologists, physicists, and anthropologists. At the symposium, the concept of artificial life was proposed and the direction for imitating natural life was pointed out. It was agreed that artificial life is a man-made system to showcase the behavioral features of natural life. Life as we know it is the classical subject of biology, whereas life as it could be is a new subject of AI. Self-reproduction and evolution are two important features of life. Creatures on earth are but one form of life. Entities with life features can be made artificially, and research can be conducted based on computers or other intelligent machines. That research includes the following subjects: life self-organization and self-replication, growth and mutation, systems with complexity, evolution and adaptive dynamics, intelligent agents, autonomic systems, robots, and artificial brains.

At present, virtual artificial lives mainly refer to digital lives by computer software and virtual computer technology, such as artificial fish and virtual TV anchorman. Artificial life entities are mainly physical beings and tangible artificial life forms, such as robots and machine cats designed and constructed with computer technology, automation, and photoelectricity.

Can artificial life be realized? Darwin's Theory of Evolution has solved the problems of evolution and the origin of species, leaving the problem of the origin of life unsolved. Research on artificial life may hold the solution to this issue. But so far, there has been no major breakthrough.[11,12]

1.3 AI ACHIEVEMENTS IN 50 YEARS

The contributions that AI has made to computer science and even to the entire information science can be best illustrated by the number of AI experts receiving Turing Awards which include Marvin Minsky in 1969, John McCarthy in 1971, Herbert Simon and Allen Newel in 1975, Edward Albert Feigenbaum and Raj Reddy in 1994. They have all made remarkable contributions in their respective fields, each with a success story to tell and to be admired.

How AI has pushed forward science and technology and social developments can also be seen from the extensive AI applications in IT. With the emergence of various opinions, AI has become a garden with a blaze of colors. This encouraging situation can be expounded from a variety of perspectives. After careful analysis, we deem it most suitable to look in retrospect at the three areas, i.e., pattern recognition, knowledge engineering, and robotics.

1.3.1 PATTERN RECOGNITION

Pattern recognition used to be a discipline that ran parallel to AI. In recent decades, it has gradually been infused into AI and become its core content. Remarkable progress has been made in pattern recognition.

The English word "pattern" comes from the French "patron," which means a model or perfect example. The phrase "pattern recognition" has extensive meaning and usually is in the physical form of entities, e.g., sound wave, cardiogram, photo, image, character, symbol, 3-D objects, scenery, etc. Patterns can be gathered and measured with physical, chemical, or biological sensors. When observing and recognizing an object or a phenomenon, people often extract its similarities to or differences from other objects or phenomena. These similarities and differences, or patterns, are then classified, clustered into different types. This human thinking ability constitutes the ability of pattern recognition. Patterns are closely linked with classification. Recognition is closely linked with uniqueness. The results of decision-making, whether correct or incorrect, are relative rather than absolute. All of this makes up the basic content of research on pattern recognition.[13,14,15]

Early research on computer pattern recognition focused on modeling. In late 1950s, Frank Rosenblatt proposed a simplified mathematical model—perceptron,[13,15,16] imitating the recognition process of the human brain. Perceptron was trained to learn how to classify unclassified patterns according to patterns that had already been classified.[13,17,18] In the 1960s, the statistical approach in pattern recognition was greatly advanced. In the 1970s, a series of works on this approach was published. In the 1980s, John Hopfield revealed the association, storage, and computational power of ANNs, providing a new approach to pattern recognition and pointing out a new direction for the study of pattern recognition through ANNs.[13,14,15]

With pervasive applications of IT, there is a tendency for pattern recognition to be diversified and varied, and pattern recognition research can be conducted on various levels of granularities. The trendiest one is the pattern recognition of biological features, including speech recognition, character recognition, image recognition, and profile recognition. For example, IBM speech recognition software, ViaVoice®, can learn the speech sound features of the speaker through training and constant self-correction during the process of actual use. As a result, the recognition rate can be improved up to 90%, thus greatly facilitating word input. Another excellent example of pattern recognition is Chinese character recognition technology. So much progress has been made that not only can the meaning of the character be recognized, but also the character in different writing styles can be recognized as well. Printed characters can be recognized, so can handwritten characters. Nowadays in China, Chinese character recognition tools, like HWPen and Shangshu, have moved a big step forward toward commercialization. A product can create a company, even an industry. One more example is the recognition of gesture language used by the deaf–mute as an important means of communication. Gesture language recognition is exploited to put gestures into words or sounds through gesture modeling, language modeling and appropriate search algorithm so as to enable the deaf–mute to communicate with normal people in an easier and quicker way. Still one more example is image matching technique of targeted objects. This technique can be used to control and guide missiles toward heat sources of attacked targets. In so doing, it can even change the patterns of war. With the extensive use of multimedia data, there is a need for multilingual recognition, musical sound recognition, and dialect recognition to retrieve phonetically relevant information. Moreover, cross-race recognition, sex recognition, and facial expression recognition are exploited to retrieve the desired human face characteristics.

With dramatically increasing demand for security information, biological identity recognition technology has become popular, including technologies such as fingerprint/palm-print recognition, facial recognition, signature recognition, iris recognition, and human posture recognition. Identity recognition has become an important means to ensure financial safety and social security. Image division, feature extraction, classification, clustering, and model matching play important roles in identity recognition. Other employed techniques are wavelet transform, fuzzy clustering, genetic algorithms, Bayesian theory, and supporting vector machine. For instance, identity recognition through fingerprints has been extensively used by the police and customs officials. Signature recognition is becoming an important security measure to secure the smooth operation of E-finance and E-business.

1.3.2 Knowledge Engineering

The rapid development of the AI discipline urgently called for its application in practical projects. Francis Bacon, a British philosopher, had the famous statement, "knowledge is power," and Edward Feigenbaum, the promoter of knowledge engineering, pointed out that, "in knowledge lies power" and "computer is an amplifier of such power." At the Fifth International AI Conference held in 1971, he elaborated on knowledge engineering in his speech entitled "The Art of AI: Themes and Case Studies of Knowledge Engineering."[19] Since then the term "knowledge engineering" has spread to every corner of the world.[20,21]

Knowledge engineering is a discipline concerned with how to use AI and software engineering to design, construct, and maintain knowledge systems. Its research content covers such areas as related theories and technology, methods and tools.[20,22]

In 1968, Edward Feigenbaum, a knowledge engineering expert, led his research group in successfully making the first expert system DENDRAL for a mass spectrometer to analyze the molecular structure of organic chemical compounds.[23] It picked the correct result out of thousands of possible molecular structures based on known molecular formula and mass spectrograph of the organic chemical compounds. Again in 1976, they successfully developed a medical expert system MYCIN to help doctors diagnose infectious diseases and give advice on treatment with antibiotics.[24] Since the 1980s, the number of expert systems has dramatically increased and their applications have extended to such areas and departments as tax revenue, customs, agriculture, mining, civil aviation, medicine, and finance.

Natural language understanding represented by machine translation is a shining example to showcase the significant achievements made in knowledge engineering in the past 30 years or so. Beginning from the Fifth International AI Conference held in 1977, the number of treatises on natural language understanding always stood at the top at all the international AI conferences.[20]

The focus of natural language understanding by computer is on how to use a computer to process, understand, and generate various natural languages familiar to humans so that the machine can communicate with people through these natural languages. The research covers such areas as lexical analysis, syntax analysis, grammatical analysis, semantics analysis, contextual analysis, phrase structure grammar, case grammar, and language data bank linguistics, computing linguistics, computational linguistics, intermediate language, and translation assessment.[25]

The research on natural language understanding has gone through three phases. The earlier phase was built on the analysis of word order and parts of speech, the main stream being keywords matching technology. In the middle phase, concepts of semantics, pragmatics and context were introduced, with the focus on syntax-semantics analysis. At present, it is mainly concerned with practicality in specific fields and its engineering development. A number of commercialized machine translation systems and natural language man–machine interfaces have entered the world market and been industrialized to a considerably large scale. Machine translation systems have become a necessity in daily office work, automatic abstract generators are widely used, and limited natural language control systems can be seen everywhere.[25,26]

With the extensive use of database and networks, people are flooded in magnanimity data, though still thirsty for knowledge. Data authenticity and security have become a major concern. However, people's quest for knowledge has made it possible for data mining (DM) to grow up quickly in the field of knowledge engineering. The term "data mining" made its first appearance in 1989 at the 11th International Joint Conference on Artificial Intelligence held in Detroit, Michigan. At first, it was called "knowledge discovery in database (KDD)," which the author of this book used as the title of the research project to apply for the 1993 National Nature Science Fund. After 1996, general consensus was gradually reached on the use of DM, which means the process of digging up valid, up-to-date and potentially useful knowledge that is friendly to people and can be understood by machine as well.[27] Up till now, such mining objects and mining tools as DM, document mining, voice mining, image mining, Web mining have become popular in the information age, with related works and reference books available everywhere. The symposium on KDD, first initiated by the American Association for Artificial Intelligence in 1989, was augmented to an annual activity. After 1995, ten symposiums have been convened. Competitions were organized and awards were given. For example, the KDD Gold Cup was won by MEDai from Orlando, Florida in 2004. It should be particularly pointed out that, from the very beginning, DM was application oriented. IBM, GTE, Microsoft, Silicon Graphics, Integral Solutions, Thinking Machine, DataMind, Urban Science, AbTech, Unica Technologies successively developed some practical KDD business systems like BehaviorScan, Explorer, MDT (Management Discovery Tool) for market analysis, Stock Selector, AI (Automated Investor) for financial investment, and Falcon, FAIS, CloneDetector for fraud warning.[28]

1.3.3 ROBOTICS

Research on robots began with the manipulator, which was a machine capable of imitating human behavior. It was a combination of mechanical structures, sensor technologies, and AI. The first generation of remote-controlled manipulator was made in 1948 at the Argonne National Laboratory. Seventeen years later, the first industrial robot was born. Its operational process could be easily changed through programming. In the 1960s, many scholars from the United States and England regarded robots as carriers of AI, and conducted research on how to equip robots with the ability of environment recognition, problem solving and planning. In the 1980s, the industrial robot industry took a great leap forward. Robots for spot welding, arc welding, spraying, loading and unloading were primarily used in the auto industry. During the 1990s, assembly machines and soft assembling technology also entered a stage of rapid progress.[29] Now we have robots all around us, doing a lot of repetitive, boring, or dangerous work. It is estimated that there are one million robots in the world so far.

Research on robots has gone through three generations. The first generation is programmable robots. They usually "learn" to work in the following two ways: controlled by preset programs or by the "demonstration-repeating" method, in which robots learn from repeated demonstrations before they can perform their duty in the order demonstrated. When there is a change in the task or in the environment, demonstrations are needed again. Programmable robots can work at the lathe, the furnace, the welder, and the assembly line. Current robots commercialized for practical applications fall into this category. As they have no perception ability, they can only accomplish their jobs inflexibly as programmed without being able to function in the changed environment. The second generation is self-adaptive robots with corresponding sensors, such as vision sensors, to obtain simple information from their surroundings. Their actions are analyzed, processed, and controlled by the computer built inside, and consequently they can be adaptive to small changes of the object. The third generation is distributed and coordinated smart robots, which have more intelligence akin to humans. As they are equipped with various types of sensors for vision, hearing, and touching, they can perceive multidimensional information on a number of platforms. These robots are highly sensitive in the fact that they can precisely perceive information of the surroundings, analyze it in real-time and coordinate their various kinds of actions. They also have a certain degree of learning ability to deal with changes in the environment and interact with other robots for accomplishment of various complicated and difficult tasks. The Robot World Cup held yearly has greatly enhanced the research on the third-generation robots. Nevertheless, these robots have only limited intelligence, and there is still a long way to go before artificial life and natural intelligence can be realized. Robot vision and communication with natural language remain two problems to be solved.[30,31]

1.4 MAJOR DEVELOPMENT OF AI IN THE INFORMATION AGE

1.4.1 IMPACTS OF AI TECHNOLOGY ON THE WHOLE SOCIETY

AI impact can be measured by answering the following two questions:

1. Are AI products useful to society?
2. How many products come from the implementations and realizations of AI?

In industry, especially in the manufacturing sector, successfully implemented AI technologies include intelligent design, virtual production, soft production, agile production, on-line analysis, intelligent workflow, simulation and planning, etc. All these have considerably increased production efficiency.

AI has exerted tremendous impact on economy and finance through extensive use of expert systems. It is estimated that more one billion U.S. dollars are saved throughout the world due to the implementation of this technology. For example, shareholders use AI systems to help analyze, determine, and decide buying and selling shares. Credit card fraud detection systems are widely used as well.

AI has already infiltrated into our daily lives, including education, medical care, and telecommunications. The great changes brought about by AI technologies can be easily seen and felt. AI has enabled computers to have a variety of flexible and friendly interfaces, and to communicate with people more easily and naturally. The intellectualization and automation of domestic appliances with embedded computers is freeing people from trivial household chores. AI technologies are helping people with their medical care and children's education. They are helping people find real and useful information from the vast sea of the Internet. They have changed the traditional means of communication. Voice dialing and handwritten text messages have endeared people who are engaged in communication. Moreover, the intelligent mobile phone becomes increasingly friendly and personal, featuring more and more smart functions.

AI has impacted the cultural life and entertainment, leading people to think more deeply in spiritual and philosophical ways. From the *Terminator* movie series starred by Arnold Schwarzenegger, *The Matrix* starred by Keanu Reeves, to *A.I. Artificial Intelligence* directed by Steven Spielberg, they have all raised the same questions although through different stories: How to deal with AI? How to deal with machines with intelligence? Will they some day outdo humans in intelligence? The answers may vary, but the popularity of these movies not only reflects the pleasure people get from AI, but it also shows that people have already begun to think in earnest about the issue of AI with both awe and fear.

1.4.2 FROM THE WORLD WIDE WEB TO THE INTELLIGENT GRID

While the advent of the computer provided an entity for AI to be materialized, the emergence and development of the Internet provided AI with more space. The year 1969 witnessed the birth of ARPANET, the precursor to the Internet. In 1972, Ray Tomlinson invented e-mail. In 1973, Vinton G. Cerf and Robert E. Kahn published their thesis entitled "A Protocol for Packet Network Intercommunication," and proposed Transmission Control Protocol/Internet Protocol (TCP/IP) for the first time. Later, Vinton G. Cerf was commonly referred to as the "father of the Internet." In 1991, the commercialization of the Internet began. After that, Web sites and Internet users grew exponentially. In 1992, the World Wide Web (WWW) was born. In 1999, the number of Internet users worldwide reached 150 million and Web pages reached 800 million.[32] By 2004, in China alone, there were more than 600,000 Web sites. Individual users reached a record high of more than 80 million. The Internet has become a symbol of informatization of society. The Internet-based Web has become a "digital library" for more and more people. Such search engines as Google™, Yahoo®, and Baidu™ are commonly used in our daily work. However, the Web is unlike a traditional library where books are arranged and can be retrieved in an organized way. On the contrary, it is like a large warehouse in which information is in disorder rather than systematical. Moreover, it is difficult to tell the truth from the false. In this warehouse, information is not classified according to different fields of knowledge. No consideration is given to the users' types and their preferences. Repetition exists in retrieved results. To address these problems, many people are trying to develop all sorts of intelligent search engines based on AI technologies, providing users with such functions as correlation ordering, role registration, recognition of individual interests, semantic understanding of contents and smart information filtering and push.

The term "grid" is derived from power grid, which is used to separate electricity suppliers from consumers who are not interested in the origins of the power. It is hoped that the Web will function like a power grid where people are only concerned with the information contents. All networks, regardless of their structures (asterisk structure, bus structure, or grid structure) and physical distributions, are combined by high-speed networks into a huge grid for people to share resources and solve problems of individual concern. In this huge grid, resources are no longer isolated and separated; instead, they are coordinated and integrated to help people face more sophisticated problems. Research on grid is just in the beginning. Its research contents mainly include the structure of a grid system, grid computing, peer-to-peer computing, grid security and the development of grid-based applications. Further research will enable the grid to be intelligent, i.e., to construct an intelligent grid. To each individual, the intelligent grid is like a super brain where all resources — including computing resources, stored resources, communication resources, software resources, and knowledge resources — can be transmitted to each other, similar to the process between neuron cells. In this case, resources will be shared, integrated, and renascent.

The Web's grid is expected to be an encyclopedia on demand. Using it, people can customize the search result, search the hidden Web page, locate the user, search for multimedia information, and obtain personal services.

1.4.3 FROM DATA TO KNOWLEDGE

With the rapid development of network technologies, applications of database are continuing to expand in terms of scale, scope, and depth. The spread of E-business, the management of enterprise and government affairs as well as the development of data gathering tools all contribute to the generation of large volumes of data. Millions of databases are used in business management, in government departments, in national defense and in data processing for science and industry. Behind the dramatic expansion of data lie hidden information and knowledge. Data entry, data enquiry, and data analysis can be realized in a highly efficient way. However, the relations and rules among data can hardly be discovered. Prediction of future trend based on existing data cannot be made, and useful information and knowledge hidden in traditional databases cannot be dug out. Thus, although the exploration has gathered a huge quantity of data, the number of discovered knowledge is still minor. As a result, people desire a higher level of data analysis function that can turn data into useful information and knowledge. To cater to this need, DM and knowledge discovery came into being and grew quickly.

DM is an exciting direction of research. It can satisfy our desire by discovery of hidden, unknown, but potentially useful information and knowledge out of a large quantity of data. Not only can data mining be exploited to look on specific database for simple require and transference, statistical calculation and analysis, synthesis and deduction of data can also be made available on different scales (microscopic, macroscopic and in-between) so that the inter-relationship can be discovered to help solve practical problems, even to predict future events based on historical and existing data. By so doing, the usage of data will move from a lower level of enquiry operation to a higher level of discovering useful information and knowledge, and move on to providing necessary support for decision-makers at various levels. The demand for DM is more common and deep going than that for traditional data enquiry. Here DM means data aggregation in a specific area of application. Although data are usually magnanimous, yet they may be incomplete, noisy, redundant, and even contradictory. Knowledge discovery neither means discovering commonly used abstract mathematical formulas, nor does it mean discovering new laws in nature and science, or discovering truth that can be applied to everything in the universe. By knowledge discovery, we mean discovering information and knowledge hidden in data. As an important branch in AI, DM will bridge data, information, and knowledge, adding more intellectual colors to the dull digital life of the human race.

1.5 THE CROSS TREND BETWEEN AI, BRAIN SCIENCE AND COGNITIVE SCIENCE

1.5.1 THE INFLUENCE OF BRAIN SCIENCE ON AI

The human brain is considered the most sophisticated and most advanced intelligence system in nature. To reveal the secret of the brain is the greatest challenge to the present natural science. Nowadays it remains one of the three mysteries in the world. Mankind has traveled a long way to explore the human brain. As early as 400 BC, Hippocrates, a doctor in ancient Greece, stated that "the brain is the organ of intelligence." In the seventeenth century, Descartes proposed the concept of "reflexion." In late nineteenth century, Cajal laid a foundation for neuron theory with a chromosome method named after him. After entering the twentieth century, Pavlov established the theory of conditioned reflexion of advanced nervous activities. In the 1940s, the invention of microelectrode made possible the research on neurophysiology, a stride forward in understanding nervous activity. In the 1960s, neuroscience grew quickly and scientists began to investigate nervous phenomenon at the cellular and molecular level. Damage-free brain imaging technology provided an unprecedented tool for scientists to study activities of a live brain and analyze its working mechanism. From the 1990s on, emphasis was laid on integration in the brain science. In 1989, the United States became the first country to launch a nationwide brain science program and declared the 1990s to be the "decade of the brain."[33] Table 1.1 lists the names of brain scientists and neurobiologists who happen to be Nobel Prize winners.

The goals of brain science are to understand the brain, to protect the brain, and to create a brain.[36] So far, AI can only simulate the human brain by computer and is trying to create an artificial brain. Therefore, it is inevitable for brain science and AI to be interwoven and convergent.

Brain science deals with the function of the brain and its related diseases in a comprehensive way, which may be at the molecular, cellular, behavioral, and integrated levels, respectively, aiming to understand the structural principle of the brain. AI is concerned with how to utilize the computer to simulate mental activities of the human brain such as consciousness, perception, reasoning, learning, thinking and planning in order to solve complex problems formerly done only by human experts. Therefore, research on the brain is an inevitable prerequisite for AI. The complexity of the brain lies in the fact that it is an information-processing and decision-making system made up of a trillion (10^{12}) neuron cells and a thousand trillion synapses. It is most likely that human cognitive activities reflected in the brain correspond to

TABLE 1.1
A List of Nobel Prize Winners Comprised of Brain Scientists and Neurobiologists

Year	Country	Name	Area of Study/Discovery
1904	Russia	I. P. Pavlov (1849–1936)	The theory of conditioned reflexion and signal
1906	Italy	C. Golgi (1843–1926)	The structure of the nervous system
	Spain	S. R. Cajal (1852–1934)	
1932	U.K.	C. S. Sherrington (1857–1952)	The functions of neurons
	U.K.	E. D. Adrian (1889–1977)	
1936	U.K.	H. H. Dale (1875–1968)	Chemical transmission of nerve impulses
	Austria	O. Loewi (1873–1961)	
1944	U.S.	J. Erlanger (1874–1965)	The highly differentiated functions of single nerve fibers
	U.S.	H. S. Gasser (1888–1963)	
1949	Switzerland	W. R. Hess (1881–1973)	The functional organization of the interbrain as a coordinator of the activities of the internal organs
1963	Australia	J. C. Eccles (1903–1997)	The ionic mechanisms involved in excitation and inhibition in the peripheral and central portions of the nerve cell membrane
	U.K.	A. L. Hodgkin (1914–1998)	
	U.K.	A. F. Huxley (1917–)	
1970	U.K.	B. Katz (1911–2003)	The humoral transmitters in the nerve terminals and the mechanism for their storage, release, and inactivation in the peripheral and central portions of the nerve cell membrane
	Sweden	U. S. V. Euler (1905–1983)	
	U.S.	J. Axelrod (1912–2004)	
1977	U.S.	R. Guillemin (1924–)	Hypothalamic hypophysiotropic hormone
	U.S.	A. V. Schally (1926–)	
1981	U.S.	R. W. Sperry (1913–1994)	The functional specialization of the cerebral hemispheres
2000	U.S.	A. Carlsson (1923–)	Signal conduction in the nervous system
	U.S.	P. Greengard (1925–)	
	U.S.	E. R. Kandel (1929–)	

some chemical and electric changes physiologically. However, life science is unable to establish a definite relation between mental activities and chemical and electric layers of subcells, e.g., how a concept is stored in the biological form and what the biological process is when a concept is connected with other concepts? Nor is life science able to decide which neuron structures determine the occurrences of which cognitive patterns. Therefore, it is the future task of brain science to study the integrated functions from different angles and push the understanding of nervous activities to the cellular and molecular level. These research subjects include: How are cognition and thinking performed in the brain? How does the brain understand the natural language? How are feelings produced in the brain?[37] All this research will greatly push forward the development of AI science.

Although the nature of consciousness remains a mystery and although people still want to develop "mind-reading machines," "memory pills," and "smart pills" through the "ten-year project of behavioral science," which is still being implemented, our efforts to use the machine to simulate human intelligence will not end up in vain. The impact of brain science development on AI is not doubtful. In dealing with the relations between brain science and AI, we must have the interdisciplinary awareness to reveal the nature of the brain functions, to prevent and cure brain diseases, and to create computers with human intelligence. In short, they are both to understand the brain, to protect the brain, and to create a brain, at the same time.[36]

1.5.2 THE INFLUENCE OF COGNITIVE SCIENCE ON AI

Cognitive science is derived from cognitive psychology. The term "cognitive science" probably made its first appearance in publications in 1975 in a book *Presentation and Understanding: Studies in Cognitive Science*, cowritten by D. G. Bobrow and A. Collins. In 1977, the journal *Cognitive Science* was published. In 1979, 23 years after the Dartmouth Symposium on AI, the first cognitive science conference was convened at the University of California, San Diego. At this conference, D. A. Norman, who chaired the meeting, made a speech entitled "Twelve Issues for Cognitive Science," in which he set an agenda for cognitive science.[38]

Cognitive science is the study of information processing in the course of human cognition and thinking, consisting of perception, memory, learning, language and other cognitive activities.[38] The brain receives information from the environment in the form of sound, light, touch and smell through various sensory organs. These are what we call perceptions, of which visual perception plays a particularly important role. Cognition is based on perception, which is the overall reaction of the brain to the objective world. The presentation of perception constitutes the basis for the study of cognitive processes at all levels. Memory is the retaining of perceptions. With memory, current response can be processed on the basis of the previous one. And only with memory, can people accumulate experience. Memory and forgetfulness are two instincts of the brain. Learning is a basic cognitive activity. The neurobiological basis of learning is the flexibility of synapses that link neural cells. Research in this direction has been a very active field in present brain science. Some people classify learning into three categories: perceptive learning, cognitive learning, and semantic learning. Learning is mainly presented in the form of languages, which take sounds and words as its carriers and grammar as its rules. Language is a system, with the most complex structure, the most flexible usage, and the most extensive applications. Thinking activities and cognitive exchange cannot be performed without the help of language. Besides, there are other cognitive behaviors such as concentration and consciousness.[39,40,41]

Psychologist H. Gardner suggests that there are six disciplines that are closely linked to cognitive science. They are philosophy, psychology, linguistics, anthropology, artificial intelligence, and neuroscience. To make breakthroughs in search, presentation, learning, optimization, prediction, planning, decision-making and self-adaptation of AI, one has to obtain support from brain science and cognitive science.[38]

1.5.3 COMING BREAKTHROUGHS CAUSED BY INTERDISCIPLINES

Today, science has developed into a stage with two significant features. On one hand, it is highly divided, i.e., there are more and more detailed disciplinary division, bringing about new disciplines and fields. On the other hand, it is highly crossing, i.e., there is a trend of intercross and integration, bringing the emergence of new brand cross-disciplines. Looking back at the history of human development, natural and social sciences are always going hand-in-hand, both being the crystallization of the human knowledge system. With the development of human civilization, natural science is more and more closely linked to human activities. The nature of science determines that natural and social sciences will be intercrossed and integrated more and more closely and extensively. During the development process of modern natural and social sciences, each has a strong desire to get some new scientific approaches from the other. Especially today when science and technology is rapidly progressing, the development of natural science is reliant on the support from social science.

The universal trend of the discipline crossing is best demonstrated in AI, which is the crystallization of multiple natural and social science disciplines, embracing philosophy, brain science, cognitive science, mathematics, psychology, information science, medical science, biology, linguistics and anthropology. Once some breakthroughs are made in simulating the most sophisticated human intellectual behaviors, the impact on human civilization will be enormous. However, it is difficult to count on the development of one discipline alone to achieve this goal. There needs to be a cooperative effort among multiple disciplines, and research achievements of one discipline can be shared by another as a research basis or auxiliary means. There are numerous examples in this respect. For instance, the application of ANNs in AI is inspired by research results from medical science and biology. Moreover, through arduous efforts, scientists working on the human genome initiative have already constructed the DNA sequence of the human being and many other creatures. However, without automatic instruments dealing with large numbers of samples, and without high-speed computer processing, storing, comparing and restoring these data, it would have been impossible to accomplish the work of sequencing the three billion base pairs of the human genome in a number of years. It can be perceived that as a source of innovation thinking, discipline crossing will bear more scientific and technologic achievements and inevitably brew major breakthroughs in AI.

REFERENCES

1. Zixing Cai and Guangyou Xu, *Artificial Intelligence and Its Applications, The 3rd Edition*, Tsinghua University Press, Beijing, 2004.
2. Xingsan Hu, Tracing back to the history of AI, *Journal of Lishui Normal School,* Vol. 18, No. 5: 20–22, 1996.
3. Heling Wu and Lin Cui, *ACM Turing Award* (1966–1999). *The Epitome of Computer Phylogeny*, High Education Press, Beijing, 2004.
4. Songde Ma and Yu Ma, Review and Preview of AI Technology, In: Chinese Academy of Science, *High Technology Development Report 2000*, 102–108, Science Press, Beijing, 2000.

5. S. Russell and P. Norvig, *Artificial Intelligence: A Modern Approach*, Prentice Hall, New York, 2003.
6. J. J. Hopfield, Neural Networks and Physical Systems with Emergent Collective Computational Abilities, In: *Proceedings of the National Academy of Science of the United States of America*, Vol. 79:2554–2558, 1982.
7. D. E. Rumelhart and J. L. McClelland, *Parallel Distributed Processing: Explorations in the Microstructure of Cognition*, MIT Press, Cambridge, MA, 1986.
8. Wenjun Wu, Mathematics Mechanization, In: Xianglin Yu and Yong Deng, eds., *The Charming of Science*, Preface, Science Press, Beijing, 2002.
9. G. Polya, *How to Solve It: A New Aspect of Mathematical Method*, Princeton University Press, New Jersey, 2004.
10. Deyi Li and Dongbo Liu, *A Fuzzy PROLOG Database System*, John Wiley & Sons, New York, 1990.
11. Yongguang Zhang, Some Problems about Artificial Life, In: Xuyan Tu and Yixin Yin, eds., *Artificial Life and Its Application*, pp. 22–26, University of Posts and Telecommunications Press, Beijing, 2004.
12. Zhongzhi Shi, Jun Shi, and Jinhua Zheng, Intelligent Problems Research of Artificial Life, In: Xuyan Tu and Yixin Yin, eds., *Artificial Life and Its Application*, pp. 27–32, University of Posts and Telecommunications Press, Beijing, 2004.
13. Xiaoxiang Zhang, *Encyclopedia of Computer Science*, Tsinghua University Press, Beijing, 1998.
14. S.Watanabe, *Pattern Recognition: Human and Mechanical*, John Wiley & Sons, New York, 1985.
15. Zhaoqi Bian and Xuegong Zhang, *Pattern Recognition*, Second Edition, Tsinghua University Press, Beijing, 2000.
16. J. Sklansky and G. N. Wassel, *Pattern Classifier and Trainable Machines*, Springer-Verlag, New York, 1981.
17. M. Minsky and S. Papert, *Perception*, Expanded Edition, MIT Press, Cambridge, MA, 1988.
18. Zhongzhi Shi, *Neural Computing*, Publishing House of Electronics Industry Press, Beijing, 1993.
19. A. Barr and E. A. Feigenbaum, The Art of AI: Themes and Case Studies of Knowledge Engineering, In: *Proceedings of the 5th International Joint Conference on Artificial Intelligence*, Vol. 5: 1014–1029, 1977.
20. Yaohua Lu, *Thinking Simulation and Knowledge Engineering*, Tsinghua University Press, Beijing, 1997.
21. Ruqian Lu, Knowledge Science and its Research Foreland, In: Dazhong Wang and Shuzi Yang, eds., *Development and Expectation of Science Technology— Academicians Discuss Science*, pp. 123–132, Shandong Education Press, Jinan, 2002.
22. A. Barr, P. R. Cohen, and E. A. Feigenbaum, *The Handbook of Artificial Intelligence*, Vol. I–IV, Addison-Wesley Publishing Company, Reading, MA, 1981–1989.
23. N. J. Nilsson, *Artificial Intelligence: A New Synthesis*, Morgan Kaufmann, San Francisco, CA, 1998.
24. Zixing Cai, *Some Development of AI Research*, In: *The Progress of Artificial Intelligence in China 2003*, pp.58–63, University of Posts and Telecommunications Press, Beijing, 2003.
25. Chunyi Shi, Changning Huang, and Jiaqing Wang, *Principles of Artificial Intelligence*, Tsinghua University Press, Beijing, 1993.
26. Rob Callan, *Artificial Intelligence*, Palgrave Macmillan, New York, 2003.

27. U. M. Fayyad, Piatesky-Shapiro, P. Smyth, and R. Uthurusamy, eds., *Advances in Knowledge Discovery and Data Mining*: AAA/MIT Press, Cambridge, MA, 1996.

28. Yi Du, *Research and Applications of Association Rules in Data Mining (Ph.D. Thesis)*, PLA University of Science and Technology, Nanjing, 2000.

29. Xinsong Jiang, *The Introduction of Robotics*, Liaoning Science and Technology Press, Shenyang, 1994.

30. Yuehong Yin, Zhongxin Wei, and Xiaoxi Huang, *Force Sensor and Force Control Technology of Intelligent Machine Systems*, National Defence Industry Press, Beijing, 2001.

31. Hao Wang and Zongyuan Mao, *Intelligent Control Approach of Robot*, National Defence Industry Press, Beijing, 2002.

32. National Academy of Engineering, *Frontiers of Engineering: Reports on Leading Edge Engineering from the 1999 NAE Symposium on Frontiers of Engineering*, 2000.

33. Zhongzhi Shi, Intelligent Science: A New Way of Artificial Intelligence, In: *The Progress of Artificial Intelligence in China 2003,* pp.42–48, University of Posts and Telecommunications Press, Beijing, 2003.

34. "100-Year Review of Nobel Medical Award," http://www.phil.pku.edu.cn/post/center/ and http://www.bioon.com/service/scienceway/200405/73599.html

35. "Nobel Physiology & Medical Award," *http://zh.wikipedia.org/wiki/*.

36. Yizhang Chen, The Strategy of the Brain Science Research, In: Tao Zhang, ed., *The Frontier and Future of Science*, Science Press, Beijing, pp. 36–47, 1998.

37. Xiongli Yang, Mystery of Brain, In: Baosheng Ye, ed., *The Beauty of Science*, China Youth Press, Beijing, pp. 305–323, 2002.

38. Nanyuan Zhao, *Cognition Science and Generalized Evolutionism*, Tsinghua University Press, Beijing, 1994.

39. F. Clark, *Striking Hypothesis*, Hunan Sci. & Tech. Press, Changsha, 2003.

40. John B. Best, *Cognition Psychology*, China Light Industry Press, Beijing, 2000.

41. Su Wang and Ansheng Wang, *Cognition Psychology*, Peking University Press, Beijing, 1992.

2 Methodologies of AI

In the 50 years of AI research, there appeared a number of dominant schools centering on basic theories and methodologies.

In 1987, in Boston, an international symposium to address the fundamental issues of AI was jointly sponsored by the Massachusetts Institute of Technology (MIT) AI Lab, the National Science Foundation (NSF) and the American Association for Artificial Intelligence (AAAI). Invited to the symposium were AI experts who had made remarkable contributions to AI development. In the proceedings, the participants elaborated on their own academic ideas and basic theories, discussed the ideological source of their theories, explained representative forms and basic models of their own theories and probed into the applicabilities and limitations.

From then on, many scholars summed up the fundamental theories and methodologies for AI proposed at the symposium as symbolism, connectionism, and behaviorism.

Symbolism is based on the physical symbol system hypothesis, i.e., symbol-operating system and limited rationality theory. Connectionism concerns itself with artificial neural networks (ANNs) and evolutionary computation. Behaviorism emphasizes particularly on relations between perception and action.[1-3]

2.1 SYMBOLISM METHODOLOGY

2.1.1 BIRTH AND DEVELOPMENT OF SYMBOLISM

The early research on intelligence was, for the most part, philosophical thinking depending on instinctive speculation and empirical observation. It was not until the rising of cognitive science that knowledge about intelligence began to move in the right direction of scientific concepts and formalized approach emphasizing the importance of computation in cognitive science. Some scholars hold that the importance of computation in science is the same as "energy" and "mass" in physics and as "protein" and "gene" in biology.

However, the mathematical description of the concept of intuitionist computability was the concept of the Turing machine in 1936. Around 1935, Alonzo Church, Stephen Cole Kleene and Kurt Gödel held a series of discussions about intuitionist computability at Princeton University and gave it a mathematical description in definability and recursive functions. In the end, Church came up with his standard "Church's thesis": "A function of positive integers is effectively calculable only if recursive."

By doing so, Church became one of the pioneers in recursive functions—the basic theory for theoretical computation.

On the other hand, totally unaware of the research work conducted by mathematicians at Princeton University, Turing was thinking about the issue of effective calculability in England and described it in the concept of the Turing Machine, i.e., "calculable by means of an LCM [logical computing machine: Turing's expression for Turing machine]." It can be expressed by the following "Turing's thesis": "LCMs can do anything that could be described as 'rule of thumb' or 'purely mechanical.'"

When he was about to submit his paper, Turing found out about the work on definability and recursive functions done at Princeton. So, he attached a note to his article, giving an equivalence proof between calculability and definability in the Turing Machine.

It may be said that when Gödel was working on the proof of his Incompleteness Theorems, the basic concept of formal systems was not yet quite clear. It was in 1936 when there emerged the concept of the Turing Machine that people began to realize that a formal system was no more than a machine program to bring about theorems. The concept of the formal system was to transform all deductions into machine computation that was then applied to formulas. Machine computation means "algorithm" precisely described for a Turing Machine. In other words, a formal system is no more than a multivalue Turing Machine that is allowed to make choices in the preset range in certain steps.[4]

Based on the concept of algorithm, some concepts and theories in theoretical computer science such as computability, computational complexity, serial and parallel processing and so on were produced, which gave a great promotion to development of cognitive science.

More importantly, it was based on the concept of an algorithm that Marvin L. Minsky and Herbert Simon, founders of cognitive science, first put forward the research guideline for computational cognition which is now still dominant in the academic circle in the west and which maintains that "the nature of cognition is computation."[5] No matter what differences there might be between the human brain and the computer in terms of hardware and software, they are both able to produce, operate, and process abstract symbols in terms of computational theory. As an information processing system, a symbol is the basic unit in describing cognitive and intellectual activities and so both the human brain and the computer are regarded as formalized systems to operate and process discrete symbols. The operation and processing is what is meant by "computation" according to the Turing Machine and any cognitive and intellectual state is merely a state of the Turing Machine. So any cognitive and intellectual activity is calculable by an algorithm. This means recognizing that all human cognitive activities can be simulated by computer. Starting from this point, some have drawn the conclusion that, some day, the computer can do everything and even outdo what humans can.

The proposal of "computational cognition" as a guideline enabled the study of human cognition to enter a regular scientific phase of research. Just as Simon remarked in 1988, when he was looking back on the history of cognitive science development, "Before the computer was regarded as a universal symbol processing system, there were very few scientific concepts and approaches for the study of the nature of cognition and intelligence." "Computational cognition" soon became the guiding principle in artificial intelligence, cognitive psychology, and mathematical linguistics, greatly advancing the progress of AI.[6]

Under the guidance of "computational cognition," there arose a study of the symbolist paradigm, believing that the basic unit in thinking is a discrete symbol, that the core of intelligence is to use knowledge and knowledge reasoning for problem solving. The basis for intellectual activity is the computation of physical symbols that both the human brain and the computer are systems of physical symbols and that human intelligence can be simulated completely by setting up a symbolic logic-based intelligent theoretical system.[7]

Symbolism holds that cognition is symbol processing and that the process of human thinking can be described by certain kinds of symbols. In other words, thinking is computation (or cognition is computation). This ideology constitutes one of the philosophical bases for artificial intelligence.

The symbolist approach is represented by Herbert Simon and Allen Newell. In 1976, they proposed the Physical Symbol System Hypothesis, maintaining that the physical symbol system is a necessary and sufficient condition to present intellectual behaviors. Using mathematical methods to study intelligence and look out for forms, patterns, and formulas of intelligent structure enables intelligence to be systemized and formalized like a mathematical symbol and formula. In this way, any information processing system can be viewed as a materialized physical symbol system which uses rule-based memory to obtain, search for, and control knowledge and operators toward general problem solving. Humans can also be looked upon as intelligent information processing systems, which are referred to as symbol operation systems or physical symbol systems. The so-called symbol is a pattern; any pattern, as long as it can be distinguished from other patterns, is a symbol. For example, different Chinese characters or English letters are symbols. To work on symbols is to compare them and find out about the same and different symbols. The task and function fundamental to a physical symbol system is to identify the same symbols and distinguish different ones. Therefore, it is necessary for the system to be able to tell the substantial differences between symbols. Symbols can be concrete, such as the patterns of electrons moving in the physical world or the patterns of neurons moving in the human brain. Symbols can also be abstract, such as concepts in human thinking.[8]

A complete symbol system should have the following six basic functions:

1. Inputting symbols
2. Outputting symbols
3. Storing symbols
4. Duplicating symbols
5. Creating symbol structures, i.e., forming symbol structures in the symbol system by finding out relations among symbols
6. Conditional migration, i.e., carrying on with its action process based on existing symbols

A symbol system capable of completing the whole process is an integrated physical symbol system (PSS). Humans possess the six functions mentioned above, so do up-to-date computers. Therefore, both the human and the computer are complete physical symbol systems.

The physical symbol system hypothesis states that any system that exhibits intelligence is certain to carry out the above-mentioned six functions and that any system with the six functions is capable of exhibiting intelligence. One provides sufficient and necessary condition for the other. Along with the hypothesis come three deductions:

1. Humans possess intelligence, so a human is a PSS.
2. A computer is a PSS, so it has intelligence.
3. Because a human is a PSS and a computer is also a PSS, we can use a computer to simulate human intellectual activities.

It should be pointed out that such a physical symbol system is merely an external representation of the system on a certain conceptual granularity. It can be constructed on a different conceptual granularity. As a PSS, the computer can simulate human intelligence on the macroscopic, intermediate, and microscopic levels. The relationship between human and machine is established when the external representation of the previously mentioned six functions is on the same conceptual granularity, where the computer is able to simulate human intelligence. However, on a smaller conceptual granularity, the intelligential mechanism between human and machine might be totally different. For example, when people are trying to solve an identical complex problem, although the thinking process of each individual may not be the same, they may arrive at the same conclusion. When the computer is used for simulation by way of some programmatic structure distinguished from a human's thinking process, the same result will be reached. In this sense, the computer can be said to have realized human intelligence. So, symbolism advocates adopting a functional simulation approach to realize artificial intelligence through analyzing functions possessed by the human cognitive system and then using the computer to simulate these functions.

For the symbolism approach of AI, its basis is symbolic mathematics, which is embodied in predicate calculus and revolution principles; its means is a program designing tool, which gives expression to logical programming language and its purpose is application, which is reflected in the expert system.[7,9]

2.1.2 PREDICATE CALCULUS AND RESOLUTION PRINCIPLE

Predicate calculus, which grows from propositional calculus, is the mathematic basis of symbolism. Proposition is a statement that affirms or denies something and is either true or false.

A proposition that is considered irreducible is referred to as an atom. Propositions and atoms can form compound propositions by virtue of some connectives, including negation ($\neg$), conjunction ($\wedge$), disjunction ($\vee$), implication ($\rightarrow$), and equivalence ($\leftrightarrow$). With these connectives, we can get the disjunction normal form and the conjunction normal form, by which the propositional calculus can be carried out, such as proving, deduction, and reasoning.

Atom is the basic element of the propositional calculus, but its granularity is too big to express the relationship between the individuals in a proposition. So the word predicate is adopted to express the correlation, which is called predicate calculus. In predicate calculus, there are two types of quantifiers: (1) existential quantifier ($\exists$), a certain individual and (2) universal quantifier ($\forall$), the whole of the individuals. An existential quantifier can be expressed as the disjunction of an instance, while a universal quantifier conjunction can be expressed as the conjunction of an instance. Atoms or their negations are the literal. A clause is composed of the literals' disjunction.[10,11]

A predicate can be used to express the details of propositions and build up the formal description of the relationship between the propositions. From this issue, predicate calculus is more detailed than proposition calculation. Predicate calculus can involve a universal quantifier and build up the formal description of their relationship. From this issue, predicate calculus is more general and more flexible than proposition. An instance sentence in predicate calculus is an assertion in proposition calculation.

The mentioned predicate calculus mainly focuses on the expression of the quantifiers, literals, and clauses. But it is resolution that realizes the reasoning process. Resolution means eventually to draw a conclusion (true or false) of all the clause sets, and prove the conclusion to be permanent true in finite steps. This function is called the "Resolution Principle." It is the basic content of symbolism methodology.

Suppose A, B, and C are atoms. Then $A \lor B \lor \neg C$ is a clause, but $(A \land B) \lor C$ is not.

The basic idea of the resolution principle can be demonstrated by the following example:

Suppose C_1 and C_2 are two clauses. If two literals L_1 and L_2 exist in C_1 and C_2, and

$$L_1 = \neg L_2$$

$$C_1 = L_1 \lor C'_1$$

$$C_2 = L_2 \lor C'_2$$

then, we have

$$C_1 \lor C_2 = L_1 \lor C'_1 \lor L_2 \lor C'_2 = C'_1 \lor C'_2$$

where C'_1 and C'_2 are both clauses, and $C'_1 \lor C'_2$ is a resolvent from the clauses C_1 and C_2.

As shown in the above sample, resolution principle is an easily operating method. Just removing the complemented literal from two clauses and then disjuncting the remains.

Syllogism is a special case of resolution principle. For example: let

$$C_1 = \neg A \lor B, \quad C_2 = A$$

Apply resolution principle to C_1 and C_2, and we end up with B.

Since $C_1 = A \rightarrow B$, $C_2 = A$, B can be deferred from C_1 and C_2. This is syllogism.

When proving some mathematic theorems by resolution principle, it is actually a contradictory process. For example, if you want to prove the theorem: $((A \rightarrow B) \wedge (B \rightarrow C) \wedge A) \rightarrow C$, you only need to prove $((A \rightarrow B) \wedge (B \rightarrow C) \wedge A \wedge \neg C)$ is permanently false. Therefore:

1. Transfer this formula to a conjunctive one: $(\neg A \vee B) \wedge (\neg B \vee C) \wedge A \wedge \neg C$, and then rewrite it to a set of clauses: S

$$S = \{\neg A \vee B, \neg B \vee C, A, \neg C\}.$$

2. Obtain B from the resolution of $\neg A \vee B$ and A.
3. Obtain C from the resolution of B and $\neg B \vee C$.
4. C and $\neg C$ are contradictory, from which a permanently false clause (null clause) can be obtained by resolution.
5. So S is permanently false.

This completes the proof.

The resolution principle can be expanded properly. On one side, with the synergetic replacing method, resolution principle can be used to describe the predicate of the predicate (so called second-order predicate). It comes into being the second-order predicate calculus. On the other side, besides the original existential quantifier and universal quantifier, some other quantifiers are added, such as minority, extremely individual, mass, etc., by which the resolution principle can be expanded to multi-value logic and fuzzy logic. Indeed, the resolution principle can even be expanded to general non-standard logic.[12,13]

2.1.3 LOGIC PROGRAMMING LANGUAGE

In 1959, based on Alonzo Church's calculation and the "list structure" first introduced by Simon and Newell, John McCarthy developed his famous LISP (list processing language), which later became the most favored language in artificial intelligence research.[14] LISP is a functional symbolic-processing language with its program made up of functional subfunctions. Its functional structure is analogous to the structure of recursive function in mathematics, which is capable of constructing new functions from a few basic ones by certain means. LISP is a functional programming language. It is a logic programming language as well because its calculation is based on symbols rather than numbers and it carries out deductions by means of symbolic calculation. LISP is characterized by the following technical features:[15,16]

1. Uses symbolic expressions rather than numbers for calculation.
2. Capable of list processing, i.e., using linked lists to represent all the data.
3. Capable of forming more complex functions into basic control structures through functional compounding.
4. Uses recursion as a way to describe a problem and the process.
5. In LISP language, EVAL function is used both as interpreter and the formal definition of this language.

6. As other data, the program itself is represented by list structure.
7. Describes the constraint of the object as late as possible.
8. Capable of running interactively.

These features of LISP are key to symbolic problem solving. In addition, the elegant list structure is also a convenient and powerful tool for further simplifying LISP programming (although with it comes the problem of too many brackets). Therefore, since its invention, LISP also has been widely used in theorem proof, predicate calculus, game theory, expert system, etc., besides being used for symbolic calculus in mathematics. Later, derived from it was a series of new products such as Visual LISP, Auto LISP, Concurrent LISP, which are extensively exploited in many specific areas. Some even attempted to make a LISP machine to simulate human intelligence, but so far without success.

PROLOG (PROgramming in LOGic) is another famous logic programming language, which was first created by Robert Kowalski, a young student of London University in the U.K., and first implemented in 1972 by the research group under Alain Colmerauer of Marseilles University in France.[17] Later, Pillipe Roussel introduced the PROLOG interpreter and David Warren contributed the first PROLOG compiler.[18] PROLOG is characterized by the following main features:

1. It is a descriptive language, focusing mainly on the description of the problem to be solved regardless of the executing sequence of the program. And unlike their advanced languages, it has no such control clauses, such as if-clause, when-clause, as if-clause, case-clause and for-clause.
2. Both the data and the program are represented by terms.
3. The basic ways of program execution are matching and backtracking, which determine the order of program execution; in fact it is a deductive reasoning machine.
4. It contains rich and powerful internal functions for the implementation of numerical and functional calculations.
5. It has a variety of interfaces for application programs, the latest version including Windows GUI function groups, ODBC/OCI, database function group and Internet function group such as Socket, FTP, HTTP, and CGI (Common Gateway Interface).

If we say that LISP language takes the functional form as its basic "hue," then PROLOG focuses more on the description of the problem to be solved. The powerful list processing function is also built in.

PROLOG resembles database operation. Performing queries on the database in structured query language (SQL) clause can be deemed as equivalent to deductive proving in PROLOG. And performing complex queries on the database in SQL clause can be regarded as advanced deductive proving in PROLOG.[19]

Since its creation, PROLOG has drawn great attention worldwide. To construct an intelligent computer, Japan used PROLOG as the system language for its Fifth Generation Computer Systems. Later, more versions of PROLOG appeared, such as ProLOGO, Visual PROLOG, and Concurrent PROLOG.

PROLOG suits expert systems perfectly and has excellent interfaces as well for SQL database systems, C++ development systems, and Delphi. Consequently, it has become a powerful universal developing tool for natural language understanding, mechanical theorem proving, and expert systems. In 1995, the International Standard Organization (ISO) issued the ISO PROLOG standard. After the creation of PROLOG, many tried in vain to invent a PROLOG machine to simulate human intelligence,[20] but did not succeed.

2.1.4 Expert System

As the mathematical basis for symbolism was brought closer to perfection with each passing day, any mathematical or logical system was able to be designed into some sort of production rule system and most categories of knowledge were able to be represented by production rules based on predicate calculus and the resolution principle, which provided a theoretical basis for the development of expert systems for assorted fields of knowledge in the information age.

The description of existence of one event (or some events) leading to the creation of another is referred to as the production rule, which is represented symbolically as follows:

$$\text{If } A \text{ then } B$$

or

$$A \rightarrow B$$

where A is called precondition, and B is called postcondition, $\rightarrow$ means if A is true then B is true.

The production system, which takes production rules as its structure, can describe experts' knowledge in a great number of areas. A production system consists of three parts: a collection of production rules, a working memory of facts, and a set of inference engines. Production rules is where expert knowledge is sorted and stored. In the working memory are stored initial data and target data, i.e., facts base as well as intermediate data produced during the execution process of production. The running of an inference engine is represented as triggering a string of rules and executing them. Usually, three steps are taken in rule choice and execution:

1. Matching: That is to match the current facts base with the precondition of the rule. If there is a perfect match, then the rule is referred to as a fired rule. It is possible that the preconditions of a number of rules are met at the same time, hence arises the conflict. Of all the fired rules, only one is executed and this one is called an enabling rule. When there is a conflict, one rule must be chosen as enabled from among a number of fired rules. So the second step is taken.
2. Conflict resolution: The task of conflict resolution is performed by the inference engine. At present, there are many ways to solve a conflict, such

as depth-first strategy, breadth-first strategy, speed-first strategy, and time-first strategy. The rationality of conflict resolution is relative. And the conflict resolution mechanism determines the performance of a production system.

3. Operation: The postcondition of the rule is executed. After the execution, some variants are instantiated and the current contents in the working memory are altered.

Then, it either stops or moves on to the next cycle of matching–conflict resolution–operation.

It is on the basis of such a production system that the expert system is developed. And logic programming languages such as LISP and PROLOG have provided the design of the system with a powerful tool. Generally speaking, the expert system is a program system with a large amount of professional knowledge and experience. It makes an inference and simulates the decision-making process to solve complex problems that usually take an expert in the field to solve using AI technology and basing itself on knowledge of one or more experts. The expert system has the following technical characteristics:[21-24]

1. Concealment of symbolic logic: Expertise is often non-mathematical. You can hardly expect specialized experts to express their expertise or reasoning procedure in mathematical symbols and terms. The expert system can achieve that by building a general purpose mathematical framework and representing each case of the specialized expert with rules. This is the natural way for humans to solve problems while discreetly concealing the reasoning procedure. From its appearance, a rule base is a knowledge base. When the problem is given, the expert system will come up with the correct result through inference to rules. The result is a resolution in the resolution principle or a proof in symbolic logic where the user cannot see the proving process. This is where the charm of mathematics lies.

2. Nonprocedural of program execution: The expert system requires only the description of a problem while the procedure of problem solving is realized by the inference engine in the system. The nature of problem solving is to seek solution to a problem by clause conjunction, matching, instantiation, and backtracking. The actual step taken in problem solving is the execution procedure of the program, which is transparent even to a programmer.

3. Flexibility in expertise enlargement: Just as the concealment of symbolic logic, the nonprocedural of program execution in the expert system enables easy capsulation of knowledge and easy update of databases. So the expert system can enlarge knowledge continually for more extensive applications.

4. Credibility and friendliness: Almost all expert systems have explanation subsystems, whose function is to explain to the user the system's behavior, including the explanation of correctness of the conclusion and the reason for its choice; although it is no more than a recurrence of the actual procedural of the resolution that has greatly enhanced the expert system's credibility and friendliness.

2.2   CONNECTIONISM METHODOLOGY

2.2.1   BIRTH AND DEVELOPMENT OF CONNECTIONISM

After the 1980s, a revolution of ANN in AI took place, enabling connectionism to exert a great impact on symbolism. In contrast to the symbolist physical symbol system hypothesis, connectionism maintains that the human cognitive activities are based on the activity of neurons in the human brain.

The earliest conception of ANNs can be traced backed to 1943, when W. S. McCulloch and W. Pitts, two American physiologists proposed the mathematical models for neurons, thus forming the basis for the neuron models and integrating them into a multilayer model called a neural network.[25] In the 1960s, the combination of artificial neural cell models with the computer made possible the production of a simple perception machine. This machine has a three-layer structure: input layer of sensory neural net, linking layer of central neural net, and output layer of motor neural net. This perception machine is capable of simple letter recognition, image recognition, and speech sound recognition through learning by example and training by showing it many examples and by giving stimulus-response-reward or punishment. But it is incapable of learning linearly nonseparable patterns.

In the 1970s, the research of perception machine and neural network became stagnant. John J. Hopfield's proposal of the brand new "Hopfield neural network" in 1982, which successfully solved the traveling salesman problem (TSP) with a calculating complexity of NP (Non-deterministic Polynomial) type, led to the resurgence of neural network research.[26,27] In 1983, Geoffrey E. Hinton and Terrence Sejnowski developed a neural network model capable of solving the optimization problem of a nonlinear dynamic system. In 1986, David E. Rumelhart and Geoffrey E. Hinton put forward error back-propagation learning algorithm of neural networks.[28] Around 1987, they first developed a multilayered perception machine for the solution of nonlinear perception and for complex pattern recognition and then developed a neural network with an excellent self-adaptation.

If the Hopfield neural network put forward in 1982 was marked as the resurgent point of neural network research, the ANN research has since gone on for 25 years. And if the convening of China's first conference on neural networks in 1990 was marked as the starting point, China's research in this field has since gone on for 17 years.

As a new type of information processing method, ANN has gained increasingly widespread use in various fields such as pattern recognition, automatic control, and combinational optimization. However, there have been very few fruitful results in ANN hardware realization and few breakthroughs have been made in intelligence representation. That is to say, so far the various ANNs constructed in the magnanimity of parallel-distributed systems of biological neural networks have not yet displayed intellectual intelligence as expected, although they are playing an increasingly important role in information processing. Therefore, some people are puzzled and disappointed at the future of ANN.

2.2.2   STRATEGY AND TECHNICAL CHARACTERISTICS OF CONNECTIONISM

The representatives of connectionism are McCulloch and Hopfield. They maintain that to simulate human intelligence, it is necessary to construct a brain model with the help of bionics. They also maintain that the basic unit of human thinking is neural cells rather than symbols and that intelligence is the result of the interconnected neural cells competing and coordinating. They hold views different from the physical symbol system hypothesis, believing that the human brain is not the same as the computer.

When the computer is used to simulate the human brain, emphasis should be laid on structural simulation, i.e., simulating the network structure of the human biological nervous system. They also believe that functions, structures, and behaviors are closely related and that different functions and behaviors are represented by different structures. In 1943, psychologist McCulloch and mathematician Pitts created a brain model and named it MP using their initials. It made research into the neural network model and the brain model starting from neural cells, opening up a new way of simulating the human brain and its functions with electronic apparatus and paving the way for the development of artificial intelligence in a new direction.[25]

The neuron in the human brain consists of two parts: cell body (also called soma) and process. The process is further divided into axon and dendrite, both projecting. The axon is responsible for outputting signals, while the dendrite for receiving them. The axon of each neuron connects to the dendrite of another neuron so that information transmission is realized. The junction across which a nerve impulse passes from an axon terminal to the dendrite is called "synapse." The neuron is said to be fired when some synapses are stimulated. Only when the total strength of all signals reaches the threshold value, say 40 millivolt, will the neuron begin to work. Whenever this value is reached, the neuron will produce a full strength nerve output impulse and transmit from the axon of the cell body to a branch axon. Then the neuron is said to have been fired. More and more evidence has shown that learning takes place near the synapse, which transforms the impulse passing it into excitement or inhibition for the next neuron. This way, the mechanism of the human brain has completed the transformation from a continuous signal into a binary signal (excitement or inhibition).

The ANN is an abstract mathematical model of the human brain and its activities. It is a large-scale, parallel/distributed, nonlinear, and self-adaptive system composed of numerous discrete processing units interconnected through fire. The processing element (PE) of the neural network is capable of local storage and local operation. An ANN can be regarded as a directed graph with the PE as the nodes interconnected by a weighted directed arc (link). In the directed graph, PE is the simulation of a biological neuron, while directed arc is the simulation of an "axon-synapse-dendrite" and the weight of the directed arc represents the strength of the interrelation between two processing units. Figure 2.1 is a diagram of ANN, in which the input from another neuron, times the weight, is summed up and compared with the threshold value. When the sum is greater than the threshold value, the output is 1, which corresponds to the excitement; otherwise the output is 0, corresponding to inhibition. In a simple ANN model, the properties of an axon are simulated by weight and multiplication, the interconnectional relation is simulated by the adder, and the switch property caused by the electrochemical reaction in a cell body is simulated by comparing it with the threshold value. The training process is one of adjustment of weight and threshold.

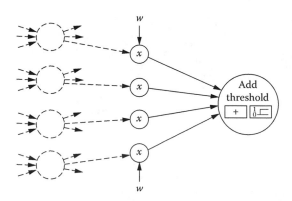

FIGURE 2.1 The mathematical description of the artificial neural network (ANN).

Each processing unit has a single output which, when necessary, can branch into a number of parallel connections with the same output signal. The output is independent of the number of branches. The operations executed in each processing unit must be locally autonomous, i.e., depending only on the current value of all the input signals into the processing unit, the local value stored in the processing unit and its operations.

The basic constituent parts of a connectionist structure can be activated to a certain degree under certain circumstances just like a simple unit of the brain neuron. Some units are interconnected with other units just as the brain neurons do. The strength of the connection varies with the activities within the system. The influence of one unit on another is constantly changing. A basic cognitive system is an integrity connected by these units.

The ANN differs from the symbolist approach in that, in a neuron network, knowledge is represented by the value of weights in interconnection between units. These weights can be continuous. The learning rule of the network depends on the active value equations taking the continuous weights as variants. Thus, the basic units of describing cognitive and intellectual activities in the learning rule are the variants of discrete subsymbol values rather than just the abstract discrete symbols that have nothing to do with biology. By doing so, the ANN has made a great leap forward toward bionics and is further approaching the neuronal constituency of the human brain on a microscale. Therefore, the proposal of ANN is regarded as a revolution, one that can be called the transformation of research methodology in cognitive science from symbolism to connectionism.

The neural network has the following three main technical characteristics:[29]

1. Distributed information storage and large-scale parallel processing. Information is distributed in the whole network with a large number of neuronal local storages. Each neuron completes its own operations with its own weights while simultaneously taking part in both distributed and parallel calculations and works.

2. Excellent self-adapting and self-organizing. Each neuron is capable of processing continuous simulating signals, even chaotic, incomplete and fuzzy information and coming up with a possible next best approximate solution. The mechanism of neuron connecting is very simple and there are various options for layers between numerous neurons. The structures are self-organizing.

3. Strong abilities of learning and fault tolerance. Through training, a neural network can form threshold value conditions for each neuron to enable itself to learn. Because of the large number of neurons, output is possible even when partial conditions exist. A fairly good result can be obtained even if some inputs contain some mistakes or if some neurons should break down.

2.2.3 HOPFIELD NEURAL NETWORK MODEL

In the connectionist approach, the Hopfield Neural Network Model is a typical representative, playing an important role in the resurgence of ANN research. The Hopfield NN is a single-layer, full-feedback model with the following main technical charactcristics:

1. The Hopfield NN is a full-connection, single-layer, and full-feedback system made up of nonlinear components. Each neuron in the network transmits its output to other neurons through connections and at the same time receives information sent from other neurons. Therefore, at time, T, the output state of one neuron in network is indirectly associated with its own output state at time, T-1.

2. One important feature of the Hopfield NN is its stability. When the energy function reaches the minima, it is a stable state for the network. Here the energy function represents a transitional tendency in the state of the network. The statc varics with thc Hopficld opcration rulcs and is finally able to reach the target function of a minimum value. When the energy function reaches the minima, it is called network convergence. If the target function in the optimization problem is converted into the energy function of the network, and if we let the variables correspond to the state of the network, then the Hopfield neural network can be used to solve the combinatorial optimization problem.

3. While a Hopfield NN is running, the connection strengths or weights of each neuron remain fixed, only the output state is updated. For the network of the same structure, with the change of the network parameters (weights and thresholds), the number of minima of the energy function in the network (called "stabilized balance point in the system") and the values of the minima also change. Therefore, the needed memory pattern can be designed with a stabilized balance point in a fixed network state. And if the network has M balance points, then it can memorize M memory patterns. Besides, the Hopfield NN is capable of associative memory. When the output provides only part of the information of a certain pattern,

the network will update the state starting from a certain initial state of the nearest memory pattern using the Hopfield operation rules until the network state is stabilized at the minimum of the energy function, thus completing the associating process caused by the incomplete information.

The main contributions of the Hopfield model are as follows:

- Proposing the energy function for the system, which takes the feedback neural network as a nonlinear dynamic system for stabilizing analysis of the system.
- Using analog electronics circuits to construct a circuitry model for the Hopfield network.
- This model is best suited for solving combinatorial optimization problems like the TSP.

2.2.4 BACK-PROPAGATION NEURAL NETWORK MODEL

Another typical structure of the connectionist approach is the back-propagation (BP) model,[30] first proposed in 1974 by Paul J. Werbos. Then David Parker and D. Rumelhart deduced the back-propagation learning algorithm after working further on it, thus solving the learning problem of connection weight values in the hidden layer units of a multilayer neural network and realizing M. L. Minsky's idea of a multilayer network.

In a conventional feed-forward propagation model, input signals are processed from one layer to the next through multiple hidden layers, and at last, propagate to the output layer. Each output of neuron in one layer only affects the state of the next layer. A back-propagation model belongs to the error correction learning type, whose learning process is made up of two parts: input feed-forward propagation and error feed-back propagation. The error is propagated backward when it appears between the input and the expected output during the feed-forward process. During the back propagation, the connection weight values between each layer of neurons are corrected and gradually adjusted until the minimum output error is reached.

Figure 2.2 is a diagram of a back-propagation network.

The training method of a back-propagation network consists of two phases: feed-forward and feed-back propagation. During the feed-forward phase, the input vector is introduced from the input layer through hidden layers to the output layer, while the output value of the network is calculated. At this time, the weighting values of the network are all fixed.

In the feed-back propagation phase, the error signal is obtained by subtracting the network output value from the expected output value and is then propagated backward through the various hidden layers to the input layer so that the weighting values are corrected.

Repeat the above two phases and recycle the learning process so that the network produces a better approximation of the desired output.

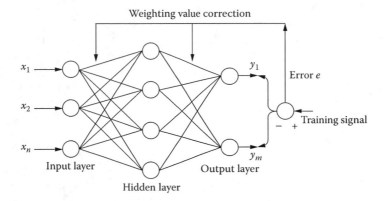

FIGURE 2.2 Mechanism chart of the back-propagation neural network.

In this training process, it is necessary to determine the condition under which the learning process will be terminated. Usually, one of the following can be set as the terminating condition:

1. When the gradient of the weighted value vector is smaller than the preset threshold.
2. In the Nth cycle of the learning process, when the mean variance of the output is smaller than the preset allowable value.
3. At the end of each learning cycle, check the network to see if the application ability has met the preset goals.
4. Integrate the above three methods and determine one terminating condition so as to avoid the weighting value vector oscillating constantly and being unable to converge or converging slowly.

In recent years, back propagation has found successful applications in pattern classification, fuzzy control, missing data restoration, function approximation, etc. At the same time, many scholars have proposed improvements on some problems in back-propagation algorithm, such as how to determine the number of hidden layers and hidden units in network structure design, and how to guarantee the global convergence with the decrease of gradient of weighted values vector in the network and how to increase the training rate.[31]

2.3 BEHAVIORISM METHODOLOGY

2.3.1 BIRTH AND DEVELOPMENT OF BEHAVIORISM

It has been long since control theory was used for AI research. Behaviorists hold that intelligence depends on perception and behavior, putting forward a "perception–behavior" model of intellectual behavior, usually called behaviorism. Tracing back to its history of development, it has roughly gone through three periods.[32]

From the 1940s to the 1960s, it was the "classical control theory" period, in which the main developments were the solution of the single-input/single-output problem, frequency analysis based on transfer functions, frequency properties, the root-locus method, and research on linear time invariant system. Theoretical accomplishments in this period, with H. W. Bode and W. R. Evans as representatives, included a fairly good solution of the single-input/single-output problem in the production process.[33]

From the 1960s to the 1970s, with the rapid development of the computer, control theory entered the period of "modern control theory." A higher order differential equation was transformed into a first order differential equation set to describe the dynamic process of the system, referred to as the state-space method. This method can be used to solve multi-input/multi-output problems, thus expanding a steady-state linear system into a time-varied nonlinear system. Representatives of this period were Lev Semenovich Pontryagin, Carl Michael Bellman, and Rudolph E. Kalman.

From the 1970s onward, control theory developed in the direction of "generalized system theory," on one hand researching into the structural representation, analytic method, and coordination of a generalized system based on the idea of control and information, and on the other hand, working on and imitating human perception processes and behaviors, developing information processing processes, and controlling with biotical functions. Representatives were Xuesen Qian, K. S. Fu and G. N. Saridis.[34]

Focus of early behaviorism was on human intellectual behaviors and functions in the control process such as self-optimizing, self-adapting, self-adjusting, self-calming, self-organizing and self-learning, and on the development of so-called "animats." In the 1980s, the intelligent control system and intelligent robots were born, pushing behaviorism in the AI research to a new height. In 1988, Rodney Brooks, a representative of behaviorism, created a six-legged walking robot based on the perception–behavior pattern and the control system imitating the behaviors of insects. At present, the inverted pendulum control system and RobotCup have become highlights in the behaviorist research on AI.[35]

2.3.2 ROBOT CONTROL

Control theory is an important branch of research in robotics. Problems dealt with in this field cover robot sensing, optimal movement of arms, and planning methods of action sequence implementation by a robot, of which control is an important part of research contents. Analogous to psychological "stimulus–action" mode, a robot will take corresponding actions through control once a firing condition is satisfied. If the firing condition is adequate enough and the difference between the actions is obvious, then the robot will react even without intelligence. Accuracy of robot control depends on the integration density of circuitry, the speed of components used for control algorithm, storage capacity, properties of programmable chips, diagnosis and communication, accuracy of the servo, etc.

The rapid development of robotic research in the direction of industrialization is pushing forward industrial automation and expansion of AI research scope. The combination of automation and intellectualization is likely to be employed to simulate processing states of industrial automation, describe the transformation from one production state to another, and program how action sequence is brought about and how the execution of the plans is supervised. With the computer taking part, the information processing and controlling activities are generalized as intellectual activities and intellectualized production.

Nowadays, robotic research is rapidly expanding to cognitive systems including those of touch, force, hearing, and especially of sight of a robot. It is also spreading to system structures, control mechanism, robotic language and robot assembly. Applications of robots are gaining more and more widespread use in industry, agriculture, commerce, tourism, and national defense. Robots are working in the air, on the sea, and in various hazardous environments.[36,37]

2.3.3 INTELLIGENT CONTROL

Traditional control theory methodology requires that the relation between input and output of the controlled object be expressed by a transfer function and demands an accurate mathematical model, which is often difficult. Some scholars researched the controlling mechanism of self-learning and self-organizing. Then, they introduced the artificially intelligent technology into the controlling system. Professor Jerry M. Mendel employed the learning mechanism on his space flight vehicle and put forward the idea of artificially intelligent control. In 1967, C. T. Leodes and Mendel first introduced the term "intelligent control." Starting from the 1970s, K. S. Fu, and Saridis suggested that intelligent control was a cross-discipline of AI and control, and constructed a system architecture of man–machine interactive hierarchical intelligent control. In the 1980s, the creation of microprocessors and built-in systems provided conditions for the development of intelligent controllers. Technological advances in knowledge expression, knowledge inference in AI research and technological progresses in the design and construction of expert systems have also provided new means for the study of intelligent control systems. In 1992, the National Science Foundation (NSF) and Electric Power Research Institute (EPRI) of the United States proposed "Intelligent Control" as a research program and issued a joint proposal on this issue. In 1993, an intelligent control group was set up in the Institute of Electrical and Electronics Engineers (IEEE) Control System Society (CSS) Technical Committee on Intelligent Control (TCIC). And in 1994, the IEEE World Congress on Computational Intelligence was convened in Orlando, integrating fuzzy logic, neural networks and evolutionary computation, thus greatly enriching the connotation of intelligent control.

Intelligent control refers to a broad category of control strategy of some devices with apery intellectual characteristics. It concerns the controlled object whose model parameters, even structures, are variable or hard to be precisely described in mathematical methods, and have nonlinear, uncertain and time-varied properties. As the intelligent control's outside environment is difficult to be restricted with mathematical parameters, it is required to be capable of self-organizing, self-learning, and self-adaptive, i.e., to be capable of intelligent behavior. The autonomous machine is such an example. There are various control methods. It may be pattern recognition-based learning control, expert system-based rule control, fuzzy set-based fuzzy control, or ANN-based neural control.

Self-organization in intelligent control concerns the architecture inside a system. Herman Haken, pioneer of system science, holds that, "Organization is a system comprised of inter-dependent variables." By "system," here we mean the inter-relation between variables expressed by parameters. By "self-organization," we refer to a system which spontaneously exchanges materials, energy, and information with the outside world to reduce its own entropy, i.e., to decrease its uncertainties so as to increase the level of orderliness within the structure. For example, living organisms constantly improve their own organizing structures through heredity, mutation, and struggle for survival of the fittest, resulting in the evolution of the species. This is what we call a self-organizing behavior. Intelligent control requires constant adjust-ment of the parameter relation between variables within the system. This relation is often nonlinear and characteristic of variable structure. The parameters are adjusted based on current deviation and deviation changing rate in terms of magnitude and direction and even the structure inside the system can be changed in the form of episodic change.

Self-learning in intelligent control mainly concerns itself with the mathematical model of the system. Learning means receiving conditions and results from the outside. It is a process of knowledge accumulation, called training by some people. From a mathematical point of view, it equals determining the parameters and vari-ables in the mathematical model of the system through the sets of condition and result. Self-learning means a process during which a corresponding result will be given based on the experience accumulated when a new input condition is deter-mined, or a process during which parameter and variable will be improved or adjusted when a new condition and result are given.

Self-adaptation in intelligent control is concerned with how a system reacts to the changes of the outside environment. Self-adaptation means that when the envi-ronment and conditions are changed, the parameters within the system structure are automatically changed by taking the information of environmental change in real time so that the running of the whole system still satisfies the stipulated characteristics.

It is hard to tell the differences among self-organization, self-learning, and self-adaptation, as they are interconnected and inseparable. For example, living organisms continuously improve their own organizing structures to lead to the evolution of the species through heredity, mutation, and struggle for survival of the fittest, which is not only a demonstration of self-organization, but also of self-learning and self-adaptation. Besides, the inverted pendulum is another typical example of intelligent control. It is an inherently unstable system of varied structure which is impossible to be described by a mathematical model. However, it can learn and be trained through a rule system. It is also capable of resistance against outside interference. Therefore, the control of the inverted pendulum can be used to exhibit self-organization, self-learning, and self-adaptation in intelligence control.

2.4 REFLECTION ON METHODOLOGIES

Symbolism, connectionism, and behaviorism mentioned above are all simulations of human deterministic intelligence. In the past 50 years, AI's development is not smooth although great achievements have been made. Up till now, there is not yet a unified theoretical system in AI. Different schools have different views over such fundamental theoretical issues of AI as its definition, basics, kernels, architectures, and relation with human intelligence.

Symbolism holds that the basic element of human cognition is the symbol and the cognitive process is equal to the operating process of symbols. A human being is a physical symbol system, so is a computer. Therefore, the computer can be used to simulate human intelligent behaviors. Knowledge is a form of information, which constitutes the basis of intelligence. The key problems of AI are knowledge representation, knowledge inference, and knowledge application. From this viewpoint, a unified theoretical system based on the knowledge of human intelligence and machine intelligence could be established.

Connectionism maintains that the basic element of human thinking is the neuron rather than the symbol. It questions the hypothesis of the physical symbol system and has proposed the working mode of the brain, i.e., using the neural network connected by plenty of multilayered parallel neurons to simulate the human brain.

Behaviorism believes that intelligence depends on perception and behavior, so behaviorists have put forward the "perception–behavior" mode. They also think that intelligence is not necessarily dependent on knowledge and that the representation, inference, and application of knowledge can be expressed by the interaction between the real world and its surroundings.

Regardless of the difference of the three aforementioned research strategies, the issue of AI that they are dealing with is only a small category of human intelligence. Talking about human intelligence in a wider view of life science, brain science, cognitive science, linguistics, philosophy, mathematics, psychology, etc., there are many aspects that have not yet been touched upon, such as human emotions, language, imagination, sudden awakening, inspiration, instinct, etc.

The widening of the concept of AI calls for a breakthrough in the study of biologic intelligence, especially in the study of human intelligence. Only when we have a fairly better understanding of the working mechanism of the two, can we simulate it more effectively.

Another more important aspect of the issue is the simulation of the uncertainties in human intelligence research, which is the focus of this book.

REFERENCES

1. A. Barr and E. A. Feigenbaum, *The Handbook of Artificial Intelligence*, Vol. 1. William Kaufmann, Inc., Los Altos, CA, 1981.
2. A. Barr and E. A. Feigenbaum, *The Handbook of Artificial Intelligence*, Vol. 2. William Kaufmann, Inc., Los Altos, CA, 1981.
3. A. Barr and E. A. Feigenbaum, The art of AI: themes and case studies of knowledge engineering, In: *Proceedings of the 5th International Joint Conference on Artificial Intelligence*, Cambridge, MA, Vol. 5: 1014–1029, 1977.
4. Kurt Gödel, *The Consistency of the Axiom of Choice and of the Generalized Continuum— Hypothesis with the Axioms of Set Theory*, Princeton University Press, Princeton, NJ, 1940.
5. M. L. Minsky, *Semantic Information Processing*, MIT Press, Cambridge, MA, 1969.

6. H. A. Simon, *The Sciences of the Artificial*, 3rd ed., MIT Press, Cambridge, MA, 1997.
7. Xiaoli Liu, Gödel *and AI*, Center for Science Communication, Peking University, http://www.csc.pku.edu.cn, 2003
8. A. Newell and H. A. Simon, Computer Science as Empirical Inquiry: Symbols and Search, *Communications of the ACM*, Vol. 19: 113–126, 1976.
9. Dixing Wang, Artificial Intelligence Theory and Technology Revolution, http://entropy.com.cn, 2002.
10. Shichang Fang, *Discrete Mathematics*, Xidian University Press, Xi'an, 2000.
11. Yuanyuan Wang and Shangfen Li, *Discrete Mathematics*, Science Press, Beijing, 1994.
12. Xiaoxiang Zhang, *Computer Science and Technology Encyclopedia*, Tsinghua University Press, Beijing, 1998.
13. Xuhua Liu and Yunfei Jiang, *Theorem Machine Proof*, Beijing Science Press, Beijing, 1987.
14. Alonzo Church, *The Calculi of Lambda Conversion*, Princeton University Press, Princeton, NJ, 1941.
15. Heling Wu and Lin Cui, *The ACM Turing Award (1966–1999) — the Development History of Computer Phylogeny*, High Education Press, Beijing, 2000.
16. Zixing Cai and Guangyou Xu, *Artificial Intelligence: Principles and Applications*, Tsinghua University Press, Beijing, 1996.
17. Alain Colmerauer, An Introduction to Prolog III, *Communications of the ACM*, Vol. 33, No. 7:69–90, 1990.
18. P. Roussel, *Prolog: Manuel de Reference et d'Utilisation. Groupe d'Intelligence Artificielle*, Faculté des Sciences de Luminy, Marseilles, France, 1975.
19. Deyi Li, *A Prolog Database System*, John Wiley & Sons, New York, 1984.
20. M. R. Genesereth and N. J. Nilsson, *Logic Foundation of Artificial Intelligence*, Morgan Kaufmann, Palo Alto, CA, 1987.
21. Yaorui Lin, Bo Zhang, and Chunyi Shi, *Expert System and Its Applications*, Tsinghua University Press, Beijing, 1988.
22. Joseph C. Giarratano and Gary D. Riley, *Expert Systems: Principles and Programming*, Thomson Course Technology, Boston, MA, 2003.
23. Wenwei Chen, *Decision Support System and Its Development*, Tsinghua University Press, Beijing, 2000.
24. Xingui He, *Knowledge Processing and Expert System*, National Defence Industry Press, Beijing, 1990.
25. W. S. McCulloch and W. Pitts, A Logical Calculus of Ideas Immanent in Nervous Activity, *Bulletin of Mathematical Biophysics*, Vol. 5: 115–133, 1943.
26. J. J. Hopfield, Neural networks and physical systems with emergent collective computational abilities, In: *Proceedings of the National Academy of Sciences*, Vol. 79: 2554–2558, 1982.
27. J. J. Hopfield, Artificial Neural Networks, *IEEE Circuit and Devices Magazine*, Vol. 4, No. 9:3–10, 1988.
28. David E. Rumelhart, Geoffrey E. Hinton, and Ronald J. Williams, Learning Internal Representations by Backpropagating Errors, *Nature*, Vol. 323, No. 99: 533–536, 1986.
29. W. T. Miller et al., *Neural Network for Control*, MIT Press, Cambridge, MA, 1990.
30. P. J. Werbos, Beyond Regression: New Tools for Prediction and Analysis in the Behavioral Sciences, Ph.D. Thesis, Harvard University, Cambridge, MA, 1974.
31. Richard O. Duda, Peter E. Hart, and David G. Stork, *Pattern Classification*, 2nd edition, Wiley Interscience, Inc., New York, 2000.

32. Zushu Li and Yaqing Tu, *Apery Intelligent Control*, National Defence Industry Press, Beijing, 2003.

33. H. W. Bode, Feedback-the history of an idea, In: *Proceedings of the Symposium on Active Network and Feedback Systems*, Brooklyn, NY, 1960.

34. Jingxun Fu, *Robotics: Control, Sensors, Vision and Intelligence*, China Science Press, Beijing, 1989.

35. Norbert Wiener, *The Human Use of Human Beings: Cybernetics and Society*, Da Capo Press, Cambridge, MA, 1988.

36. Xinsong Jiang, Development of foreign robots and our countermeasure, *Robot*, No.1:3–10, 1987.

37. Hao Wang and Zongyuan Mao, *Intelligent Control Method of Robot*, National Defence Industry Press, Beijing, 2002.

3 On Uncertainties of Knowledge

The greatest difference between human intelligence and the intelligence of other creatures lies in the fact that the former can, with the help of language, carry on knowledge accumulated over thousands of years. So, the uncertainties of intelligence will definitely be reflected in knowledge. In order to study the uncertainties of intelligence, first we must study the uncertainties of knowledge.

The uncertainties of knowledge are first and foremost reflected in the uncertainties of the language, which is the carrier of knowledge. They are also reflected in the commonsense knowledge, which usually is the knowledge of knowledge, called meta-knowledge. It is the basis of all other professional knowledge. Common sense is usually expressed in natural languages. The basic elements in a language are linguistic values, which correspond to different concepts. The uncertainties of concepts come in various aspects, mostly in randomness and fuzziness. Thus, this book starts with the discussion on randomness and fuzziness, and then moves on to discuss other uncertainties in language and common sense.

3.1 ON RANDOMNESS

3.1.1 THE OBJECTIVITY OF RANDOMNESS

What is randomness? In nature and human society, we often encounter this phenomenon: an experiment or observation (generally referred to as "test"), even if conducted under exactly the same condition, might bring out totally different results. In the case of dice rolling, you have six possible results although it is thrown under the same condition. This phenomenon is called "randomness." It is characterized by repeatability and uncertainty on the result although knowing all possible choices. So the phenomenon is determined by objective conditions. It is uncertain because the insufficiency of condition makes no necessary relation between condition and outcome.

Is randomness objective? Either in the science or philosophy field, this has been a significant question in controversies. The most famous one is the conflict between the two great physicists: Albert Einstein and Niels Bohr. "God does not play dice with the universe," Einstein asserted. "Stop telling God what to do," Bohr replied. Nevertheless, we may raise another question, "Where is God?" The three arguments may be traced back to the fundamental issues of philosophy.

Deterministic science represented by Newtonian mechanics gives an accurate description approach, in which the universe is regarded as a clockwork dynamic system in fixed, concordant, and orderly motion. In other words, once the initial state of the universe is set, its entire future for all time is determined.[1] From Newton to Laplace and Einstein, what they described were the completely deterministic views of the universe. Determinists held the belief that all events are *predetermined* and *fixed* in a world, and randomness is not natural but emerges because of people's ignorance. If given the initial states and boundary conditions of the universe, the subsequent development of the universe could be predicted with as much accuracy as desired. The doctrine is given its most striking illustration by Laplace in his *Philosophical Essays on Probabilities* in 1814: "Given for one instant an intelligence which could comprehend all the forces by which nature is animated and the respective situation of the beings who compose it — an intelligence sufficiently vast to submit these data to analysis — it would embrace in the same formula the movements of the greatest bodies of the universe and those of the lightest atom; for it, nothing would be uncertain and the future, as the past, would be present to its eyes." Even Einstein, who initiated a revolution in science, also believed that it should be possible to determine unequivocally every past and future state of the universe based on the state at a given instant.[2]

The determinists are right in some cases. For example, for such questions as, "Do aliens exist," no definite answer can be given due to the lack of knowledge. What can be given is only uncertain answers such as, "Maybe they do, maybe they don't." But there can be only one answer. Once we have had enough knowledge, we can give a definite answer. Undoubtedly, the deterministic ideas are right about this kind of pseudorandom problems. Besides, since knowledge about that system behavior may not be precisely described, the determinists still stick to the belief that dynamic systems generally have the characteristics of stability and convergence. Once the initial errors are adequately small, the future deviation can be kept within a satisfactorily small range. In some respects, their ideas are verified in successful applications, e.g., the prediction of the Halley's Comet orbit, the discovery of Neptune, etc.

The influence of deterministic science is so immense that, for quite a long period of time, it has confined people's way and perspectives on the world. Although living in a real and chaotic world, scientists can see nothing more than a clockwork mechanical world. The task of science is merely to explain the structure and the motion principle of this clockwork universe. Scientists neglect uncertainties and exclude them from the study scope of modern science.

According to determinism, all developments and present states of the universe, ranging from changes of the world situation to individual fate, were determined billions of years ago when the universe was still in chaos. Obviously, nowadays nobody would agree with them. We can cite numerous examples to refute them. For instance, no matter how knowledgeable and experienced you are, you cannot predict with certainty who will win the Olympics gold medal. Nor can you predict what will happen tomorrow, or whether the lottery ticket you have bought will win you a big prize, etc.

With the advancement of science, for example the study of molecular thermal motion, determinism has met with more and more insurmountable difficulties. When natural science encountered a multiple degree-of-freedom system composed of a huge number of elements, determinism did not fit any more because of the single-value determinism assumption, which is not applicable to the complexity inherent in the system. More importantly, this complexity will lead to a fundamental change of the being — even if we could precisely determine the tracks of the particles and their interactive forces, we could not master their accurate motions as a whole. Therefore, in the late nineteenth century, L. Boltzmann and W. Gibbs introduced the concept of randomness into physics and established the field of statistical mechanics. According to statistical mechanics, as to a group, what can be described deterministically by using Newton's law is only its general law; as to any individual in the group, no definite description can be given. What can be given is the "possibility" of individual behaviors.

The greater impact on determinism came from quantum mechanics, which further reveals that the true nature of the real world is randomness. Quantum mechanics deals with the law of motion of a group made up of atoms or particles. In the microscopic world, all particles have both wavelike and particlelike properties, i.e., the wave–particle duality. As they are so tiny, the particles under observation will be perturbed whatever methods of observation are used. So it is not possible to simultaneously determine the position and momentum of a particle. Moreover, the better the position is known, the less sure the momentum is known (and vice versa). The position and momentum of a particle cannot be simultaneously measured with arbitrarily high precision. Based on this finding, the German physicist Werner Heisenberg put forward the "uncertainty principle" in 1927. It should be noted, however, the uncertainty principle is not a statement about the inaccuracy of measurement instruments, or a reflection on the quality of experimental methods; it arises from the wave–particle duality inherent in the nature of particles. The uncertainty principle suggests that it is impossible, in principle, to obtain precise initial values. Randomness in the objective world is not a transitional state resulting from ignorance or inadequacy of knowledge. It is the true reflection of the intrinsic properties of nature, a real entity in the real world and a basic element existing in the universe. In 1928 the Danish physicist Neils Bohr deduced from philosophy his famous "complementary principle," which insisted on the wave–particle duality of microcosmic matter and pointed out that the wave and particle nature are mutually exclusive and simultaneously complementary. The uncertainty principle and complementary principle implicitly assert that the rigid causal determinism or causalism is invalid in the microcosm. The thought to unify randomness and determinism in quantum mechanics is of great significance in changing people's ideas while we try to understand the true nature of the world.[3]

Studies on chaos phenomena provided the most up-to-date and powerful proof for scientists to overcome the impact of determinism. Chaos theory has thrown new light on the origin and nature of randomness and its relationship with determinism. The randomness in statistical mechanics and quantum mechanics is an external one. Before the discovery of the chaos phenomenon, people believed that randomness originated from the "great number" phenomenon or the group effect. Giant systems composed of masses of molecules or particles have various complicated causal nexus and incomprehensible interplays at a microscale level, which result in the behavior of particles being highly random. Surprisingly, studies on the chaos phenomenon, the inherent randomness of a deterministic system, led to an interesting finding that randomness may occur in very simple systems, although the great number phenomenon is not involved. The chaos or inherent randomness stems from the nonlinear property of the deterministic systems. As nonlinear property is common in most systems, randomness has a vast source. Therefore, it is the common attribute inherent in the objective world.[4]

Since the objective world is random, the subjective world, which is the reflection of the objective world in the human mind, is also random. Thus, there must be randomness in the intelligence and the knowledge expressed in the cognitive process of human beings.

3.1.2 THE BEAUTY OF RANDOMNESS

Randomness has made it more arduous for mankind to explore the universe, as scientists will have to produce more sophisticated theories to understand the world. However, at the same time, randomness has made the world more colorful and charming. Both in the objective world and the subjective world, randomness is everywhere.

People often say that there still remain three difficult problems to be solved in the world, namely: How life begins, where the universe originates from, and how the human brain works. Up till now, scientists have not yet given a clear explanation on how the universe was formed. There is a great deal of randomness in the formation of earth and the advent of human beings. The earth has experienced at least six times massive extinction of creatures. The most remarkable one was the extinction of dinosaurs 60 million years ago. Had it not been for the catastrophic change, could it be that the earth was still dominated by dinosaurs? Could human beings become what they are today? Nobody knows how many random catastrophes the earth has experienced since then. As a matter of fact, many random factors were present in all events such as the formation and positioning of the earth and the sun, as well as the other stars and the galaxy, the advent of life and the evolution of species.

In real-world situations, you might have a nose like your grandpa's while your sister's eyes might resemble those of your uncle's. Both of you may look alike, but you are not the same. This is called genetic variation. Creatures of the species have similar attributes, but their differences are obvious; they are not identical in details. This is because sudden random changes have occurred in the genetic attributes of their genes in the process of copy and transformation, resulting in some dissimilarity of new cells or entities from their ancestors. In the evolution of species, it is because of this relentless change that species adapt themselves to nature and become the fittest to survive in it. Without this randomness in evolution, there would not be so many different kinds of species and picturesque landscapes.

In social life, in history, or even in individual life, there exists randomness. In the course of history of each country, there are always some turning points. If, at a certain turning point, a different choice had been made, the history of that country, even the histories of its neighboring countries would have to be rewritten. Human society is a world so full of randomness that the interactions and mutual influence between one person and another, or between people and events are random, totally unpredictable. For instance, the birth of any individual is the result of a series of coincidences. In the process of growing up, it is all random what kind of schoolmates, friends, workmates and spouse one will encounter, which way one will choose at each crossroad, what sort of person one will grow up to be, and finally what way one will choose to leave the world. It is this randomness that has become our driving force for pursuit and struggle in life.

Randomness fills the world and our life with charms of the unknown and provides us with all kinds of opportunities. While determinism may tell us the general laws about events, such as statistical laws of a group or a relative truth, for an individual an opportunity will change his or her life. The so-called "opportunity" that everyone seeks is in essence a random event of a special kind, the low probability event. This opportunity of the low probability rarely shows up in life. When it does show up, it will work wonders. So it often leads to the success of an individual. By "seizing the opportunity," we actually mean to snatch the randomness, make use of, or even create such incidents of low probability.

Humans are born with a desire to pursue knowledge. The omnipresent randomness has greatly incited the curiosity of humans and has become what life is all about. Just imagine how boring life would be if you already knew the result before a sports match's start. What a boring life it would be if you already knew the outcome of something before you ever begin to do it. And how uninterested you would be if you knew beforehand who and what you would come across in your life ahead. We are sure nobody would like such a totally deterministic life without any randomness or fancy.

3.2 ON FUZZINESS

Early studies of uncertainty focused only on randomness. Probability theory and mathematic statistics already have a history of more than a hundred years. With more in-depth studies, people found a kind of uncertainties that could not be described with randomness. That was "fuzziness."

Fuzziness is a characteristic feature of modern science to describe quantitative relationships and space formation by using precise definitions and rigidly proven theorems, and to explore the laws of the objective world by using precisely controlled experimental methods, accurate measurements, and calculation so as to establish a rigorous theoretic system. It was believed that everything should and could be more precise and there was nothing that need not and could not be more precise. If things should go to the contrary, it was because people's understanding of the problems had not reached such a depth.

Fuzziness had long been excluded from the sanctuary of science until the twentieth century when people began to realize that fuzziness was not something negative, rather it was something positive because it could convey more information at a smaller cost and make judgment on complicated problems and solve them efficiently. That is to say, fuzziness helps improve efficiency. Both accuracy and fuzziness are characterized by dualism and both approaches can be regarded as scientific. The shift from viewing fuzziness as something negative to recognizing its positive role was a profound revolution both in scientific thinking and in methodology, laying a philosophic foundation for the establishment of fuzzy theory. Bertrand Russell's thesis titled "Vagueness" published in 1923 marked a starting point.[5] And in 1937, Max Black dwelt on it in his thesis with the same title.[6] What they meant by vagueness was roughly the fuzziness we are speaking of nowadays. In 1951, Gaspard Monge, a French mathematician, first used the term "fuzzy sets."

Lotfi Zadeh, as the founder of fuzzy logic, has long been active in system science. He appreciates adequately the contradiction between and unity of accuracy and fuzziness. He realized that a complex system was difficult to be dealt with in the framework of precise mathematics. He analyzed fuzziness, approximation, randomness, and ambiguity. He maintained that fuzziness should become a basis research object, put forward the basic concepts of degree of membership and membership function, and produced the fuzzy set, thus being considered as the creator of fuzzy theory. His paper titled "Fuzzy Sets" was regarded as one of the first works in fuzzy theory.[7] Since then, this discipline has witnessed a booming development.

3.2.1 THE OBJECTIVITY OF FUZZINESS

The following is a famous *falakros* ("bald" in Greek) puzzle of the Bald Man derived from the ancient Greek scholars:

Proposition A: A man without hair on his head is bald.
Proposition B: A man with one more hair on his head than a bald man is bald.
Proposition A is true. Proposition B is also true because one hair more or less will not change the fact of being bald or not. With Propositions A and B as premises, a conclusion can be deduced by repeating precise reasoning.
Proposition C: A hirsute man is bald.

Obviously, Proposition C is false. That is what we call a paradox. Innumerable paradoxes can be expressed in this way, e.g., the paradoxes of the age, the paradox of the height, etc. They could not be explained with the precise reasoning due to lack of the notion of fuzziness. Predicates "is bald" and "is not bald" are different concepts, easy to distinguish in our daily life. However, the two concepts cannot be defined precisely because they both embody the characteristic feature of fuzziness. Changes between the two are gradual, not sudden and there is no clear boundary between them. If you use binary logic to describe these concepts and make judgment and reasoning based on them, it will no doubt lead to a paradox, for traditional logic and precise thinking have proved useless before them.

Although we are familiar with the ever-changing shapes of clouds in the sky, the slowly rising smoke, and a fog that comes from nowhere, we cannot describe their profile accurately. The reason for this is that they have no clear boundary, or their boundary, if any, is not regular or smooth. This is what we call fuzziness in nature.

Seasons come, seasons go. People may say a certain month is spring or a certain day is summer; however, it is hard to determine on which day spring becomes summer. How is it that today is spring and tomorrow turns summer? Likewise, the same holds true for rotation of daytime and nighttime, kids growing up into adults. What time is the clear boundary of day and night? How can a kid grow up to be an adult overnight? Generally speaking, all kinds of microcosmic transformations are gradual continuous processes. This is another kind of fuzziness in nature.

The few examples above cannot cover the universality of fuzziness. Not only is fuzziness reflected in the categorization of things of objective existence, but it is also reflected in people's thinking process and in the understanding of the subjective and objective world.

Some believe that fuzziness comes into being in the process of people trying to perceive the objective world, reality independent of the mind. It does not reflect the inherent feature of reality, but rather it is an uncertainty that comes into existence during the process of cognition and expression of the cognitive subject. According to the understanding, fuzziness is no more than the feeling and judgment of the cognitive subject and the objective reality or existence itself is not characterized as clear or fuzzy. This is a one-sided view.

Human cognition is the reflection of things that exist independent of human consciousness. As for the things in the objective world, some present the characteristics of one or the other while others exhibit the properties of one and the other. These differences are an objective reality. The subjective feeling of sharpness or vagueness is only the reflection of the objective differences. If things of objective existence were all labeled "one or the other" with a clear-cut boundary, there should not exist such things as fuzziness and fuzzy concept. Therefore, it should be said that fuzziness strikes root in the intermediate transition of the differences in the objective world. It is an objective reality inherent in the things that exist independent of the mind.[8]

Things of objective existence are extensively interconnected and continuously developing. They are interwoven with such extensive connections and mutual reactions. These characteristic features, together with continuous development, make it possible to bring about fuzziness to the nature and categorization of objective facts through objective cognition. For example, to those things having the continuity in time or in state, people cannot analyze the whole time domain or all its states. But the continuous objects can be simplified to be a discrete model so as to analyze a lot of objects with this model. The infinite, continuous and transitional objects can be classified into finite, discrete, and neutral-exclusive sets. This simplified, the precise approach is actually the approach of taking preciseness and fuzziness as special cases.

3.2.2 THE BEAUTY OF FUZZINESS

When arguing about whether light was particle or wave, Einstein once said, "Why 'this or that'? Why not 'this and that'?" This remark can help us better understand the relationship between fuzziness and accuracy. Fuzziness and accuracy are a unity of contradiction. Sharpness is "this or that" in the condition and category of things, while fuzziness is "this and that" in the condition and category of things, i.e., neutral exclusion. "This and that" of fuzziness in the condition and category of things is neutral transition. Therefore, in essence, fuzziness is "this and that."

The fuzziness existing in both the objective world and the human mind is not an obstacle to science development and cognition of human beings. On the contrary, with the dramatic development of modern science and gradual progress of the human society, "fuzziness," a word with a fuzzy meaning in itself, is attracting more and more interest and attention.

Accuracy can be the dreamboat of scientists. But going too far in seeking accuracy while ignoring fuzziness will run counter to one's wishes. In 1923 philosopher Russell addressed in his thesis titled, "Vagueness" that "It would be a great mistake to suppose that vague knowledge must be false." and "All traditional logic habitually assumes that precise symbols are being employed. It is therefore not applicable to this terrestrial life, but only to an imagined celestial existence." Russell, as a symbolic and logic scientist, deeply realized the significance of fuzziness and criticized the blind adoration of preciseness. In the 1950s, Norbert Wiener, the initiator of control theory, pointed out that, compared with computer, human brain is superior in that it can grasp the unclear and fuzzy concepts.[9] It confirms the positive signification of fuzziness. In 1957, Daniel Jones, an English linguist, wrote that we all (including the preciseness pursuers) use imprecise, vague, and indefinable terms and principles while speaking and writing. However, it does not hinder that the words we use are effective and necessary.[10] This is the criticism toward the precise transformation of every natural linguistic concept in the academic field.

With the development of science and technology, scientists have realized the truth that if fuzzy things are to be made precise deliberately, we will not only pay the price of complexity in methods, but the significance of the result will also be reduced. When it has reached a certain point, it will become something glamorous in theory, yet of little use in practice. The incompatibility theory points out that the more complex a system is, the lower the ability to describe it with precision and significant understanding.[11]

Fuzziness makes our lives easier and more efficient. With the help of fuzziness, complex events can be judged and managed efficiently. So, people can recognize different handwritings easily, figure out the meaning of an incomplete utterance, and recognize friends they have not seen for a long time. Thanks to fuzziness, painters can paint picturesque landscapes and lifelike portraits without precise measurement and calculation, and doctors can make right diagnoses from the fuzzy symptoms of the patients, etc.

When talking about the relationship between art and science, most people agree that works of art, such as literature, painting, and music are less precise than the theorems and principles in mathematics, physics, and chemistry. But we all enjoy the fuzzy artistic mood in works of art which can be sensed, but not explained in words. We will use all the imagination and intellect we have to appreciate and feel them, thus bringing about aesthetic joy. No matter how fast your central processing unit is and how large the memory of your computer is, the computer cannot understand the feeling that people have when enjoying a beautiful sunset. Science and art have a close relationship. To appreciate great works of art or to understand great science, intelligence and wisdom are needed. Both pursue the universality, the depth, and the meaningfulness. Both seek truth and beauty. It is a great enjoyment to appreciate the amazing scenery created by the convergence of different disciplines, even by the convergence of science and art. The unity of science and art has created a splendid and glamorous picture of human knowledge.

3.3 UNCERTAINTIES IN NATURAL LANGUAGES

Randomness and fuzziness are two basic aspects of uncertainties, which are involved in natural languages. The uncertainties of natural languages are important in the research on the uncertainties of knowledge, and the understanding of natural languages becomes significant in the research of artificial intelligence (AI).

3.3.1 LANGUAGES AS THE CARRIER OF HUMAN KNOWLEDGE

Natural languages emerge with the rise of mankind for the communication, expression of ideas, and construction of minds. We have not yet found a people group with no language of its own. There are two kinds of languages: oral and written. So far, the explanations of the origins of all oral languages are merely presumptions. But there is one affirmation that, apart from the vocal organs, the brain is also involved in the origin of oral languages.

How many languages are there in the human world? A linguist in the Soviet Union devoted his lifetime to learning more than a hundred languages. This amazing figure, however, is only one-fortieth of the total number of the known human languages! There are approximately 4,200 languages acknowledged by linguists, without counting local dialects.

Nevertheless, the situation of written languages is quite different. They emerged only in a certain stage during the human development process. The earliest language existed 3,000 years ago. Their origins are pictures and symbols, e.g., Chinese characters are hieroglyphs tightly related to pictures, and English words composed of letters are tightly related to symbols. The pictures and symbols were notional in the early days, and turned into the current characters and words after long periods of evolution and development. All the written languages in the world, although various, can be categorized into two kinds in general: the Chinese character system representative of the Chinese civilization, and the Latin letter system standing for the western civilization.[12]

In long-term evolution, human beings, among all the creatures, became the unique and highly intelligent kinds. The reason for this lies in vocal languages and words. Language, as the approach to construct the mind and express ideas, is the key communication tool for humans, as well as one of the distinguishing characteristics between humans and other animals. Other animal languages and communication means, although existent, cannot be compared to those of humans. Human languages are effective codes. They enable humans to communicate effectively, passing down the ancestors' experience, information, and knowledge generation by generation. Civilization comes from memory, and memory comes from written languages. The emergence of written languages helps humans to learn the knowledge accumulated in the past, as well as to record their own experiences for the next generation. Human experience and knowledge can last longer by words than by vocal languages. For instance, ancient inscriptions of Chinese characters on oracle bones and carapaces record the ancient king in the Shang Dynasty combating in a war, and the arrowheaded characters reveal the codes of Hammurabi in ancient Babylon to the current world. Words construct a shared knowledge database for humans rather than storing the knowledge in the individual's brain. Consequently, the human civilization can be developed rapidly as human intelligence does. One apparent evidence is the development of human intelligence within the recent thousands of years, which surpasses the development within the ancient hundreds of thousands of years. Ever since the invention of vocal languages and words, human brains have evolved rapidly, which has formed the material foundation for the human intelligence enhancement. Thereafter, various abstract languages are created on the basis of words, e.g., mathematics and computer languages, and consequentially propel the human intelligence to a higher level. As a result, AI has been given birth by human intelligence, and has become the supplement to human intelligence.

Derived from all the statements above, we think that languages are essential embodiments of human intelligence and carriers of human thoughts. Other animals may possess intelligence, memory, consciousness, sense, emotion, temper, and simple languages, but not written languages. Hence other animal intelligences are resting on simple biological repetition, whereas for humans, our development is based on knowledge accumulation and civilization evolution through written languages.

3.3.2 UNCERTAINTIES IN LANGUAGES

Uncertainties are the inherent features of the objective world, and thus, as the expression tools of the objective world and the carriers of human thoughts, natural languages are inevitably uncertain. Secondly, the limitation of an individual's cognition results in the uncertainties of human expression of the world, and consequently makes the linguistic outputs different. Even for the same event, the difference in the cognitions of different individuals makes the linguistic expression different. Uncertainty is a natural characteristic in human languages, which is an essential feature in human thoughts.

There are neither definite structures in the organization of languages, nor fixed orders in the expression of thoughts. A structured sentence, although grammatically constrained, will vary its meaning in different contexts. Even in grammar, there is no constant and no non-exceptionally prevalent regularity. As the basic units in sentence, linguistic values usually correspond to concepts, which are generally expressed by nouns. The relationships between concepts are expressed by predicates. Uncertainty exists in concepts and predicates, as well as other constructive factors in sentences, e.g., adverbs.

The research in uncertainties of concepts, which are the basic constructive units of natural languages, is the key research in uncertainties of languages. There are various kinds of uncertainties in concepts, within which the uppermost are fuzziness and randomness.

Concepts are generally expressed by the connotation and the extension. The concept of fuzziness mainly refers to the uncertainty of the extension, i.e., no definite meaning in the essence, and no clear boundary in the quantity. There are many fuzzy concepts in our daily lives, where clear quantitative boundaries do not exist. For instance, in order to determine the completion of steel in furnace, apart from some precise information such as temperature, ingredient proportion, and smelting time, we also need to know some fuzzy information, such as color, boiling extent. In general, for the representation of continuous and infinite objects by discrete and finite concepts, the overlapping of the concept boundaries is inevitable, and consequentially the concepts become fuzzy. These include the concepts of young, tall, fat, beautiful, good, hot, far, etc.

Conceptual fuzziness is most typically involved in the sensational words. Human sensation signals such as temperature, color, smell, sound, etc., are generally continuous, while the linguistic symbols are discrete. The representation of continuous sensation by discrete symbols makes the boundary vague, and thus results in fuzziness at the boundary. For example, there are finite words for colors, while the color spectrum is continuous. The representation will not provide clear boundaries for different color words. The colors within the spectrum between red and orange are difficult to be classified into red or orange. Other similar sensation words are fuzzy as well, including cold, hot, beautiful, and ugly.[13]

The linguistic expressions of numbers are also fuzzy, e.g., "a pile of," "a few minutes past three," "in his or her thirties," etc. Such kind of usage does not mean that speakers are reluctant to convey the precise number, but the simple expressions by fuzzy numbers make them easier to be memorized. According to the "principle of economy," this is to achieve the maximum understanding effect by minimum psychological investment.

Besides, adverbs such as "very," "extremely," "maybe," "generally," "about," "probably," etc., are frequently used for the fuzzy expression of objects.

Moreover, concepts also involve randomness. Concepts are connected with the objective world rather than isolated, and have a concrete background. The connection with time makes them constantly in the making. Due to the difference in people's life experiences and social backgrounds, the concepts formed after a series of perceptual activities will differ. Different individuals will have different understandings of the same concept, and even the same individual will have different understandings of the same concept at different times, which is especially obvious in the concepts in humanity activities. Besides, the abstract feature of concepts makes it possible to represent lots of concepts by the same linguistic value. There are different themes in different occasions, and the same linguistic value can represent different concepts for different objects. This is the reason why concepts have the feature of randomness.

Here are some examples. If we translate the English word "uncle" into Chinese, there can be a few different meanings, e.g., father's brother, mother's brother, father's brother-in-law, mother's brother-in-law, etc. The choice in these meanings is dependent on the context. Apart from those aforementioned, many words can be used to describe frequency, e.g., "often," "probably," "seldom," etc. They are used to reveal the randomness of the objective world.

More often, the uncertainties of concepts combine randomness and fuzziness, which are not obviously separable. For example, the word "sometimes" conveys randomness; however, for different individuals in different occasions the understanding of its boundary will be fuzzy.

Although uncertainties exist in word selection, sentence expression, mood usage, and intersentence organization in the usage of languages, it does not hinder the communication. This phenomenon indicates that human intelligence is strongly capable of expressing, processing, and understanding uncertainties. It would be impossible to carry on the communication if precision was desired for every linguistic value in every sentence.

Research on a computer's understanding of natural language, and machine translation have been carried out for more than 60 years since the 1940s. Despite the progress, we are still far from the goal of complete understanding of human languages because of too many uncertainties involved in languages. AI with certainties established in the past century provides a variety of symbolic languages, which are more precise and stricter than natural languages and lacking in uncertainties. If the breakthrough in uncertainty research on natural languages is achieved, computers will be able to "think" in natural languages rather than in precise and strict symbolic languages, and there will be essential progress in natural language understanding and even in AI. Hopes are laid for the breakthroughs in the research on uncertainties of linguistic values, which represent concepts. This is probably the direction of "computing with words" pursued by Dr. Zadeh.[14]

3.4 UNCERTAINTIES IN COMMONSENSE KNOWLEDGE

Research on the uncertainty of knowledge will surely touch on common sense, which is related to any one in any discipline. Human intellectual activities, including judgment, reasoning, abstracting, etc., are all related to common sense. First of all, let's see what common sense is.

3.4.1 COMMON UNDERSTANDING ABOUT COMMON SENSE

In our daily lives, common sense means simple, general, and prevalent knowledge, which is self-explaining. Nevertheless, it is extremely difficult to represent, process, and verify common sense in AI because the more prevalent and more basic common knowledge is, the more difficult it is to be proved. The definitions of common sense are different according to different people.

As defined in *Ci Hai**, common sense, compared with specialty knowledge, is the knowledge required for and comprehensible to every person. In philosophy, common sense is the normal judgment ability, natural reasons, the beginning of reasoning, the preliminary reason of normal issue, and the middle status between stupidity and cleverness. In *Oxford English-Chinese Dictionary*, common sense is "the ability to think about things in a practical way and make sensible decisions."[15]

The first definition treats common sense as the knowledge which is known to common persons. It is invariant according to time and environment. In the second definition, the phrases "natural reasoning," "the beginning of reasoning," and "the preliminary reasoning of normal issues" reveal that common sense is for the general public. The last one to take into account is life experiences, which can explain the variant features based on place, time, and people. Nevertheless, the excessive relying on life experience makes common sense specialized, and hence this definition is not completely appropriate. As a summary of the aforementioned explanations, we think

---

* *Ci Hai* is a set of large-scale synthetical cyclopaedia on Chinese words and different subjects.

that common sense should have at least the properties of universality and directness. The position of common sense in the whole region of knowledge is like that of axiom in the logic system, which is self-evident.

First, in general, normal people have common sense, so common sense should be universal to the largest degree. This universality is not the universality in the theoretical summarization and abstraction, but the universality that is accepted by most people. The connection between the common sense and the experiences in daily lives makes this universality subject to era, region, social life status, and knowledge levels of people. The most prevalent common sense is the one possessed by the majority of people. Secondly, common sense is self-evident. It should be accepted directly through intuition and instinct. If it can be acquired only through verification, it will be distorted or bifurcated, as different understandings of the verification will emerge, and consequentially will not be accepted universally. Finally, people have arguments about whether common sense is the most fundamental. In one aspect, common sense is the knowledge of knowledge, and thus it is the most fundamental; nevertheless, there are so many occasions that common sense is only the prejudice in the public. In this case, common sense is not the truth. So, sometimes disobedience can lead to innovation.

Actually, AI experts do not care about the psychological debate on common sense definition. Instead, they focus on the problem of what kind of common sense should be involved in AI research, after the understanding of the important position that common sense takes in the simulation of AI. In the research on common sense, J. McCarthy divided human commonsense abilities into two parts: commonsense knowledge and commonsense reasoning,[16] and he listed valuable research problems related to common sense, i.e., knowledge of status which is variant according to changes of time and events; knowledge of the results of concurrent events; knowledge of animal survival and death, their position and change in shape; knowledge of how to represent and exploit knowledge; knowledge of how to represent knowledge, faiths, objectives, hobbies, motivations, and abilities; and the commonsense knowledge of scientific knowledge.[15]

As can be inferred, McCarthy was interested in the formalized representation of common sense, and the methodology for commonsense-based reasoning using mathematical tools.

3.4.2 RELATIVITY OF COMMONSENSE KNOWLEDGE

Generally, one item of common sense is the same as one item of true proposition. Proposition is composed of sentences. The uncertainties of a sentence have been discussed before. In this section we are going to discuss on a higher level uncertainty in common sense, i.e., the relativity of commonsense knowledge.

Common sense is different from professional knowledge because of its universality and directness. It is not necessarily strict, profound, and systematic, which professional knowledge must have. It is also influenced by the factors of time, region, cognition subject, etc. In a word, this is the uncertainty because of relativity.

The boundary between commonsense knowledge and professional knowledge is relative as well. Professional knowledge can turn into commonsense knowledge as time changes, and vice versa. The current commonsense knowledge that the earth moves around the sun is a remarkable scientific discovery in the seventeenth century. In the nineteenth century, we discovered that many diseases are caused by bacteria, which is now common sense. Quantum physics, which is abstruse to the public now, may be widely accepted by the common people in the future. From another perspective, there are cases where common sense turns into professional knowledge, e.g., the difference between Jinshi and Juren*. The difference between common sense and professional knowledge is also relative according to people's professional backgrounds and educational levels. For a historian, the order of Eastern Jin Dynasty** and Western Jin Dynasty is his commonsense knowledge, while it is not necessarily so for a chemistry professor.

Commonsense knowledge is also regional, related to local cultures and customs. For the Chinese people, the "Mid-Autumn Festival" is a festival for family reunions in which people enjoy moon cakes and stare at the moon. However, in western culture, it is quite different. The common sense in the West that we should hold the fork with the left hand and the knife with the right may be perceived as something strange for Asians. Knowledge regarded as common sense in one culture may become the academic research topic in another culture.

The vast range of content of commonsense knowledge and the tight connection with environment, time, and problem background make it uncertain which units of common sense are selected in the human's thinking activity, so that the formalization of common sense is extremely difficult. The representation and development of commonsense knowledge are acknowledged as foundational difficulties in AI. There are two main approaches dealing with commonsense knowledge. First, McCarthy proposed to establish a logical system of common sense, and to introduce a complete set of formalized systems, e.g., nonmonotonic logics, cognition logics, etc. The second approach is proposed by Feigenbaum, which realizes the AI plan by constructing a huge scale of commonsense database. None of the approaches is practically promising due to the tremendous difficulties in realization. The representation methods on various knowledge, such as one-order logic, production system, semantic networks, neural networks, etc., and various formulized reasoning methods, such as qualitative reasoning, fuzzy reasoning, monotonic reasoning, hypo-coordinate reasoning, faith reasoning, and case-based reasoning, etc., although implemented in the commonsense research, are far away from the utilization of human commonsense knowledge.

Currently, there is a common understanding in AI, which is the possession of common sense is the essential distinction between human and machine, and the concretion of human commonsense knowledge will determine the realization of AI. Therefore, we cannot avoid the research on common sense, which will be a prosperous direction of AI research in this new century.

---

* Jinshi and Juren are two ranks of scholars in feudatorial China, and means first degree scholars and imperial scholars respectively. Jinshi is superior to Juren.
** Eastern Jin and Western Jin are two feudatorial dynasties in China within the time periods of 317 BC-420 BC and 265 BC-316 BC respectively.

3.5 OTHER UNCERTAINTIES OF KNOWLEDGE

It is of much difficult to describe clearly all the uncertainties present in knowledge. As addressed before, randomness and fuzziness are the two most basic uncertainties, and are involved in both the uncertainty of language and in the uncertainty of common sense. Nevertheless, there are uncertainties with higher level in the framework of knowledge system, especially incompleteness, incoordination, and impermanence.

3.5.1 INCOMPLETENESS OF KNOWLEDGE

In the sense of human cognitive to the objective world and himself, the accumulated knowledge has not been complete yet, and also will not be completed. The knowledge system ought to be open. The activity of knowledge accumulation is only a process approaching completeness but not achieving that. Kurt Gödel addressed in his "incompleteness theorem" that for every mathematic axiom system that contains no contradictory axioms, no matter how formalized it is, there exist theorems that cannot be proven. Although the scientific knowledge system based on mathematics cannot be completed, it does not mean that the knowledge is incomplete in any concrete occasion. Starting from a concrete problem with specific background, the completeness of related knowledge is normally required, especially for the mathematic abstraction of this problem. We cannot let go of the requirement for relative completeness of specific knowledge only because of the non-existence of absolute completeness.

The incompleteness of knowledge is composed of incompleteness of knowledge content and incompleteness of knowledge structure. The incompleteness of knowledge content probably originates from the insufficient observation, imprecise equipment, and local information constraint in the knowledge acquisition. As a result, some parts of the information content are totally not acquired, or the quality is found but not the quantity. The incompleteness of knowledge structure may be caused by the limitation in understanding and acquisition approaches. For the incomplete of knowledge structure, it may be due to the fact that some key factors are neglected in the incomplete understanding process of the background and structure while solving a specific problem. Moreover, people often make judgment based on some self-evident common sense or without consulting certain knowledge sources. As a result, the knowledge will be incomplete.

How to treat the uncertainties of knowledge? Does it mean that the more intelligent people are, the more complete that knowledge is? Professor Daniel Kahneman, the 2002 Nobel Prize winner in economics, discovered uncertainties in the thinking process during judgment and the rational feature within irrational events, i.e., knowledge completeness is not compulsory for the thinking process. Individual cognition varies greatly, and there are many differences between self-learning and supervised learning, familiarity and unfamiliarity, activeness and passiveness, positive knowledge and negative knowledge rational and emotional components, the present and the past, etc. With all this diversity, data and knowledge become preferable and result in different personalized procedures in knowledge acquisition, accumulation, processing and exploitation. All these differences enable people of unlimited abilities to understand the objective world and themselves, and make it possible to approach completeness.

3.5.2 INCOORDINATION OF KNOWLEDGE

Another representation of knowledge uncertainty is incoordination, which refers to the internal contradiction in the knowledge. There are different levels of incoordination: redundance, disturbance, and conflict.

Redundance means that there exist some phenomena of redundant and excessive knowledge while people solve problems. From the logical reasoning perspective, redundant knowledge might not be exploited, redundance is inevitable in the process of knowledge replication, accumulation, and utilization. Redundance is universal, and represents a waste of resources. It is considered uncoordinated as we have to spend time processing the redundant knowledge and sometimes the judgment will be misled by it. In knowledge engineering, redundant knowledge can be eliminated by knowledge reduction. Nevertheless, there is still one advantage that redundance has, i.e., the system robustness can be enhanced. Knowledge redundance in human society will not reduce the importance and necessity of knowledge accumulation in the individual.

Disturbance means that the knowledge is not only helpless to the current problem, but also harmful to other knowledge, or even leading to mistakes. For instance, the disturbance caused by noise in knowledge acquisition, the disturbance caused by the incompatibility between old and new knowledge during learning, and the inter-disturbance while using similar knowledge, will cause the uncertainties in using knowledge.

Conflict is contradiction, which means that knowledge may have states that oppose each other. Knowledge is the summarization of human activities in the objective world, which is limited by the capability of self, and subject to time and location. There exist contradictions between knowledge in different disciplines; therefore, conflicts within the totality of human knowledge are unavoidable.

Within the same theoretical logic frame, conflict should not be allowed. For an enclosed and specific knowledge system, conflicts will lead to contradictory results, and break down the axiom system in this knowledge system. However, for the human knowledge system as a whole, conflicts are the stairs leading to progress because they can inspire human desire for knowledge and ignite the passion for exploration. In the process of scientific development, a new discovery or assumption is often contradictory to the previous theories. By this iteration between contradiction and unification, scientific discovery can approach truth.

Incoordination is an important embodiment of knowledge uncertainty. It is impossible and unnecessary to eliminate the knowledge incoordination in any occasion. Incoordination should be treated as a normal status of knowledge, and allowed to be contained and compromised.

3.5.3 IMPERMANENCE OF KNOWLEDGE

Impermanence means that knowledge varies with time. Human cognition of nature, society, or even oneself is a continuously updating process. Like any biological system, human knowledge also has metabolism. On one hand, correct knowledge in one era might become wrong in another. For instance, people in the past believed that earth was the center of the universe, and that heavier objects had larger acceleration. Now this knowledge is abandoned. On the other hand, some knowledge could be outdated. For example, the frontier knowledge on vacuum tube computer and relay switch in the past is obsolete now. For individuals, the dated knowledge might be meaningless; however, it is an indispensable part of the chain in the human knowledge system. The present knowledge is evolved out of the past. Impermanence becomes more apparent in the present information era, as knowledge accumulation speeds up. We must keep studying in our lifetime because of this knowledge uncertainty.

Let's consider memory, which is the storage of human knowledge and the foundation of human cognition and intelligence. For an individual, the brain is in the process of growing, maturing, and decaying. Humans have different memorizing abilities in different periods. For all humankind, the brain is also in the process of evolution. Besides, the brain has the tendency of forgetting. The memorized information will fade away, shift, shake, and disappear eventually, just as a photograph blurs as time passes by. As a consequence, knowledge stored in the human brain varies with time, i.e., the knowledge that is frequently used will be more impressed and gradually intensified, while the one that is seldom used will be eliminated from the memory.

Besides the aforementioned time-related variation, person-dependence is another embodiment of knowledge impermanence. Because different persons have different cognition abilities and even one person can be in different external environments, the knowledge will be understood, applied and verified in different ways, and consequentially knowledge impermanence will emerge. Knowledge impermanence makes it more difficult to formalize the knowledge. Nevertheless, it is also impermanence that propels knowledge evolution. During the process in which old knowledge is being amended and new knowledge is being acquired, human intelligence evolves.

Nowadays, knowledge incompleteness, incoordination, and impermanence are vividly manifested in the fact of prevalent dependence on the Internet. The information and knowledge on the Internet are for the most part unstructured or hemi-structured. They exist in the forms of image, text, sound, and data, which are translated in multiple languages, distributed on billions of Web sites. The contents on millions of Web sites are increased, deleted or modified quickly. Almost all the knowledge uncertainties are presented there. The research spotlight is now focusing on how to share and exploit the efficient and reliable uncertain knowledge within the open and dynamic environment.

The uncertainties of knowledge originate from the uncertainties of the objective world, in which the majority of phenomena are uncertain. The certain and regular phenomena will only occur under some particular preconditions, and exist within a short period of time. Although there are researchers in fields of certainty, such as the natural science fields of physics, mathematics, biology, and in the social science fields of philosophy, economy, society, psychology, cognition, almost nobody places suspicion on the uncertain essence of the world. An increasing number of scientists believe that uncertainty is the charm of the world and only uncertainty itself is certain! Given this background, the science of chaos, the science of complexity, and AI with uncertainty can be developed prosperously.

Knowledge uncertainties inevitably lead to the research of AI with uncertainty. It is an important task for AI researchers to represent, process, and simulate uncertain knowledge, formalize the regularity in the uncertain knowledge, simulate the human cognition process of understanding the world and oneself, and enable the machine to process uncertain intelligence.[17] In this book, we will start with the mathematic foundation of uncertain knowledge, and introduce the cloud model which is a model for qualitative-quantitative transformation. Later, physical approaches of knowledge discovery with uncertainty will be established. Thereafter, we present the beneficial attempts in data mining and intelligent control.

REFERENCES

1. Isaac Newton and Andrew Motte, *Sir Isaac Newton's Mathematical Principles of Natural Philosophy and His System of the World*, University of California Press, CA, 1960.
2. Liangying Xu and Dainian Fan, *Einstein Corpus*, Volume 1, The Commercial Press, Beijing, 1976.
3. Dongsheng Miao and Huajie Liu, *Introduction in Chaos*, China Renmin University Press, Beijing, 1993.
4. Ilya Prigogine, (transl. by Lan Zhan), *The End of Certainty*, Free Press, New York, 1997.
5. B. Russell, Vagueness, *Australasian Journal of Psychology and Philosophy*, No. 1: 84–92, 1923.
6. M. Black, Vagueness, *Philosophy of Science*, No. 4: 422–431, 1937.
7. L. A. Zadeh, Fuzzy sets, *Information and Control*, No. 8: 338–353, 1965.
8. Dongsheng Miao, *Introduction of Fuzziness*, China Renmin University Press, Beijing, 1987.
9. Norbert Wiener, (transl. by Ren Zhong), *The Selection of Wiener's Composings*, Shanghai Translation Publishing House, Shanghai, 1978.
10. Tieping Wu, *Fuzzy Linguistics*, Shanghai Foreign Language Education Press, Shanghai, 1999.
11. Xiaoming Li, *Fuzziness — the Enigma in Human Cognition*, People's Publishing House, Beijing, 1985.
12. The origin and species of the language, Web of Literature Views, http://www.white-collar.net/wx_hsl/whfk/040.htm, 2004
13. Feisheng Ye, Tongqiang Xu, *Compendium of Linguistics*, Peking University Press, Beijing, 1997.
14. L. A. Zadeh, Fuzzy logic = computing with words, *IEEE Transactions on Fuzzy Systems*, No. 2: 103–111, 1996.
15. Ruqian Lu, *The Knowledge Engineering and Knowledge Science across the Century*, Tsinghua University Press, Beijing, 2001.
16. J. McCarthy, *Formalizing Commonsense*, Alebex, Norwood, New Jersey, 1990.
17. Deyi Li, Changyu Liu, and Yi Du, Artificial intelligence with uncertainty, *Journal of Software*, 15:11, 1583–1594, 2004.

4 Mathematical Foundation of AI with Uncertainty

In research or in daily life, humans search certain mathematical modules in order to describe phenomena or solve problems. Both with the rapid development of communication, computer, and network and the widespread application of basic software, middle part and application software, the capability of the computer used in value computation, data processing, information searching, industry control, decision support, and knowledge engineering has greatly improved. However, the problems mentioned in the above fields mostly have certain preconditions and exact mathematical modules and can be described in computer programming language.

Artificial Intelligence (AI) has been developed based on mathematics. In order to solve different kinds of uncertainty problems in AI, we also need the support of mathematics. In this chapter, we will address the key point in foundational mathematical knowledge related to uncertainty.

4.1 PROBABILITY THEORY

Randomness is the most essential uncertainty in human knowledge and intelligence. Probability theory is the main mathematical tool to solve the problem of randomness. A gambler's dispute in 1654 led to the creation of probability theory. The Helvetic mathematician Jacob Bernoulli, the founder of the probability theory, demonstrated the stability of frequency using strict mathematics that we call "Bernoulli's law of large numbers" today. P. S. Laplace and J. W. Lindeberg demonstrated the central limit theorem. P. L. Chebyshev, A. A. Markov, Khinchine, etc. established the general form of the law of large numbers and central limit theorem, and illustrated that a large number of random phenomena obtain normal distribution. One of the difficulties in developing a mathematical theory of probability has been to arrive at a definition of probability that is precise enough to use in mathematics. Russian mathematician A. N. Kolmogorov finally solved this matter in the twentieth century by treating the probability theory on an axiomatic basis. He outlined an axiomatic approach that forms the basis for statistics and stochastic processes. K. Pearson conducted the research on biological statistics by means of mathematics, and introduced the basic terms of mathematical statistics, e.g., standard deviation, normal curve, and mean-squared error. In 1901, he published *Biometrika*, which is the forum for mathematical statistics. R. A. Fisher established the approach for parameter estimation of model and experiment design, which made experiments more scientific and contributed to mathematical statistics. R. Brown, who is a biologist, noticed that pollen particles had irregular motions in water. Einstein and Wiener conducted their research on this phenomenon from the physical and mathematical aspects, respectively. Wiener proposed the mathematical model of Brown motion and initiated the stochastic process. A. K. Erlan et al. did research on the Poisson process of telephone calls and established the foundations of queueing theory. With the research in birth–death process, stationary process, Markov process, and martingale theory, the stochastic process became a significant branch that was extensively applied in the probability theory.

Probability theory includes probability, statistics and stochastic processes, which provide a mathematical basis for the randomness study[1] and a tool for the research on uncertainty.

4.1.1 Bayes' Theorem

4.1.1.1 Relationship and Logical Operation of Random Event

In nature and societal activities, inevitable phenomena denote the situations that must happen under certain conditions. That is to say, the result of a inevitable phenomenon can be predicted as long as it satisfies certain conditions. However, many other phenomena when repeatedly observed under some conditions lead to different results. It is such phenomena, which we think of as being random, that are called "random phenomena." The representations of random phenomena are random events.

If the random events are represented by sets, the relationships between events in probability theory and sets in set theory are as follows:

$\bar{A}$ corresponds to the event that A does not occur.
$A \subset B$ corresponds to the event that A is a proper subset of B.
$A = B$ corresponds to the event that A equals B.
$A \cup B$ corresponds to the event that either A or B occurs.
$A \cap B$ corresponds to the event that both A and B occur.
$A - B$ corresponds to the event that A occurs but B does not occur.

Let A, B, and C be three events. Basic properties of event operations are as follows:

Commutative laws: $A \cup B = B \cup A, A \cap B = B \cap A$
Associative laws: $A \cup (B \cup C) = (A \cup B) \cup C, A \cap (B \cap C) = (A \cap B) \cap C$
Distributive laws: $A \cup (B \cap C) = (A \cup B) \cap (A \cup C), A \cap (B \cup C) = (A \cap B)$
$\cup (A \cap C)$
De Morgan's laws: $\overline{A \cup B} = \bar{A} \cap \bar{B}, \ \overline{A \cap B} = \bar{A} \cup \bar{B}$

Normally, there are three approaches to calculate the probability of event A, denoted $P(A)$.

Classical probability: $P(A) = \frac{k}{n}$, where k is the number of elementary events involved in A, and n is the total number of the elementary events.

Frequency approach: $P(A) = \frac{m}{n}$, here n is the number of repeated times of the experiment, and m is the number of times that A happens.

Subjective determination approach: $P(A) = $ the value given by experts. It is usually used for random events that cannot be repeated in large quantity.

4.1.1.2 Axiomization Definition of Probability

Basic axioms of probability introduced by Kolmogorov reflects the essential law of probability.

A probability measure P on a σ-field of subsets F of a set Ω is a real-valued function satisfying the following properties:

1. $\forall\ A \in F, P(A) \geq 0$
2. $P(\Omega) = 1$
3. If $A_i \cap A_j = \varnothing (i \neq j)$ for $\forall\ A_m \in F, m = 1, 2, 3,...,$ then

$$P\left(\bigcup_{m=1}^{\infty} A_m\right) = \sum_{m=1}^{\infty} P(A_m)$$

A probability space, denoted by (Ω, F, P), is a set Ω, a σ -field of subsets, and a probability measure P defined on F. Now it is quite easy to find a probability space that corresponds to each random experiment.

Some probability space (Ω, F, P) is given and the properties of probabilities are as follows:

1. The relationship of probabilities between two opposite events

$$P(\overline{A}) = 1 - P(A)$$

2. If A is a proper subset of B, i.e., $(A \subset B)$, then

$$P(A) \leq P(B), \quad P(B - A) = P(B) - P(A)$$

3. Add formula

$$P(A \cup B) = P(A) + P(B) - P(AB)$$

4. Semi-addability

$$P\left(\bigcup_{m=1}^{n} A_m\right) \leq \sum_{m=1}^{n} P(A_m)$$

5. Continuous theorem

Let $\{A_n\}(n = 1,2,...)$ be an arbitrary sequence of monotonic events and $\lim_{n \to \infty} A_n = A$
Then

$$\lim_{n \to \infty} P(A_n) = P(\lim_{n \to \infty} A_n) = P(A)$$

4.1.1.3 Conditional Probability and Bayes' Theorem

Definition 4.1

Independence of random events: Let (Ω, F, P) *be a probability space. Let A and B be two arbitrary events in F. If* $P(A \cap B) = P(A)\,P(B)$*, then A and B are independent.*
The properties of independent events are as follows:

1. Any event is independent of certain events or impossible events.
2. If A and B are independent, then A and $\bar{B}$, $\bar{A}$ and B, $\bar{A}$ and $\bar{B}$ are also independent.
3. If A and $B_i (i = 1, 2,..., n)$ are independent and B_i does not intersect with B_j, then A and $\bigcup_{i=1}^{n} B_i$ are independent.

Event A is independent of B if and only if the happening of event A is not affected by the happening of event B.

Definition 4.2

Let (Ω, F, P) *be a probability space. Let A and B be two arbitrary events in F. Suppose* $P(B) > 0$*, then the conditional probability of A given B is defined as* $P(A|B) = \frac{P(AB)}{P(B)}$*.*

The significance of conditional probability is that the uncertainty of event A can be identified by using the probability of event B.
The properties of conditional probability are as follows:

1. $0 \le P(A|B) \le 1$ for any $A \in F$
2. $P(\Omega|A) = 1$
3. If $A_i \cap A_j = \varnothing (i \ne j)$ for $A_m \in F$, $m = 1, 2,...$, then

$$P\left(\bigcup_{m=1}^{\infty} (A_m|B) \right) = \sum_{m=1}^{\infty} P(A_m|B)$$

Bayes' theorem can be demonstrated by using the above properties of conditional probability.

Theorem 4.1: Bayes' Theorem.

Let B_i *be a mutually disjoint event in F.* $\bigcup_{i=1}^{n} B_i = \Omega$*;* $P(B_i) > 0$ *(*$i = 1, 2,..., n$*). Let A be an arbitrary event in F and* $P(A) > 0$*, then*

$$P(B_i|A) = \frac{P(B_i)P(A|B_i)}{\sum\limits_{j=1}^{n} P(B_j)P(A|B_j)}$$

In general, Bayes' theorem can be used to explain the following questions:

Suppose B_i is the set of all possible reasons resulting in the happening of event A. Let the probability of B_i be $P(B_i)$, which is called prior probability. In random experiments, assume that we can only observe the happening of A which is related with B_i instead of the happening of B_i. Under this condition, we can calculate the possibility of event B_i in terms of the conditional probability $P(B_i|A)$, which is called posteriori probability of B_i. Bayes' formula shows the relationship between the prior probability and posteriori probability, from which we can make a decision about what is the most important reason causing event A.

For example, symptom A may be caused by disease B_i. In order to confirm the exact disease resulting in symptom A, we can calculate the posteriori probability of B_i in the condition of A happening using Bayes' formula. The most possible disease that causes symptom A can be judged according to the maximal value of posteriori probability.

Bayesian statistical approach is developed based on the above thought. Subjective Bayesian reasoning approach is based on the Bayes formula. As represented in forms of rules, it is:

$$(Rulename) \ E \to H(P(H), LS, LN)$$

where E is the evidence, H is the conclusion, LS is the degree to which E supports H, LN is the degree to which $\neg E$ supports H, $P(H)$ is the prior probability of H, and $P(H)$ is the probability of the event that H is true.

The values of $P(H)$, LS and LN are given subjectively. The trust on H is dependent on the updated information. The subjective Bayesian reasoning is the process in which the prior probability of H is updated into the posteriori probability $P(H|E)$ based on $P(E)$ and the rules LS and LN. But this approach is subject to the shortage of prior probability.

A Bayesian network which combines probability theory and graphic theory provides a new approach to deal with the uncertainty information in AI. The Bayesian theorem is the foundation of this probability network.

A Bayesian network is composed of a set of nodes and directed edges. The nodes represent events or variables. The edges of Bayesian network prospect for causalities or probability relation among nodes. All of the edges are directed edges and there are no cycles in the graph. The Bayesian network is the specific type of graphical model that is used to qualitatively describe the complex causality and probability among events. It can also be used to quantificationally represent these relationships under the condition that the prior information was already known. The topology of a Bayesian network usually depends on the problem that is defined. Nowadays, one of the hottest research orientations of the Bayesian network is how to automatically confirm and optimize the topology through learning.

4.1.2 PROBABILITY DISTRIBUTION FUNCTION

Definition 4.3

Let X be a random variable and x be an arbitrary real number. The distribution function of X is defined as $F(x) = P\{X \leq x\}$. The random variable is continuous if the distribution function is absolutely continuous. The differential f(x) of the distribution function is called "probability density function" and

$$F(x) = \int_{-\infty}^{x} f(t)\,dt$$

Theorem 4.2

The distribution function $F(x)$ of any arbitrary random variable has the following properties:

1. Monotone nondecreasing:

$$F(a) \leq F(b); \ \forall -\infty < a < b < +\infty$$

2. Right continuous:

$$\lim_{x \to a+0} F(x) = F(a); \ \forall -\infty < a < +\infty$$

3. $F(-\infty) = 0; F(+\infty) = 1$

Distribution function is the most important tool to describe random phenomena. If we get the distribution function or probability density function of the random variable, the probability of this random variable in any range can be calculated. That is to say, we can obtain all of the probability properties for the random variable, but we will face the following problems in the application of probability distribution function:

1. Distribution function usually cannot fully represent some properties of random variables, such as the position of value, decentralization degree, and so on.
2. In many applications, the distribution function is too complex to obtain. In another situation, we only need to know the probability of some ranges.
3. The mathematical formalism of distribution function of some important distribution, such as binomial distribution, normal distribution, Poisson distribution, and so on are already known, but with some unknown parameters which may represent important mathematical properties.

It is necessary to study numerical characters of random variables. The most important numerical characters are expectation, variance, and correlation coefficient.

Definition 4.4

Let X be any random variable. The mathematical expectation of X denoted by EX is defined as

$$EX = \int_{-\infty}^{\infty} x\,dF(x)$$

where F(x) is the probability distribution function of X.

If X is continuous, EX can also be defined as

$$EX = \int_{-\infty}^{\infty} xf(x)dx$$

where f(x) is the probability density function of X.
The variance DX of X is defined as

$$DX = E(X - EX)^2$$

The correlation coefficient of two random variables X_1 and X_2 is defined as

$$r = \frac{E(X_1X_2) - EX_1EX_2}{\sqrt{DX_1}\sqrt{DX_2}}$$

Mathematical expectation *EX* represents the mean with probability for all possible values of the random variable. Variance *DX* shows the dispersive degree of the values of the random variable. The correlation coefficient *r* represents the dependence degree between the random variables.

Moment is another important numerical character of the random variable. EX^k is the *k*th order origin moment of X. $E|X|^k$ is the *k*th order absolute origin moment. $E(X - EX)^k$ is the *k*th order central moment. $E|X - Ex|^k$ is the *k*th order absolute central moment, where *k* is positive integer and $k \geq 1$.

4.1.3 NORMAL DISTRIBUTION

Normal distribution is one of the most important distributions in probability theory. It is used as an approximation to a large variety of problems. Its probability density function is symmetric at the expectation, and decreases to the bi-directions.

4.1.3.1 The Definition and Properties of Normal Distribution

Definition 4.5

If the probability density function of random variable X is

$$f(x) = \frac{1}{\sqrt{2\pi}\sigma} e^{-\frac{(x-\mu)^2}{2\sigma^2}}, \quad -\infty < x < +\infty$$

where $\mu, \sigma(\sigma > 0)$ are constants, then X subjects to the normal distribution with parameters μ, σ, denoted as

$$X \sim N(\mu, \sigma^2)$$

If $\mu = 0$, $\sigma = 1$, X subjects to standard normal distribution.

If X is a normal distribution $N(\mu, \sigma^2)$, the properties of X are as follows:

1. The probability density function $f(x; \mu, \sigma^2)$ is symmetrical in terms of the line $x = \mu$, i.e.,

$$f(\mu - x) = f(\mu + x)$$

2. $f(x; \mu, \sigma^2)$ is increasing in $(-\infty, \mu)$ and decreasing in $(\mu, +\infty)$. The maximal value $\frac{1}{\sqrt{2\pi}\sigma}$ is achieved when x equals μ. There are inflexions when $x = \mu - \sigma$ and $x = \mu + \sigma$ and

$$\lim_{x \to \infty} f(x) = \lim_{x \to -\infty} f(x) = 0$$

3. The distribution function $F(x; \mu, \sigma^2)$ is central symmetric about the point $(\mu, \frac{1}{2})$, i.e.,

$$F(\mu - x) = 1 - F(\mu + x)$$

4. The expectation and variance of X are $EX = \mu$ and $DX = \sigma^2$, respectively. The parameter μ determines the central position, while σ determines the steepness.

5. If $X_i \sim N(\mu_i, \sigma_i^2)$, $(i = 1, 2, ..., n)$, and they are independent of each other, then

$$\sum_{i=1}^{n} k_i X_i \sim N\left(\sum_{i=1}^{n} k_i \mu_i, \sum_{i=1}^{n} k_i^2 \sigma_i^2 \right)$$

That is to say, any linear combination of independent normal random variables is also normal distribution.

Especially, if $X \sim (\mu, \sigma^2)$, $Y = \alpha X + \beta$, the distribution of Y is also normal distribution. The expectation and variance of Y is $\alpha \mu + \beta$ and $\alpha^2 \sigma^2$. If the distribution of the sum of independent random variables is normal distribution, then the distribution function of each random variable is also normal distribution.

6. Any normal distribution function can be transferred into standard normal distribution using the property: $\frac{X - \mu}{\sigma} \sim N(0, 1)$, and

$$P\{\mu - 3\sigma \leq X \leq \mu + 3\sigma\} \approx 0.9973$$

i.e., if the random variable subjects to normal distribution, 99.73% of its values are located in the interval with the center μ and length 3σ. This is called the "3σ principle," which is widely applied in mathematical statistics.

4.1.3.2 Multidimensional Normal Distribution

For multirandom variables, we need to know not only the probability property of single random variable, but also their joint probability property. The most important multidimensional random variable is n-dimensional normal distribution.

Definition 4.6

n dimensional random vector $X = (X_1, X_2,..., X_n)$ subjects to the n-dimensional normal distribution with parameter (μ, C), if its probability density function is

$$f(x) = (2\pi)^{-\frac{n}{2}} |C|^{\frac{1}{2}} \exp\left[\frac{1}{2}(x-\mu)^T C^{-1}(x-\mu)\right]$$

where C is a $n \times n$ symmetric order positive matrix, C^{-1} is the inverse matrix of C, $(x - \mu)^T$ is the transpose of $(x - \mu)$, and

$$x = \begin{pmatrix} x_1 \\ \vdots \\ x_n \end{pmatrix}, \quad \mu = \begin{pmatrix} \mu_1 \\ \vdots \\ \mu_n \end{pmatrix}$$

The properties of n-dimensional normal distribution are as follows:

Theorem 4.3

Let X be a random vector $(X_1, X_2,..., X_n)$. The distribution function of X is n-dimensional normal distribution if and only if any linear combination $Y = \sum_i a_i X_i + b$ is one-dimensional normal distribution, where a_i, b are real numbers and they cannot both be equal to 0.

Theorem 4.4

Let X be a n-dimensional vector $(X_1, X_2,..., X_n)$ obtaining n-dimensional normal distribution. Let

$$Y_l = \sum_{j=1}^{n} a_{lj} X_j \quad (l = 1, 2,..., r; \ r \le n; \ a_{lj} \in R)$$

The random vector $(Y_1, Y_2,...,Y_r)$ is an r-dimensional normal distribution.

Two-dimensional normal distribution is the simplest and most important distribution in multidimensional normal distributions.

Definition 4.7

The distribution function of the vector $X = (X_1, X_2)$ is defined as two-dimensional normal distribution (with parameters $(\mu_1, \mu_2, \sigma_1^2, \sigma_2^2, r)$), if its probability density function is

$$f(x) = f(x_1, x_2)$$

$$= \frac{1}{2\pi\sigma_1\sigma_2} \exp\left\{-\frac{1}{2(1-r^2)}\left[\frac{(x_1-\mu_1)^2}{\sigma_1^2} - \frac{2r(x_1-\mu_1)(x_2-\mu_2)}{\sigma_1\sigma_2} + \frac{(x_2-\mu_2)^2}{\sigma_2^2}\right]\right\}$$

where $\sigma_1 > 0$; $\sigma_2 > 0$; $|r| \le 1$.

When $r = 0, \mu_1 = \mu_2 = 0, \sigma_1 = \sigma_2 = 1$, it is called a two-dimensional standard normal distribution.

The two marginal distributions of X_1 and X_2 are both one-dimensional normal distribution, with probability density functions as

$$f(x_1) = \frac{1}{\sqrt{2\pi}\sigma_1} e^{-\frac{(x_1-\mu_1)^2}{2\sigma_1^2}}$$

$$f(x_2) = \frac{1}{\sqrt{2\pi}\sigma_2} e^{-\frac{(x_2-\mu_2)^2}{2\sigma_2^2}}$$

The parameters $(\mu_1, \mu_2, \sigma_1^2, \sigma_2^2, r)$ are, respectively, the expectation, variance, and correlation coefficient of the two marginal distributions.

4.1.4 Laws of Large Numbers and Central Limit Theorem

4.1.4.1 Laws of Large Numbers

In probability theory, laws of large numbers imply that the average of a sequence of random variables converges to their expectations, as the size of the sequence goes to infinity. We aim to describe the two main and widely used laws of large numbers, namely the Poisson law of large numbers and the Khinchine law of large numbers.

Theorem 4.5 Poisson's Law of Large Numbers

Let μ_n be the times that event A occurs in the n independent experiments. If the probability that A occurs in the ith experiment is p_i, then $\frac{\mu_n}{n}$ converges in probability to $\frac{1}{n}\sum_{i=1}^{n} p_i$.

This theorem indicates that the frequency of event is stable in the repeated experiments. Thus, the frequency can be the estimation of probability in practical applications.

Theorem 4.6 Khinchine's Law of Large Numbers

Let $\{X_i\}(i = 1,2,..., n)$ be independent random variables with the same distribution. Their mathematical expectations are a. Then $\frac{1}{n}\sum_{i=1}^{n} X_i$ converges in probability to a.

This theorem indicates that the average result of a large quantity of random phenomena is stable. A single random phenomenon can hardly affect the overall result of a large number of random phenomena. In other words, although a single random phenomenon can result in random deviation, these deviations will be compensated for after a large number of experiments, and the average result will be stable.

4.1.4.2 Central Limit Theorem

Central limit theorem, as one of the most important theorems in probability theory, shows the reasons of causing a normal distribution. It is the theoretical foundation of normal distribution.

People find that many problems can be solved with the limit distribution of the sum of independence random variables, denoted as $\sum_{i=1}^{n} X_i$. In order to avoid getting infinite expectation and variance of the random varieties, we need to normalize $\sum_{i=1}^{n} X_i$. So, we assume that X_i has finite expectation and variances. Let

$$EX_i = \mu_i, \quad DX_i = \sigma_i^2, \quad B_n^2 = \sum_{i=1}^{n} \sigma_i^2$$

The random variable

$$Y_n = \sum_{i-1}^{n} \left(\frac{X_i - \mu_i}{B_n} \right)$$

is the normalized sum of independent random variable sequence $X_1, X_2,..., X_n$. If the corresponding normalized sum sequence $Y_1, Y_2,...,Y_n$ is asymptotic to standard normal distribution, $X_1, X_2,..., X_n$ satisfy the central limit theorem.

Generally, the theorems, which determine whether the limit distributions of the summations of random variables are normal distributions, are called "central limit theorems."

There are lots of forms for central limit theorems. They have the same conclusion, only with different constraints on $X_1, X_2,..., X_n$.

For independent random variables with the same distribution, the central limit theorem is the simplest and most commonly applied, as called "Levy-Lindeberg theorem."

Theorem 4.7 Levy-Lindeberg Theorem

For independent random variables with the same distribution, i.e., $X_1, X_2,...,X_n$, if their expectations are μ, and the variance σ^2 is finite, then the limit distribution of $\frac{1}{\sqrt{n}\sigma}\sum_{j=1}^{n}(x_j - \mu)$ is a standard normal distribution.

In history, the De Moivre-Laplace theorem is the earliest central limit theorem and a special example of the Levy-Lindeberg theorem.

Theorem 4.8 De Moivre-Laplace Theorem

Let μ_n denote the times of success in the n-Bernoulli experiments. Let p be the probability of each successful experiment. Then the limit distribution of μ_n subjects to the normal distribution.

This theorem demonstrates that normal distribution is the limit distribution of binomial distribution.

The following theorem provides the most generalized conditions for the independent random variables with different distribution to satisfy the central limit theorem.

Theorem 4.9 Lindeberg Theorem

Let $X_1, X_2,\ldots$ be independent random variables that satisfy the Lindeberg condition, i.e.,

$$\lim_{n\to\infty}\frac{1}{B_n^2}\sum_{i=1}^{n}\int_{|x-\mu_j|\geq\tau B_n}(x-\mu_j)^2 dF_j(x)=0, \quad \forall\tau>0$$

Then, $X_1, X_2,\ldots$ obey the central limit theorem.

The probability meaning of the Lindeberg condition is that if the independent random variables $X_1, X_2,\ldots$ satisfy the condition, for arbitrary $\varepsilon>0$,

$$\lim_{n\to\infty}P\left\{\max_{1\leq i\leq n}\left|\frac{X_i-\mu_i}{B_n}\right|\geq\varepsilon\right\}=0$$

That is, when n is adequately large, the normalized sum is composed of terms that are equally small.

The Lindeberg condition is the mathematical expression of this intuitionistic fact: if the random variable is determined by the sum of a large quantity of independent occasional factors, and every factor has equally minor effects on it, then this random variable approximately subjects to normal distribution.

The central limit theorem not only shows the reason for causing normal distribution, but also demonstrates many important distributions, e.g., the limits of binomial and Poisson distribution are normal distributions. Besides, many important distributions are normal distribution functions, such as χ^2 distribution, t-distribution and F-distribution. Therefore, normal distribution can as well describe many random phenomena in nature.

The problems related to normal distribution can be well solved because of the good mathematical properties and simple mathematical format of normal distribution density, so that normal distribution plays an essential part in probability theory, mathematical statistics, and stochastic process. The significance of it has already gone beyond the range of probability theory.

4.1.5 POWER LAW DISTRIBUTION

Definition 4.8

Power law distribution is defined as,

$$f(x) = kx^{-a}, \quad (x > 0)$$

where $f(x)$ is the probability density function, k is a constant, and a is a positive constant.

Power law distribution is simple in probability theory. Although it is expressed in the form of elementary function, it reflects the property of self-similarity and scale-free in nature, and society. Thus, it has important application prospect.
The properties of power law distribution are as follows:

1. When $k > 0$ and $x > 0$, if we take logarithm on both sides of the above equation,

$$\ln f(x) = \ln k - a \ln x$$

   i.e., it is a line under bi-logarithm coordinate, as shown in Figure 4.1.
2. Self-similarity and scale-free. If we take the logarithm on both sides of the power law distribution function, followed by differentiating the result, we can get

$$d \ln f(x) = -a d \ln x$$

Because

$$d \ln x = dx/x, \quad d \ln f(x) = df/f$$

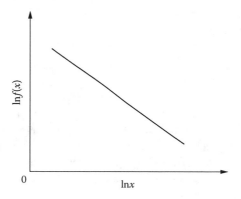

FIGURE 4.1 Power law distribution under bi-logarithm coordinate.

So,

$$(df/f)/(dx/x) = -a$$

That is to say, there is a linear relationship between relative change of function (df/f) and variable (dx/x). This is the mathematical definition of self-similarity. Thus, power law distribution has the property of self-similarity, which is also called scaling free.

Power law distribution not only attenuates slowly, but also has the same proportional attenuation to different degree. Distribution function in other forms, such as exponent function and Gaussian function, does not take on this scaling invariance. After having changed their scale, the new function is not simply proportional to the original function. All these functions contain a characteristic length, which attenuates rapidly in this range. Power law distribution does not have this characteristic length.

Zipf law is a specific power law distribution, which was first discovered in glossology.[2]

Zipf Law: In a certain range, if the vocabulary used is large enough, we compose the order of words according to their appearance probability; thus, it is power law distribution between the probability of certain word appearance $P(r)$ and the corresponding serial number r:

$$P(r) \propto 1/r^a$$

where a is a positive constant, called "Zipf exponent."

The value of a depends on the concrete usage. In the English language, $a \approx 1$. That is, in the English language, the word "the" is used with highest probability, almost twice as much as "of," which comes in second place. Zipf law shows that words frequently used only occupy a small proportion of the whole vocabulary; most of the words are seldom used. Afterwards, people discovered that, in nature language, etyma, and alphabets that are much smaller than words in scale and phrases and sentences that are much larger than words in scale also obey the power law distribution generally.

Today, especially after 1998, articles published in *Nature* and *Science* have revealed that, a complex network in real world has the property of scale-free. Thus it has drawn interests from many different domains like mathematics, statistics, computer science, and ecology. Some people even put the same importance on power law distribution as on normal distribution.

4.1.6 ENTROPY

Entropy is an important parameter in the research field of AI with uncertainty. This concept was originally introduced in 1864 by the Germanic physical scientist R. J. Clausius, in the study of classical thermodynamics. Clausius defined the entropy ΔS of a thermodynamic system, during a reversible process in which an amount of heat Q is applied at constant absolute temperature T, as

$$\Delta S = \frac{\Delta Q}{T}$$

Here entropy represents the average distribution degree of any energy in space. Entropy increases as the uniformity of the energy spreads. The Second Law of Thermodynamics tells us that no system can convert from one form to another with 100% efficiency.

In 1877, Boltzmann proposed the new concept of entropy in the field of statistics, a named Boltzmann formula:

$$S = k \ln W$$

where k is Boltzmann's constant and W is the number of arrangements of the atoms or molecules. From the formula, we can find that entropy is proportional to the logarithm of W.

Because the W increases with the system situation becoming more disordered, entropy in the field of thermodynamics represents the unordered degree of system.

In 1948, in a fundamental paper on the transmission of information, C. E. Shannon proposed the definition of information entropy:

Definition 4.9

Let X be a random variable with range $\{X_i\}(i = 1, 2,..., n)$. Consider the event X_i with probability $p(X_i)$, the information entropy or uncertainty of X is

$$H(X) = -\sum_{i=1}^{n} p(X_i) \log p(X_i)$$

The basic concept of entropy in information theory has to do with how much randomness there is in an event. An alternative way to look at this is to talk about how much information is carried by the signal. The bigger the entropy is, the more information the signal carries.

Information entropy describes the average of probability of a certain event occuring in the event set X. Entropy is the indicator of the level of the uncertainty: the larger the entropy, the higher the uncertainty. In the area of communication, entropy is the parameter for the uncertainty of the system state. The "state" we refer to here is the extended version of the entropy's definition, not as being limited in the thermodynamics system. In the formula of entropy, if we use 2, 10, or natural number e as base, for the log term, the units of information entropy are Bit, Hartley or Nat, respectively. Information entropy reaches maximum when the probability of the occurrence of events in sample X is equal.[3]

By the 1990s, the definition of entropy has further extended to statistical physics and quantum physics, e.g., thermo-entropy, electronic entropy, mobile entropy, vibration entropy, self-spin entropy, as well as to some other areas, such as topology entropy, geography entropy, meteorologic entropy, black hole entropy, society entropy, economy entropy, human body entropy, spirit entropy, cultural entropy, etc.[4]

Einstein defined entropy as the essential principle of science. The definition and application of entropy evolved from the measurement of uniformity of distribution, to the measurement of level of disorderliness, and further to the measurement of uncertainty. It is clear to see that the research on entropy is popular throughout.

4.2 FUZZY SET THEORY

Probability theory is a powerful mathematical tool of dealing with randomness. For a long time, humans thought uncertainty was equal to randomness. In 1965, system theorist Lotfi A. Zadeh, who is called "father of fuzzy logic," published *Fuzzy Sets*,[5] thereby laying out the mathematics of fuzzy set theory and, by extension, fuzzy logic. Since its launching in 1978, the journal *Fuzzy Sets and Systems*, which was organized by the International Fuzzy Systems Association (IFSA), has been devoted to the international advancement of the theory and application of fuzzy sets and systems. From 1992, IEEE International Conference on Fuzzy Systems is held annually. IFSA is held once every two years. The eleventh IFSA was held for the first time in China in 2005. Scientists and researchers have shifted their attention to fuzzy algebra, fuzzy logic, fuzzy function, and fuzzy measurement. From 1993 to 1995, there were debates on fuzzy logic between the fuzzy school and the statistical school, resulting in literature collections.[6] At the same time, applications of fuzzy control, fuzzy computer, etc. were booming throughout the world.

4.2.1 MEMBERSHIP DEGREE AND MEMBERSHIP FUNCTION

As defined in the previous section, the characteristic function of classical (nonfuzzy) sets assigns a value of either 1 or 0 to each individual in the universal set, thereby discriminating between members or nonmembers of the classical sets under consideration. However, in the viewpoint of fuzzy logic, there is the other relationship between the elements and the set. Such a function is called a "membership function," and the set defined by it a "fuzzy set." The most commonly used range of values of membership functions is the unit interval [0, 1]. Each membership function maps elements into real numbers in [0, 1]. The real number is called a "membership degree."

Definition 4.10

Let U be the universal set. Any mapping from U to the real interval [0, 1]

$$\mu_{\tilde{A}} : U \to [0, 1]$$

$$\forall x \in U, x \to \mu_{\tilde{A}}(x)$$

determines a fuzzy set $\tilde{A}$ on U. $\mu_{\tilde{A}}$ is the membership function of $\tilde{A}$, $\mu_{\tilde{A}}(x)$ is the membership degree of x for $\tilde{A}$. The set is denoted as

$$\tilde{A} = \left\{ \int \frac{\mu_{\tilde{A}}(x)}{x} \right\}$$

So, classical sets are the special case of fuzzy sets when the membership is in $\{0, 1\}$.

Definition 4.11

If $\tilde{A}$ is a fuzzy set on U, the definitions of the kernel, support set, boundary set, and external sets of $\tilde{A}$ are defined as follows:

1. *Ker $\tilde{A} = \{x | x \in U, \mu_{\tilde{A}}(x) = 1\}$*
2. *Supp $\tilde{A} = \{x | x \in U, \mu_{\tilde{A}}(x) > 0\}$*
3. *Bound $\tilde{A} = \{x | x \in U, 0 < \mu_{\tilde{A}}(x) < 1\}$*
4. *Out $\tilde{A} = \{x | x \in U, \mu_{\tilde{A}}(x) = 0\}$*

The fuzzy set $\tilde{A}$ divides U into three parts: Kernel consists of the elements that belong to $\tilde{A}$ totally, external consists of all the elements that do not belong to $\tilde{A}$, and boundary consists of the elements that partly belong to $\tilde{A}$.

Let $\tilde{A}$, $\tilde{B}$ and $\tilde{C}$ be fuzzy sets on U. The logic operations are defined by the following membership functions:

Union: $\mu_{\tilde{A} \cup \tilde{B}}(x) = \mu_{\tilde{A}}(x) \vee \mu_{\tilde{B}}(x)$

Intersection: $\mu_{\tilde{A} \cap \tilde{B}}(x) = \mu_{\tilde{A}}(x) \wedge \mu_{\tilde{B}}(x)$

Complement: $\mu_{\bar{\tilde{A}}}(x) = 1 - \mu_{\tilde{A}}(x)$

The operations of fuzzy sets have the following characteristics:

Commutativity laws: $\tilde{A} \cup \tilde{B} = \tilde{B} \cup \tilde{A}$, $\tilde{A} \cap \tilde{B} = \tilde{B} \cap \tilde{A}$

Associativity laws: $\tilde{A} \cup (\tilde{B} \cup \tilde{C}) = (\tilde{A} \cup \tilde{B}) \cup \tilde{C}$, $\tilde{A} \cap (\tilde{B} \cap \tilde{C}) = (\tilde{A} \cap \tilde{B}) \cap \tilde{C}$

Distributivity laws: $\tilde{A} \cup (\tilde{B} \cap \tilde{C}) = (\tilde{A} \cup \tilde{B}) \cap (\tilde{A} \cup \tilde{C})$, $\tilde{A} \cap (\tilde{B} \cup \tilde{C}) = (\tilde{A} \cap \tilde{B})$
$\cup (\tilde{A} \cap \tilde{C})$

Idempotence laws: $\tilde{A} \cup \tilde{A} = \tilde{A}$, $\tilde{A} \cap \tilde{A} = \tilde{A}$

Laws of Identity: $\tilde{A} \cup \varnothing = \tilde{A}$, $\tilde{A} \cup U = U$, $\tilde{A} \cap \varnothing = \varnothing$, $\tilde{A} \cap U = \tilde{A}$

Transitivity laws: if $\tilde{A} \subseteq \tilde{B} \subseteq \tilde{C}$, then $\tilde{A} \subseteq \tilde{C}$

Complementary laws: $\bar{\bar{\tilde{A}}} = \tilde{A}$

De Morgan's laws: $\overline{\tilde{A} \cap \tilde{B}} = \bar{\tilde{A}} \cup \bar{\tilde{B}}$, $\overline{\tilde{A} \cup \tilde{B}} = \bar{\tilde{A}} \cap \bar{\tilde{B}}$

But they do not obey the law of excluded middle. In other words, $\tilde{A} \cap \bar{\tilde{A}} \neq \varnothing$, $\tilde{A} \cup \bar{\tilde{A}} \neq U$.

The foundational problem of fuzzy sets is how to confirm a certain membership function. However, there is no strict method for that. The only existing way is very subjective. The six types of functions normally used are as follows:[7]

1. Linear membership function:

$$\mu_{\tilde{A}}(x) = 1 - kx$$

2. *Gamma* membership function:

$$\mu_{\tilde{A}}(x) = e^{-kx}$$

3. Concave/convex membership function:

$$\mu_{\tilde{A}}(x) = 1 - ax^k$$

4. Cauchy membership function:

$$\mu_{\tilde{A}}(x) = 1/(1 + kx^2)$$

5. Mountain-shaped membership function:

$$\mu_{\tilde{A}}(x) = 1/2 - (1/2)\sin\{[\pi/(b-a)][x-(b-a)/2]\}$$

6. Normal (bell) membership function:

$$\mu_{\tilde{A}}(x) = \exp[-(x-a)^2/2b^2]$$

4.2.2 DECOMPOSITION THEOREM AND EXPANDED PRINCIPLE

Definition 4.12

Let $\tilde{A}$ be a fuzzy set on U, $\forall \lambda \in [0, 1]$

$$A_\lambda = \{x | x \in U, \tilde{A}(x) \geq \lambda\}$$

It is called the λ cut of $\tilde{A}$, and λ is called "the confidence level."

Definition 4.13

Let $\tilde{A}$ be a fuzzy set on U, and $\lambda \in [0, 1]$. $\lambda\tilde{A}$ is the multiple of λ and the fuzzy set $\tilde{A}$. Its membership function is defined as

$$\mu_{\lambda\tilde{A}}(x) = \lambda \wedge \mu_{\tilde{A}}(x)$$

Theorem 4.10 Decomposition Theorem

Let $\tilde{A}$ be a fuzzy set on U, A_λ is the λ cut of $\tilde{A}$, $\lambda \in [0, 1]$. Then

$$\tilde{A} = \bigcup_{\lambda \in [0,1]} \lambda A_\lambda$$

It also shows a possibility of how the fuzziness comes into being, i.e., the overlap of a large number of or even infinite events can create fuzzy things.

Definition 4.14

Let U and V be both universal sets. F(U) denotes all the fuzzy sets on U, and F(V) denotes all the fuzzy sets on V. Given mapping f: UV, fuzzy mapping from F(U) to F(V) can be induced by f, i.e.,

$$f: F(U) \to F(V)$$

$$\tilde{A} \mapsto f(\tilde{A})$$

where $f(\tilde{A}) = \bigcup_{\lambda \in [0,1]} \lambda f(A_\lambda)$.
  f can also induce the fuzzy mapping from F(V) to F(U), denoted as f^{-1}, i.e.,

$$f^{-1}: F(V) \to F(U)$$

$$\tilde{B} \mapsto f^{-1}(\tilde{B})$$

where $f^{-1}(\tilde{B}) = \bigcup_{\lambda \in [0,1]} \lambda f^{-1}(B_\lambda)$.

Theorem 4.11 Expanded Theorem

Let f and f^{-1} be the fuzzy mappings induced by f: U → V. The membership functions of $f(\tilde{A})$, and $f^{-1}(\tilde{B})$ are

$$\mu_{f(\tilde{A})}(y) = \bigvee_{f(x)=y} \mu_{\tilde{A}}(x), \quad (y \in V, x \in U)$$

$$\mu_{f^{-1}(\tilde{B})}(x) = \mu_{\tilde{B}}(f(x)) \quad (x \in U)$$

The expanded theorem provides the general principle of expanding classical set operation into fuzzy sets. It is an important principle in fuzzy sets theory having a wide application in the field of fuzzy logic, fuzzy integral, and fuzzy probability.

4.2.3 Fuzzy Relation

Definition 4.15

Let U and V be both universal sets, and U × V be the Cartesian product. Any fuzzy set $\tilde{R}$ on U × V is called the fuzzy relation between U and V, i.e.,

$$\mu_{\tilde{R}}: U \times V \to [0, 1]$$

$$(x, y) \mapsto \mu_{\tilde{R}}(x, y)$$

where $\mu_{\tilde{R}}(x,y)$ is called the relation strength of x and y corresponding to $\tilde{R}$.

If $U = V$, $\tilde{R}$ is called the fuzzy relation on U.

Fuzzy relationship is the mapping from U to V by through $U \times V$. The relation strength is measured by [0, 1] instead of {0, 1}.

Let $\tilde{R}$ and $\tilde{S}$ be fuzzy relations on the Cartesian space, the operations are defined as follows:

Union: $\mu_{\tilde{R} \cup \tilde{S}}(x, y) = \max\{\mu_{\tilde{R}}(x, y), \mu_{\tilde{S}}(x, y)\}$

Intersection: $\mu_{\tilde{R} \cap \tilde{S}}(x, y) = \min\{\mu_{\tilde{R}}(x, y), \mu_{\tilde{S}}(x, y)\}$

Complement: $\mu_{\overline{\tilde{R}}}(x, y) = 1 - \mu_{\tilde{R}}(x, y)$

Inclusion: $\tilde{R} \subseteq \tilde{S} \rightarrow \mu_{\tilde{R}}(x, y) \leq \mu_{\tilde{S}}(x, y)$

Composition: let $\tilde{R}$ be a fuzzy relation in $X \times Y$, $\tilde{S}$ be a fuzzy relation in $Y \times Z$, and $\tilde{T}$ be a fuzzy relation in $X \times Z$. The max-min composition $\tilde{T} = \tilde{R} \circ \tilde{S}$ is defined as

$$\mu_{\tilde{T}}(x, z) = \bigvee_{y \in Y} (\mu_{\tilde{R}}(x, y) \wedge \mu_{\tilde{S}}(y, z))$$

Fuzzy relations satisfy the laws such as commutativity, associativity, distributivity, idempotence, and De Morgan's laws; however, they do not obey excluded middle law.

The fuzzy relation $\tilde{R}$ on U is called "fuzzy equivalence relation," if it concurrently satisfies:

1. Reflexivity: $\mu_{\tilde{R}}(x_i, x_i) = 1$
2. Symmetry: $\mu_{\tilde{R}}(x_i, x_j) = \mu_{\tilde{R}}(x_j, x_i)$
3. Transitivity: if $\mu_{\tilde{R}}(x_i, x_j) = \lambda_1$ and $\mu_{\tilde{R}}(x_j, x_k) = \lambda_2$, then $\mu_{\tilde{R}}(x_i, x_k) = \lambda$, where $\lambda \geq \min\{\lambda_1, \lambda_2\}$

If it only has reflexivity and symmetry, it is called a "similarity relation."

For any fuzzy similarity relation $\tilde{R}_1$, we can obtain the fuzzy equivalence relation $\tilde{R}_1^{n-1} = \tilde{R}_1 \circ \tilde{R}_1 \circ \cdots \circ \tilde{R}_1$ by at most $n - 1$ iterations.

Fuzzy relations, a basic approach for presenting propositions, can be used to describe various relations of various elements. These elements refer to fuzzy objects, fuzzy events, fuzzy properties, fuzzy factors, and so on. Any event or object can be described by using properties and membership degree:

Object: {property1, membership1; property2, membership2; ...; property n, membership n}.

How to confirm the membership of fuzzy relations is also a problem. The general approaches include Cartesian product, closed expression, table searching, lingual rule of knowledge, classification, similarity approach in digital process, etc. The membership plays a really important role in fuzzy theory, but its determination is still much too subjective, so this problem has to be solved to consolidate the foundation of fuzzy theory.

4.2.4 POSSIBILITY MEASURE

Based on fuzzy sets theory, Zadeh proposed the concept of possibility measure in 1978. It uses possibility to describe the uncertainty instead of probability. This is a simple example. Event A is described as one eating 5 eggs for breakfast. Then the possibility of event A is 1. But the probability of event A is 0. Being similar to probability measure, possibility measure is also an approach of getting set values.

Definition 4.16

Let U be the universal set. Poss is defined on U and it is a set function with values in [0, 1]. Poss is called "possibility measure" if it satisfies:

Condition 1: $\text{Poss}(\varnothing) = 0$ *and*
Condition 2: $\text{Poss}(V \cup W) = \max(\text{Poss}(V), \text{Poss}(W))$

where V, W are two nonintersected sets involved in U.
If it satisfies the third condition, i.e., $\text{Poss}(U) = 1$, *the possibility measure is said to be regular.*

The essential difference between possibility measure and probability measure is that the probability sum of all the nonintersected events in probability measure is 1, while it may not be 1 in possibility measure.

If U and V are not intersected, $\text{Poss}(U \cup V)$ is the maximum of the two, while $P(U \cup V)$ is the sum of the two.

Possibility measure has the following properties:

Monotonicity: $A \subseteq B \rightarrow \text{Poss}(A) \leq \text{Poss}(B)$
Down continuity: Let $A_1 \subseteq A_2 \subseteq \cdots \subseteq A_n \subseteq \cdots$, and $A = \bigcup_{n=1}^{\infty} A_n$. Then

$$\lim_{n \to \infty} \text{Poss}(A_n) = \text{Poss}(A)$$

Definition 4.17

Let $\tilde{A}$ be the fuzzy set on U. If Poss is the possibility measure and $x \in U$, the fuzzy statement "x is $\tilde{A}$" can induce a possibility distribution Poss_x, where $\text{Poss}_x = \mu_{\tilde{A}}(x)$.

By this way, possibility measure and fuzzy set are connected. The possibility distribution of x itself is a fuzzy set. Hence, possibility distribution and fuzzy set are consistent in the form, and we can compute the possibility distribution by the laws in fuzzy set.[8]

4.3 ROUGH SET THEORY

Fuzziness and randomness are both uncertainty. Fuzziness, being different from randomness can be described in mathematics by using fuzzy set theory. Accordingly, we can use a new theory and approach to describe the uncertainty. However, fuzzy set theory cannot do any operation without the prior information such as membership degree or membership function. So could we study uncertainty just in terms of the information provided by uncertainty itself? In the early 1980s, Zdzislaw Pawlak introduced rough set theory based on boundary region thoughts.[9] The annual international conferences on Rough Sets and Current Trends in Computing (RSCTC) held annually gather researchers and practitioners from academia and industry to discuss the state of the art in rough set theory and its applications. The first RSCTC conference held in Warsaw, Poland in 1992 provided an opportunity to highlight the basic thoughts and applications of set approximation definition and the basic research of machine learning in the environment of rough set. The second RSCTC conference was held in Banff, Canada. The aim was to discuss the problem of the relation between rough sets and other soft computing approaches, especially the application problem in the field of data mining. In 1995, the Association for Computing Machinery lists "rough set" as a new research topic in the research area of computing science.

Fuzzy set theory studies uncertainty based on the relationship between sets and elements. However, rough set theory studies uncertainty based on knowledge classification. The ability of classification for objects in rough set theory is to find a set of subsets of the universe objects such that each object answers to at least one subset in the sense that it is an element of this subset. In other words, classification case happens when the covering of the universe objects consists of disjoint categories as in this case each object answers to a unique category, thus classification acquires a functional character. This is the original idea that leads to rough set theory. In rough set theory, we may say that classification of objects consists of finding a covering of the universe objects by a set of categories using indiscernibility relation and lower and upper approximation based on the given data samples.

4.3.1 Imprecise Category and Rough Set

In rough set theory, knowledge is interpreted as an ability to classify some objects that form a set and their nature may vary from case to case. Classification becomes the key point of reasoning, learning, and decision making. From a mathematical point of view, "class" and "equivalence class" are individually called "relation" and "equivalence relation." The subset $X \subseteq U$ is called a "category of U." Any conceptual cluster in U is called "abstract knowledge," or "knowledge" in short. Capital letters, such as $\mathbf{P}$, $\mathbf{Q}$, $\mathbf{R}$ represent relations and bold capital letters such as $\mathbf{P}$, $\mathbf{Q}$, and $\mathbf{R}$ are dense clusters of relations." $[x]_R$ or $R(x)$ represents the equivalent class containing the element $x \in U$.

Definition 4.18

An approximation space is defined as a relation system $K = (U, R)$, where nonempty set U is a universe of objects and R is a set of equivalent relations on U.

Definition 4.19

Let $P \subseteq R$ and $P \neq \varnothing$, the intersection of all equivalence relations on P is called the indiscernibility relation and it is denoted as $ind(P)$, i.e., $[x]_{ind(P)} = \bigcap_{R \in P} [x]_R$, where $ind[P]$ is an equivalence and unique relation.

Indiscernibility relation is the foundation of rough set theory. It tells us the truth that because of the limitation of comprehension degree or imperfectness of data samples, we do not have enough knowledge to classify certain objects in the universe. In rough set theory, these sets that have the same information on a certain attribute subset are called "indiscernible equivalent classes."

Definition 4.20

For a given similarity space $K = (U, R)$, the subset $X \subseteq U$ is called the "concept on U." In the form, the empty set $\varnothing$ can also be seen as a concept. Elementary knowledge is the set of equivalent classes of the indiscernibility relation ind(P) generated by the nonempty subset cluster $P \subseteq R$, i.e., U/ind(P). The corresponding equivalent classes are called the "elementary concepts" or "elementary categories." Especially if the relation $Q \in R$, Q is called "junior knowledge," and the corresponding equivalent class is called "junior concept" or "junior category."

According to the definition above, concept is the set of objects. The clusters of concepts are classification, which is the knowledge on U. The clusters of classifications are knowledge base, or in another word, knowledge base is the set of classification approaches.

Definition 4.21

Let $X \subseteq U$, and R be an equivalence relation on U. If the operation of union on a some elementary categories of R can be expressed in terms of R, X is said to be R-definable. Otherwise, X is R-undefinable. The definable set of R is also called "R-exact," and the undefinable set is called "R-rough."

For example, as shown in Figure 4.2, the region enclosed by real line represents R-rough set; the little square represents elementary categories.

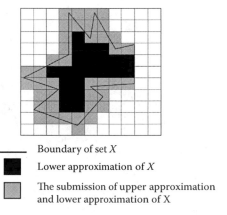

——— Boundary of set X

▪ Lower approximation of X

▫ The submission of upper approximation and lower approximation of X

FIGURE 4.2 Approximation partition of set X in knowledge space.

According to the rough set, knowledge has certain granularity. If the granularities of the knowledge under research and the understood knowledge match, the knowledge under research is precise, otherwise it has no precise boundary, i.e., it is rough. In rough set theory, R-rough can be defined using two exact sets called, respectively, the "R-lower-approximation" and the "R-upper-approximation."

Definition 4.22

For a given knowledge database, $K = (U, R)$, *for every subset* $X \subseteq U$ *and an equivalent relation* $R \in \text{ind}(K)$, *we define two sets:*

$$\underline{R}X = \bigcup \{Y \in U / R \mid Y \subseteq X\} = \{x \in U \mid [x]_R \subseteq X\}$$

$$\overline{R}X = \{Y \in U / R \mid Y \cap X \neq \varnothing\} = \{x \in U \mid [x]_R \cap X \neq \varnothing\}$$

They are called the lower-approximation set and upper-approximation set of X, respectively. The set $bn_R(X) = \overline{R}X - \underline{R}X$ *is called the R boundary region of X,* $\text{pos}_R(X) = \underline{R}X$ *is the R positive region of X, and* $\text{neg}_R(X) = U - \overline{R}X$ *is the R negative region of X.*

The lower- and upper-approximation set operations satisfy the following properties:

Theorem 4.12

1. $\overline{R}(U) = \underline{R}(U) = U$ $\overline{R}(\varnothing) = \underline{R}(\varnothing) = \varnothing$
2. $\overline{R}(X \cup Y) = \overline{R}(X) \cup \overline{R}(Y)$ $\underline{R}(X \cap Y) = \underline{R}(X) \cap \underline{R}(Y)$
3. $\overline{R}(X \cap Y) \subseteq \overline{R}(X) \cap \overline{R}(Y)$ $\underline{R}(X \cup Y) \supseteq \underline{R}(X) \cup \underline{R}(Y)$

A lower approximation set is also named as positive region composed of the elements in U, which are judged to definitely belong to X according to the knowledge R, as illustrated by the black part in Figure 4.2. Upper approximation consists of the elements in U, which are judged as possibly belonging to X according to the knowledge R, as shown by the sum of black part and gray part in Figure 4.2. The negative region consists of the elements in U, which do not belong to X according to R, shown as the white part in Figure 4.2. Boundary region is the set of the elements that cannot be classified definitely into X or $(U - X)$ according to R, as shown in the gray part in Figure 4.2.

Thus, we can see that the basic category in rough set is considered as precise and contains the smallest granularity. Based on this, any concept can be expressed in terms of some already known knowledge. In general, given a knowledge base, the object to be classified can usually be roughly defined by two precise categories, i.e., upper approximation and lower approximation. This is a concrete approach for uncertainty expression by precise categories.

4.3.2 Characteristics of Rough Sets

In rough sets, the existence of boundary causes the imprecision of sets. The bigger the boundary, the worse the accuracy. We use the concept of precision to describe the situation mentioned above: the bigger the precision, the better the accuracy. The precision of sets X is defined as follows:

$$d_R(X) = \frac{card(\underline{R}X)}{card(\overline{R}X)}$$

where, *card* is the unit number of the set, and $X \neq \emptyset$.

Obviously, $0 \leq d_R(X) \leq 1$. If $d_R(X) = 1$, the boundary region of X is null. The set X is definable by R. If $d_R(X) < 1$, the set X is indefinable by R.

We can also measure the uncertainty using roughness defined as follows:

$$r_R(X) = 1 - d_R(X)$$

Roughness represents the rough degree of sets: the bigger the roughness, the worse the precision.

We need a more precise, local measurement indicating the roughness degree of a set at particular objects. This purpose is served by the rough membership function, which is different from the membership function in fuzzy set theory.

Let X be a rough set. $X \subseteq U$ and $x \in U$. The rough membership function is defined as:

$$\mu_X^R(x) = \frac{|X \cap R(x)|}{|R(x)|}$$

where R is a indiscernibility relation, and $R(x) = [x]_R = \{y : (y \in U) \wedge (yRx)\}$. Obviously, $\mu_X^R(x) \in [0,1]$.

Here, the measurement of uncertainty, either the precision or the rough membership function, does not require subjective determination ahead of time. Instead, it is calculated according to the present classification knowledge objectively. This is a significant difference between the rough set theory and fuzzy set theory.

Besides precision and rough membership function, we also can describe the topological structures of rough set using the lower approximation and the upper approximation. Four important rough sets are shown as follows:

1. If $\underline{R}X \neq \emptyset$ and $\overline{R}X \neq U$, X is roughly R-definable. At this time, it can be determined whether some elements in U belong to X or $\overline{X}$.
2. If $\underline{R}X = \emptyset$ and $\overline{R}X \neq U$, X is R-undefinable. At this time, it can be determined whether some elements in U belong to $\overline{X}$. But whether any element in U belongs to X cannot be judged.
3. If $\underline{R}X \neq \emptyset$ and $RX = U$, X is roughly out of R-definable. At this time, it can be determined whether some elements in U belong to X. But whether any element in U belongs to $\overline{X}$ cannot be judged.
4. If $\underline{R}X = \emptyset$ and $\overline{R}X = U$, X is all R-undefinable. At this time, it cannot be determined whether any element in U belongs to X or $\overline{X}$.

4.3.3 ROUGH RELATIONS

Rough relations mainly consist of membership relation, rough equality, and rough inclusion which are defined as follows:

Membership relation: $x \bar{\in} X \Leftrightarrow x \in \bar{R}X$, $x \underline{\in} X \Leftrightarrow x \in \underline{R}X$. $\bar{\in}$ is the upper-membership relation, and $\underline{\in}$ is the lower-membership relation. In a word, $\bar{\in}$ means that x may belong to X according to R, and $\underline{\in}$ means that x definitely belongs to X according to R.

Roughly equality: let $\mathbf{K} = (U, \mathbf{R})$ be a knowledge base. $X, Y \subseteq U$ and $R \in \text{ind}(\mathbf{K})$:

1. If $\underline{R}X = \underline{R}Y$, the sets X and Y are R lower roughly equal.
2. If $\bar{R}X = \bar{R}Y$, the sets X and Y are R upper roughly equal.
3. If X and Y are both lower roughly equal and upper roughly equal, they are R roughly equal, denoted as $X \approx Y$.

The three roughly equalities are all equivalent.

We can express upper-approximation set and lower-approximation set according to the equivalence of rough sets.

Theorem 4.13

For any equivalent relation R:

1. *$\underline{R}X$ is the intersection of all the subsets in U, which are lower roughly equal to X.*
2. *$\bar{R}X$ is the union of all the subsets in U, which are upper roughly equal to X.*

Roughly inclusion: let $\mathbf{K} = (U, \mathbf{R})$ be a knowledge base. $X, Y \subseteq U$ and $R \in \text{ind}(\mathbf{K})$:

1. If $\underline{R}X \subseteq \underline{R}Y$, the sets X and Y are R lower roughly inclusion.
2. If $\bar{R}X \subseteq \bar{R}Y$, the sets X and Y are R upper roughly inclusion.
3. If X and Y are both lower roughly inclusion and upper roughly inclusion, they are R roughly inclusion, denoted as $X \tilde{\subseteq} Y$.

The three roughly inclusions above are all relations of order.

Compared with the classical set, the relations of membership, equality, and inclusion are dependent on the knowledge in the universal set. As a result, it is relative to say whether an element belongs to a certain rough set because it is dependent on the initial knowledge base. If the knowledge granularity in the initial database changes, all the relations will change. Figure 4.3 illustrates the change of knowledge granularity. The upper-approximation set, lower-approximation set, and the boundary set all change. Figure 4.3(a), (b), and (c) reflect the classification in rough, median, and precise granularities for the same knowledge K. In (a), the lower-approximation set contains 32 units, and the boundary set contains 320 units. In (b), the lower-approximation set contains 88 units, and the boundary set contains 160 units. In (c), the lower-approximation set contains 125 units, and the boundary set contains 80 units. Table 4.1 shows the calculated parameters. It can be seen that the more precise the background knowledge, the smaller the boundary, and the lower the roughness.

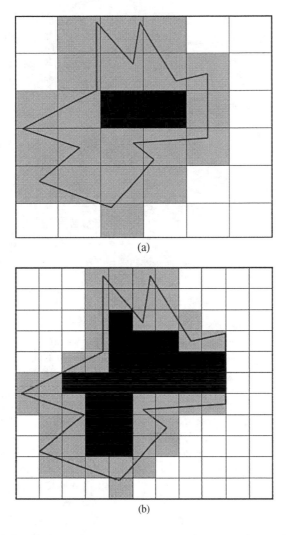

(a)

(b)

FIGURE 4.3 Relationship between rough set and granularity: (a) rough granularities, (b) median granularities, and (c) precise granularities.

Rough set theory is based on classification understood as equivalence relation used for dividing the certain universe. Rough set theory has the following characteristics:

1. The granularity of knowledge results in the nonprecise description of a certain concept with current knowledge.
2. The uncertainty in classification problem can be efficiently described and calculated using concepts of indiscernibility relation, lower and upper approximations, positive, negative, and boundary regions.

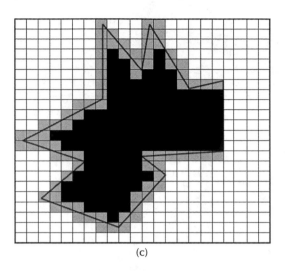

(c)

FIGURE 4.3 (Continued)

3. Different from fuzzy set theory, rough set membership function is calculated impersonally based on the known data only. In other words, fuzzy
   set solves problems in the research of uncertainty from the viewpoint of
   connotation. However, the viewpoint of rough set is concept extension.

In comparison with probability and fuzzy set, rough set theory based on granularity from the starting point of indiscernibility relation aims to do research in
knowledge roughness, which enriches the research content of uncertainty. Although
rough set theory has been successfully applied in many research fields, it still has
disadvantages. Because this theory has strict requirement for the precision of data
sample in information systems, it does not have the ability to deal with the stochastic
or fuzzy samples. Many extension modules have been proposed in the research of
rough set theory, such as precision-variable rough set, probability rough set, fuzzy
rough set, and so on.

TABLE 4.1
**Related Parameters of the Same Rough Set under Different
Knowledge Granularities**

Parameters	Units in Lower-Approximation Set	Units in Upper-Approximation Set	Units in Boundary Set	Accuracy	Roughness
Fig. 4.3(a)	32	352	320	0.091	0.909
Fig. 4.3(b)	88	248	160	0.355	0.645
Fig. 4.3(c)	125	205	80	0.601	0.399

4.4 CHAOS AND FRACTAL

Chaos is another uncertainty, which originated from the ancient Chinese mythology. It refers to the formless and disordered state of matter before the creation of the cosmos. Subsequently, in a scientific context, the word "chaos" has a slightly different meaning than it does in its general usage as a state of confusion, lacking any order. Chaos, with reference to chaos theory, refers to an apparent lack of order in a system that nevertheless obeys particular laws or rules. Philosophers consider chaos as the foggy state of the early development of recognition. Latter-day physical scientists regard chaos as the basic state of all objects. For a more daring hypothesis, chaos is the time and space for packing basic particles. In the viewpoint of modern cosmography, chaos represents heat balance. Some complex and uncertain phenomena are generally defined as chaos.

The first true experimenter in chaos was a French mathematician and physical scientist, Henri Poincaré. When he did the research in celestial mechanics, he found that some answers of certainty dynamical equations are unforeseen, which is dynamical chaos now. In 1954, A. N. Kolmogorov published the paper "On the Conservation of Conditionally Periodic Motions for a Small Change in Hamliton's Function,"[10] and outlined the Kolmogorov–Arnold–Moser (KAM) theorem. In 1963, I. Arnold and J. Moser gave the strict proof of the KAM theorem almost at the same time. KAM theorem is regarded as the symbol of chaos theory foundation. E. N. Lorenz, an American meteorologist, first found chaos in dissipative system. In 1963, he published "Deterministic Nonperiodic Flow"[11] explaining the basic characters of chaos. He also discovered the first chaotic attractor: Lorenz Attractor. He also was the first person studying chaos using the approach of computer simulation. In 1971, Frenchman David Ruelle and Netherlandish Floris Takens published the famous paper "On the Nature of Turbulence,"[12] first proposed using chaos to study turbulence and found a class of new-style attractors which were very complicated and proven that the movement related to these attractors is chaos. In 1975, Tianyan Li and J. Yorke's article, "Period Three Implies Chaos,"[13] describing the mathematical characters of chaos caused a little shock in the academic circles. In 1967, the pioneer of fractal geometry, French mathematician and physical scientist Benoit Mandelbrot published his paper "How Long Is the Coast of Britain? Statistical Self-Similarity and Fractional Dimension"[14] in *Science* and subsequently released the books: *Les Objets Fractals: Forme, Hazard, et Dimension*[15] and *The Fractal Geometry of Nature*.[16] All of these are foundations of fractal.

Mitchell Jay Feigenbaum is a mathematical physicist whose pioneering studies in chaos theory led to the discovery of the Feigenbaum constant. He discovered that the ratio of the difference between the values at which such successive period-doubling bifurcations occur tends to be a constant of around 4.6692. He was then able to provide a mathematical proof of the fact, and showed that the same behaviour and the same constant would occur in a wide class of mathematical functions prior to the onset of chaos. For the first time, this universal result enabled mathematicians to take their first huge step to unraveling the apparently intractable "random" behaviour of chaotic systems. This "ratio of convergence" is now known as the "Feigenbaum constant." Bolin Hao, a Chinese academician, developed the symbolic dynamics to be a concrete tool in the research of chaotic dynamics. It is applied in the numerical research of periodically driven and self-consistent differential function. The numerical and experimental research of all kinds of real dynamic systems were conducted on a deeper and more integral scale. Chaos theory progressed more rapidly after the 1980s. As chaos changed from a little-known theory to a full science of its own, it has received widespread publicity. More and more papers of chaos are published in journals, such as *Science, Nature, Physics Transaction, Progress in Physics,* and so on. Chaos theory has become the forefront of nonlinear science research, moving out of the traditional boundaries of physics, and nearly covers every scientific subject.[17]

4.4.1 Basic Characteristics of Chaos

In the past, people thought that the uncertainty of dynamical systems was represented by random force term, random coefficients, and random initial conditions of equations. Therefore, the system without random force term, random coefficients, and random initial conditions is regarded as the one that can be definitely confirmed and predicted. However, more and more research results exhibit that most of the certain systems would generate random and complex behaviors, which are called "chaos." Thus far, Li–Yorke theorem is the most systemic and rigorous mathematical definition of chaos in the field of nonlinear dynamics.

Theorem 4.14 Li–Yorke Theorem

Let f(x) be continuous self-mapping on [a,b]. If f(x) has a point of period 3, f(x) has a point of period n for any positive integer.

Definition 4.23

Let f(x) be continuous self-mapping in the closed interval I. The system described by f(x) will be considered as chaos system with S being the chaos set of f, if the following conditions are satisfied:

1. *There is no upper boundary for the period points of f.*
2. *Uncountable subset S exists in the closed interval I satisfying:*
   For any x, y ∈ s, if x ≠ y, then $\limsup\limits_{x\to\infty}|f^n(x)-f^n(y)|>0$
   For any x, y ∈ s, $\liminf\limits_{x\to\infty}|f^n(x)-f^n(y)|=0$
   For any x ∈ s and any period point y of f, $\limsup\limits_{x\to\infty}|f^n(x)-f^n(y)|>0.$

According to the theorem mentioned above, for continuous function $f(x)$ on the closed interval I, the existence of period-three orbit implies chaos.

This definition represents that a chaotic motion consists of:

1. Many countable stable periodic orbits
2. Many uncountable stable nonperiodic orbits
3. At least one unstable nonperiodic orbit

In general, the three states for certain movements are balance, periodic motion, and quasiperiodic motion. The normal behaviors of chaos are different from certain ones. They are the motions always limited in a finite range on an unrepeated orbit.

Sometimes, the normal behaviors of chaos are described as infinite periodic motion or randomlike motion. Normally, chaos has the following basic characteristics:

1. **Inner-randomness:** The randomness generated from the interior of a certain system is called "inner-randomness."

    In the traditional viewpoint, a certain system will not generate randomness without outside random function. However, chaos tells us that a certain system will generate randomness even if there is no outside disturbance. Randomness exists in certainty.

    Local unstability is one of the most important representations of inner-randomness. It refers to the behaviors of a system heavily dependent on initial conditions. Such sensitivity to initial conditions is the so-called "butterfly effect."

2. **Self-similarity:** "Self-similar" means that the chaotic attractor's geometric shape is the order underlying the apparent chaos. If we exhibit all possible statuses of one system using phase space, the variation of the system can be described as a trajectory. After infinite iterations in phase space, chaos generates self-similar structure with infinite levels, which we call the "strange attractor." Chaotic attractors have fractal structures and fractal dimension.

3. **Universality and Feigenbaum constant:** "Universality" refers to the universal characters appearing in the tendentious process of chaotic motion. It is independent of movement equation and coefficient. Universality has three aspects. "Structure universality" means that orbit bifurcation and quantitative characters only depend on the mathematical structure. "Measure universality" means that the same mapping or iteration will have the same nesting structure among different dimensions. The structure's characteristics only depend on the order of power progression for nonlinear function. "Self-similar" universality will be found on different levels of the same mapping. It is independent of transformation for levels.

Feigenbaum constant represents the dynamic invariability in the tendentious process of chaotic motion. That is to say, we will see the same geography structure even if we magnify or reduce the observation dimension. The parameter for each bifurcation is denoted as a_n, a_{n+1}, then the value of $\frac{a_{n+1}-a_n}{a_{n+2}-a_{n+1}}$ will be different corresponding to different n. However, when $n \to \infty$, the limit will be an irrational number denoted as $delta = 4.669201609....$ Feigenbaum constant represents the deeper law of chaos.

How does a certain system generate chaos? At present, there are three kinds of evolvement processes:

1. Quasi-period process: Chaos can be regarded as oscillation phenomena that consist of infinite frequencies. The coupling of just three irrelevant frequencies will lead to the coupling of infinite frequencies, which we call "chaos."

2. Period-doubling process: Dual-period is generated by system bifurcation. Many dual-period coupling will lead to chaos.

3. Intermittent chaos: System tangent bifurcation may result in chaos.

4.4.2 STRANGE ATTRACTORS OF CHAOS

Chaotic attractors are helpful in deeper research on basic characteristics of chaos. The importance of chaotic attractors is similar to the importance of normal distribution for probability.

If we consider the phase space of a system, i.e., all possible states of the system, then a strange or chaotic attractor is a set of states in a system's phase space with very special properties. First of all, the set is an attracting set, so that the system, starting with its initial condition in the appropriate basin, eventually ends up in the set. Second, and most important, once the system is one attractor nearby, states diverge from each other exponentially fast. For example, if we consider the system's phase space, i.e., the current of a downpour, a strange or chaotic attractor is a great river. The rainwater cannot be stable until it inflows into the great river. Even if the system is perturbed off the attractor, it eventually returns. From the viewpoint of entropy in uncertainty, this is a reduced process of entropy.

There are many kinds of chaotic attractors having fractal structures and fractional dimension. They are sensitive to initial conditions. The space of chaotic attractors is discrete. It will change a lot even under slight disturbance.

Lyapurov exponents are one possible quantitative measure of strange attractor. They represent the rate of orbital divergence from the initial point.

For example, for one-dimensional mapping $x_{n+1} = f(x_n)$, after n times iterations, the distance between two nearby points are denoted as

$$\frac{df^n(x_0)}{dx}\delta = e^{\lambda(x_0)n}\delta$$

where x_0 is the initial point, and δ is the distance between x_0 and its adjacent neighbor.

From the equation, we can find that the distance changes exponentially in time. The exponential item $\lambda(x_0)$, called "Lyapurov exponent," is a real number representing the statistical characteristic, and

$$\lambda(x_0) = \lim_{n\to\infty}\frac{1}{n}\log|f^{(n)}(x_0)| = \lim_{n\to\infty}\frac{1}{n}\log\left|\prod_{i=0}^{n-1}f^{'}(x_i)\right| = \lim_{n\to\infty}\frac{1}{n}\sum_{i=0}^{n-1}\log|f'(x_i)|$$

Lyapurov exponent is the result of averaging along the orbit in a long term.

Thus we can see that if $\lambda(x_0) > 0$, the initial error speeds up rapidly, the two adjacent trajectories diverge rapidly, generating chaotic attractors, so the positive Lyapurov exponent can be the criteria of chaos; if $\lambda(x_0) = 0$, the initial error does not change and the boundary is stable; if $\lambda(x_0) < 0$, the two trajectories converge representing one period orbit motion which is insensitivity with initial conditions. The turning of Lyapurov exponent from negative to positive indicates that the motion is changing to chaos.

Besides, we can also measure chaos according to the generation speed of uncertainty information, which is called "measure entropy." Because the chaotic motion is unstable locally, the adjacent orbits diverge at an exponential rate, when the initial points are very close, the number of orbits cannot be discerned. After divergence at the exponential rate, the number of orbits increases, and the degree of uncertainty increases as well. Chaos motions generate information that relates to the distinguishable orbit number, denoted as N. N increases exponentially with time, i.e.,

$$N \propto e^{Kt}$$

where the constant K is the measurement entropy, representing the rate at which information is generated.

The measurement entropy K is defined as follows:

Definition 4.24

Let $x(t)$ be orbits in the dynamical system on the chaotic attractor, and $x(t) = x_1(t)$, $x_2(t)$, ..., $x_d(t)$. The d-dimensional phase space is divided into boxes with the scale of 1d. We can observe the state of the system in the time interval τ. $p_{i_0,i_1...i_n}$ is the joint probability of the event that $x(0)$ is in the box i_0, $x(\tau)$ in the box i_1,..., and $x(n\tau)$ in the box i_n. Let

$$K_n = -\sum_{i_0,i_1,...,i_n} p_{i_0,i_1,...,i_n} \ln p_{i_0,i_1,...,i_n}$$

then $K_{n+1} - K_n$ is the measurement of the information variance from time n to n + 1.

Measure entropy K represents the average variance rate of the information:

$$K = \lim_{x \to 0} \lim_{i \to 0} \lim_{n \to \infty} \frac{1}{n\tau} \sum_i (K_{i+1} - K_i)$$

For regular motion, absolute random motion, and chaotic motion, the values of K are zero, infinite and the constant bigger than zero individually. The degree of chaos and the variation ratio of information become large with the increasing of K. In a one-dimensional map, measure entropy is a positive Lyapurov exponent.

4.4.3 GEOMETRIC CHARACTERISTICS OF CHAOS AND FRACTAL

In the system evolvement process, chaos generated by stretching, distorting, and folding results in the diversity of nature. We are sure about the result of each step for stretching, distorting, and folding. However, after infinite repetitions of the above transformation, the behavior of the system becomes uncertain resulting in fantastic characters. For example, we put a red line in a piece of dough. After countless dough kneading, we cannot image the pattern composed of the red line in the dough.

Fractal geometry is a powerful tool for describing undifferentiable, unsmooth, and discontinuous phenomena. Fractal has the following properties:[18]

1. Complex details and precise structure under any small dimension.
2. Self-similarity, in approximate or statistics meaning.
3. Scrambling. Both the integral and partial are hard to be described using traditional geometrical language.
4. The dimension of fractal is bigger than the one of topology. The dimension of fractal is defined as the measurement of fractal's scrambling. We can describe scrambling from different angles, such as similar dimension, capacity dimension, information dimension, correlative dimension, and so on. The value of fractal can also be fraction.
5. In most situations, fractal can be generated using simple approaches, such as iteration.

Fractal in nature is usually represented by physical phenomena. After the theoretical abstractor, fractal geometry is formed, which can reflect the property of "graphics" more deeply in nature.

4.5 KERNEL FUNCTIONS AND PRINCIPAL CURVES

Kernel functions and principal curves are the main approaches for data statistics and analysis. They are also important tools to deal with uncertainty problems.

4.5.1 KERNEL FUNCTIONS

The internal reason plays a foundational role in the generation and development of events. For instance, kernel affects the evolvement of plants. In mathematics, the concept of kernel is used in many fields of mathematics, such as sets theory, abstract algebra, category theory, and integral equation. Here we give the kernel functions of integral equations.

$K(x, t)$, as the kernel function of the three following integral equations, determines their properties.

$$\int_a^b K(x,t)\varphi(t)dt = f(x)$$

$$\varphi(x) = \lambda \int_a^b K(x,t)\varphi(t)dt + f(x)$$

$$a(x)\varphi(x) = \lambda \int_a^b K(x,t)\varphi(t)dt + f(x)$$

The Fourier-transformation equation is commonly used for the solution of physical problems

$$F(\lambda) = \frac{1}{\sqrt{2\pi}} \int_{-\infty}^{+\infty} f(t)e^{-i\lambda t}dt$$

where $e^{-i\lambda t}$ is the kernel function of the Fourier-transformation equation.

In 1909, James Mercer first proposed the Mercer theorem and developed the theory of kernel.[19]

Definition 4.25

Let $K(x, y)$ be a symmetrical function in R^N, $K(x, y)$ is the Mercer kernel of nonlinear map Φ, when

$$K(x_i, y_j) = \Phi(x_i) \bullet \Phi(y_j)$$

where x_i, y_j are training data in R^N space, R^N is a N-dimensional real number space, $\bullet$ is the dot product in the space transformed by Φ. The space after transformation is called "feature space."

Theorem 4.15

Mercer theorem for an arbitrary square integratable function $f(x)$, it is true that

$$\iint\limits_{C \times C} K(x, y) f(x) f(y) dx dy \geq 0$$

where C is the compact subset in domain of definition. $K(x, y)$ is the Mercer kernel, and

$$K(x, y) = \sum_{i-1}^{N} \lambda_i \varphi_i(x) \varphi_i(y)$$

where λ_i is the positive eigenvalue of $K(x, y)$, φ_i is the corresponding eigenfunction, and N is the number of positive eigenvalues.

From the Mercer theorem, it is straightforward to construct a nonlinear mapping Φ into a potentially infinite dimensional space that satisfies the inner-integral operation without knowing the detailed information about Φ.

In general, it is easy to transform the data in initial space into feature space via mapping Φ if the mapping Φ is known. For instance, as shown in Figure 4.4, we can obtain 3-D feature space which is shown in Figure 4.4(b) via the nonlinear mapping Φ to an initial 2-D space

$$\Phi: (x_1, x_2) \rightarrow \left(x_1^2, \sqrt{2} x_1 x_2, x_2^2 \right)$$

The unseparable vectors in Figure 4.4(a) can be classified in Figure 4.4(b) by a classification plane. The charm of the Mercer function is that it does not require the expression of Φ for classification. In this example, the kernel function is $K(X, Y) = (X \cdot Y)^2$, where vectors $X = (x_1, x_2)$ and $Y = (y_1, y_2)$.

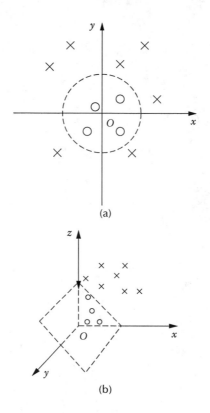

FIGURE 4.4 An example of nonlinear mapping: (a) unseparable vectors in low-dimension space and (b) separable vectors in high-dimension space.

Of course, we also can map the data from 2-D initial space into higher-dimensional feature space via kernel functions. For instance, we map the data into 6-D feature space via this nonlinear mapping

$$\Phi: (x_1, x_2) \rightarrow (x_1, x_2, \sqrt{2}\, x_1 x_2, 2x_1, 2x_2, 2)$$

The kernel function is $K(X, Y) = (X \cdot Y + 2)^2$.

From the viewpoint of machine learning, the training data $\bar{x}_k \in \mathbf{R}^N (k = 1, 2, ..., K)$ in initial space can be transferred into the vector sets $\Phi(\bar{x}_1), \Phi(\bar{x}_2), ..., \Phi(\bar{x}_K)$ in high-dimensional space H via a nonlinear constant map Φ. The kernel in initial space is denoted as:

$$K(\bar{x}_i, \bar{x}_j) = (\Phi(\bar{x}_i) \cdot \Phi(\bar{x}_j))$$

Gaussian kernel is the most commonly used Mercer kernels,

$$K(x, y) = \exp(-\beta \|x - y\|^2)$$

where $\beta > 0$ and it is the self-defined parameter.[20]

Note that when using Gaussian kernels, the feature space is infinite dimensional space. That is to say, the finite training data must be separable in this feature space. Therefore, Gaussian kernels are used normally in classification problems directly mapping the low-dimension space into infinite dimensional space (Hilbert space). However, Hilbert space is just a virtual approach to think and understand problems and medial process of solving problems. In fact, we do not need to solve problems in Hilbert space, all things still can be done in low initial space, which avoids complication.

There are other commonly used Mercer kernels, such as polynomial kernel, denoted as $K(x, y) = (x \bullet y + 1)^d$, where d is the integer parameter that can be self-defined; Sigmoid kernels, denoted as $K(x, y) = \tanh(b(x \bullet y) + c)$, where b and c are parameters that can be self-defined.

Mercer kernels are very widely applied. If the problem involves only dot products, kernel function can be used to change the definition of dot product when required, and solve the problem in another space (usually with higher dimension). Yet the computational complexity is not increased, and the generalization in the high-dimensional space is not constrained by the dimension.

However, the first application of the Mercer theorem was only in 1992 when Boser, Guyon, and Vapnik applied it in the classification learning and proposed support vector machine.[21] This is 100 years after the birth of the Mercer theorem.

4.5.2 SUPPORT VECTOR MACHINE

To design machine learning algorithms, one needs to come up with autocomputing functions. "Binary classification" is the basis problem in classification. The criteria of binary classification is the spacial distances between the objects, i.e., the distances of the objects in the same classes should be minimized, while those in the different classes should be maximized. Because the calculation of distance mainly involves dot product, the linearly nonseparable problem in the low-dimensional space can be transformed into a linearly separable problem in a higher-dimensional space by nonlinear transformation, which is realized by kernel functions. The classification functions depend on support vectors, so this is called "support vector machine." Different kernel functions can result in different algorithms.[22]

Suppose $(x_i, y_i), i = 1, 2, \ldots, n$, is the sample set, where $x \in \mathbf{R}^d$. If the samples can be separated linearly, and $y_i \in \{1, -1\}$ is the class label, then general form of linear discriminant function is

$$g(x) = w \bullet x + b$$

Hyperplane function is

$$w \bullet x + b = 0$$

where w is the normal vector of the hyperplane and $\bullet$ is dot product for vectors.

Rescaling w and b such that the points closest to the hyperplane satisfy $|g(x)| \geq 1$, we obtain a canonical form (w, b) of the hyperplane, satisfying $|g(x)| = 1$. Note that in this case, the margin, measured perpendicularly to the hyperplane, equals $\frac{2}{\|w\|}$.

The hyperplane is the optimal classification plane if it can separate all the samples correctly and maximize the distance between the classes. Let H_1 and H_2 be two hyperplanes that contain the points closest to the classification plane and are parallel with the classification plane. The samples on H_1 and H_2 are called "support vectors." So only a few samples that consist of support vectors are contributive to classification, while all other samples can be neglected.

According to the definition of optimal classification plane, its solution can be expressed as the following constrained optimization problem.

Minimize

$$\Phi(w) = \frac{1}{2}\|w\|^2 = \frac{1}{2}(w \bullet w)$$

s.t.

$$y_i(w \bullet x_i + b) - 1 \geq 0 \qquad (i = 1, 2, \ldots, n) \tag{4.1}$$

This is a quadratic programming problem, which can be solved by a Lagrangian multiplier approach.

Let Lagrangian function be

$$L(w, b, \alpha) = \frac{1}{2}(w \bullet w) - \sum_{i=1}^{n} \alpha_i(y_i(w \bullet x + b) - 1)$$

where the Lagrangian coefficient $\alpha_i \geq 0$.

Calculate the partial derivatives of w and b and set them to be 0. The original problem turns into a simpler dualization problem.

Maximize

$$W(\alpha) = \sum_{i=1}^{n} \alpha_i - \frac{1}{2}\sum_{i,j=1}^{n} \alpha_i \alpha_j y_i y_j (x_i \bullet x_j)$$

s.t.

$$\alpha_i \geq 0, \qquad \sum_{i-1}^{n} \alpha_i y_i = 0$$

Let α_i^* be the optimal solution, then

$$w^* = \sum_{i=1}^{n} \alpha_i^* y_i x_i$$

Solving the limit of the quadratic function of the inequality constraint in (4.1), there exists a unique solution that satisfies Karush–Kuhn–Tucker (KKT) condition:

$$\alpha_i(y_i(w \bullet x_i + b) - 1) = 0 \quad (i = 1, 2, \dots, n)$$

It can be inferred from (4.1) that support vectors only consist of a few samples satisfying $\alpha_i^* > 0$ contribute to the classification, and the other sample with $\alpha_i^* = 0$ does not contribute to the classification.

When α_i^* and w^* are acquired, we select one support vector sample, and calculate $b^* = y_i - w^* \bullet x_i$. As a result, finally we get the optimal classification function as

$$f(x) = (w^* \bullet x) + b^* = \sum_{i=1}^{n} \alpha_i^* y_i (x_i \bullet x) + b^*$$

If the sample data set is not linear separable or with bad separation effect, we can also apply the kernel function approach. In the process of computing the optimal classification plane, the samples only emerge in the dot product operation. To improve the classification, we map the data into a higher-dimensional space by the mapping Φ, which retains the dot product operation:

$$x_i \bullet x_j \rightarrow \Phi(x_i) \bullet \Phi(x_j)$$

According to the Mercer theorem, the form of Φ is not required, and the dot product in the feature space can be obtained by kernel function

$$K(x_i, x_j) \rightarrow \Phi(x_i) \bullet \Phi(x_j)$$

In this way, the linearly unseparable problem in the original space is changed into a linearly separable problem in a higher-dimensional space, i.e.,

Maximize

$$W(\alpha) = \sum_{i=1}^{n} \alpha_i - \frac{1}{2} \sum_{i,j=1}^{n} \alpha_i \alpha_j y_i y_j K(x_i, x_j)$$

s.t.

$$\alpha_i \geq 0, \quad \sum_{i-1}^{n} \alpha_i y_i = 0$$

and the corresponding KKT conditions are

$$y_i(w \bullet x_i + b) - 1 \geq 0, \quad \alpha_i \geq 0$$

$$\alpha_i(y_i(w \bullet x_i + b) - 1) = 0, \quad (i = 1, 2, ..., n)$$

The final classification function is the support vector machine:

$$f(x) = w^* \bullet x + b^* = \sum_{i=1}^{n} \alpha_i^* y_i K(x_i, x) + b^*$$

It can be concluded that the complexity of this function is only dependent on the number of support vectors, but not on the dimension of feature space.

In classical statistical approaches, success is only guaranteed when the number of samples increases to infinity. Nevertheless, in practical applications, the number of samples is usually finite or even small, so statistical approaches based on the large number theorem cannot achieve satisfactory results. However, support vector machine, based on the Mercer kernel theorem, searches for the optimal linear hyperplane in the high-dimensional feature space. It conducts classification based on a few samples that consist of the support vectors. In a word, the advantages of SVM (Support Vector Machine) are raising dimension, linearization, and small sample number.

4.5.3 PRINCIPAL CURVES

Principal curve was first proposed by Trevor Hastie from Stanford University in his Ph.D. thesis "Principal Curves and Surfaces" in 1984.[23] In 1988, this report was published in *Journal of the American Statistical Association*.[24] Because the author employed complicated mathematical knowledge while illustrating this idea, scholars in computer science were not attentive enough to it at that time.

The statistical analysis on a data set by principal curve can be originated from the principal component analysis (PCA).

PCA, as an important tool in classical data statistical analysis, is based on a linear assumption. The first principal component of a data set is a vector, onto which data are projected and generate the least mean squared error (MSE). In 1-dimensional space, the principal component is a line (as shown in Figure 4.5), in 2-dimensional space, it is a plane (as shown in Figure 4.6), and in multidimensional space, it is a hyperplane. There are two significant merits of PCA. First, it the whole data set can

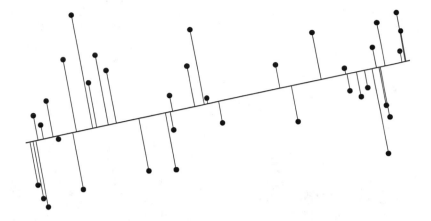

FIGURE 4.5 1-Dimensional principal component.

be represented by a vector. Second, we can calculate the eigenvalue equations of the self-correlation matrix in order to orderly compute the first and second principal component, which is easily realized in mathematics. Due to those two aspects, as well as the statistical significance of MSE, PCA is applied extensively. However, the linear assumption results in a very rough description in the internal structure of the data set. The details are not retained in the compressed data.

Though PCA reminds people of regression analysis, PCA and regression analysis are still different. Regression analysis is to find the line that minimizes the sum of the squares of the vertical distances of the points from the line. PCA is to find the line that minimizes the sum of squared distance from the points to their projection onto this line. Similar to the nonlinear extension of linear regression approach in 1994, Hastie

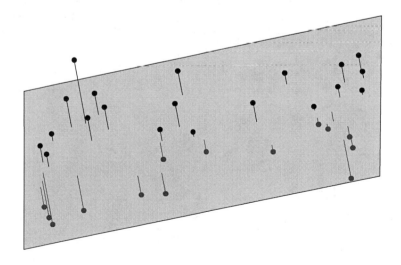

FIGURE 4.6 2-Dimensional principal component.

proposed to extend PCA to a nonlinear aspect, i.e., principal curve approach, which substituted the line with a smooth curve. The curve smoothly goes through the central region of the data, which can reflect the real state and the internal structure of the data set. So we can see that principal component is a special example of principal curve.

Definition 4.26 HS Principal Curve

Given a smooth curve f(x), it is a principal curve if the following conditions are all satisfied:

1. *f does not intersect with itself and there is no closed loop on it.*
2. *In the bounded subset in real domain R^d with arbitrary d-dimension, the length of f is finite.*
3. *f is self-consistent, i.e., $f(t) = E(X|t_f(X) = t), \quad \forall t \in T$*

where T is a closed interval in real domain, and $t_f(x)$ is the projection of x onto the curve f(x).

According to self-consistency, every point on the principal curve is the conditional mean of all the data points that are projected on this point. Hence this definition is consistent with the intuitive understanding of the "middle" of data distribution, as shown in Figure 4.7. According to this definition, when the curve turns into a line, the principal curve becomes a principal component.

Let X be the data set in a d-dimensional space. The curve f can be expressed by a single variable function in terms of parameter method, i.e.,

$$f(t) = (f_1(t), f_2(t),..., f_d(t)), \quad t \in \mathbf{R}$$

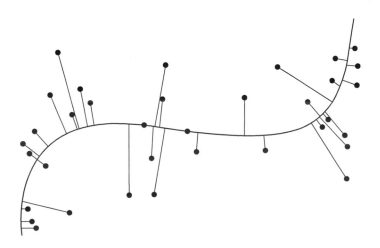

FIGURE 4.7 Principal curve.

The distance of any point x in X to the curve f can be calculated as $d(x, f) = \|x - t_f(x)\|$, where $t_f(x)$ is the projection of x on $f(x)$. Thus, the problem to find the principal curve is to find f which minimizes $\sum_{x \in X} \|x - t_f(x)\|^2$. It is also equivalent to minimizing $E\|X - f(t)\|^2$.

The solution of $t_f(x)$ depends on the concrete form of f; however, f itself is the object to be solved, in order that we can hardly get the principal curve through directly calculating the target function. In fact, the computation process is usually realized by iterations. The real principal curve is approximated by fractional linearization. However, due to the difference between curve and surface, this approach on curves cannot be extended to high-dimensional surfaces. There is hardly any essential progress in either theory or application, even though some scholars are trying to extend the principal curve to high-dimensional surface by means of differential manifold.

The principal curve proposed by Hastie is a creative work, but theoretical analysis is required to prove whether the principal curve exists in an arbitrarily distributed data set. Hastie does not give the strict proof for the existence of principal curve. Moreover, considering the noise in the raw data, it may not be appropriate to describe the data distribution by the principal curve. Besides, the assumption that the principal curve is continuous, differentiable, and smooth will result in a series of problems, such as bias, low efficiency, un-uniqueness, convergence, etc. All of these make people improve the theory of principal curve. T principal curve, C principal curve, and K principal curve are proposed sequentially, but they cause other problems while solving some problems in HS principal curve.[25]

Although it poses many questions in theory, principal curve still inspires us a lot. It contains an integral analysis approach, which describes the properties of the data set from the overall structure. Besides this, it also emphasizes the non-parameter analysis and may consider that to be inappropriate, which assumes that the data sets are subject to certain distributions. As the foundational theory in nonlinear data processing, principal curves should be given sufficient attention.

In conclusion, the research topics of mathematics are number and graph, which are the abstraction of the phenomena in the world. Mathematics becomes the most extensive fundamental subject, as number and graph are ubiquitous. Although mathematics have not been classified as mathematics of certainty or mathematics of uncertainty, there exist knowledge and intelligence of uncertainty, which can be analyzed by means of probability theory, fuzzy set theory, rough set, chaos and fractal, kernel and principal curve, etc.

In probability theory, the subject is random phenomena. Fuzzy set theory studies fuzziness in uncertainty. In rough set theory, "roughness" is analyzed by the rough boundary under a given knowledge background. Chaos and fractal do research on the internal randomness in a system of certainty. In kernel function and principal curve theory, the linear statistical analysis is extended to nonlinear area.

All these mathematical tools provide foundations to deal with human knowledge and intelligence of uncertainty. However, they have their limitations as well. For instance, in probability theory, a large number of samples and a certain traditional probability distribution are required. It can hardly deal with the random phenomenon that are not traditional. The membership function in fuzzy set theory is still dependent on precise computation, and thus it is only the accurate solution of fuzzy problems. In the rough set theory, the background knowledge database is totally certain, without considering the fact that elementary knowledge and concepts are uncertain. The research in chaos and fractal deals with only part of uncertain phenomena. Principal curve is hard to deal with noise and cannot be solve problems in high dimension. Kernel functions are still linear statistical analyses.

Moreover, in almost all the advanced axiomatic mathematical systems, the main goal is to prove theorems under the precondition of axioms. However, the emphasis of human intelligence lies in the understanding of problems in complex environments based on commonsense knowledge, solution searching, and knowledge extraction by experience. We are not thinking in a preset mathematical system.

People make cognition, expression, communication, and solution via natural languages, so we are considering studying AI with uncertainty from the angle of natural languages as a linkage between mathematics and human natural languages. This will be discussed in Chapter 5.

REFERENCES

1. Zikun Wang, *Probability Theory and Its Applications*, Beijing Normal University Press, Beijing, 1995.
2. G. K. Zipf, *Psycho-Biology of Languages*, MIT Press, Cambridge, MA, 1965.
3. C. E. Shannon, A mathematical theory of communication, *Bell System Technical Journal*, Vol. 27, No. 6 and 10, pp. 379–423, 623–656, 1948.
4. Wanhua Qiu, *Management Decision and Applied Entropy*, China Machine Press, Beijing, 2002.
5. L. A. Zadeh, Fuzzy sets, *Information and Control*, Vol. 8, pp. 338–353, 1965.
6. Yingming Liu, *Fuzziness: Another Half of Preciseness*, Tsinghua University Press, Beijing, 2001.
7. Hongxing Li and Peizhuang Wang, *Fuzzy Mathematics*, National Defence Industry Press, Beijing, 1994.
8. Peizhuang Wang and Liyan Han, *Applied Fuzzy Mathematics*, Beijing Economics University Press, Beijing, 1989.
9. Z. Pawlak, Rough sets, *International Journal of Computer and Information Science*, No. 11, pp. 341–356, 1982.
10. A. N. Kolmogorov, On the conservation of conditionally periodic motions for a small change in Hamliton's function, *Dokl. Akad. Nauk SSSR*, No. 98, pp. 525–530, 1954.
11. Edward N. Lorenz, Deterministic Nonperiodic Flow, *Journal of the Atmospheric Sciences*, Vol. 20, No. 2, pp. 130–141, 1963.
12. David Ruelle and Floris Takens, On the nature of turbulence, *Communications in Mathematical Physics*, Vol. 20, No. 3, pp. 167–192, 1971.
13. Tianyan Li and J. Yorke, Period three implies chaos, *American Mathematic Monthly*, No. 82, pp. 985–992, 1975.
14. Benoit B. Mandelbrot, How long is the coast of Britain? Statistical self-similarity and fractional dimension, *Science*, No. 156, pp. 636–638, 1967.
15. Benoit B. Mandelbrot, *Les Objets Fractals: Forme, Hazard, et Dimension*, Flammarion, Paris, 1975.

16. Benoit B. Mandelbrot, *The Fractal Geometry of Nature*, W. H. Freeman and Company, New York, 1982.
17. Xiangxing Wu and Zhong Chen, *Introduction of Chaos*, Shanghai Science and Technology Literature Press, Shanghai, 2001.
18. Xia Sun and Ziqin Wu, *Fractal Theory and Its Applications*, University of Science and Technology of China Press, Hefei, 2003.
19. J. Mercer, Functions of positive and negative type and their connection with the theory of integral equations, *Philosophical Transactions of the Royal Society of London*, No. 209, pp. 415–446, 1909.
20. Yongyi Chen, *The Approach of Support Vector Machine and Its Applications in Climate*, China Meteorological Administration Training Center, Beijing, 2004.
21. B. E. Boser, I. Guyon, and V. Vapnik, A training algorithm for optimal margin classifiers, *Proceedings of the 5th Annual ACM Workshop on Computional Learning Theory*, pp. 144–152, MIT Press, Pittsburgh, PA, 1992.
22. Nello Cristianini and John Shawe-Taylor, *An introduction to Support Vector Machines*, Cambridge University Press, Cambridge, MA, 2000.
23. T. Hastie, Principal Curves and Surfaces, Ph.D. thesis, Stanford University, Stanford, 1984.
24. T. Hastie and W. Stuetzle, Principal curves, *Journal of the American Statistical Association*, Vol. 84, No. 406, pp. 502–516, 1989.
25. Junping Zhang and Jue Wang, An overview of principal curves, *Chinese Journal of Computers*, Vol. 26, No. 2, pp. 1–18, 2003.

5 Qualitative and Quantitative Transform Model — Cloud Model

Natural languages, particularly written languages, in which qualitative words play an important role, are powerful tools for human thinking, and the use of means is the fundamental difference between the intelligence of humans and other creatures. Human brains and computers are the carriers of human intelligence and artificial intelligence (AI), respectively. If AI based on the quantitative calculation could take natural language as a way of thinking, then we have to work out a bridge to fill the gap between the two carriers, which is performed by qualitative and quantitative formalization.

5.1 PERSPECTIVES ON THE STUDY OF AI WITH UNCERTAINTY

5.1.1 MULTIPLE PERSPECTIVES ON THE STUDY OF HUMAN INTELLIGENCE

In the research of human intelligence, there are different perspectives depending on specific disciplines.

In the cognitive science, especially in cognitive psychology, research may involve sensation, attention, consciousness, memory, knowledge organization, etc. Dr. U. Neisser published the well-known book titled *Cognitive Psychology* in 1967. He thought that sensation was one perspective of human cognition. Cognition starts at sensation, followed by all the other processes such as input transformation, reduction, explanation, storage, resumption, and usage. It is mainstream in cognitive psychology that in order to understand the relationship between the creature's psychological activities and appearing phenomena, we can carry out biological contrast experiments.

In brain science, especially in neural science, research is conducted on various levels of cells, molecules, and feedback paths, etc. There are around 10^{11} to 10^{12} neurons and 10^{15} synapses in the human brain. People have also deeply understood several fundamental processes in neural activities, for instance, the signal transmission process of neurons, communication within the signal transmission, the generation and transmission of neuron activation, the transmission and modulation through synapses, the cellular and molecular mechanisms of learning and memorization, the plasticity of neural activities, the fast/slow reactions caused by neurotransmitters, the cellular mechanism of slow reactions, and so on. On the molecular level, there have also been some progresses on the ion channel, neuron receivers, and the clone of transfer proteins.

If the research of life science could be carried out on a more microcosmic level, the cognitive activities may be corresponding to the electronic or chemical variances in the cellular or subcellular levels, or even related to genes. Nevertheless, currently, life science is unable to determine such relationships between thinking activities and activities of subcellular on electronic or chemical levels, for instance, the way to store a concept, corresponding to a word in a language in the biological form, the biological process to connect this concept with other concepts, and the determinative relationships of neural constructions on cognitive activities.

Obviously, we cannot derive an e-mail behavior in a complex network simply based on the most fundamental activities in the entire silicon chips of computers which finally constructed the complex network. And similarly, with only the property analysis of single ion, synapse, protein, gene, cell, neuron, and organ, we can neither infer the cognitive and thinking activities of human brains. System theory suggests the principle that characteristics of an overall system are not simply the sum of all elements at a low level. People often oppugn reductionism in this way.

The perspective of human intelligence research in the academic circle of AI is based on mathematics and computer architecture. Mathematicians extract numbers and shapes out of various phenomena in the subjective and objective world, and originate branches such as mathematical analysis, topology, functional analysis, graph theory, differential geometry, manifold, etc. All these branches are established based on a specific axiomatized system, and pursue formalization and strictness. The major work of a modern axiomatized mathematical system is to prove theorems, and its outcomes are usually in the form of theorems. Generally, the theorem proof will turn into a pure algebraic problem.

Excellent mathematical ability is generally considered a distinguishing talent for highly intelligent human beings, so people think that if a computer can solve mathematic problems, it will possess human intelligence. Driven by this belief, mechanical research activities and extensive realizations in mathematics mechanization came into being, e.g., theorem proof by machines. As a result, a new stage of formalized system was established on the formalized system composed of symbolic systems. Various computer languages were derived thereafter, such as machine language, assembly language, and computer platform-dependent languages, e.g., Algol, Fortran, Pascal, SmallTalk, Cobol, Basic, Lisp, Prolog, Ada, C, C++, Java, Delphi, and XML. The emergence of these languages, especially the emergence of the advanced and specialized languages, enables computers to communicate in a friendly way with human beings to some extent. These machines, essentially based on Turing's computing mechanism, seem to obtain intelligence increasingly.

During the 50 years since the development and growth of AI, people have been seeking different perspectives in research techniques (Figure 5.1). The "logical school" conducts research at the symbolic level, and it takes symbols as the elements of cognition, which implement the intelligent behaviors by symbolic operations. The logicians emphasize on the heuristic search and reasoning. Another school, "biometric school" investigates at the neural constructional level and treats neurons

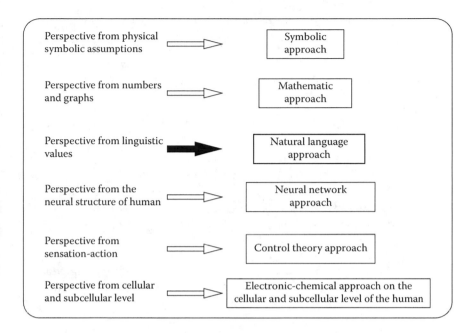

FIGURE 5.1 Various perspectives in the research of artificial intelligence.

as the basic cognitive elements. These researchers have invented artificial neural networks (ANNs), and emphasize the structural mimetism. Intelligence, as they explain, is the result of competitions and cooperation of the neurons. Neural properties, structure topology, learning methods, nonlinear dynamics of the network, and adaptive cooperative behaviors are the research subjects. Scholars in the "control school" believe for sure that there cannot be intelligence without feedback. They emphasize the interaction between a system and its environment. The intelligent system acquires information from the environment by sensations, and affects the environment by its actions.

As a matter of fact, mathematical axioms and formulas are always tightly conditioned by the environment which is very often described by natural language. To carry out the research in mathematics to a certain extent, people are used to focusing on the formalized symbols and formulas that are more and more complicated, but they often neglect the fact that the natural language still plays an important role in that descriptive proof, involving improvability and uncertainty, which are even more fundamental in the axiom system.

From the linguistic aspect, natural language is the essential embodiment of human intelligence and it is not substitutable. No science or technology in the world could exit without the description of natural language. As a result, natural language is an inevitable perspective for the research on human intelligence. The foundation of AI with uncertainty lies in the research on the uncertainties and their formalization of natural language.

5.1.2 The Importance of Concepts in Natural Languages

Since natural languages are the carrier of human thought, the development of any natural language becomes a cultural phenomenon. Hence, as the basic unit of natural language, the linguistic value or concept is essential in human thought.

Generally speaking, philosophy and cognitive scientists consider that the objective world involves physical objects, and the subjective world, starting from the cognitive units and the objects that they are pointing at, reflect the inherent and extrinsic relationships between the two worlds. Every thinking activity points to a certain object, and the subjective sensation of the existence of the object is perceived due to the existence of that object. The case of language, which is an invention during human evolution, also obeys this rule. The interactions between humans and the environment, including all body motions, sensations and so on, are reflected in neural activities. The objective features, e.g., the shape, color, and sequence, and the subjective emotional states, are categorized by the human brain. A new level of representation is then generated based on the categorization result. This may be called an "abstract concept," which is represented by linguistic values. Thereafter, the brain will select a concept and activate the related words, or in reverse, extract the corresponding concept out of words received from other people. The linguistic value, directly connected with the concept, can "condense" the cognition and reclassify the objective world. It would reduce the complexity of conceptual structure to an acceptable degree.[1,2] Thus the concept plays a key role in the activities of processing the sensations on objects and phenomena, and supplementing the sensational organs.

As a high-level productive activity in the human brain, the concept is the reflection of the object in the brain. Although the concept might look subjective, it essentially contains certain regularity in categorization, as it reflects the generalized and most significant feature of the object. While utilizing the concept, people abstract and classify various objects in the real world according to their essential feature, and construct a cognitive framework that is not too psychologically complex. This way, cognition evolves from a low-level sensational stage to a high-level rational stage. This process of concept generation in the brain is a representation of thinking.

As the evolution of human beings goes on, natural language is also evolving. Human beings, inventors of languages, utilize language symbols in the process of thinking. From the aspect of human evolution, the concept-based languages, theories, and models become tools to describe and understand the objective world.

In natural language, the concept is usually represented by the linguistic value, i.e., the word. In this book, we use linguistic value, word, and concept interchangeably. To this extent, soft computing, or computing with words, or thinking with natural language is all toward the same direction.

5.1.3 The Relationship between Randomness and Fuzziness in a Concept

The most significant and distinctive difference between the group of linguistic values, and the group of mathematic symbols, is that the first group involves a great number of uncertainties, while the second one does not.

There are many approaches in the research of uncertainties, among which probability theoretics is the earliest and most mature. It starts from the research on the inevitability and the occasionality of event occurrence, and forms three branches, namely, probability theory, stochastic study, and mathematical statistics. Thereafter, theories of fuzzy set and rough set start from the uncertain event, and introduce the membership function and upper/lower approximate set. The more often used measurement of uncertainties is entropy, such as entropy in thermodynamics and information entropy. Besides, approaches of chaos and fractal are used for the research of uncertainty in certain systems. All these approaches lead the research of uncertainty from different perspectives. Although they have clear perspectives and clear constraints on boundary conditions, and research can be conducted in depth by these approaches, the view's local confinement is noticeable.

For example, in the past, research on fuzziness did not consider of randomness and vice versa. Nevertheless, fuzziness and randomness are usually tightly related and inseparable.

In the fuzzy set, membership functions are applied to describe the extent of uncertainty, and hence the fuzzy set is more developed compared with the determinative theory. However, the determination of membership functions is often accompanied by subjective thought, as it is dependent on the experience of experts or acquired by statistics.

Chinese scholars such as Nanlun Zhang calculated the membership of the fuzzy concept "youth" by statistical approach. This large-scale experiment is a classical one for membership function computation. Zhang selected 129 valid candidates in the Wuhan Institution of Constructional Materials. These candidates independently gave their own age as a definition for the term "youth." The data were grouped and the relative frequencies were calculated. Within each group, the median was applied to represent the membership frequency, i.e., the membership value at each point. The result is shown in Table 5.1.

This experiment reflects differences of subjective cognitions, environmental conditions, etc. in the process of membership acquisition, and thus the resulting membership must involve these differences which can be investigated by probability theoretics.

In probability theoretics, the most fundamental axiomatic presumption is the neutral exclusive law, i.e., the sum of probabilities of event A and non-A is strictly equal to 1. However, while we are talking about the concepts used in natural languages, it is not necessarily with the same case. For example, for the same person, the sum of probabilities of events, i.e., the statement that he or she is a youth and the one that he or she is not a youth, is not necessarily equal to 1. In the discussion of possibility measurement

---

TABLE 5.1
The Membership Degree of "Youth"

Age X_i	24	25	26	27	28	29	30
Membership degree Y_i	1	0.9922	0.7981	0.7829	0.7674	0.6202	0.5969
Age X_i	31	32	33	34	35	36	37
Membership degree Y_i	0.2093	0.2093	0.2016	0.2016	0.2016	0.0078	0

of fuzziness, membership and possibility measurement are different. In short, it is difficult to clarify the differences within memberships, possibility measurement and probability. In logic theory, the terms "and" and "or" are distinctive, but while used in natural languages for daily activity expression, they may be difficult to be distinguished sometimes. While using uncertain words, e.g., about, maybe, probably, sometimes, usually, around, etc., people do not care whether they are used for expression of fuzziness or randomness, especially in the case of emotional and mental descriptions.

Actually, concepts in natural languages are qualitative. For understanding uncertainties in natural languages, we do not have to conduct research from the perspectives of randomness and fuzziness, respectively. In comparison with qualitative and quantitative difference, the gap between randomness and fuzziness is not so restricted and impotent. Therefore, we propose a more significant approach to establish a transformation model of uncertainty between the qualitative concept and the quantitative description.

5.2 REPRESENTING CONCEPTS USING CLOUD MODELS

Describing the uncertainty between variables by concepts is more natural and more generalized than doing it by mathematics which is of certainty. In that case, how do we express qualitative knowledge by natural languages? How do we realize the inter-transformation between qualitative and quantitative knowledge? How do we represent the soft-reasoning ability in thinking with languages? To answer these questions, we introduce an important qualitative–quantitative transformation model with uncertainty. The model can show the uncertain mechanism during the transformation between qualitative concepts and quantitative values.

5.2.1 CLOUD AND CLOUD DROP

Definition 5.1

Let U be a universal set described by precise numbers, and C be the qualitative concept related to U. If there is a number $x \in U$, which randomly realizes the concept C, and the certainty degree of x for C, i.e., $\mu(x) \in [0, 1]$, is a random value with stabilization tendency

$$\mu: U \to [0,1] \quad \forall x \in U \quad x \to \mu(x)$$

then the distribution of x on U is defined as a cloud, and every x is defined as a cloud drop.[3–7]

The cloud has the following properties:

1. The universal set U can be either one-dimensional or multidimensional.
2. The random realization in the definition is the realization in terms of probability. The certainty degree is the membership degree in the fuzzy set, and it also has the distribution of probability. All these show the correlation of fuzziness and randomness.
3. For any $x \in U$, the mapping from x to [0; 1] is multiple. The certainty degree of x on C is a probability distribution rather than a fixed number.

4. The cloud is composed of cloud drops, which are not necessarily in any order in the universal set. A cloud drop is the implementation of the qualitative concept once. The more cloud drops there are, the better the overall feature of this concept is represented.

5. The more probable the cloud drop appears, the higher the certainty degree is, and hence the more contribution the cloud drop makes to the concept.

For better understanding of the cloud, we utilize the united distribution of (x, μ) to express the concept C. In this book, the united distribution of (x, μ) is also denoted as $C(x, \mu)$.

Cloud is a model described by linguistic values for representation of the uncertain relationships between a specific qualitative concept and its quantitative expression. It is introduced to reflect the uncertainties of the concepts in natural languages. We can explain it by means of the classical random theory and fuzzy set theory. The cloud, as a reflection of the correlation of randomness and fuzziness, constructs the mapping between quality and quantity.

The cloud model leads the research on intelligence at the basic linguistic value, and focuses on the approach to represent qualitative concepts by quantitative expressions. It is more intuitive and pervasive. In this way, the concept is transformed into a number of quantitative values, or more vividly speaking, into the points in the space of the universal set. This process, as a discrete transition process, is random. The selection of every single point is a random event, and can be described by the probability distribution function. Besides, the certainty degree of the cloud drop is fuzzy and can be described by the probability distribution function as well. This cloud model is flexible, boundless, and its global shape rather than its local region can be well observed. These attributes located in the universe are very much similar to the cloud in the sky showing uncertainties, so we name this mathematic transform a "cloud."

The cloud can be expressed graphically by a cloud graph. The geographical shape of the cloud is of much assistance in understanding the transform between quality and quantity. Here, we would like to give an example, i.e., "the neighborhood at the origin" on a two-dimensional plane. It can demonstrate the way to express a concept by cloud drops. There are three visualization methods of the cloud graph.[8]

Figure 5.2(a) shows the position of cloud drops in the two-dimensional space. Every point represents a drop, and its gray-level intensity shows the certainty degree to which this drop can represent the concept. In Figure 5.2(b), every circle represents a cloud drop. The position and the certainty degree of the drop can be inferred from the location and the size of the circle, respectively. Figure 5.2(c) illustrates the united distribution of the drop and certainty degree, i.e., $C(x,\mu)$, where x is the drop location in the two-dimensional space, and μ is the certainty degree, at the third domain, to which the drop can represent the concept C.

5.2.2 NUMERICAL CHARACTERISTICS OF CLOUD

The overall property of a concept can be represented by the numerical characters, which are the overall quantitative property of the qualitative concept. They are of

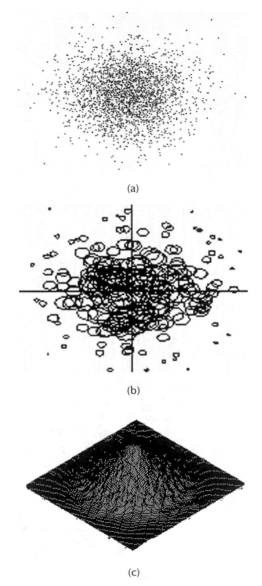

FIGURE 5.2 Three visualization approaches of the cloud graph: (a) gray-level representation, (b) circle representation, and (c) three-dimensional representation.

great significance for us to understand the connotation and the extension of the concept.

In the cloud model, we employ the expected value Ex, the entropy En, and the hyper-entropy He to represent the concept as a whole.

The expected value Ex: The mathematical expectation of the cloud drop distributed in the universal set. In other words, it is the point that is most representative of the qualitative concept, or the most classical sample while quantifying the concept.

The entropy *En*: The uncertainty measurement of the qualitative concept. It is determined by both the randomness and the fuzziness of the concept. From one aspect, as the measurement of randomness, *En* reflects the dispersing extent of the drops, and from the other aspect, it is also the measurement of "this and that," representing the value region in which the drop is acceptable by the concept. As a result, the correlation of randomness and the fuzziness are reflected by using the same numerical character.

The hyper-entropy *He*: This is the uncertainty measurement of the entropy, i.e., the second-order entropy of the entropy, which is determined by both the randomness and fuzziness of the entropy.

Generally speaking, the uncertainty of the concept can be represented by multiple numerical characteristics. We can say that the mathematical expectation, variance and high-order moments in the probability theory reflect several numerical characters of the randomness, but not of the fuzziness. While the membership function is a precise descriptive approach of the fuzziness and does not take the randomness into account; the rough set measures the uncertainty by the research of two precise sets that are based on the background of precise knowledge rather than the background of uncertain knowledge. In the cloud model approach, we may express the uncertainty of the concept by higher-ordered entropy aside of the expectation, entropy and hyper-entropy, so research can be conducted with more depth if necessary.

In general, people undertake reasoning with the help of a natural language, rather than excessive mathematic calculus. So, it is more adequate to employ these three numerical characteristics to reflect the uncertainty in common concepts, while the use of excessive numerical characters will contradict with the essence of the fact that people take qualitative thinking with natural languages.

The uncertainties in a natural language do not prevent an audience from understanding the content, neither do they keep people from making correct conclusions or decisions. On the contrary, they bring more imaging space for people's intercommunion and understanding. This is the beauty of uncertainties indeed.

5.2.3　Types of Cloud Model

The discreet implementation of the cloud is the cloud model, which is the foundation of cloud computation, cloud clustering, cloud reasoning, cloud control, etc. To express the qualitative concept by the quantitative method, we generate cloud drops according to the numerical characteristics of the cloud. This is called "forward cloud generator." The reverse one, i.e., from the quantitative expression to the qualitative concept, is called "backward cloud generator," which extracts the numerical characteristics from the group of cloud drops.

There are various implementation approaches of the cloud model, resulting in different kinds of clouds, for example, the symmetric cloud model, the half-cloud model, and the combined cloud model.

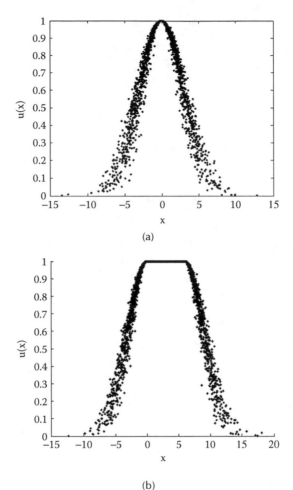

(a)

(b)

FIGURE 5.3 Symmetric cloud model.

The symmetric cloud model, as shown in Figure 5.3, represents the qualitative concept with symmetric features.

The half-cloud model, as shown in Figure 5.4, represents the concept with uncertainty on only one side.

There are various mathematical characteristics representing uncertainties, and the variation also exists in natural languages and the real world, for instance, the representation region of some concepts are asymmetric. As a result, we can construct the varying cloud model, i.e., the combined cloud model. Figure 5.5 illustrates a combined cloud model.

The cloud model can be multidimensional as well. Figure 5.6 shows the joint relationship of the two-dimensional cloud and its certainty degree with the third dimension.

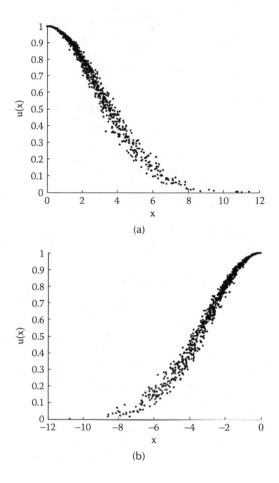

(a)

(b)

FIGURE 5.4 Half-cloud model.

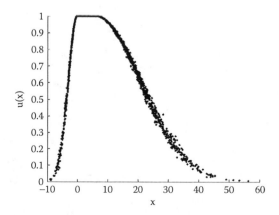

FIGURE 5.5 Combined cloud model.

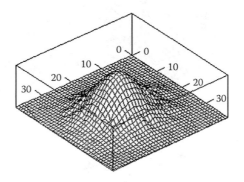

FIGURE 5.6 Two-dimensional cloud model.

5.3 NORMAL CLOUD GENERATOR

Normal distribution is one of the most important distributions in probability theory. It is usually represented by two numerical characteristics, i.e., the mean and the variance. While the bell-shaped membership function is the one used the most in the fuzzy set, and it is generally expressed as $\mu(x) = e^{-\frac{(x-a)^2}{2b^2}}$. The normal cloud is a brand new model developed based on both the normal distribution and the bell-shaped membership function.

Cloud generator (CG) may be an algorithm implemented in the computer, or a piece of hardware made by integrated circuits (ICs).[9]

5.3.1 FORWARD CLOUD GENERATOR

Forward normal CG is a mapping from quality to quantity. It generates as many cloud drops as you like according to *Ex*, *En*, *He*. The forward normal cloud is defined as follows:

Definition 5.2

Let U be a quantitative universal set described by precise numbers, and C be the qualitative concept related to U. If there is a number x ∈ U, which is a random realization of the concept C, and x satisfies x ~ N(Ex, En²), where En′ ~ N(En, He²), and the certainty degree of x on C is

$$\mu = e^{-\frac{(x-Ex)^2}{2(En')^2}}$$

then the distribution of x on U is a normal cloud.

The algorithm of the forward normal CG (Figure 5.7) is as follows:

Algorithm 5.1 Forward normal cloud generator CG(Ex, En, He, n)

Input: (*Ex*, *En*, *He*), and the number of cloud drops *n*
Output: *n* of cloud drops *x* and their certainty degree μ, i.e., Drop(x_i, μ_i), $i = 1, 2,\ldots, n$

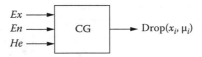

FIGURE 5.7 Forward cloud generator (CG).

Steps:

1. Generate a normally distributed random number En'_i with expectation En and variance He^2, *i.e.*, $En'_i = \text{NORM}(En, He^2)$
2. Generate a normally distributed random number x_i with expectation Ex and variance En'^2_i, *i.e.*, $x_i = \text{NORM}(Ex, En'^2_i)$
3. Calculate

$$\mu_i = e^{-\frac{(x_i - E_x)^2}{2(En'_i)^2}}$$

4. x_i with certainty degree of μ_i is a cloud drop in the domain
5. Repeat steps 1 to 4 until n cloud drops are generated

This algorithm is applicable to the one-dimensional universal space situation, and also applicable to the two- or higher dimensional situations.

The key point in this algorithm is the second-ordered relationship, i.e., within the two random numbers, one is the input of the other in generation.

Generally speaking, the variance should not be 0 while generating normal random numbers. That is why En and He are required to be positive in CG algorithm. If $He = 0$, step 1 will always give out an invariable number En, and as a result x will become a normal distribution. If $He = 0$, $En = 0$, the generated x will be a constant Ex and $\mu \equiv 1$. By this means, we can see that certainty is the special case of the uncertainty.

Here we give the source code of the one-dimensional normal cloud in MATLAB® and VC++®.

Source Code 1: One-Dimensional Normal CG in MATLAB

```
//*********************************************//
// This function generates one-dimensional cloud drops.
// Input Parameters:
// Ex: Expectation of cloud.
// En: Entropy of cloud.
```

```
// He: Hyper-Entropy of cloud.
// n: number of drops we want to generate.
// Output Values:
// x,y: matrix of cloud drops.
//*************************************************//


function cloud(Ex,En,He,n)
for i = 1:n
// Step 1
Enn = randn(1)*He + En;
// Step 2
x(i) = randn(1)*Enn + Ex;
// Step 3
y(i) = exp(-(x(i)-Ex)^2/(2*Enn^2));
end
```

Source Code 2: One-Dimensional Normal CG in VC++

```
//*************************************************//
// This function generates one-dimensional cloud drops.
// Input Parameters:
//     Ex: Expectation of cloud.
//     En: Entropy of cloud.
//     He: Hyper-Entropy of cloud.
//     n: number of drops we want to generate.
// Output Values:
//     drop[][2]: Global matrix of cloud drops.
//*************************************************//
void cloud(Ex,En,He,n)
{
float Enn,x,y;
// Sets a random starting point.
```

```
srand((unsigned)time(NULL));

for(int i=0; i<n; i++)

{

// Step 1

Enn=(sqrt(-2*log(rand()*1./RAND
MAX))*cos(2*Pi*rand()*1./RAND MAX))*He+En;

// Step 2

x=(sqrt(-2*log(rand()*1./RAND
MAX))*cos(2*Pi*rand()*1./RAND MAX))*abs(Enn)+Ex;

// Step 3

y=exp(-(x-Ex)*(x-Ex)/(2*Enn*Enn));

// Save (x,y) to the Global Matrix drop[][2] (Defined
outside of this func.)

drop[i][0]-x;

drop[i][1]=y;

  }

}
```

The foundation of the algorithm lies in the way random numbers are generated with normal distribution. In almost all programming languages, there are functions to generate random numbers with uniform distribution in [0, 1]. However, to generate normally distributed random numbers by uniformly distributed numbers, we have to investigate the seed of uniformly random function, as it determines whether the generated random numbers are the same each time. There are many literatures in statistical computation on the problem of generating normally distributed random numbers or other distributed random numbers by uniformly distributed ones.[10,11] With the inputs $Ex = 20$, $En = 3$, $He = 0.1$, and $N = 1,000$, the aforementioned algorithm produces the cloud graph of the joint distribution $C(x,\mu)$ illustrated in Figure 5.8.

For an example, the qualitative concept "approximately 20" can be understood by 1,000 cloud drops described quantitatively here.

It is not difficult to extend a one-dimensional normal cloud to a two-dimensional case. With the given numerical characteristics of a two-dimensional normal cloud,[12] i.e., expectation (Ex, Ey), entropy (Enx, Eny), and hyper-entropy (Hex, Hey), we can generate cloud drops by a two-dimensional forward normal CG.

Algorithm 5.2 Two-dimensional forward normal CG

Input: $(Ex, Ey, Enx, Eny, Hex, Hey, n)$
Output: $Drop(x_i, y_i, \mu_i)$, $i = 1,...,n$

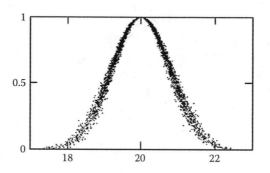

FIGURE 5.8 The cloud graph $C(x,\mu)$ generated by CG(20; 3; 0.1; 1,000).

Steps:

1. Generate a two-dimensional normally distributed random vector (Enx'_i, Eny'^2_i) with expectation (Enx, Eny) and variance (Hex^2, Hey^2).
2. Generate a two-dimensional normally distributed random vector (x_i, y_i) with expectation (Ex, Ey) and variance (Enx'^2_i, Eny'^2_i).
3. Calculate

$$\mu_i = e^{-\left[\frac{(x_i-Ex)^2}{2Enx'^2_i} + \frac{(y_i-Ey)^2}{2Eny'^2_i}\right]}$$

4. Let (x_i, y_i, μ_i) is a cloud drop, and it is one quantitative implementation of the linguistic value represented by this cloud. In this drop, (x_i, y_i) is the value in the universal domain corresponding to this qualitative concept, and μ_i is the degree measure of the extent to which (x_i, y_i) belongs to this concept.
5. Repeat steps 1 to 4 until n cloud drops are generated.

The corresponding two-dimensional forward normal CG is shown in Figure 5.9.

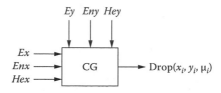

FIGURE 5.9 Two-dimensional forward cloud generator (CG).

5.3.2 CONTRIBUTIONS OF CLOUD DROPS TO A CONCEPT

In the forward normal cloud model, cloud drop communities contribute to the concept with difference. To understand the forward normal cloud model in even more depth, we are going to discuss the different contributions made in the different drop communities, based on one-dimensional forward normal cloud model.[13]

Definition 5.3

Within the one-dimensional universal domain, the cloud drop cluster Δx in any small region will make contribution to the qualitative concept A by ΔC, which satisfies:

$$\Delta C \approx \mu_A(x) * \Delta x / \sqrt{2\pi En}$$

Obviously, the total contribution C to the concept A by all the elements in the universal domain is

$$C = \frac{\int_{-\infty}^{+\infty} \mu_T(x)\,dx}{\sqrt{2\pi En}} = \frac{\int_{-\infty}^{+\infty} e^{-(x-Ex)^2/2En^2}\,dx}{\sqrt{2\pi En}} = 1$$

Because

$$\frac{1}{\sqrt{2\pi En}} \int_{Ex-3En}^{Ex+3En} \mu_T(x)\,dx = 99.74\%$$

the contributive cloud drops to the concept A in the universal domain U lie in the interval $[Ex - 3En, En + 3En]$.

As a result, we can neglect the contribution to the concept C by the cloud drops out of the domain $[Ex - 3En, Ex + 3En]$. This is named "the 3En rule" of the forward normal cloud.

According to calculation, the drops located within $[Ex - 0.67En, Ex + 0.67En]$ take up 22.33% of the whole quantity, and their contribution to the qualitative concept occupies 50% of the overall contribution. This part of cloud drops is called "key elements." The drops within $[Ex - En, Ex + En]$ take up 33.33% of the whole quantity, and contribute 68.26% to the concept. They are called "basic elements." The drops within $[Ex - 2En, Ex - En]$ and $[Ex + En, Ex + 2En]$ are called "peripheral elements," which contribute 27.18% while taking up 33.33% of the whole quantity. The drops within $[Ex - 3En, Ex - 2En]$ and $[Ex + 2En, Ex + 3En]$ are called "weak peripheral elements" because these 33.33% of the total quantity make up only 4.3% of the whole contribution. The contribution to the concept by the cloud drops in different regions is illustrated in Figure 5.10.

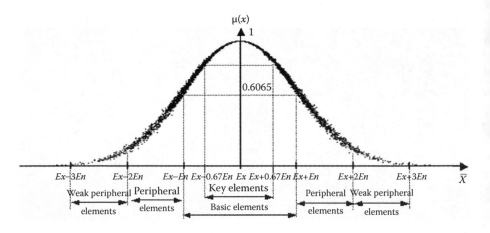

FIGURE 5.10 Contributions to the qualitative concept by cloud drops in different regions.

5.3.3 Understanding the Lunar Calendar's Solar Terms through Cloud Models

With the help of the forward normal cloud model, we are happy to understand a lot of qualitative concepts, which are words or terms in a natural language, for instance seasonal concepts, i.e., spring, summer, autumn, and winter. The ancient Chinese accumulated abundant experience in farming activities and climate variation, and summarized all that into 24 solar terms, which are the deeper understanding of the four seasonal concepts. We can employ 4 normal cloud models to represent the 4 seasonal linguistic values, with 5 as their entropies and 0.3 as their hyper-entropies. The certainty degree of a cloud drop represents the extent degree to which a specific date belongs to one season.

As recorded in the Spring and Autumn Period*, there are four dates in the lunar calendar called "vernal equinox," "summer solstice," "autumnal equinox," and "winter solstice." They stand for the expectation of the four qualitative concepts of spring, summer, autumn, and winter, respectively. At these four points, the season belongs to spring, summer, autumn, or winter, respectively with a certainty degree of 1. In the cloud graph, the rising trend before each point means that the climate is more like the expected one in that season, and the falling trend after that means that the season is gradually passing. The symmetry of the graph at these points reflects the turning of the seasons.

At the end of Warring States Period, i.e., 500 years later, for the description of the ending of a season and the beginning of the following season, four other temporal points were added, i.e., "spring begins," "summer begins," "autumn begins," and "winter begins." In the Qin Dynasty and Han Dynasty, the solar terms became more complete. Within each temporal period between the 8 existing terms, 2 more terms

---

* The Spring and Autumn Period represents an era in Chinese history between 722 BC and 481 BC.

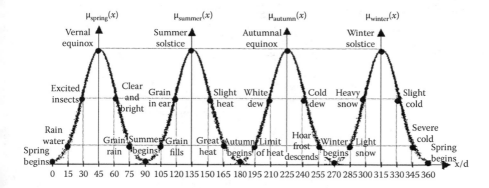

FIGURE 5.11 Twenty-four solar terms represented by the cloud model.

were added. They describe the climate in terms of temperature (e.g., "slight heat," "great heat," "limited heat," "slight cold," and "severe cold"), moisture (e.g., "white dew," "cold dew," and "hoar frost descends"), rain/snow (e.g., "rain water," "grain rain," "light snow," and "heavy snow") and the growth of plants (e.g., "excited insects," "clear and bright," "grain fills," and "grain in ear"). Let's take the concept of "spring" as an example and give a detailed discussion. The expectations of certainty degree of "rain water" and "grain rain" for the concept of spring are both 0.1353, while those of "excited insects" and "clear and bright" are both 0.6065. The contributions to spring by the durations from "excited insects" to "clear and bright," from "rain water" to "grain rain," and from "spring begins" to "summer begins," are 68.26, 95.44, and 99.74%, respectively. Figure 5.11 shows the 24 solar terms represented by the cloud model. We can see that the points of the 24 solar terms are located on the multiples of *En*. They are all distributed as the specific points on the expectation curve of the normal cloud, which will be discussed in detail in Section 5.4.3.

5.3.4 BACKWARD CLOUD GENERATOR

Backward cloud generator (CG^{-1}) is the model of transformation from a quantitative value to a qualitative concept.[14] It maps a quantity of precise data back into the qualitative concept expressed by *Ex*, *En*, *He*, as shown in Figure 5.12.

There are two kinds of basic algorithms of CG^{-1} based on statistics, classified by whether algorithms utilize the certainty degree.

FIGURE 5.12 Backward cloud generator (CG).

Algorithm 5.3 Backward normal CG with the certainty degree

Input: x_i and the certainty degree μ_i, $i = 1,\ldots,n$
Output: (Ex, En, He) representative of the qualitative concept
Steps:

1. Calculate the mean of x_i for Ex, i.e., $Ex = \text{MEAN}(x_i)$
2. Calculate the standard variance of x_i for En, i.e., $En = \text{STDEV}(x_i)$
3. For each couple of (x_i, μ_i), calculate

$$En'_i = \sqrt{\frac{-(x_i - Ex)^2}{2\ln\mu_i}}$$

4. Calculate the standard variance of En'_i for He, i.e., $He = \text{STDEV}(En'_i)$

In the algorithm, MEAN and STDEV are functions for mean and standard variance of the samples.

There are drawbacks to the one-dimensional backward CG algorithm:

1. The certainty degree μ is required for recovering En and He; however, in practical applications we can usually get only a group of data representative of the concept, but not the certainty degree μ.
2. It is difficult to extend this algorithm to higher dimensional situations, and the error in the higher dimensional backward cloud is larger than that of the one-dimensional backward cloud.

To overcome the drawbacks of the algorithm requiring a certainty degree, we propose the following backward cloud algorithm, which utilizes only the value of x_i for backward cloud generation based on the statistical characters of the cloud.

Algorithm 5.4 Backward normal CG without certainty degree

Input: Samples x_i, $i = 1,\ldots,n$
Output: (Ex, En, He) representative of the qualitative concept
Steps:

1. Calculate the mean and variance of x_i, i.e., $\bar{X} = \frac{1}{n}\sum_{i=1}^{n} x_i$ and $S^2 = \frac{1}{n-1}\sum_{i=1}^{n}(x_i - \bar{X})^2$
2. $Ex = \bar{X}$
3. $En = \sqrt{\frac{\pi}{2}} \times \frac{1}{n}\sum_{i=1}^{n} |x_i - Ex|$
4. $He = \sqrt{S^2 - En^2}$

Here we provide the validity for the algorithm:

Let random variable X be the cloud drops generated by the cloud $\{Ex, En, He\}$.

Since the expectation of X is Ex, we can estimate Ex by the mean of the samples, i.e., $\bar{X}$ shown in step 2.

Then we can compute the first-order absolute central moment $E\,|X-Ex|$. From the statistical characters of the normal cloud model, we can get the probability density of X as:

$$f(x) = \frac{1}{2\pi He} \int_{-\infty}^{+\infty} \frac{1}{y} \exp\left[-\frac{(x-Ex)^2}{2y^2} - \frac{(y-En)^2}{2He^2}\right] dy$$

So,

$$E|X - Ex| = \int_{-\infty}^{+\infty} |x - Ex| f(x) dx$$

$$= \frac{1}{2\pi He} \int_{-\infty}^{+\infty} \int_{-\infty}^{+\infty} |x - Ex| \frac{1}{y} \exp\left[-\frac{(x-Ex)^2}{2y^2} - \frac{(y-En)^2}{2He^2}\right] dy dx$$

$$= \frac{1}{2\pi He} \int_{-\infty}^{+\infty} \exp\left[-\frac{(y-En)^2}{2He^2}\right] dy \int_{-\infty}^{+\infty} \frac{|x-Ex|}{y} \exp\left[-\frac{(x-Ex)^2}{2y^2}\right] dx$$

where

$$\int_{-\infty}^{+\infty} \frac{|x-Ex|}{y} \exp\left[-\frac{(x-Ex)^2}{2y^2}\right] dx = \int_{-\infty}^{Ex} \frac{Ex-x}{y} \exp\left[-\frac{(x-Ex)^2}{2y^2}\right] dx$$

$$+ \int_{Ex}^{+\infty} \frac{x-Ex}{y} \exp\left[-\frac{(x-Ex)^2}{2y^2}\right] dx$$

$$= \int_{+\infty}^{0} - te^{-\frac{1}{2}t^2} y dt + \int_{0}^{+\infty} te^{-\frac{1}{2}t^2} y dt$$

$$= 2\int_{0}^{+\infty} ye^{-\frac{1}{2}t^2} d\left(\frac{1}{2}t^2\right) = 2y$$

So,

$$E|x - Ex| = \frac{1}{\pi He} \int_{-\infty}^{+\infty} ye^{-\frac{(y-En)^2}{2He^2}} dy = \sqrt{\frac{2}{\pi}} \times \frac{1}{\sqrt{2\pi He}} \int_{-\infty}^{+\infty} ye^{-\frac{(y-En)^2}{2He^2}} dy$$

$$= \sqrt{\frac{2}{\pi}} En$$

When the amount of sample cloud drops is n, $En = \sqrt{\frac{\pi}{2}} \times \frac{1}{n} \sum_{i=1}^{n} |x_i - \overline{X}|$. As a result, step 3 in the algorithm has been proved.

The variance of X is

$$DX = \int_{-\infty}^{+\infty} (x-Ex)^2 dx \int_{-\infty}^{+\infty} \frac{1}{2\pi Hey} \exp\left[-\frac{(x-Ex)^2}{2y^2} - \frac{(y-En)^2}{2He^2}\right] dy$$

$$= \frac{1}{\sqrt{2\pi}He} \int_{-\infty}^{+\infty} y \exp\left[-\frac{(y-En)^2}{2He^2}\right] dy \int_{-\infty}^{+\infty} \frac{1}{\sqrt{2\pi}} \frac{(x-Ex)^2}{y^2} \exp\left[-\frac{(x-Ex)^2}{2y^2}\right] dx$$

$$= \frac{1}{\sqrt{2\pi}He} \int_{-\infty}^{+\infty} y^2 \exp\left[-\frac{(y-En)^2}{2He^2}\right] dy \int_{-\infty}^{+\infty} \frac{1}{\sqrt{2\pi}} t^2 \exp\left[-\frac{t^2}{2}\right] dt$$

$$= En^2 + He^2$$

Substitute DX with the sample variance $S^2 = \frac{1}{n-1}\sum_{i=1}^{n}(x_i - \overline{X})^2$, we can get step 4.

Here we provide the source codes of Algorithms 5.3 and 5.4 in both MATLAB and VC++.

Source code 3: Backward normal cloud generator (with certainty degree) in MATLAB

```
//************************************************//
// This function retrieves parameters from cloud
drops(with certainty degree).
// Intput Values:
// x,y: matrix of cloud drops.
// Output Parameters:
//     b_Ex: Expectation of cloud.
//     b_En: Entropy of cloud.
//     b_He: Hyper-Entropy of cloud.
//************************************************//
function back cloud(x,y)
// Step 1
b_Ex=mean(x);
// Step 2
b_En=std(x);
// Step 3
```

```
b_Enn=sqrt(-(x-b_Ex).^2./(2*log(y)));
b_He=std(b_Enn);
```

Source code 4: Backward normal cloud generator (with certainty degree) in VC++

```
//*************************************************//
// This function retrieves parameters from cloud
drops(with certainty degree).
// Input Values:
//    drop[][2]: Global matrix of cloud drops.
//    n: number of drops.
//    Output Parameters:
//    b_Ex: Expectation of cloud.
//    b_En: Entropy of cloud.
//    b_He: Hyper-Entropy of cloud.
//*************************************************//
void back cloud()
float b_Ex=0, b_En=0, b_He=0;
float b_Enn[n], b_Enn_Ex=0;
// Step 1, retrieve Ex
for (int i=0; i<n; i++)
  b_Ex+=drop[i][0];
b_Ex/=n;
// Step 2, retrieve En
for (i=0; i<n; i++)
  b_En+=(drop[i][0]-b_Ex)*(drop[i][0]-b_Ex);
b_En=sqrt(b_En/(n-1));
// Step 3, retrieve He
for (i=0; i<n; i++)
```

```
    b_Enn[i]=sqrt(-(drop[i][0]-b_Ex)*(drop[i][0] -
    b_Ex)/(2*log(drop[i][1])));

for (i=0; i<n; i++)

    b_Enn_Ex+=b_Enn[i];

b_Enn_Ex/=n;

for (i=0; i<n; i++)

    b_He+=(b_Enn[i]-b_Enn_Ex)*(b_Enn[i]-b_Enn_Ex);

b_He=sqrt(b_He/(n-1));
```

Source code 5: Backward normal cloud generator (without certainty degree) in MATLAB

```
//****************************************************//

// This function retrieves parameters from cloud
drops(without certainty degree).

// Intput Values:

//    x: matrix of cloud drops.

// Output Parameters:

//    b_Ex: Expectation of cloud.

//    b_En: Entropy of cloud.

//    b_He: Hyper-Entropy of cloud.

//****************************************************//

function back_cloud(x)

//step 1

b_Ex=mean(x);

//step 2

b_En=mean(abs(x-b_Ex))*sqrt(pi/2);

//step 3

b_He=sqrt(var(x)-b_En^2);
```

Source code 6: Backward normal cloud generator (without certainty degree) in VC++

```
//***************************************************//
// This function retrieve parameters from cloud
drops(without certainty degree).
// Intput Values:
//    drop[]: Global matrix of cloud drops.
//    n: number of drops.
// Output Parameters:
//    b_Ex: Expectation of cloud.
//    b_En: Entropy of cloud.
//    b_He: Hyper-Entropy of cloud.
//***************************************************//
void back_cloud()
float b_Ex=0, b_En=0, b_He=0;
float Sn=0;
// Step 1, retrieve Ex
for (int i=0; i<n; i++)
  b_Ex+=drop[i];
b_Ex/=n;
// Step 2, retrieve En
for (i=0; i<n; i++)
  b_En+=abs(drop[i]-b_Ex);
b_En=sqrt(Pi/2)*b_En/n;
// Step 3, retrieve He
for (i=0; i<n; i++)
  Sn+=(drop[i]-b_Ex)*(drop[i]-b_Ex);
Sn=sqrt(Sn/(n-1));
b_He=sqrt(Sn*Sn-b_En*b_En);
```

5.3.5 PRECISION ANALYSIS OF BACKWARD CLOUD GENERATOR

According to statistical principles, the more samples there are, the less the error in the backward cloud algorithm is. As a result, constrained by the limit of samples, the error is inevitable, no matter which algorithm is used:

1. Error estimation of *Ex:* Mean approach is employed in both algorithms for calculation of *Ex*. We can see that the mean of samples, i.e., $\bar{X} = \frac{1}{n}\sum_{i=1}^{n} x_i$, satisfies normal distribution with *Ex* and $\frac{1}{n}(En^2 + He^2)$ as the expectation and variance. As a result, when we take $\bar{X}$ as the estimation of *Ex*, the estimation error will be

$$P\left\{|\bar{X} - Ex| < \frac{3}{\sqrt{n}}\sqrt{En^2 + He^2}\right\} = 0.9973$$

Since *En* is also the parameter to be estimated, we can substitute it with the standard variance of the samples, i.e.,

$$P\left\{|\bar{X} - Ex| < \frac{3}{\sqrt{n}}S\right\} \approx 0.9973$$

Furthermore, if the amount of cloud drops is *n*, the significance level is α, the $(1-\alpha)$ confidence interval of *Ex* is,

$$\left(\bar{X} - t_\alpha(n-1)\frac{S}{\sqrt{n}}, \bar{X} + t_\alpha(n-1)\frac{S}{\sqrt{n}}\right)$$

that is,

$$P\left\{|\bar{X} - Ex| < t_\alpha(n-1)\frac{S}{\sqrt{n}}\right\} = 1-\alpha$$

where $\bar{X}, S$ are the mean and standard variance of the samples, as calculated from the drops. α takes the values of 0.1, 0.05, 0.01, 0.005, and 0.001. $t_\alpha(n-1)$ is the α-level percentile of the *t*-distribution with $n-1$ degree of freedom, and it can be acquired from the probability distribution table or directly computed. If $n > 200$, t_α is close to a constant for a given α. At this time, we can figure out the probability with which *Ex* lies in a certain interval.

Since

$$DX = \frac{1}{n^2}\sum_{i=1}^{n} En_i'^2 = \frac{1}{n}(En^2 + He^2)$$

the error of *Ex* will decrease if the *n* increases, and it will increase if *En* and *He* increase.

2. The error analysis of *En* and *He:* In Algorithm 5.3, we figure out *En′* first, and then its expectation *En* and standard variance *He*.

$$En' = \sqrt{\frac{-(x-Ex)^2}{2\ln\mu}} = \frac{|x-Ex|}{\sqrt{-2\ln\mu}}$$

If $x \to Ex$, $\mu \to 1$, then $\sqrt{-2\ln\mu} \to 0$, so $En' \to +\infty$. Because *He* = *STDEV* (En'_i), so *He* $\to +\infty$. We can see that the estimation error is huge in this case. Due to the fact that while estimating the error of *En* and *He* we have to employ En'_i, the error of which is difficult to be precisely calculated, we can hardly improve the computation for the error of *En* and *He*.

In the Algorithm 5.4, as not using middle variable, the error of *En′* is not extended, so the accuracy is higher than the previous one. The accuracies of *En* and *He* are only related to the estimation of *Ex*. The more cloud drops there are, the more precise *Ex* will be, and thus the less the estimation error of *En* and *He* will be.

Because the backward cloud algorithms are based on the statistical result of a large quantity of cloud drops, the performance is determined by the amount of drops. In general, the errors of the three parameters will all decrease with the increasing of cloud drop numbers.

3. The solution of *n* (number of cloud drops) with the given errors and confidence level: We can derive from the first point that if α is given, the necessary amount of drops can be figured out in order to reduce the error of *Ex* estimation below Δ.

Usually, *En* and *He* are unknown, and can only be calculated with the help of the standard variance of the samples. In real applications, it is good enough to set $\alpha = 0.001$. If $t_{0.001}(n-1)\frac{S}{\sqrt{n}} \le \Delta$, the error in *Ex* estimation will not exceed Δ. On the other hand, $t_{0.001}(n-1) < 4.45$, so $n \ge \frac{20S^2}{\Delta^2}$ (S^2 is the standard variance of the samples). If the calculated *n* is larger than 200, we can substitute the cloud drop number with $n = \max(200, \frac{9S^2}{\Delta^2})$. This will reduce the computational cost. The confidence degree of the result above is 99.999%.

If *En* and *He* are known, the minimal number of cloud drops is only required to satisfy $n \ge \frac{9(En^2+He^2)}{\Delta^2}$.

5.3.6 MORE ON UNDERSTANDING NORMAL CLOUD MODEL

Cloud is a description approach aiming at the uncertainty problems with concepts. In the beginning of the cloud study, people will probably compare the cloud with the approaches in statistics or fuzzy theory, and simplify the cloud model as randomness compensated by fuzziness, fuzziness compensated by randomness, second-order fuzziness, or second-order randomness. Here, we will advance an example to clarify the possible misunderstandings.

Shooting
results   5 0 7 6 6 6 5 6 7 5

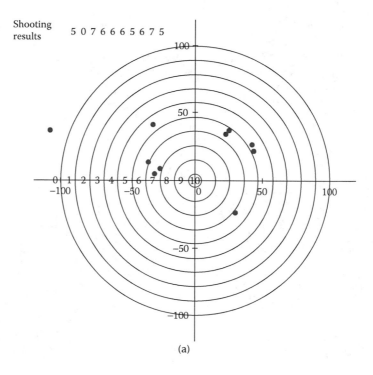

(a)

Shooting
results   5 9 7 8 6 6 3 9 5 7

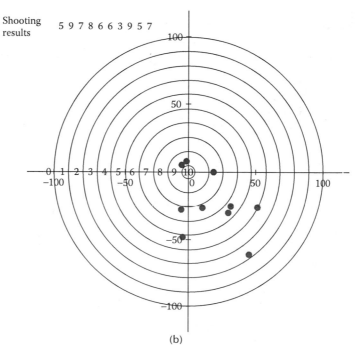

(b)

FIGURE 5.13 The records of shooters A, B, and C.

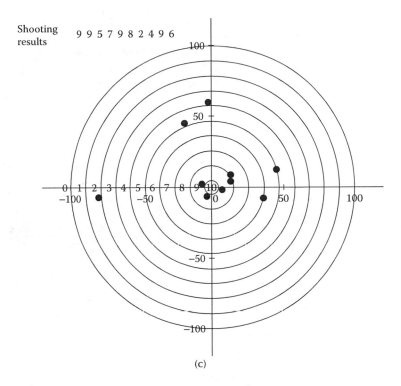

Shooting results   9 9 5 7 9 8 2 4 9 6

(c)

FIGURE 5.13 (Continued)

For example, in a shooting competition, three scholars—one statistician, one fuzzy scholar, and one cloud model researcher—are invited as judges. The three competitors, named A, B, and C, respectively, and perform as shown in Figure 5.13.

Probability theory and mathematical statistics are subjects used to discover statistical regularity in random phenomena. After a large quantity of repeated experiments, the values of variables turn out to be statistically regular. The statistician thinks that "on" and "off" are unambiguous. If it is not on/off, it is off/on. There is no status between the two. However, for even single shot, it is uncertain whether it is on or off, which is called "randomness." The experimental results are random. Let U be the experimental sample space, i.e., $U = x$, x is the event in the sample space. For every result, we introduce the variable u with values 0 or 1. For every event, u is variable, so u can be treated as s function defined on the sample space, i.e., $u(x)$ is a random variable. The overall performance of the competitor is measured in terms of the number of "on", i.e., frequency. For instance, after 10 shots, A got 9 "on" and 1 "off". The probability of "on" for A is 0.9. The score is 90 if put into the 100 scale. All the shots of B and C are "on", so their scores are both 100. As a result, the performances of B and C are equal, both better than that of A.

In the events that can be classified into either this or that, there exists uncertainty called "fuzziness." Fuzzy theory is a subject dealing with the regularity within fuzzy phenomena. The fuzzy scholar will treat the shooting results in a different way. He thinks that "on" and "off" are relative rather than absolute, and they are related to the distance from the shot point and the center of the target. There is no precise boundary between "on" and "off." Let x be the element in the sample space $U = x$. He represents the events "definitely on" and "definitely off" by 1 and 0, respectively. In this case, some part of the elements in the sample space will have an extent degree to which they can be classified into "on." This kind of transition is expressed by the numbers between 0 and 1.15 In this approach, "on" and "off" are represented by the membership degrees of the shot points. The target is divided into 10 concentric circles, which are marked from the inside to the outside with scores from 10 to 1. The respective membership degrees are from 1 to 0.1. "Off" is marked with 0 and its membership degree is 0 too. Figure 5.14(a) illustrates the two-dimensional membership function. In this case, even a single shot can reveal the skill of the competitor.

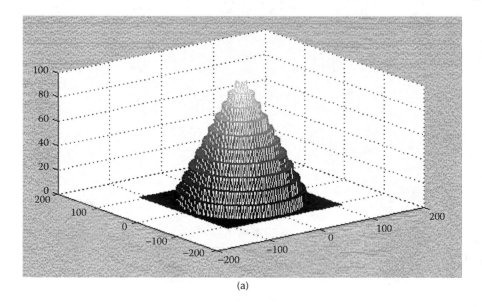

(a)

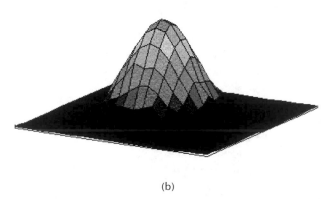

(b)

FIGURE 5.14 The comparison of (a) two-dimensional membership function and (b) two-dimensional cloud model.

Considering the two factors of randomness and fuzziness, people calculate the total score by the formula $score = \sum_{i=1}^{n} w_i$, where n is the shooting times, w_i is the score of the ith shot. The records of A, B, and C are 5/0/7/6/6/6/5/6/7/5, 5/9/7/8/6/6/3/9/5/7, and 9/9/5/7/9/8/2/4/9/6, respectively, so their total scores are 53, 65, and 68, respectively. As a result, C performs the best, and A performs the worst. The total score in this approach is quite different from the total scores such as 90 and 100 given by the statistician, resulting in different judgment.

Nevertheless, people are more used to evaluating the shooter's skill by natural languages rather than numerical ways. With this consideration, the cloud model scholar thinks that it is random in the event of "on" or "off," and it is fuzzy on the "on" level. Every shot point can be treated as a cloud drop. After a number of shots, the generated cloud contains the overall characteristics which can reflect the skill of the competitor. People would like to describe the cloud in terms of qualitative languages; for instance, a backward cloud can extract from the shot points the numerical characteristics $(Ex_1, Ex_2, En_1, En_2, He_1, He_2)$, which is representative of the shooting skills. Figure 5.14(b) shows the corresponding two-dimensional cloud model. Table 5.2 illustrates the numerical characters representative of the shooting skill. The expectation (Ex_1, Ex_2) is the coordinates of the average shot point of all the cloud drops, reflecting the aiming skill. The entropy (En_1, En_2) represents the extent degree to which the shot is "on", and it also reflects the dispersion degree relative to the average point. The hyper-entropy (He_1, He_2), which reflects uncertainty of the certainty degree, and the dispersion degree of the entropy. From these characteristics, we can infer that A shoots a little to the up-right and is not stable enough, B shoots a little to the down-right but is stable, and C shoots closer to the center but is not stable enough.

With the numerical characteristics extracted by the backward cloud generator, we can also configure another forward cloud generator to produce drops for more shots of the 3 shooters. Figure 5.15 shows the 10 and 100 shot points of the 3 shooters. We can see that the increasing in the shooting will reflect the skill with more truth.

TABLE 5.2
Numerical Characters Representative of the Shooting Skill Extracted by the Backward Cloud Generator

Characters ⟍ Shooter	A	B	C
Ex_1, Ex_2	(0.08,0.1)	(0.1,0.12)	(0,0.3)
En_1, En_2	(0.45,0.3)	(0.25,0.2)	(0.4,0.3)
He_1, He_2	(0.05,0.07)	(0.02,0.02)	(0.05,0.07)
	Up-right	Down-right	Close to the center
	Dispersive	Concentrated	Dispersive
Performance	Unstable	Stable	Unstable

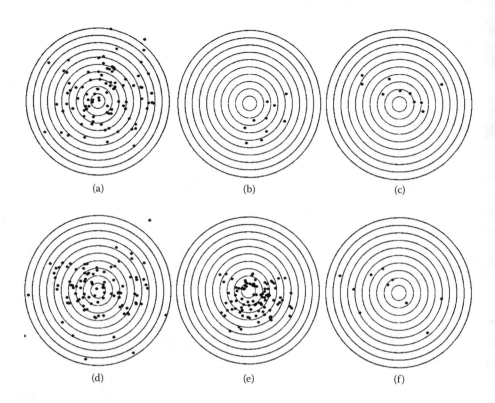

FIGURE 5.15 The three visualization approaches of the cloud graph: 10 shot points of A   10 shot points of B   10 shot points of C   100 shot points of A   100 shot points of B   100 shot points of C.

5.4 MATHEMATICAL PROPERTIES OF NORMAL CLOUD

Since the normal cloud plays a significant role in the cloud model, it is necessary to analyze its mathematical properties.

The normal CG produces a quantity of cloud drops, which are composed of a random variable. The degree of certainty of the drops is also a random variable. These two random variables have their own mathematical properties. Viewed from statistics, they both have distribution functions.

5.4.1 STATISTICAL ANALYSIS OF THE CLOUD DROPS' DISTRIBUTION

According to the algorithm of the normal CG, all the cloud drops x are composed of a random variable X.

En' obtains the normal distribution with expectation En and variance He^2, so the probability density function of En' is

$$f_{En'}(x) = \frac{1}{\sqrt{2\pi}He} e^{-\frac{(x-En)^2}{2He^2}}$$

When *En'* is fixed, *X* obtains the normal distribution with expectation *Ex* and variance *En'²*. Thus the probability density function of *X* is

$$f_X(x|En') = \frac{1}{\sqrt{2\pi}\,|En'|} e^{-\frac{(x-Ex)^2}{2En'^2}}$$

Since *En'* is a random variable, from the conditional probability density function formula,[16] we may infer the probability density function of *X* as

$$f_X(x) = f_{En'}(x) \times f_X(x|En')$$

$$= \int_{-\infty}^{\infty} \frac{1}{2\pi He\,|y|} e^{-\frac{(x-Ex)^2}{2y^2} - \frac{(y-En)^2}{2He^2}} dy$$

This probability density function has no analytical expression and for each *x*, the function value can be calculated through numerical integration. For the case of *n* cloud drops, the probability density function of *X* can be estimated by utilizing the Parzen window.[17]

In a more special case, i.e., when *He* = 0, the probability density function of *X* is

$$f(x) = \frac{1}{\sqrt{2\pi}En} e^{-\frac{(x-Ex)^2}{2En^2}}$$

Because all the cloud drops *x* originate from the normal random variable with expectation *Ex*, the expectation of *X* is

$$EX = Ex$$

The variance *DX* is

$$DX = \int_{-\infty}^{+\infty} (x-Ex)^2 dx \int_{-\infty}^{+\infty} \frac{1}{2\pi Hey} \exp\left[-\frac{(x-Ex)^2}{2y^2} - \frac{(y-En)^2}{2He^2}\right] dy$$

$$= \frac{1}{\sqrt{2\pi}He} \int_{-\infty}^{+\infty} y \exp\left[-\frac{(y-En)^2}{2He^2}\right] dy \int_{-\infty}^{+\infty} \frac{1}{\sqrt{2\pi}} \frac{(x-Ex)^2}{y^2} \exp\left[-\frac{(x-Ex)^2}{2y^2}\right] dx$$

$$= \frac{1}{\sqrt{2\pi}He} \int_{-\infty}^{+\infty} y^2 \exp\left[-\frac{(y-En)^2}{2He^2}\right] dy \int_{-\infty}^{+\infty} \frac{1}{\sqrt{2\pi}} t^2 \exp\left[-\frac{t^2}{2}\right] dt$$

$$= En^2 + He^2$$

The above expressions indicate the fact that the generated cloud drop is a random variable with expectation *Ex* and variance *En² + He²*. This is an extremely important property of the normal cloud.

5.4.2 Statistical Analysis of the Cloud Drops' Certainty Degree

According to the algorithm of the normal CG, the certainty degrees of all the drops are composed of a random variable Y, and every certainty degree can be considered as a sample generated by the random variable

$$Y_i = e^{\frac{-(X-Ex)^2}{2(En_i')^2}}$$

The first step is to calculate the distribution function of Y_i, i.e., $F_{Y_i}(y)$. If

$$y \in (0,1)$$

$$F_{Y_i}(y) = P\{Y_i \le y\} = P\{e^{\frac{-(X-Ex)^2}{2(En_i')^2}} \le y\}$$

$$= P\left\{\frac{X-Ex}{En_i'} \ge \sqrt{-2\ln y}\right\} + P\left\{\frac{X-Ex}{En_i'} \le -\sqrt{-2\ln y} \le\right\}$$

Because

$$X \sim N(Ex, En_i'^2)$$

thus

$$\frac{X-Ex}{En_i'} \sim N(0,1)$$

As a result,

$$F_{Y_i}(y) = \int_{-\infty}^{-\sqrt{-2\ln y}} \frac{1}{\sqrt{2\pi}} e^{-\frac{t^2}{2}} dt + \int_{\sqrt{-2\ln y}}^{+\infty} \frac{1}{\sqrt{2\pi}} e^{-\frac{t^2}{2}} dt$$

At this time, the probability density function of Y_i is

$$f_{Y_i}(y) = F_{Y_i}(y)' = \frac{1}{\sqrt{2\pi}} e^{-\frac{(-2\ln y)^2}{2}} (-\sqrt{-2\ln y})' - \frac{1}{\sqrt{2\pi}} e^{-\frac{(-2\ln y)^2}{2}} (\sqrt{-2\ln y})'$$

$$= \frac{1}{\sqrt{-\pi \ln y}} \quad y \in (0,1)$$

If $y \geq 1$, $F_{Y_i}(y) = 1$, and if $y \leq 0$, $F_{Y_i}(y) = 0$. So, the probability density function of Y_i is

$$f(y) = \begin{cases} \dfrac{1}{\sqrt{-\pi \ln y}}, & 0 < y < 1 \\ 0, & \text{otherwise} \end{cases}$$

So, whatever En'_i is, the probability density function of Y_i is not variant, i.e., all the certainty degrees are connected to a random variable with the density above. As a result, $f(y)$ is the probability density function of Y, and its shape is shown in Figure 5.16.

From the analysis above, we can see that the probability density function of certainty degree is independent on the three numerical characters of the normal cloud. This is another important property of the normal cloud.

We can also investigate the probability density function of the joint distribution $C(x_i, \mu_i)$ for x_i within the universal space U.

If U is one dimensional, $C(x_i, \mu_i)$ is a two-dimensional random variable, and we can compute its joint-probability density function. From what we have discussed above, we can see that

$$f_Y(y) = \begin{cases} \dfrac{1}{\sqrt{-\pi \ln y}}, & 0 < y < 1 \\ 0, & \text{otherwise} \end{cases}$$

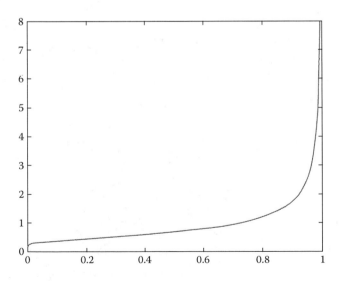

FIGURE 5.16 The probability density function curve of certainty degree.

For any $\mu = y$,

$$X = Ex \pm \sqrt{-2 \ln y} \; En'$$

Since $En' \sim N(En, He^2)$, X obtains normal distribution as well and its probability density function is

$$f_X(x|\mu = y) = \begin{cases} \dfrac{1}{\sqrt{2\pi} \times \sqrt{-2 \ln y} He} \exp\left\{ \dfrac{-(x - Ex - \sqrt{-2 \ln y} En)^2}{2(\sqrt{-2 \ln y} He)^2} \right\} & Ex \leq x < +\infty \\[4mm] \dfrac{1}{\sqrt{2\pi} \times \sqrt{-2 \ln y} He} \exp\left\{ \dfrac{-(x - Ex + \sqrt{-2 \ln y} En)^2}{2(\sqrt{-2 \ln y} He)^2} \right\} & -\infty < x \leq Ex \end{cases}$$

As a result, the joint-probability density function of $C(x_i, \mu_i)$ is

$$f_{X,\mu}(x,y) = f_\mu(y) f_X(x|\mu = y)$$

$$= \begin{cases} \dfrac{1}{2\pi He \ln y} e^{\frac{(x - Ex - \sqrt{-2 \ln y} En)^2}{4 He^2 \ln y}} & 0 < y \leq 1,\; Ex \leq x < +\infty \\[4mm] \dfrac{1}{2\pi He \ln y} e^{\frac{(x - Ex + \sqrt{-2 \ln y} En)^2}{4 He^2 \ln y}} & 0 < y \leq 1,\; -\infty < x < Ex \end{cases}$$

If the universal space becomes high-dimensional, the joint-probability density function will be more complicated.

5.4.3 EXPECTATION CURVES OF NORMAL CLOUD

Although the format of the joint distribution $C(x_i, \mu_i)$ is rather complex, the cloud graph (x, μ) by the normal CG is rich in geometrical properties. We can investigate the overall property by means of the recursive curve and the principle curve.

From Section 4.5.3, we have known that the recursive curve is of normal cloud formed in this way: for every fixed x_i, the corresponding certainty degree μ_i has expectation of $E\mu_i$, various couples of $(x_i, E\mu_i)$ form the recursive curve. The normal cloud has recursive curve as follows:

$$f(x) = \int_{-\infty}^{+\infty} \frac{1}{\sqrt{2\pi} He} e^{-\frac{(y - En)^2}{2 He^2}} \times e^{-\frac{(x - Ex)^2}{2y^2}} \, dy$$

It is difficult to figure out its analytical form, but it can be approximated by linear estimation.

From Section 4.5.3, we have understood that the principle curve is formed in this way: every point on the principle curve is the expectation of every point that is projected to this point. We can also approximately get the principle curve of the normal cloud by linear estimation, although the analytical form is not available.

The overall property of the cloud geometric shape is reflected in both the recursive curve and the principle curve. The former deals with the expectation in the perpendicular direction, and the latter is about the expectation in the orthogonal direction. Nevertheless, can we define an expectation curve in the horizontal direction? Here, we will address this perspective. As

$$\mu = e^{\frac{(x-Ex)^2}{2En'^2}}$$

for an arbitrary $0 < \mu \leq 1$, $X = Ex \pm \sqrt{-2\ln\mu}\, En'$.

Since En' is a random variable, X is a random variable located symmetrically on both sides of Ex. We can discuss the case of $X = Ex + \sqrt{-2\ln\mu}\, En'$ and similarly transplant into the case of $X = Ex - \sqrt{-2\ln\mu}\, En'$.

As $En' \sim N(En, He^2)$, X obtains normal distribution with expectation $EX = Ex + \sqrt{-2\ln\mu}\, En$ and standard deviation $B = \sqrt{DX} = \sqrt{-2\ln\mu}\, He$.

According to $EX = Ex + \sqrt{-2\ln\mu}\, En$, we can get

$$\mu = e^{-\frac{(EX-Ex)^2}{2En^2}}$$

This explains the formation of the curve $y = e^{-\frac{(x-Ex)^2}{2En^2}}$, the expectation of the related cloud drop is Ex_i, which is one point on the so-called "expectation curve" of the normal cloud.

Expectation curve can be utilized to investigate the statistical regularity of the spatial distribution of the data. It can reveal some key geometrical properties of the normal cloud as well. Though the recursive curve and the principle curve of a normal cloud may not be expressed analytically, the expectation curve has the analytical representation. All three curves go through the "center" of drops smoothly, and illustrate the overall outline of the cloud. They construct the framework of the drop set, as all the drops fluctuate randomly around the expectation curve. There are slight differences in the definition of "center" in the recursive curve, the principle curve and the expectation curve, regarding to the perpendicular direction, the orthogonal direction and the horizontal direction, respectively.

The curve in Figure 5.17 is the expectation curve of $C(x, \mu)$ corresponding to the concept $C(Ex = 0, En = 3, He = 0.5)$.

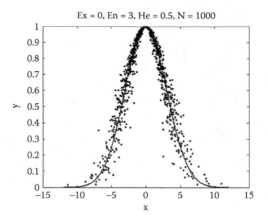

FIGURE 5.17 The expectation curve of the normal cloud.

5.5 ON THE PERVASIVENESS OF THE NORMAL CLOUD MODEL

Randomness and fuzziness used to be the two research topics of probability theory and possibility theory, respectively. Based on these two topics, the cloud model, as a new qualitative–quantitative transition model, focuses on the relationship between randomness and fuzziness, and seeks their correlation in a unified way. The normal cloud, which is the most important kind of cloud model, is universal because of the universalities of the normal distribution and the bell membership function.

5.5.1 PERVASIVENESS OF NORMAL DISTRIBUTION

Normal distribution plays a significant role in academic researches and practical applications of probability theory and stochastic process. As the most important probability distribution, normal distribution obtains the following form

$$F(x; \mu, \sigma^2) = \frac{1}{\sqrt{2\pi}\sigma} \int_{-\infty}^{x} \exp\left(-\frac{(x-\mu)^2}{2\sigma^2}\right) dx$$

Its probability density function is

$$f(x; \mu, \sigma^2) = (2\pi)^{-1/2}\sigma^{-1}\exp[-(x-\mu)^2/2\sigma^2]$$

where μ is the expectation representative of the most possible value of the random variable, and σ^2 is the variance showing the dispersive degree of all the possible values.

Normal distribution exists universally in natural phenomena, social phenomena, science and technology, and production activities. There are many examples of obtaining normal distributions, such as the product quality index under normal production conditions, the random error in measurement, a certain feature within a biological species, the annual temperature of a certain place, etc.

The central limit theorem theoretically explains the conditions under which the normal distribution is obtained. To simplify the theorem, we can interpret it this way. If the value of a random variable is determined by the sum of a quantity of minor and independent random factors, and if every factor has equally minor influence, i.e., there is no dominant factor, then this random variable generally obtains normal distribution approximately. For instance, if the production conditions, e.g., technique, equipment, manipulation, and raw material, are normal and stable, the product quality index shall obtain the normal distribution, and if the normal distribution is not obtained, the production condition must have been changed or unstable. In applications, people judge the satisfaction of normal distribution in this way.

Normal distribution is the limit distribution of many important probability distributions. There are a lot of un-normal random variables that are expressed in terms of normal ones. Due to the good properties and the simple mathematical formula of its probability density function and distribution function, normal distribution is widely employed in theoretical research and practical applications.

It should be pointed out that there are still many random phenomena that do not obey normal distributions. Once the determinant factors influence the random phenomena unequally, or they are dependent on each other to some extent, then the conditions of normal distribution will not be satisfied. In this case, normal distribution can be employed only to approximate the distribution. In probability theory, people deal with such a case by means of joint distribution, whose probability density function is too complex to be of practical application. Attention should be shifted to another interesting distribution named "power law distribution." In the study of scale-free networks given by Dr. A. L. Barabasi, there are some important properties caused by the growth and preferential attachment in a network.

5.5.2 Pervasiveness of Bell Membership Function

The concept of membership function is one of the foundations in fuzzy theory. However, there has not been a well-accepted approach to determine specific membership functions of fuzzy concepts in applications. Instead, they are usually determined case by case according to experience. We have mentioned six typical analytical formations in Section 4.2.1, i.e.:

1. Linear membership function

$$\mu_{\tilde{A}}(x) = 1 - kx$$

2. Γ membership function

$$\mu_{\tilde{A}}(x) = e^{-kx}$$

3. Concave/convex membership function

$$\mu_{\tilde{A}}(x) = 1 - ax^k$$

4. Cauchy membership function

$$\mu_{\tilde{A}}(x) = 1/(1 + kx^2)$$

5. Mountain-shaped membership function

$$\mu_{\tilde{A}}(x) = 1/2 - (1/2)\sin\{[\pi/(b-a)][x - (b-a)/2]\}$$

6. Bell membership function

$$\mu_{\tilde{A}}(x) = \exp[-(x-a)^2/2b^2]$$

Although the three former membership functions are self-continuous, there are some uneven points in the membership curves, and their one order derivatives are discontiguous, i.e., the left derivative and the right derivative are not equal at these points. If the fuzziness is natural at multiscales, the transition in the membership curve should be smooth, so such a sudden change is not allowed. From another aspect, if fuzziness is considered to be existent in both the macro- and microscopes, concepts should be continuous in terms of all scales, so even higher-order derivatives ought to be continuous. Moreover, these three membership functions are changing relatively fast in the ambiguous intervals, which disobey the common perception regularity. Hence, these three membership functions may only be suitable to some simple occasions.

Therefore, we only provide comparison analysis on the other three membership functions.

Let's discuss the typical example of "youth" as shown in Section 5.1.3. Nanlun Zhan et al. calculated the membership data of "youth" by a statistic approach. According to the given data, we approximate the polynomial curve of the membership function as

$$\mu_0(x) = 1.01302 - 0.00535(x - 24) - 0.00872(x - 24)^2 + 0.0005698(x - 24)^3$$

With the aim of minimizing

$$\left(\int_a^b [\mu(x) - \mu_0(x)]^2 \, dx/(b-a)\right)^{1/2}$$

Instantly, the Cauchy function, mountain-shaped function, and bell function are utilized to approximate $\mu_0(x)$. As computation results, Cauchy membership function is

$$\mu_1(x) = 1/[1 + (x - 24)^2/30]$$

TABLE 5.3
The Mean Squared Errors (MSEs) between Different Membership Functions and $\mu(x)$

Membership Function	MSE
Cauchy	0.042 181 118 428 255
Mountain-shaped	0.060 183 795 103 931
Bell	0.030 915 588 518 457

the mountain-shaped membership function is

$$\mu_2(x) = 1/2 - (1/2) \sin\{[\pi/(37 - 24)][x - (37 - 24)/2]\}$$

and the bell membership function is

$$\mu_3(x) = \exp[-9(x - 24)^2/338]$$

Let's calculate the mean squared errors (MSE) of the membership functions and $\mu_0(x)$ by numerical integration and get 1,400 sample points in total, shown in Table 5.3. These MSEs are the comparison of the analytical formulas and the approximated curve $\mu_0(x)$. Among the three functions, the bell membership function has the least MSE.

Furthermore comparing the three membership functions with the test value (X_i, Y_i), as shown in Table 5.4. it is always the bell membership function that obtains the least MSE.

The use of the bell membership functions is very appropriate for the fuzzy concepts such as "youth," since their membership functions are extracted statistically, and usually have a shape with a large middle part plus two small side parts. Actually, during recent decades, the bell membership function is the most frequently discussed in the fuzzy journals for membership functions. In applications, many practical fields are consistent with the bell membership function. As a matter of

TABLE 5.4
The Mean Squared Errors (MSEs) between Different Membership Functions and (X_i, Y_i)

Membership Function	MSE
Polynomial approximation	0.083 742 138 813 298
Cauchy	0.101 253 101 730 926
Mountain-shaped	0.095 237 099 589 215
Bell	0.080 769 137 104 025

fact, the sum of low-order terms in the Taylor series of $\mu_{\tilde{A}}(x) = \exp[-(x-a)^2/2b^2]$ at the point of a, i.e.,

$$\mu_{\tilde{A}}(x) = 1 - \frac{1}{b^2}(x-a)^2 + \frac{1}{b^4}(x-a)^4 - \ldots$$

is an approximation of the bell membership function. Compared with other membership functions, the bell membership function has more universal application in many fields.

5.5.3 SIGNIFICANCE OF NORMAL CLOUD

It is of much interest to understand the universality of the normal cloud. We have seen that the normal cloud is a useful transitional model between quality and quantity. Are there any constraints in doing so? As for linguistic values, concepts or words, what is the case that normal cloud is applicable to?

According to the mathematical property of normal cloud, given above, the expectation of random variable X which is composed of drops is

$$EX = Ex$$

Its variance is

$$DX = En^2 + He^2$$

Nevertheless, the distribution of X is not normal. Thus, how to understand the distribution of X? As we know, normal distribution is universally existent in areas of natural phenomena, human society, science and technology, and production, etc. It should obtain one precondition, i.e., if the phenomenon is determined by the sum of a quantity of minor and independent random factors, and if every factor has equally minor influence, then this phenomenon approximately obtains normal distribution approximately. In applications, people judge the satisfaction of normal distribution in this way. Take the bulb production as an example. If the production conditions, e.g., technique, equipment, manipulation, raw material, and environment, are normal and stable, the product quality index (e.g., bulb life, power, size, etc.) shall obey the normal distribution.

However, there exist many occasions in which there are some relational factors with great influence. If we simply apply the normal distribution for analysis, we may not reflect what is really going on. For instance, in the shooting case, if every shot is independent, the skill can be represented by the shot points, those that are expressed by a normal distribution. However, every shot may be influential on the next shot. In this case, the psychological effect would be kept in mind, especially in an important competition. Thus, the precondition of normal distribution does not follow. To solve this problem, we propose the parameter of hyper-entropy in order to relieve the precondition of normal distribution. For example, we may use He to represent the psychological power in different shooting. If He is small, the difference between $En^2 + He^2$ and En^2 is small, and thus the shots will be closer to the normal distribution. If He is big enough, the shot distribution may be far away from normal, showing the instability in the shooting competition.

In other words, He can reflect the inequality or dependence among the effective factors. It is to measure the degree to which the distribution is deviant to the normal one. We can call the normal cloud "the weakened normal distribution."

The precondition of the weakened normal distribution is not as strict as the normal one. Compared with the general joint distribution in the probability theory, the weakened distribution is simpler, extensive, more general, and feasible. Thus, the weakened distribution is more universal than the normal distribution. Once $He = 0$, the cloud X returns to a normal distribution. That is to say the normal distribution is only a special case of the cloud model.

As we mentioned before, the probability density function of the certainty degree of the normal cloud drop is fixed and has nothing to do with the three numerical characteristics. According to this mathematical property, we discover an important rule in human cognitive process, i.e., for any qualitative concept represented by linguistic values (e.g., "youth" and "around 30 degrees"), it can always be described roughly by normal cloud models, even though there are differences in the conceptual or physical meaning, the quantitative distributions in the universal space, and certainty degrees of the cloud drops, the statistical distributions are generally the same. This means that although the concepts with linguistic values may have different understandings by different persons and in different periods, if we neglect the discreet physical meanings, they still reflect the same cognitive regularity in the brain. There are regularities in the uncertainties of cognition, i.e., the consistent common rules within the different qualitative representations by different linguistic concepts.

Generally speaking, there are two pieces of commonsense knowledge in classical science: repeatability and preciseness. Any unrepeatable temporary phenomenon is not considered scientific. And any phenomenon without using a precise mathematical tool for description is not considered scientific as well. Nevertheless, in the cloud model, there is a mathematical approach to overcome such difficulties. It relieves the presumption under which a certain probability distribution is obtained, and prevents the embarrassment that the membership function in fuzzy theory is artificially determined. This approach has found the regularity of probability density functions for membership functions, which is independent on discreet concepts. The marriage and universalities of normal distribution and bell membership function is the theoretical foundation for the universality of normal cloud model.[18]

Any new creation cannot be the sudden idea of an individual. Rather, it has deep foundations in practice, and also requires long-term accumulation and evolution. In 1923, Bertrand Russell, a famous English logician, started to challenge the traditional thought. In the paper titled "Vagueness," he pointed out that traditional logic made the assumption that the symbols used were precise; however, this was too ideal to be applicable in reality. Russell made mathematical logic comprehensive. He criticized those who overly emphasized preciseness, pointing out that it was definitely wrong to say that the vague understanding was surely undependable, and oppositely vague understanding was probably more real than precise because it could be proved by more potential facts. In 1937, Max Black introduced the concept of consistency profiles, which could be considered as the former of a membership function. Since 1965, L. A. Zadeh, a system scientist, had proposed a set of concepts, such as membership degrees, membership function, fuzzy set, soft computing, computing with words, etc. In 1982, a Polish mathematician, Z. Pawlak introduced rough set. We have benefited from the prosperous applications of statistics for one-hundred years and fuzzy theory for forty years. The consistency profile on a much higher level is the universality of normal cloud. We may say today that it is definitely wrong to treat qualitative understanding as something surely undependable, and conversely, it is probably more real than the quantitative understanding, since it can be proved by more potential facts.

As a mater of fact, the exploration of concepts and knowledge with uncertainty representation is not just the subject in AI, we need more scientists and engineers from different disciplines of cognitive science, computing science, mathematics, linguistics, psychology, or even philosophy to focus on the same subject.

REFERENCES

1. E. R. Kandel and R. D. Hawkins, The biological basis of learning and individuality, *Scientific American*, pp. 79–86, September 1992.
2. G. E. Hinton, How neural networks learn from experience, *Scientific American*, pp. 145–151, September 1992.
3. Deyi Li, Xuemei Shi, and Haijun Meng, Membership clouds and membership cloud generators, *Journal of Computer Research and Development*, Vol. 32, No. 6: 15–20, 1995.
4. Deyi Li, Xuemei Shi, and M. M. Gupta, Soft inference mechanism based on cloud models, *Proceedings of the 1st International Workshop on Logic Programming and Soft Computing: Theory and Applications, LPSC'96*, Bonn, Germany, pp. 38–62, 1996.
5. Deyi Li, J. Han, and X. M. Shi, Knowledge Representation and Discovery Based on Linguistic Models, In: H. J. Lu and H. Motoda, eds., *KDD: Techniques and Applications*, World Scientific Press, Singapore, pp. 3–20, 1997.
6. Deyi Li, Jiawei Han, Xuemei Shi et al., Knowledge representation and discovery based on linguistic atoms, *Knowledge-Based Systems*, pp. 431–440, October 1998.
7. Deyi Li, Knowledge representation in KDD based on linguistic atoms, *Journal of Computer Science and Technology*, Vol. 12, No. 6: 481–496, 1997.
8. Deyi Li, Ye Wang, and Huijun Lü, Study on Knowledge Discovery Mechanism, In: *The Progress of Artificial Intelligence in China 2001*, Beijing University of Posts and Telecommunications Press, pp. 314–325, 2001.
9. Deyi Li, Intellectual Property: Membership Cloud Generator and the Controller Composed by It. Chinese Intellectual Property Number ZL95 1 03696.3.
10. Guofu Wu, Anfu Wan, and Jinghai Liu, *Applicable Approaches for Data Analysis*, China Statistics Press, Beijing, 1992.
11. Huixuan Gao, *Statistical Computation*, Peking University Press, Beijing, 1995.
12. Zhaohui Yang and Deyi Li, Planar model and its application in prediction, *Chinese Journal of Computers*, Vol. 21, No. 11: 962–969, 1998.
13. Deyi Li, Uncertainty in knowledge representation, *The Chinese Engineering Science*, Vol. 2, No. 10: 73–79, 2000.

14. Huijun Lü, Ye Wang, Deyi Li, and Changyu Liu, The Application of Backward Cloud in Qualitative Evaluation, *Chinese Journal of Computers*, Vol. 26, No. 8: 1009–1014, 2003.
15. Zhongfu Li, Analysis of the meaning of degree of membership, *Fuzzy Systems and Mathematics*, Vol. 1, No. 1: 1–6, 1967.
16. Zikun Wang, *The Basic Probability Theory and Its Application*, Beijing Normal University Press, Beijing, 1996.
17. Zhaoqi Bian, *Pattern Recognition*, Tsinghua University Press, Beijing, 1998.
18. Deyi Li and Changyu Liu, Study on the university of the normal cloud model, *The Chinese Engineering Science*, Vol. 6, No. 8: 28–34, 2004.

6 Discovering Knowledge with Uncertainty through Methodologies in Physics

6.1 FROM PERCEPTION OF PHYSICAL WORLD TO PERCEPTION OF HUMAN SELF

To understand the whole world is a strong craving and desire of human beings. People perceive the real world as a long evolutionary process that has passed a number of significant milestones in science, for example, the atom structure model and the divisibility of matter in physics, the periodic table of chemical elements in chemistry, the Big Bang theory, the continental drift theory, the theory of evolution, and so on.[1]

Research in modern physics has led to a scientific world-view in which the basic structure of matter is hierarchical with the observable objects at a macro-scale, the celestial bodies at a cosmic scale, and the subatom particles at a micro-scale. Physicists are still making an effort to divide matter into even smaller pieces, especially to break apart atoms, nuclei, protons, and even electrons. As early as 1897, J. J. Thomson developed a rough but scientific atom model, which challenged the atom model using only philosophical speculation. Thereafter, Ernest Rutherford overturned Thomson's model with his well-known "Rutherford model," in which the atom consisted of an extremely small, positively charged nucleus at the center, surrounded by a swirling ring of even smaller electrons with equivalent but opposite charges.

The famous physicist Tsung-Dao Lee, 1957 Nobel laureate in Physics, has addressed in his lecture "The Challenges from Physics" that the essence of physical progress in the twentieth century is simplicity and induction. All sciences, including physics, astronomy, chemistry, and biology, are essentially some systematic approaches by which the new, quite accurate abstraction about nature can be achieved. A simpler abstraction means more far-reaching scientific inventions, which can further result in more extensive applications.

The above incisive remark inspired us with a profound question in cognitive science, i.e., whether there exists some similarity between the subjective perception of humans and the objective events of the world, and whether it is possible to borrow ideas from objective cognition to understand human self-cognition, and as a result it promotes the research on artificial intelligence (AI). Perhaps, it will become a significant aspect in the development of cognitive science in the tweny-first century. In this book, we call it the "physical methodologies of cognition" or "cognitive physics."[2]

6.1.1 Expressing Concepts by Using Atom Models

Under the influence of the startling development in physics, the realm of brain science has taken the initiative in the research of self-cognitive mechanism, which is usually considered as the exploration of the brain and neural system. The brain is really a complicated system, which is made up of tera-scale (10^{12}) interconnected neurons (or neural cells) and supports roughly peta-scale (10^{15}) neural connections. Recently, a noteworthy shift in brain research is to elucidate the information-processing and decision-making mechanisms of brain systems at the cellular and molecular levels, and make clear how neurons interact with each other by synapses for signal transmission. Since the 1980s, the novel molecular biological methods, for example recombinant DNA technology, have resulted in better understanding of the ion channels in the membrane of neurons and the electrophysiological techniques even can directly reveal the structure and properties of various ion channels.[3]

However, brain research at the cellular and molecular scales seems too microcosmic for the exploration of human cognitive mechanism, while AI research on symbolic problem solving and expert systems seems too macrocosmic. In contrast, cognitive physics takes the concept, i.e, the word in natural language, as the departure point, and conducts research on the knowledge representation and cognitive modeling from quantitative data to qualitative knowledge.

Natural language is the medium through which human understanding and knowledge are constructed, and the fundamental linguistic value usually is related to the fundamental concept in human thought. Considering the role of atom models in the physical world, we prefer to take the most fundamental linguistic value or concept as the basic model of natural language. By this way, we do not care about the concrete physical form, such as the electrons rotating around the nucleus, but rather emphasize a fundamental model for concepts represented by the cloud model, in which the kernel can be considered as the expectation, while the entropy and the hyper-entropy may be something attached to the kernel.

Given a group of quantitative data with the same property, however, one key challenge is presented: how to form the relevant qualitative concepts, which can reflect the essence and internal relation of the data. According to feature-list theory, concepts are the common properties shared by a class of objects, which can be characterized by the typical and significant features. On the other hand, prototype theory holds that concepts can be modeled as a most exemplary case, as well as the degree to which its members deviate from the prototype, i.e., membership degree. In this book, we prefer the cloud model, which, as a transforming model between qualitative concepts and quantitative expressions, it can not only directly extract concepts from original data and formally describe the uncertainty of concepts, but it can also represent the imprecise background knowledge impermissible for the classical rough set theory. In Chapter 5, we have expatiated upon the numerical characteristics of cloud models, cloud generators, the mathematical properties and pervasiveness of normal cloud models, and so on.

6.1.2   DESCRIBING INTERACTION BETWEEN OBJECTS BY USING FIELD

Until now, physicians have found four fundamental forces in the universe: the gravitational force, the electromagnetic force, the weak force, and the strong force. Newton's law of universal gravitation states that all particles in a multiparticle system attract each other with a gravitational force, and further all objects in the universe will converge due to the gravitational attraction between them. Coulomb's law is about the electric field between charged points at a distance, which can be visually portrayed with the help of electric field lines and equipotential lines (or surfaces) where the electrical potential has the same value everywhere. Nuclear physics models the strong force or the nuclear force between nucleus and mesons as an exchange force between quarks in which the basic exchange particle is gluon. The Fermi theory described the weak interaction as a pointlike interaction, involving no field, but later on people found it flawed. In 1984, Carlo Rubbia and Simon van der Meer were awarded the Nobel Prize in Physics for their outstanding contribution to the discovery of the quantum of weak field.

Although the four fundamental forces exist at different scales and belong to different physical branches, the attempt to incorporate the associated theories has become an important trend in modern physics research. Scientists are in search of a theory to unify the four fundamental forces. Einstein devoted his later life to unify gravitational and electromagnetic forces, but did not succeed. In the late 1960s, Steven Weinberg and colleagues introduced the electroweak theory to combine weak and electromagnetic interactions into a single, electroweak interaction, which greatly encouraged physicists to produce a grand unified theory (GUT) in the 1970s. According to the GUT, at extremely high energy (almost as high as 10^{24} eV), electromagnetic force, strong force, and weak force can be linked together. The Big Bang theory even points out that the gravitational force also can be unified with the other three at the very early stage of the universe.

Since the interaction of particles in physics can be described with the help of a force field, we are wondering whether it is possible to formalize the self-cognition of the human brain in terms of the idea of field. If so, we can probably establish a virtual cognitive field to model the interactions of data objects, and visualize the human mind's perceptual, memorial, and thinking processes. Starting with the wonderful ideas, we would consider all concepts, linguistic values, lexical words, and data points in the cognitive mind as interacting objects by means of the universal field space.

Let's take the knowledge discovery in a relational database for example. Given a logic database with N records and M attributes, the process of knowledge discovery may begin with the underlying distribution of the N data points in the M-dimensional universal space. If each data object is viewed as a point charge or mass point, it will exert a force on other objects in its vicinity. And the interaction of all data points will form a field. If further data is reduced by cloud models, a simplified knowledge discovery process can be presented to mimic the cognitive process of humans by exploring the interaction of data points with fields at different granularities.

As illustrated in Figure 6.1, there are 3,000 objects described by two attributes (salary and service age). They create a two-dimensional data field, in which the

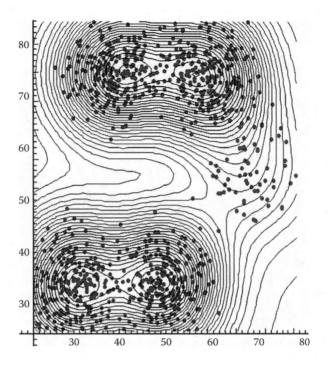

FIGURE 6.1 The equipotential plot of a data field created by 3,000 data objects.

global topology of equipotential lines can reveal straightforward the clustering properties of the underlying data.

6.1.3 DESCRIBING HIERARCHICAL STRUCTURE OF KNOWLEDGE BY USING GRANULARITY

The hierarchy is something universal in nature, society and the human mind. As Engels wrote in his *Dialectics of Nature*,

> ...whatever view one may hold of the constitution of matter,..., it is divided up into a series of big, well-defined groups of a relatively massive character in such a way that the members of each separate group stand to one another in definite finite mass ratios, in contrast to which those of the next group stand to them in the ratio of the infinitely large or infinitely small in the mathematical sense....[4]

Today Engels's viewpoint of the stratum of matter has been proved right and human cognition of the material universe has grown greatly on both the macro- and micro-scales. On the macro-scale, scientists devote themselves to exploring cosmic-scale structures, such as planets, stars, galaxies and even the universe as a whole, while on the micro-scale, the material particles are continuously broken down into molecules, atoms, nuclei, neutrons, protons, quarks, and even tinier components of particles. It is the same situation in life science. Structurally, all living systems are both super-systems — which are comprised of a number of smaller systems — and subsystems — which are systems that comprise part of a larger whole. A typical hierarchy of life systems includes molecules, cells, tissues, organs, individuals, populations, ecosystems, and the biosphere. Currently, microbiology has plunged into the molecular level and some new fields at an even deeper subatomic level have emerged, such as quantum biology and nanobiology. On the other hand, macrobiology research focuses on cosmic biology, which aims at revealing the extraterrestrial origin of life. As far as human society is concerned, there also exist various social hierarchies, communities, or stratifications depending on different perspectives. From the administrative perspective, the social system is composed of individuals, households, towns, cities, regions, states, nations, and international organizations. Of course, from the economic or educational perspective, the associated social hierarchy will be quite different.

Of course, as subjective perception is the reflection of objective reality within human consciousness, there inevitably exist various hierarchies of knowledge, which should be clarified at first in the human cognitive mechanism. For example, the hierarchy of knowledge in the human mind perhaps involves engineering, science, and philosophy, etc. Moreover, the process of cognitive development essentially is hierarchical with successive stages, such as sensation, perception, appearance, concept, and abstraction.

From a physical point of view, hierarchy is related to the concept of granularity, which is a measure of the relative size of material particles. In this book, we refer to it as a measure of information contained in a linguistic value, concept, or word. Starting with this idea, data exploration at different conceptual levels can be considered as the process of manipulating and understanding the information at different granularities. Furthermore, if we take the cloud model as the fundamental model of concepts, the expectation as the kernel or typical value of concepts, the entropy can be considered as the granularity of concepts, i.e., the measure of the relative size of concepts, while the hyper-entropy may represent the preciseness of the granularity.

As is well known, to switch among different granularities is a powerful ability of human intelligence in problem solving. That is to say, people not only can solve problems based on information at a certain granularity, but they also can deal with problems involving information at extremely different granularities. People may even jump up and down across different granularities while thinking. Just like the zooming of a telescope or microscope, the cross-layer thinking ability helps people to clarify the problems at macro-, meso-, and micro-levels, respectively.

The change from a finer up to a coarser granularity means data reduction and abstraction, which can greatly simplify the amount of data in problem solving. A coarser granularity scheme will help to grasp the common properties of problems and obtain a better global understanding. On the other hand, in a finer granularity scheme, more individual properties can be discerned to precisely distinguish each individual, which, though more abundant and complicated, is always easy to be generalized to some generic concepts and knowledge describing the common properties.

Moreover, it is important to point out that the hierarchical structure of concepts at different granularities is not fixed. In a real world, it is hard for the concept hierarchy in fixed, discrete, and steplike fashion to describe the uncertainty and gradualness of human cognitive process, as well as its infinite extendibility at the micro- or macro-scales. The world around us is so magical and beautiful that the macro can be more macroscopic and the micro can be even more microscopic.

6.2 DATA FIELD

6.2.1 FROM PHYSICAL FIELD TO DATA FIELD

The idea of field was first proposed by an English physicist, Michael Faraday, in 1837. In his opinion, the non-contact interaction between particles, such as gravitational force, electrostatic force, and magnetic force, is mediated through a certain medium called "field." With the development of the field theory, people have abstracted the notion as a mathematical concept.

Definition 6.1

The field of a physical variable or mathematical function is defined in space Ω if every point in Ω corresponds to a determinate value of the variable or function.

Obviously, the field describes the distribution of a physical variable or mathematical function throughout space. If every point in field space is associated with a single number or magnitude, the related field is called a "scalar field," for example, temperature field, density field, and electric potential field. By contrast, if the field is characterized by vectors closely related to magnitude and direction, we call it a "vector field." In physics, vector field is a general concept that can represent a certain material attribute, such as electric field, magnetic field, gravitational field, or velocity field. According to the variation in properties or conditions, the most general vector field always can be viewed as either an irrotational field or a solenoidal field or some mixture of the two. For instance, gravitational field, static electric field, and static nuclear force field are irrotational fields, magnetic field is a solenoidal field, and the field produced by a time-dependent electric flux is both irrotational and solenoidal.

The irrotational field is the most frequently discussed vector field in fundamental physics, which has been elaborated on in some basic theorems, such as Newton's law of universal gravitation and Coulomb's law. Its main characteristics include that every object located in an irrotational field will exert a certain force, and field lines start from the sources and end at the sinks. By a constant irrotational field, we mean a field independent of the time, in which the vector intensity function $F(r)$ may always be constructed out of scalar potential function $\varphi(r)$ by gradient operator $F(r) = \nabla \varphi(r)$. Thus, constant irrotational field also can be called "conservative field" or "potential field," where potential means the work done to move a unit object, such as a mass point of the unit mass in a gravitational field or a point charge with unit charge in a static electric field, from some position A to the reference point. In a potential field, the distribution of potential energy is determined uniquely by the relative position of interactive particles in space. Since the potential energy difference between some position and the reference point is a definite value, it is clear that potential function is only a function of the coordinates, regardless of whether objects exist.

For example, the scalar potential of a gravitational field produced by a mass point of mass m can be expressed as

$$\varphi(r) = \frac{G \times m}{\|r\|}$$

where r is the spherical coordinate of any point in the spherical coordinate system with its origin at the mass point m, and G is the gravitational constant.

If n mass points are present in the space, the total potential at point r is just the algebraic sum of the potentials due to the individual mass point,

$$\varphi(r) = G \times \sum_{i=1}^{n} \frac{m_i}{\|r - r_i\|}$$

where, $\|r - r_i\|$ is the distance from point r to the mass point m_i.

Let's consider the simplest electrostatic field created by a single point charge of charge Q. The electric potential or voltage at any location in the field can be determined as following by referencing to a zero of potential at infinity,

$$\varphi(r) = \frac{Q}{4\pi\varepsilon_0 \|r\|}$$

where r is the radial coordinate of a point in the spherical coordinate system with its origin at point charge Q, and ε_0 is the permittivity of free space.

In the cases of electric field for multiple point charges, the electrical potential also superposes linearly, so that the electric potential at a point r for n point charges is equal to the sum of the potentials due to the individual point charge,

$$\varphi(r) = \frac{1}{4\pi\varepsilon_0} \sum_{i=1}^{n} \frac{Q_i}{\|r - r_i\|}$$

where $\|r - r_i\|$ is the distance from point r to the point charge Q_i.

Another example is the central force field of a single nucleon, in which the central potential at any point in space can be calculated by the following optional formulas:

Square-well potential:

$$\varphi(r) = \begin{cases} V_0 & \|r\| \leq R \\ 0 & \|r\| > R \end{cases}$$

Gaussian potential:

$$\varphi(r) = V_0 \cdot e^{-\left(\frac{\|r\|}{R}\right)^2}$$

Exponential potential:

$$\varphi(r) = V_0 \cdot e^{-\frac{\|r\|}{R}}$$

where V_0 and R indicate the strength and range of the nuclear force, respectively.

From all the physical fields mentioned above, we may see that the potential at any point in space is directly proportional to a measure of the strength of an object's interaction, such as the mass or charge, and decreases as the distance of the source increases. In the case of the gravitational field and electrostatic field, the potential is inversely proportional to the distance of the source and tends to zero as the distance goes to infinity. The associated force, as the gradient force with potential function, in essence is a long-range force, which decreases slowly with increase of distance and exerts influence over an arbitrarily large distance. By contrast, in the case of the nuclear force field, the potential falls off much faster as the distance increases and the nuclear force quickly decreases down to zero, which indicates a short-range field. Moreover, in the above fields, the potential at any point in space is isotropic, which means the potential is same in every direction, and the associated force field can be modelled as a spherical force field.

Inspired by the knowledge in physics above, we introduce the interaction of particles and their field model into the data space in order to describe the relationship among data points and reveal the general characteristics of the underlying data distribution. Given a dataset containing n objects in space $\Omega \subseteq \mathbf{R}^p$, i.e., $D = \{x_1, x_2, \ldots, x_n\}$, where $x_i = (x_{i1}, x_{i2}, \ldots, x_{ip})$, $i = 1, 2, \ldots, n$, each data object can be considered as a mass point or nucleon with a certain field around it and the interaction of all data objects will form a data field through space.

As for the time-independent data points, the associated data field can be regarded as a constant irrotational field, which can be analytically modeled by scalar potential function and vector intensity function. Considering that the calculation of scalar potential is inherently simpler than that of vector intensity, we prefer to adopt scalar potential to describe a data field at first.

6.2.2 POTENTIAL FIELD AND FORCE FIELD OF DATA

According to the field theory in physics, the potential in a conservative field is a function of position, which is inversely proportional to the distance and is directly proportional to the magnitude of the particle's mass or charge. Thus, we can give the following principles about the potential function of a data field. Thus, we can set up some general rules[5,6] for the potential in a data field:

Given a data object in space Ω, let $\varphi_x(y)$ be the potential at any point $y \in \Omega$ in the data field produced by x, then $\varphi_x(y)$ must meet all the following rules:

1. $\varphi_x(y)$ is a continuous, smooth, and finite function in space Ω.
2. $\varphi_x(y)$ is isotropic in nature.
3. $\varphi_x(y)$ monotonically decreases in the distance $\|x - y\|$. When $\|x - y\| = 0$, it reaches maximum, but does not go infinity, and when $\|x - y\| \to \infty$, $\varphi_x(y) \to 0$.

In principle, all functional forms obeying the above rules can be adopted to define the potential of a data field. Referring to the potential functions of the gravitational field and the central potential field of a nucleon, we propose two optional potential functions for a data field:
Potential function of a gravitational-like data field:

$$\varphi_x(y) = \frac{m}{1 + \left(\frac{\|x-y\|}{\sigma}\right)^k}$$

Potential function of a nuclear-like data field:

$$\varphi_x(y) = m \times e^{-\left(\frac{\|x-y\|}{\sigma}\right)^k}$$

where the strength of interaction $m \geq 0$ can be regarded as the mass of data objects, $\sigma \in (0, +\infty)$ is the influence factor that indicates the range of interaction, and $k \in N$ is the order of distance term.

Figure 6.2 illustrates the curves of the two potential functions in the case of m, $\sigma = 1$. In Figure 6.2(a) with $k = 1$, the potential function of the gravitational-like field decreases slowly as the distance increases, representing a long-range field. In Figure 6.2(b) with $k = 5$, both of the potential functions decrease down to zero sharply, indicating the short-range fields. Intuitively, the potential function representing a short-range field will help to describe the interaction of data objects better.

Considering the relationship between the functional forms and the distribution properties of associated potential fields, as shown in Figure 6.3, each equipotential line plot depicts a potential field created by the same 390 data points of unit mass with different functional form and different parameter setting. It can be found that the associated potential fields, except in the case of the gravitational-like potential function with $k = 1$, are quite similar in topological structure if the influence factor σ is selected appropriately. Taking the nuclear-like functional form as example, we can further discuss the influence range of a data object of unit mass in respect to various k. As illustrated in Figure 6.4, in the case of $k = 2$, potential $\varphi_x(y) = m \times e^{-\left(\frac{\|x-y\|}{\sigma}\right)^2}$ is a Gaussian-like or nuclear-like potential function

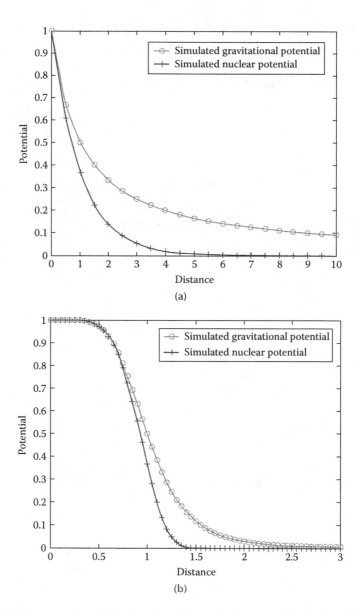

FIGURE 6.2 A comparison of two functional forms for the potential of a data field with *m,* σ = 1. (a) *k* = 1 and (b) *k* = 5.

and, according to 3σ law of Gaussian function, each data object has an influence vicinity of radius $\frac{3}{\sqrt{2}}\sigma \approx 2.12\sigma$. The range of object interaction will gradually decrease as the order of distance term k increases. When $k \to \infty$, potential $\varphi_x(y)$ will approximate to a square-well potential of width σ, i.e., the range of object

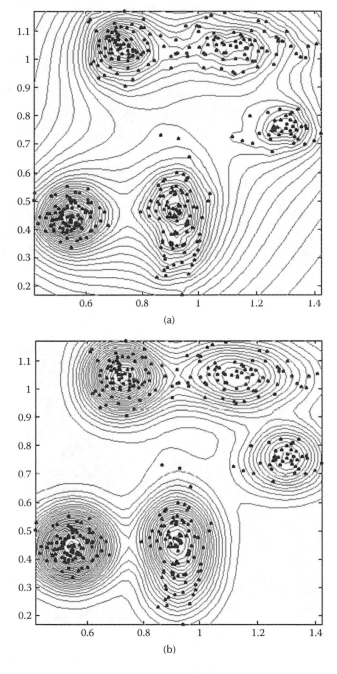

(a)

(b)

FIGURE 6.3 The effect on the distribution of data potential field by the selection of potential functions. (a) Potential function of gravitational-like field ($k = 1$, $\sigma = 0.009$), (b) potential function of gravitational-like field ($k = 5$, $\sigma = 0.095$), (c) potential function of nuclear-like field ($k = 1$, $\sigma = 0.039$), and (d) potential function of nuclear-like field ($k = 5$, $\sigma = 0.129$).

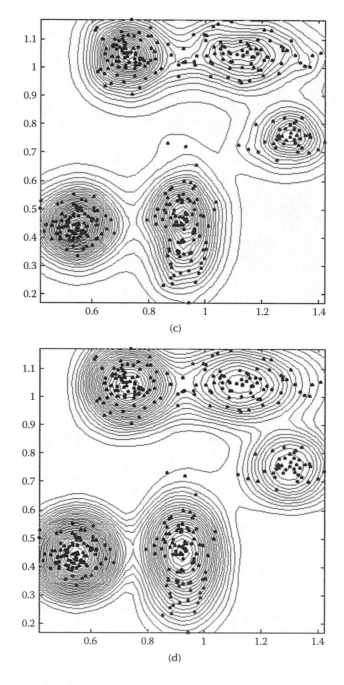

(c)

(d)

FIGURE 6.3 (Continued)

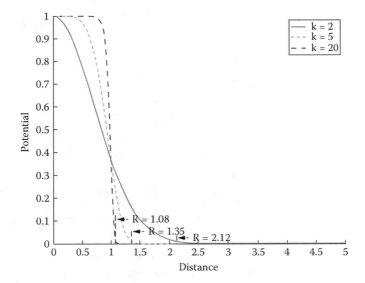

FIGURE 6.4 Nuclear-like potential functions with respect to k and its influence radii (m, $\sigma = 1$).

interaction tends to σ. Consequently, a new measure called "influence radius" could be introduced to describe the range of interaction between objects in a data field:

$$R = \sigma \times \sqrt[k]{\frac{9}{2}}$$

where R is monotonic decreasing in the order of the distance term k if σ is fixed, and $\forall k \in N$, $\sigma < R \leq \frac{9}{2}\sigma$.

For example, the influence radii in Figure 6.3(c) and (d) are $R_c \approx 0.176$ and $R_d \approx 0.174$ respectively, which means that data potential fields similar in topological structure have similar influence radii.

According to the discussion above, since Gaussian function has been widely applied for its good mathematic properties, we prefer to adopt the Gaussian function, i.e., nuclear-like potential function with $k = 2$, to model the distribution of data fields involved in human cognitive behavior.

Definition 6.2

Given a data field produced by a set of data objects $D = \{x_1, x_2, \ldots, x_n\}$ in space $\Omega \subseteq \mathbf{R}^p$, the potential at any point $x \in \Omega$ can be calculated as,

$$\varphi(x) = \varphi_D(x) = \sum_{i=1}^{n} \varphi_i(x) = \sum_{i=1}^{n} \left(m_i \times e^{-\left(\frac{\|x - x_i\|}{\sigma}\right)^2} \right)$$

where $\|x - x_i\|$ is the distance between object x_i and point x, usually given by Euclidean or Manhattan distance; $m_i \geq 0$ is the mass of object x_i ($i = 1,2,...,n$),which meets a normalization condition $\sum_{i=1}^{n} m_i = 1$.

Generally each data object is supposed to be equal in mass, indicating the same influence over space, thus a simplified potential function can be given as,

$$\varphi(x) = \frac{1}{n} \sum_{i=1}^{n} e^{-\left(\frac{\|x-x_i\|}{\sigma}\right)^2}$$

Just like a scalar field in physics is depicted with the help of isolines or iso-surfaces, we adopt equipotential lines or surfaces to represent the overall distribution of data potential fields. Given a potential ψ, an equipotential can be extracted as one where all points on it satisfy the implicit equation $\varphi(x) = \psi$. Thus, by specifying a set of discrete potentials $\{\psi_1, \psi_2,...\}$, a series of nested equipotential lines or surfaces can be drawn for better understanding of the associated potential field as a whole form.

As shown in Figure 6.5, the equipotential map for a potential field produced by a single data object consists of a family of nested, concentric circles or spheres centered on the data object. From the figure, we may find that the equipotentials closer to the object have higher potentials and are further apart, which indicates strong field strength near around the object. Another example shown in Figure 6.6 is for a potential field created by 180 data points in a three-dimensional space. Obviously, equipotential surfaces corresponding to different potentials are quite different in topology. For instance, the equipotential at potential $\psi = 0.381$ is composed of many small topological components enclosing different data objects. As we go farther, small components will be nested into larger ones and the equipotentials start to enclose more and more data objects. When the potential equals 0.279, the equipotential is composed of only five components comprising all the data objects. Eventually when the potential decreases down to 0.107, all data objects "fall" inside an equipotential.

As a special supplement, we will discuss the relationship between the potential function of data field and nonparametric density estimation in the following part.

According to the superposition principle of scalar potential, if data objects are equal in mass, the denser regions of data will have higher potential, and vice versa. In this sense, potential function can be approximately considered as a density estimation of the underlying data distribution.

Let $K(x)$ be a basis potential, corresponding to $K(x) = e^{-\|x\|^k}$ and $K(x) = \frac{1}{1+\|x\|^k}$ in terms of nuclear-like and gravitation-like potentials, respectively, we can obtain the superposition of n basis potentials as,

$$\varphi(x) = \sum_{i=1}^{n} \left(m_i \cdot K\left(\frac{x - x_i}{\sigma}\right) \right)$$

According to the properties of probability density function, it can be proved that the difference between the potential function and the probability density function is

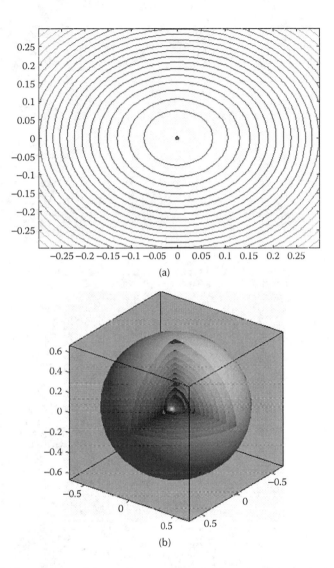

FIGURE 6.5 The equipotential map for a potential field produced by a single data object ($\sigma = 1$). (a) Equipotential lines and (b) equipotential surfaces.

only a normalization constant if $K(x)$ has finite integral in space $\Omega \subseteq \mathbf{R}^p$, i.e., $\int_\Omega K(x)dx = M < +\infty$. The proof is given as follows:

Since $K(x) \geq 0$ and $\forall i, m_i \geq 0$, $\varphi(x)$ is non-negative, i.e., $\varphi(x) \geq 0$, according to the requirements mentioned above $\int_\Omega K(x)dx = M < +\infty$ and $\sum_{i=1}^n m_i = 1$, it is easy to see directly that

$$\int_\Omega \varphi(x)dx = \int_\Omega \sum_{i=1}^n (m_i \cdot K(x-x_i))dx = \sum_{i=1}^n \left(m_i \int_\Omega K(x-x_i)dx \right) = M$$

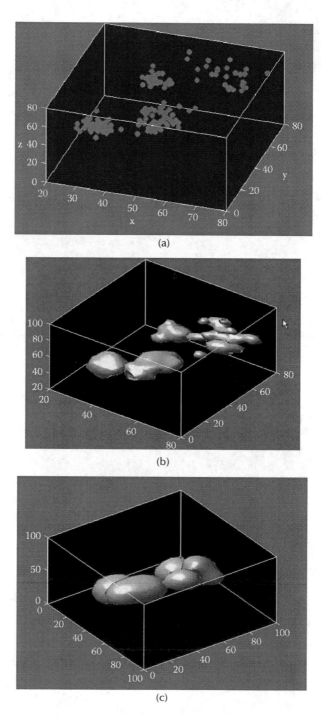

(a)

(b)

(c)

FIGURE 6.6 Equipotential surfaces for a three-dimensional potential field ($\sigma = 2.107$). (All the coordinates are nominal distances.) (a) 180 data points in a three-dimensional space, (b) equipotential at $\psi = 0.381$, (c) equipotential at $\psi = 0.279$, and (d) equipotential at $\psi = 0.107$.

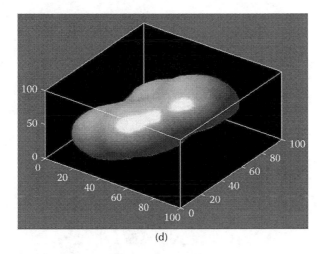

(d)

FIGURE 6.6 (Continued)

Let's take a basis potential in the form of nuclear-like potential $K(x) - e^{-\|x\|^k}$ as example and consider the integral of the basis potential over space Ω: if the order of distance term $k = 1$ or 2, the integral $\int_\Omega K(x)dx$ equals 1 or $(\sqrt{\pi})^p$, respectively, which is obviously finite. As the case of $k \geq 3$, we can divide the space Ω into two subspaces $\|x\| \leq 1$ and $1 < \|x\| < +\infty$. In the subspace $\|x\| \leq 1$, we have $e^{-\|x\|^k} \leq 1$, thus we can give $\int_{\|x\|\leq 1} e^{-\|x\|^k} dx < +\infty$. In the subspace $1 < \|x\| < +\infty$, considering that $0 < e^{-\|x\|^k} < e^{-\|x\|}$ and $e^{-\|x\|}$ has finite integral, we can derive $\int_{1<\|x\|<+\infty} e^{-\|x\|^k} dx < +\infty$. Consequently, a basis nuclear-like potential satisfies $\int_\Omega K(x)dx < +\infty$ for any k, which means that a nuclear-like potential can be viewed as the overall density estimation in a sense. In particular, if each data object is equal in mass, the overall nuclear-like potential and the kernel density estimation in non-parametric density estimation are quite similar actually.

Given n independent and identically distributed d-dimensional samples $x_1, x_2, \ldots, x_n$, the kernel density estimation of the overall density $p(x)$ can be written as

$$\hat{p}(x) = \frac{1}{n \times h^d} \sum_{i=1}^{n} \mu\left(\frac{x - x_i}{h}\right)$$

where $\mu(x)$ is the kernel function and $h > 0$ is its bandwidth.

Usually, the kernel function $\mu(x)$ is chosen to be a smooth unimodal function with a peak at the origin, such as Gaussian kernels, uniform kernels, triangle kernels, and so on. Essentially, kernel density estimation is the superposition of the basis kernel functions centered at each data point and the estimated density at any point x in space is equal to the average contribution of each data point, which depends on how apart the data point and point x are. Obviously, if $K(x) = \mu(x)$ and each data object equals in mass, the potential of a data field actually gives a physical explanation of the kernel density estimation, in which the requirements for a potential function are not as strict as that of the kernel density estimation, for example basis function $K(x)$ is not required to be a density function and each basis function must not have equal weight or mass.

Due to the fact that the vector intensity always can be constructed out of scalar potential by gradient operator, the vector intensity $F(x)$ at any point $x \in \Omega$, can be given as,

$$F(x) = \nabla \varphi(x) = \frac{2}{\sigma^2} \sum_{i=1}^{n} \left((x_i - x) \cdot m_i \cdot e^{-\left(\frac{\|x-x_i\|}{\sigma}\right)^2} \right)$$

Since the term $\frac{2}{\sigma^2}$ is a constant, the above formula can be simply rewritten as,

$$F(x) = \sum_{i=1}^{n} \left((x_i - x) \cdot m_i \cdot e^{-\left(\frac{\|x-x_i\|}{\sigma}\right)^2} \right)$$

For a data force field produced by a single data object, the associated vector intensity function may be plotted as Figure 6.7, which reaches its maximum value at the distance $r = 0.705$ and quickly decreases to zero as the distance exceeds $R \approx 2.121$, indicating a strong force on the sphere with radius 0.705.

Figure 6.8 shows a plot of force lines for a data force field produced by a single object ($m, \sigma = 1$), the radial field lines always are in the direction of spherical coordinate toward the source and perpendicular to the equipotentials, which indicates an attractive force. The force lines are uniformly distributed and spherically symmetric

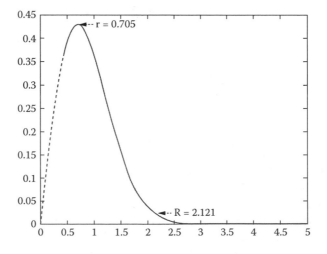

FIGURE 6.7 The vector intensity function produced by a data object with parameters $m, \sigma = 1$.

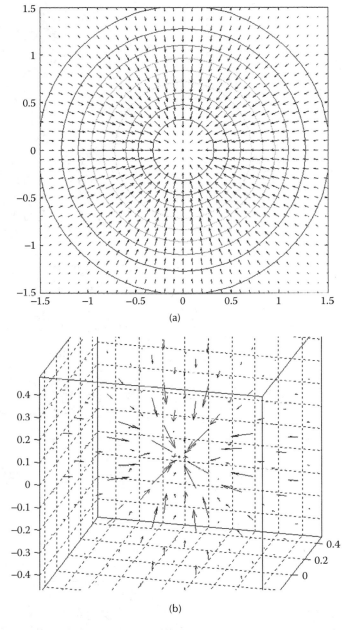

(a)

(b)

FIGURE 6.8 The plot of force lines for a data force field produced by a single object (m, $\sigma = 1$). (a) A two-dimensional plot of force lines and (b) a three-dimensional plot of force lines.

on any equipotential surface, whose norm reaches its maximum value nearly at the positions with the radial distance 0.705 and decreases as the radial distance further increases, which indicates a strong attractive force on the sphere centered on the object and with the radius 0.705.

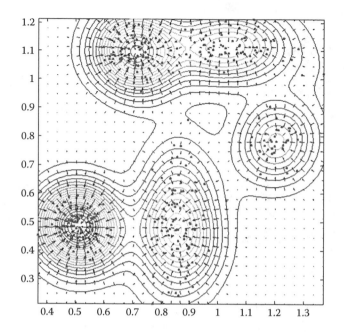

FIGURE 6.9 The plot of force lines for a two-dimensional data field ($\sigma = 0.091$).

Figure 6.9 shows the plot of force lines for a data force field generated by 390 data points in two-dimensional space. The force lines always point toward the five local maximums of the associated potential field, which can be nearly considered as a data field produced by five "virtual point sources." Due to the attraction of the "virtual sources," all the data objects in the field will tend to converge toward each other and exhibit certain features of self-organization. It is the same for the data field produced by the 280 data points in three-dimensional space shown in Figure 6.10.

6.2.3 INFLUENCE COEFFICIENT OPTIMIZATION OF FIELD FUNCTION

Given a data set $D = \{x_1, x_2, \ldots, x_n\}$ in space Ω, the distribution of the associated data field is primarily determined by the influence factor σ once the form of potential function is fixed. Examples of different potential fields produced by variance of σ are shown in Figure 6.11, where the fields are generated by five data objects in the form of Gaussian potential. If σ is too small, the range of interaction is very short, and potential function $\varphi(x)$ will become the superposition of n sharp pulses centered at the data objects. The extreme is that there exists no interaction between the objects and the potential at the location of each data object nearly equals to $\frac{1}{n}$.

On the other hand, if σ is very large, there is strong interaction between the objects, and $\varphi(x)$ will become the superposition of n broad, slowly changing functions. The extreme is that the potential at the location of each object approximates 1. Since the difference between the probability density function and the potential function in the

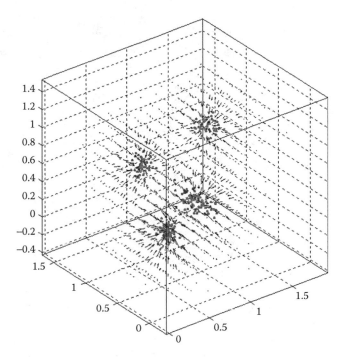

FIGURE 6.10 The plot of force lines for a three-dimensional data field ($\sigma = 0.160$).

form of Gaussian function is only normalization constant, obviously, the potential in the above extreme cases cannot produce a meaningful estimation of the underlying distribution. Thus, the choice of σ should make the distribution of potential field as consistent with the underlying distribution of original data as possible.

Entropy used to be a measure of the amount of thermal energy showing the disorder or randomness in a closed thermodynamic system. However, Shannon's entropy is a useful measure of uncertainty in an information system. The higher the entropy is, the more uncertain the associated physical system. For the data field generated by the data objects $x_1, x_2, \dots, x_p$, if the potentials at the positions of all objects are equal to one another, we are most uncertain about the underlying distribution. And Shannon's entropy is the highest in this case. Conversely, if the distribution of the potential field is highly skewed, the uncertainty and the entropy will be low. Thus, we introduce the potential entropy to measure the uncertainty about the distribution of potential field.

Let $\psi_1, \psi_2, \dots, \psi_m$, respectively, be the potentials at the positions of the objects $x_1, x_2, \dots, x_n$. The potential entropy can be defined as

$$H = -\sum_{i=1}^{n} \frac{\psi_i}{Z} \log\left(\frac{\psi_i}{Z}\right)$$

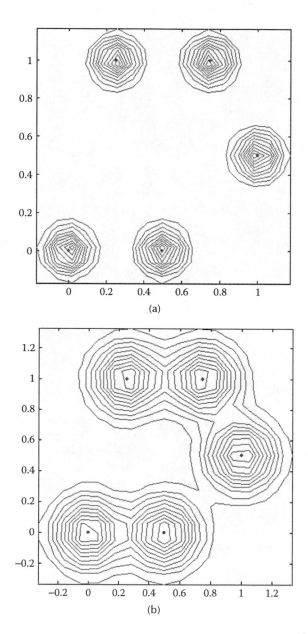

FIGURE 6.11 Different potential fields produced by five data objects with the variance of influence factor σ. (a) σ = 0.1, (b) σ = 0.2, and (c) σ = 0.8.

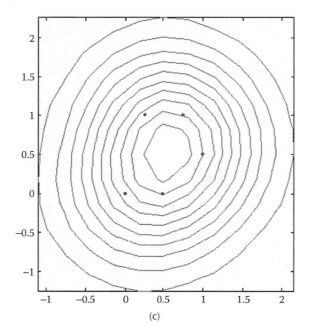

(c)

FIGURE 6.11 (Continued)

where $Z = \sum_{i=1}^{n} \psi_i$ is a normalization factor. For any $\sigma \in [0,+\infty]$, the potential entropy H satisfies $0 \leq H \leq \log(n)$, and $H = \log(n)$ if and only if $\psi_1 = \psi_2 = \ldots = \psi_n$.

Figure 6.12 illustrates an example of the optimal choice of influence factor σ for a data field produced by 400 data points. Obviously, when $\sigma \to 0$, potential entropy H tends to $H_{max} = \log(400) \approx 5.992$; H decreases at first as σ increases from 0 to ∞; and at a certain σ ($\sigma_{opt} \approx 0.036$), H achieves a global minimum $H_{min} \approx 5.815$; thereafter, H increases as σ further increases, and tends to the maximum again when $\sigma \to \infty$. Figure 6.12(b) demonstrates the data potential field with optimal σ, which obviously fits the underlying distribution very well.

In nature, optimal choice of σ is a minimization problem of a univariate, non-linear function H, i.e., $\min H(\sigma)$, which can be solved by standard optimization algorithms, such as simple one-dimensional searching method, stochastic searching method, and simulated annealing method, etc. In this chapter, we adopt the golden section search method with initial interval $[\frac{\sqrt{2}_{min}}{3^{i \neq j}} \|x_i - x_j\|, \frac{\sqrt{2}_{max}}{3^{i \neq j}} \|x_i - x_j\|]$ and the detailed algorithm is described as follows:[7,8]

Algorithm 6.1 Optimization algorithm of influence factor σ (Optimal_Sigma)

Input: data set $D = \{x_1, x_2, \ldots, x_n\}$
Output: optimized σ

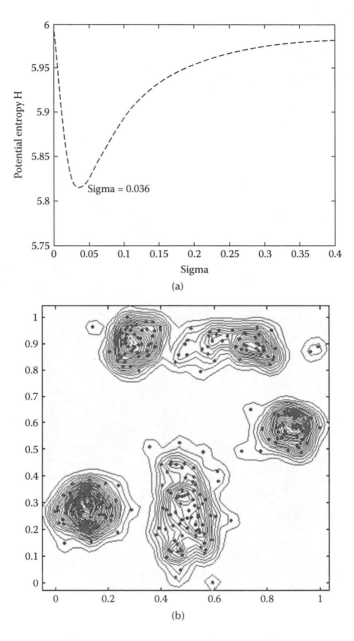

FIGURE 6.12 An example of optimal choice of influence factor σ. (a) Optimal choice of σ and (b) the data potential field with optimal σ.

Steps:

BEGIN

Let $a = \dfrac{\sqrt{2}}{3} \min_{i \neq j} \|x_i - x_j\|$, $b = \dfrac{\sqrt{2}}{3} \max_{i \neq j} \|x_i - x_j\|$, and $\varepsilon = error\ threshold;$

Let $\sigma_l = a + (1 - \tau)(b - a)$, $\sigma_r = a + \tau(b - a)$, $\tau = \dfrac{\sqrt{5} - 1}{2}$;

Calculate $H_l = H(\sigma_l)$ and $H_r = H(\sigma_r)$;

While $|b - a| > \varepsilon$ do

If $H_l < H_r$ then {

      Let $b = \sigma_r$, $\sigma_r = \sigma_l$,   and $H_r = H_l$;

      Calculate $\sigma_l = a + (1 - \tau)(b - a)$ and $H_l = H(\sigma_l)$

}

Else {

      Let $a = \sigma_l$, $\sigma_l = \sigma_r$, $H_l = H_r$;

      Calculate $\sigma_r = a + \tau(b - a)$ and $H_r = H(\sigma_r)$

}

End While

If $H_l < H_r$, then $\{\sigma = \sigma_l\}$;

      Else $\{\sigma = \sigma_r\}$;

Return σ.

END

    For the above algorithm, let t be the number of iteration, the time complexity of computing the potential entropy H at each iteration is $O(n^2)$ and thus the total time complexity is $O(t \cdot n^2)$. Obviously, the algorithm is not effective in the case with large n. In practical applications, we can adopt random sampling technique with sample size $n_{sample} \ll n$ to reduce the computational cost. Generally speaking, in the case that n is very huge, the sampling rate should be no less than 2.5% in order to keep the properties of underlying distribution of original data.[9]

6.2.4 Data Field and Visual Thinking Simulation

With the development of AI, more and more expectations are imposed from time to time. In general, the research of AI may be divided into three major catalogs: mathematical computing, logical thinking, and thinking in image. Nowadays, no one is doubtful about mathematical computing abilities by computers. In the past 50 years, machine simulation of logical thinking has achieved great success. However, little has been done in the machine simulation of thinking in image, which means the perception deriving from the image of objects, imagination, comparison, association, and inspiration etc.

Let's take the chess machine as example. In 1977, IBM's Deep Blue chess machine defeated the human world chess champion, Garry Kasparov, but until now we could hardly find any report about the human vs. machine Go match. Why?

1. The ultimate aim in the game of chess is to win by capturing the opponent's king. But the idea of Go is not to necessarily overwhelm the opponent. It is rather to control more of the board than he or she does using stones as markers. And the player with most stones at the end of the game is the winner.
2. The rules of chess seem complicated at first glance — each type of piece has its own method of movement. On the other hands, Go has only a few of simple rules. But Go is more challenging than chess for the huge number of possibilities for board positions. The rules of Go are elegant, which means you can leave large chunks of territory to your opponent, while securing your own.
3. Generally in chess, those chessmen that have been killed cannot appear again, while in Go, the stones that are captured can be replaced at the same position again.
4. The game of chess emphasizes on the logic reasoning, in which, given an opening move, if you have enough search depths and computational abilities, it is possible to search forward all the possible moves and evaluate all positions at the end of the sequence of moves. Hence, the chess program can search and evaluate many moves in order to choose a good chess move. But in the game of Go, the possibilities for board positions are so huge (said to be 10 to the 75th power) that it is quite difficult to search a good move. Moreover, in the game of Go, both logical reasoning and visual thinking are very important. So, thinking in images, overall intuition, and high computational capabilities are necessary for intelligent Go machines, and sometimes emergence computations indicating a phase transition are also demanded.

In conclusion, there still seems to be a long way to go for machines to think in images. It is well known that intuition and imagination is closely related to vision and graphics, the residue of which may form an image space of thinking in the brain. Can we borrow the ideas of physical fields to describe the interaction between pixels in the space of visual thinking? As an effective approach to visually model the interaction between objects in data space, data field has been used to formally describe the human cognitive process from data, to information, and then to knowledge. Similarly, we will demonstrate some examples about how to simulate visual thinking in way of a data field.

Vision plays the most important role in human perception and thinking. Our impression of one person can be divided into a series of cognitive processes, such as visual perception, visual residue, visual memory, or visual loss at last. How to describe this process by means of a data field?

Given a gray-scale face image in size $m \times n$ pixels $A_{m \times n}$, if each pixel is considered as a data object in two-dimensional image space and the associated gray value $\rho_{ij} = A(i, j)$ ($i = 1, 2, \ldots, m$ $j = 1, 2, \ldots, n$) is considered as the mass of associated data objects (assume that ρ_{ij} has been normalized into the interval [0, 1]), the interactions between all the pixels will form a data field in image space and the potential at any point can be calculated as

$$\varphi(x) = \sum_{i=1}^{m} \sum_{j=1}^{n} \rho_{ij} \times e^{-\left(\frac{\|x - x_{ij}\|}{\sigma} \right)^2}$$

where the influence factor σ is a time-variant function and thus the associated potential field also is time variant. If the potential field at any time is known, we can calculate the gray value at any pixel point and restore the memorized image at different times.

According to the discussion above, we can simulate the fading process of visual memory in way of data field as time goes on. As shown in Figure 6.13, the visual memories about Einstein are produced by the data field of Einstein's face image. Obviously, the visual residue decreases as time passes through 10, 20, 30, and 40 units, and the impression of his face will gradually reduce to only a pair of profound eyes.

On the other hand, for some given face images with certain expression, we can also produce new face images with somehow different expressions based on field operations of the associated data field, such as linear or nonlinear composition. For example, for the two face images of the same girl with different expression shown in Figure 6.14, we first transform them into data fields, and combine the fields by some nonlinear operators, and then transform the combined field into new face

FIGURE 6.13 Visual fading with respect to time. t = 10, t = 20, t = 30, and t = 40.

FIGURE 6.14 Different facial expressions generated from raw images based on data fields.

images with new expressions, such as, crying more, smiling more, and half-crying to half-smiling.

Moreover, the method of data field can be used for main feature extraction of an image as well. For example, in order to extract primary features of the normalized facial image in size 128×128 pixels shown in Figure 6.15(a), we first apply a nonlinear transformation $f(\rho_{ij}) = (1 - \rho_{ij})^2$ to the gray image and calculate the potential at any pixel x as

$$\varphi(x) = \sum_{i=1}^{m} \sum_{j=1}^{n} \left(f(\rho_{ij}) \times e^{-\left(\frac{\|x - x_{ij}\|}{\sigma}\right)^2} \right)$$

Figure 6.15(b) and (c) show the corresponding equipotential lines plot and its three-dimensional view. Obviously, the transformed facial data field emphasizes the significant facial features, such as eyes, mouth, eyebrows, and nose, which correspond to some facial region with lower gray values.

Suppose that the facial data field is mainly determined by the interaction between significant feature points, some weight variable $w_{ij} \in [0,1]$ can be introduced to measure the contribution of each pixel to the global distribution of the facial data field, where w_{ij} is assumed to satisfy the constraint $\sum_{i=1}^{m} \sum_{j=1}^{n} w_{ij} = 1$. According to the

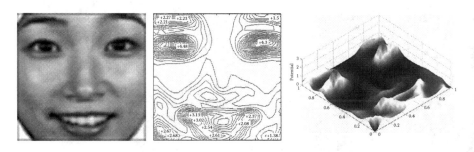

FIGURE 6.15 Nonlinear transformation of the facial data field ($\sigma = 0.05$). (a) The normalized facial gray image, (b) equipotential lines plot of facial data field, and (c) three-dimensional view of a two-dimensional potential field.

potential field of facial image data, w_{ij} can be considered as a set of functions of the pixel positions and can be optimized with the following optimization objective:

$$\min_{\{w_i'\}}\left(\frac{1}{2\cdot\left(\sqrt{2}\right)^d}\sum_{i=1}^{m\times n}\sum_{j=1}^{m\times n}w_i'\times w_j'\times f(\rho_i')\times f(\rho_j')\times e^{-\left(\frac{\|x_i'-x_j'\|}{\sqrt{2}\sigma}\right)^2}\right.$$

$$\left.-\frac{1}{m\times n}\sum_{i=1}^{m\times n}\sum_{j=1}^{m\times n}w_i\times f(\rho_i')\times e^{-\left(\frac{\|x_i'-x_j'\|}{\sigma}\right)^2}\right)$$

This way, a set of optimum estimation of w_{ij} can be calculated, and the pixel points with non-zero estimated values could be considered as the significant feature points of the facial image.

From the raw facial image (128×128 pixels) illustrated in Figure 6.16(a), we can extract 250 significant feature points, as shown in Figure 6.16(b). Similarly, the significant feature points can be reduced further into 48 points and 25 points, as in Figure 6.16(c) and (d).

Of course, the above examples are only a few trials of data field approaches in the simulation of thinking in image. We still have a long way to go in the simulation of human thinking, perception, intuition, inspiration, imagination, innovation, prediction, adaptation, and coordination, etc.

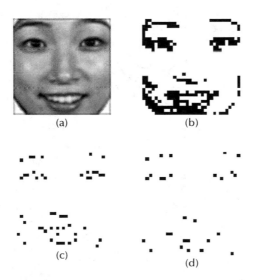

(a) (b) (c) (d)

FIGURE 6.16 Feature extraction of facial image. (a) 128×128 pixels, (b) 250 feature points, (c) 48 feature points, and (d) 28 feature points.

6.3 UNCERTAINTY IN CONCEPT HIERARCHY

Another important issue in cognitive physics is something related to the hierarchy with uncertainty, on which the knowledge granularity or the concept hierarchy is reflected referring to the granularity in physics.

In physics, the world views are very different at different scales. All observable objects in human scale falls within a fairly narrow range of scales from 10^{-7}m to 10^7m, while as currently reported, the material universe covers a very wide range from 10^{-30}m to 10^{30}m. Of course, it is possible to extend the range of scales further as new research progress is made.

Ideology and consciousness in human beings' brain are the reflection of the objective world, and there are a quantity of hierarchical knowledge series in our mind. One subject on cognitive mechanisms of humans is to deal with the hierarchical structure of knowledge. Due to the close relationship between knowledge hierarchy and concept granularity, we can discover the more pervasive and generalized knowledge by means of enhancing the granularity of concept. Nevertheless, there is still a fundamental problem in knowledge discovery, that is how to describe the hierarchical relationship of uncertainty among the concepts with different granularities.

Hierarchy is usually represented by a partial sequential set $(H, \prec)$, where H denotes the set of finite objects, and $\prec$ is the sequential relation, which is irreflexive and transitive. Object hierarchy in rules can be divided into several nonintersected object sets $H = \cup \, H_i$ based on the sequential relation $\prec$, so that it can be represented by a tree structure.

There are some serious drawbacks in the application to data mining by means of the traditional concept tree structure based on the aforementioned hierarchical idea:

1. The value intervals of different concepts on a concept tree are distinctive, and transitional phenomena, which will result in either this concept or that one, are prohibited. That is to say, fuzziness is not allowed in the concept. However, the understanding of knowledge by humans is not in the case. For instance, if the ages of 36 to 38 are defined as middle age, then 35 and 36 will be in different age categories if the concept tree is applied.
2. Membership relationships among the concepts on different hierarchies are unique. There cannot be phenomena in which one single attribute value or concept belongs to multiple higher hierarchical concepts, neither can it reflect the phenomena in which one attribute value belongs to different higher hierarchical concepts. It is not this way in human thinking at all. A strict tree structure in which a node can only belong to a father node is unacceptable, and must give up.
3. A concept tree is generally defined statically; however, the concept in cognitive process is of case by case relativity. For example, it is commonly agreed that a 40-year-old person is not young, but a 40-year-old scientist is still "young." As a result, the absolute value of the data cannot be utilized to establish a fixed concept tree, due to the fact that the applying occasions may vary.

In conclusion, it is neither realistic nor appropriate to establish a permanent fixed structure of a concept tree beforehand. But if the automatic generation of a realistic concept tree is adopted during the data mining process, there are three key problems that have to be conquered, including how to extract discrete concepts from continuous data, how to establish the structure of a flexible concept pan-tree which can provide such membership relations that a child concept may belong to multiple parent concepts, and how to climb up or even jump up from a fine level to a rough level by means of granularity change.

6.3.1 Discretization of Continuous Data

The approach of equal distance interval is one common discretization approach for continuous data. It divides the universal set into some subintervals with the same width according to human subjective will. Another approach is that of equal frequency interval, which subjectively divides the universal set into subintervals with the same frequency width based on the occurrence frequency of attribute values. In both approaches, the width and number of subintervals are user-specified, which don't take the real distribution of data into consideration. Therefore, the two discretization approaches can not effectively describe the uncertainty in the process of extracting qualitive concepts from raw continuous data. To solve the above-mentioned problems, a method based on cloud transformation can be introduced for discretization of continuous attributes.

In physics, Fourier transformation is well known as it can transform a subject in time domain into another subject in frequency domain and vice versa. This suggests that a complex issue in one state space may become simplified in another state space. It has been confirmed in mathematics that an arbitrary probability distribution can be decomposed into the sum of some normal distributions. Considering the universality of normal cloud, we can treat a frequency distribution as a combination of some normal cloud with different magnitudes, and consequentially realize the transformation from quantitative data to qualitative concepts.

Let $f(x)$ be the frequency distribution function of a data attribute X in a given universal set. Cloud transformation[11-13] is in progress from continuous quantitative domain to discrete concepts, in which different clouds $C(Ex_i, En_i, He_i)$ with different granularities are generated automatically to compose the distribution of the attribute frequency of X. The mathematical expression of this process is

$$f(x) \rightarrow \sum_{i=1}^{n} (a_i * C(Ex_i, En_i, He_i))$$

where a_i is the magnitude coefficient, and n is the number of discrete concepts after transformation.

For simplicity, let He_i be zero, and n be the minimal one under a certain preciseness desired.

From the view of data mining, cloud transformation is the process to extract concepts from data distribution of a certain attribute. It is the transformation from quantitative to qualitative expression, and is the process of concept inductive learning as well.

The transformation result might not be unique, however, it is in common sense that the contribution of the data value with higher occurrence frequency to the qualitative concept is more than the contribution of the one with lower occurrence frequency. According to this commonsense knowledge, we can develop a heuristic cloud transformation algorithm, i.e., the local maximum in the frequency distribution is the convergent center of the data, which can be considered as the center of the concept, that is the mathematical expectation of the cloud model; the higher peak shows that more data converge at this point, so the concept represented by this peak ought to be considered with higher priority; the data reflected by this concept are deleted thereafter, and the local maximum is searched iteratively until the asked preciseness is satisfied. The algorithm for cloud transformation is given below.

Algorithm 6.2 Cloudtransform

Input: The data set D of attribute X
     The error threshold allowed for the transformation ε
Output: n discrete concepts $C_i(Ex_i, En_i, He_i)$ $(i = 1,2,...,n)$
Steps:

BEGIN

     CLOUDS = $\varnothing$;

     //Generate the frequency distribution function $f(x)$ based on the data set.

     $f(x) = \text{FREQUENCY}(D)$;

     //Initialization

     $h(x) = f(x)$

     $i = 1$;

     //Iteration judgement with respect to the error threshold ε.

     WHILE(MAX($h(x)$) > ε)

     {

          //Search for the peak value of $h(x)$ as the expectation of the cloud model

          $Ex_i = \text{FIND\_Ex}(h(x))$;

          //a_i denotes the amplitude coefficient.

          $a_i = h(Ex_i)$;

          //Calculate the entropy and type of cloud model which can approximate

          $En_i = \text{CALC\_En}(h(x), Ex_i, \varepsilon)$;

          //Calculate He

          $He_i = \text{CALC\_He}(Ex_i, En_i, a_i, D)$;

CLOUDS = CLOUDS∪{$C(Ex_i, En_i, He_i)$};

//Calculate the approximation error

$h(x) = h(x) - a_i * CLOUD\_EXP(Ex_i, En_i)$;

$i = i + 1$;

    }

END

where the function CLOUD_EXP(Ex_i, En_i) approximates $h(x)$ by the expectation curve of the cloud $y = e^{\frac{-(x-Ex)^2}{2En^2}}$. The error threshold ε, as given by the user according to his knowledge, is used to control the construction of entropy and iteration times. The smaller ε is, the more precise the approximation will be. The function CALC_He(Ex_i, En_i, a_i, D) determines the set of attribute values which belong to a certain concept based on the descriptive expectation curve of the cloud model. Then, we calculate He_i by means of the backward cloud algorithm without certainty degrees (see Section 5.3.4).

Hereafter, we provide a concrete example to illustrate the approach of cloud transformation. Let T be the statistical database table for the flux of a thousand programmed controlled switchers, and the quantitative attribute A_k be the maximum occupied number with domain [0, 254] (the maximum number of switcher lines are 254). The total records in T amounts to $m = 251100$.

Step 1: For each possible value $x(x = 0,1,2,...,254)$ in the universal set of attribute A_k, calculate the number y of the records which contain such attribute value, and the frequency distribution function $f(x)$ of A_k can be acquired, as shown in Figure 6.17.

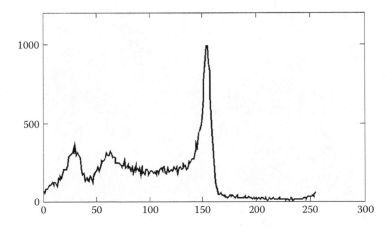

FIGURE 6.17 Experimental data distribution.

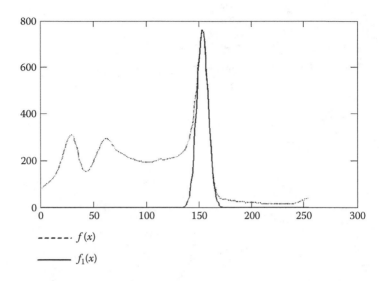

FIGURE 6.18 The data distribution function $f(x)$ based on a cloud model.

Step 2: Search for the location of maximum point in the data distribution function $f(x)$, and define the attribute value for this location as the center of mass (expectation) Ex_i ($i = 1,2,\ldots,n$). Calculate the entropy of cloud model with expectation Ex_i for approximation of $f(x)$, and then calculate its distribution function $f_i(x)$, as shown in Figure 6.18.

Step 3: Subtract $f_i(x)$ from $f(x)$ and get the updated data distribution function $f'(x)$. Repeat steps (2) and (3) on $f'(x)$, we can get several data distribution functions, as shown in Figure 6.19.

Step 4: Based on the given $f(x)$, we can get the final approximation error function $f'(x)$ and the distribution functions of each cloud model. Compute the three characteristics of the qualitative concept based on the cloud model. Figure 6.20 illustrates the transformation result.

In this way, cloud transformation can help to map an arbitrary and irregular distribution into the combination of some clouds with different scales according to a set of rules. The more clouds are in the mapping, the more precisely the data distribution is reflected and the less the error is.

6.3.2 Virtual Pan Concept Tree

Knowledge discovery is essential in data mining. Knowledge in different hierarchies is acquired due to different granularity in knowledge discovery. So, the virtual pan concept tree has to be established before setting the climbing-up strategy and algorithm.

The cloud model can be utilized to represent the qualitative concept so as to deal with the universal uncertainty in the concept. Concept set can be defined as being composed by the fundamental concepts in the universal set; in other words,

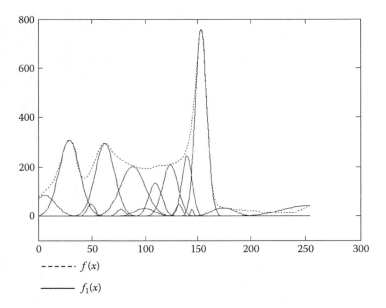

FIGURE 6.19 The data distribution function $f_i(x)$.

the concept set C can be expressed by $C\{C_1(Ex_1, En_1, He_1), C_2(Ex_2, En_2, He_2),...,$
$C_m(Ex_m, En_m, He_m)\}$, where $C_1, C_2, ..., C_m$ are the fundamental concepts represented
by cloud models. Different concept sets can be constructed at different abstract
levels, and layer by layer, the concept tree can be generated gradually.

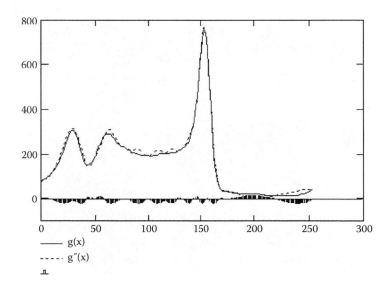

FIGURE 6.20 Experimental result.

The concept tree constructed by means of a cloud model is a kind of virtual pan tree which is of uncertainty. Rather than a common tree structure in which there is distinct and strict difference between the concepts in the same level, there is some overlapping in the pan tree. The attribute values may belong to different concepts at the same time, and the contribution to the concept by different concept values is different as well. In the pan tree, the climbing level of a concept is also flexible, i.e., either extracting in a bottom-up way, layer by layer, or directly jumping up to the level required. In other words, although the virtual pan concept tree constructed by the cloud model has a hierarchical relationship, it is not a static tree without invariance. And the granularities in the pan concept tree are continuous, which means that it is possible to climb to any level of granularity.

6.3.3 CLIMBING-UP STRATEGY AND ALGORITHMS

In Section 6.3.1, we have introduced the approach of cloud transformation, which automatically generates a series of fundamental concepts expressed by cloud models based on the distribution of data values in attribute domain and softly divides the universal set. In the process of knowledge discovery, such fundamental concepts can be considered as the leaf nodes in a pan concept tree. The concept of climbing-up is the process that may directly climb up the desired conceptual granularity or conceptual level based on the leaf node of the pan concept tree. The detailed strategy is as follows:

1. The conceptual granularity for climbing-up is given by the user before-hand, i.e., the climbing-up is carried out according to the concept number instructed by the user.
2. Automatic climbing-up. The conceptual granularity to climb up to is not pre-given. Instead, the data mining process will automatically propel the concept to an appropriate granularity, based on the situation of the pan concept tree and the related features in human cognitive psychology. From a psychological point of view, if the pan concept tree permits, the conceptual granularity of 7 ± 2 concepts will be most suitable to the psychological characters in human cognition.
3. Human–machine interactive climbing-up. The user will supervise the climbing-up process according to the mining result. In the whole process, the conceptual granularity climbs step-by-step and eventually reaches a satisfactory level.

In the conceptual climbing-up process based on pan concept tree, it is only necessary to explore the raw data set once or several times, and thus when the raw database is huge, this approach can reduce the I/O (Input/Output) cost efficiently. Specifically, in policies 1 and 2, the data set is only accessed once. In policy 3, several more visits to the data set are required, and the I/O access number is mainly dependent on the frequency of human–machine interaction. The climbing-up algorithms of the first two strategies are illustrated in detail hereafter. Policy 3 is composed of the iteration of strategy 1, so we omit that algorithm here.

Algorithm 6.3 ConceptRise1(the conceptual climbing-up algorithm based on policy 1)

Input: the leaf node set of the pan concept tree $C^{(1)}\{C_1(Ex_1,En_1,He_1),C_2(Ex_2,En_2,He_2),...,C_m(Ex_m,En_m,He_m)\}$
the concept number num given by the user, and $1\leq num < m$
Output: the conceptual level C^{lay} with concept number *num*
Steps:

BEGIN

    $C^{lay} = C^{(1)}$;

    WHILE ($|C^{lay}| > num$)

    {

        //Select the two closest concepts in the current conceptual level.

        $(C_x, C_y) = \text{min\_dist}(C^{lay})$;

        //Judge whether the two concepts can be combined

        If Is_Synthesize (C_x, C_y)

        {

            $C_z = \text{Synthesized\_Cloud}(C_x, C_y)$;

            //Combine the adjacent two concepts into a new synthesized concept.

            $lay = \text{del}(C^{lay},\{C_x,C_y\})$;

            $C^{lay} = C^{lay} \cup \{C_z\}$;

        }

        ELSE

            break;

        End IF

    }

END

In this algorithm, the function Synthesized_Cloud(C_x, C_y) combines the two neighboring concepts into one synthesized concept at a higher level. Because concept synthesization depends on the combination of cloud models, we briefly provide a combination operation of clouds.

Let $C_1(Ex_1, En_1, He_1)$ and $C_2(Ex_2, En_2, He_2)$ be the two neighboring cloud models. Then we have

$$Ex = \frac{Ex_1 En_1' + Ex_2 En_2'}{En_1' + En_2'}$$

$$En = En_1' + En_2'$$

$$He = \frac{He_1 En_1' + He_2 En_2'}{En_1' + En_2'}$$

En_1' and En_2' are calculated as follows.

Let $MEC_{C_1}(x)$ and $MEC_{C_2}(x)$ be the equations of the expectation curves for C_1 and C_2. Let

$$MEC_{C_1}'(x) = \begin{cases} MEC_{C_1}(x) & when\ MEC_{C_1}(x) \geq MEC_{C_2}(x) \\ 0 & otherwise \end{cases}$$

$$MEC_{C_2}'(x) = \begin{cases} MEC_{C_2}(x) & when\ MEC_{C_2}(x) > MEC_{C_1}(x) \\ 0 & otherwise \end{cases}$$

Then, we can get

$$En_1' = \frac{1}{\sqrt{2\pi}} \int_U MEC_{C_1}'(x)dx$$

$$En_2' = \frac{1}{\sqrt{2\pi}} \int_U MEC_{C_2}'(x)dx$$

From a geometric point of view, En_1 and En_2 are the products by $1/\sqrt{2\pi}$ and the areas covered by $MEC_{C_1}(x)$ and $MEC_{C_1}(x)$, respectively. En_1' and En_2' are the products by $1/\sqrt{2\pi}$ and the areas covered by $MEC_{C_1}'(x)$ and $MEC_{C_2}'(x)$, respectively. $MEC_{C_1}'(x)$ and $MEC_{C_2}'(x)$ are the nonoverlapped parts by $MEC_{C_1}(x)$ and $MEC_{C_2}(x)$, and they are acquired by cutting at the interaction points of $MEC_{C_1}(x)$ and $MEC_{C_2}(x)$. As a result, En_1' and En_2' can be called the "cutting entropy." The entropy of the new cloud model C is the sum of the two cutting entropies. Its expectation and hyperentropy are the weighted averages with cutting entropies as the weights. Particularly, we have $En_1' = En_1 = En_2 = En_2'$ when the two combined clouds are the same.

The climbing-up algorithm of strategy 2 is mainly different from that of the strategy 1 in the selection of a conceptual level. From a psychological point of view, humans prefer to understand 7 ± 2 categories or concepts at a level. Taking this into consideration, in the determination of conceptual level to climb to, we can select a random number for a concept that takes 7 as the expectation and 1 as the variance. Obviously, the choice on a conceptual level should satisfy the detailed situation of the pan concept tree.

Algorithm 6.4 ConceptRise2(the conceptual climbing-up algorithm based on policy 2)

Input: the leaf node set of the pan concept tree $C^{(1)}\{C_1(Ex_1,En_1,He_1),C_2(Ex_2,$ $En_2,He_2),..., C_m(Ex_m,En_m,He_m)\}$
Output: the conceptual level C^{lay}
Steps:

BEGIN

$C^{lay} = C^{(1)}$;

//Generate a normally random number with expectation 7 and variance 1, and make it an integer.

$num = 0$;

WHILE ($num < 1$)

{

$num =$ Round (Rand norm(7,1));

}

WHILE ($|C^{lay}| > num$)

{

//Select the two concepts which are nearest in the current conceptual level.

$(C_x, C_y) =$ min_dist(C^{lay});

//Judge whether the two concepts can be combined

If Is_Synthesize(C_x, C_y)

{

//Combine the two concepts into a new synthesized concept.

$C_z =$ Synthesized_Cloud(C_x, C_y);

$lay =$ del($C^{lay},\{C_x, C_y\}$);

$C^{lay} = C^{lay} \cup \{C_z\}$;

}

ELSE

break;

End IF

}

END

Once the concept climbs to an appropriate conceptual granularity or conceptual level, the remaining problem is to determine at which concept in this conceptual level the attribute values are. There are two methods for solution: random determination and maximum determination. The first one calculates the membership values of the attribute value to all the concepts in the set, and randomly selects one from several concepts with large memberships. If the membership degree of this attribute value to a certain concept is large, the probability that the attribute value belongs to it is larger than the probability to the other concepts. Maximum determination considers the membership degrees of the attribute to all the concepts in the set, and selects the concept corresponding to the maximum value.

Let A be a quantitative value attribute, and $C\{C_1(Ex_1, En_1, He_1), C_2(Ex_2, En_2, He_2),..., C_m(Ex_m, En_m, He_m)\}$ be the concept set that A corresponds to at a certain conceptual granularity. For an arbitrary attribute value x, maximum determination can be represented by the chart in Figure 6.21. For each concept in C, calculate the membership of attribute value x to each concept based on the precondition cloud generators (please refer to Chapter 8 for details) $CG_1, CG_2,..., CG_m$. Denote them as $\mu_1, \mu_2,..., \mu_m$. If $\mu_i = \max_{k=1,2,...,m} \mu_k$, then x belongs to concept C_i. If $\mu_i = \mu_j = \max \mu_k$, x is classified into either C_i or C_j randomly. According to the property of cloud, $\mu_1, \mu_2,..., \mu_m$ are random numbers with stabilization trend, rather than fixed values. Hence, it is possible for the attribute values in the overlapping interval to be classified into different clouds. This phenomenon apparently fits the classification occasions in human thinking.

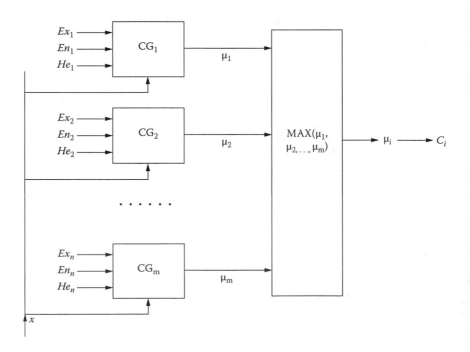

FIGURE 6.21 The theoretical chart of maximum determination.

Maximum determination is only a special case of random determination in implementation, so we only provide the algorithm of random determination.

Algorithm 6.5 CloudMap

Input: attribute value x

cloud-based concept set $C\{C_1(Ex_1, En_1, He_1), C_2(Ex_2, En_2, He_2),..., C_m(Ex_m, En_m, He_m)\}$

the number of concept candidates k

Output: *CONCEPTS* which is the concept that x is classified into

Steps:

BEGIN

$\quad CONCEPTS = \emptyset;$

$\quad$ FOR $i = 1$ TO m DO

$\quad$ {

$\quad\quad$ //Calculate the membership of x with respect to each concept by means of X-conditional cloud generator.

$\quad\quad \mu_i = X\_CLOUD(C_i, x);$

$\quad\quad CONCEPTS = CONCEPTS \cup \{(C_i, \mu_i)\};$

$\quad$ }

$\quad$ //Choose the k concepts at the front, based on the membership values.

$\quad CONCEPTS = MAX\_K(CONCEPTS, k);$

END

Obviously, when $k = 1$, Algorithm 6.5 is degenerated into maximum determination. Either maximum or random determination can obtain the membership degree of a certain attribute value to an arbitrary concept set. Classical classification approaches can only figure out an invariant concept for one attribute value, while the two cloud-based approaches can provide random concepts in some distribution. The main difference between the two cloud-based approaches lies in that the first one is more random and it will determine random concepts at any circumstance, while the latter is less random and the random occasion only exists at the overlapping area of two clouds.

For validating the effectiveness of the aforementioned thoughts in conceptual climbing-up and soft division, we apply the algorithms to the spatial database related to Chinese geography and economy. What we are interested in is the relationship between the geographical information and economical situation. Based on a small quantity of practical data, we obtain a large quantity of simulated data by means of random number generation. There are 10,000 records, and the properties are location x, y, altitude, density of road net, distance from the ocean, annual income per capita.

TABLE 6.1
Database of the Chinese Geography and Economical Situation

x	y	Altitude	Density of Road Net/ (m/km²)	Distance to the Ocean/ km	Annual Income per Capita/ Yuan
1091708.29	2420920.22	27.82	950.06	19.33	16000
349979.58	1450967.29	200.41	916.18	60.06	18000
1038667.52	1992814.97	51.97	848.49	24.51	17000
549675.77	3333817.10	29.82	1049.66	149.24	12000
1224839.09	3828302.91	187.72	899.34	458.45	8000
102736.67	3447929.21	2300.30	485.09	581.90	7500
−562917.30	2877368.66	3503.85	460.90	1439.41	5600
−838688.23	2972462.09	4297.27	402.57	1619.54	4800
−1818150.51	3904377.65	3603.35	349.92	2590.17	4900
−1979809.33	3676153.43	3501.82	178.71	2700.18	3800
292923.52	2706200.50	69.83	911.39	538.71	8200
131264.70	2430429.57	86.35	398.55	762.52	4200
−1865697.22	2363864.17	6202.52	280.81	2200.32	4800
−1780113.14	2496994.96	5897.91	168.97	2098.59	3700
292923.52	1897906.39	208.59	792.15	720.79	8100
435563.67	2183186.66	175.14	581.12	698.01	5500
...	...	...	...	...	...

The total data quantity is 600 KB. Location x, y are the rectangular coordinates, which are obtained by projective transformation of the geographical coordinates (longitude and latitude). The six attributes are all quantitative, and the density of road net is expressed by the length of road in every km^2. Table 6.1 shows part of the experimental data.

Obviously, it is difficult to discover the regularity inside these data if they are directly exploited in the process of data mining. Hence, we firstly make the cloud transformation to discretize the continuous attributes, and raise the fundamental concepts onto an appropriate conceptual level. Thereafter, we employ the maximum determination to softly divide the raw data set. In detail, the attributes x and y are combined as one linguistic variable "location," and define eight two-dimensional concepts or linguistic values for this variable: "southwest," "northeast," "north to east," "southeast," "northwest," "north," "south," and "middle." Due to the irregular shape of a Chinese map, we manually set the numerical character value for the eight cloud models representative of "location," as shown in Table 6.2. The attributes other than location are considered one-dimensional linguistic variables, and three concepts or linguistic values are defined for each. The aforementioned approaches, such as attribute discretization and concept climbing-up are carried out in this step. Altitude, density of road network, and annual income per capita are represented by "low," "middle," and "high." The distance to the ocean is represented by "near," "middle," and "far." The concept of "low" and "near" is shown by the half-decreasing cloud,

TABLE 6.2
The Numerical Characteristics of the Two-Dimensional Cloud Model Representing "Location"

Linguistic Value	Ex	Ey	Enx	Eny	θ
Southeast	612352	1690355	536037	134515	49.6
North to east	680245	3084104	225304	202876	0
Northeast	1367016	3901125	339692	157973	52.9
North	319098	3622864	443097	121059	35.8
Northwest	−1252779	3232115	703410	257936	−34.4
Middle	336859	2462458	266114	149601	−9
Southwest	−1640568	2300169	816926	266968	−37.2
South	−24288	1944419	225827	168074	−2

while "high" and "far" are illustrated by the half-rising cloud. There is partial overlapping by the neighboring cloud models.

Table 6.3 is the attribute table after soft division on the raw attribute values based on the concept set. Due to the uncertainty of model-based soft division, the percentage column may vary a little at different times. In Table 6.3, the percentage

TABLE 6.3
The Attribute Table after Soft Division

Location	Altitude	Density of Road Net	Distance to the Ocean	Annual Income per Capita	Percentage (%)
Southeast	middle	high	near	high	4
Southeast	middle	high	near	middle	2
Southeast	low	high	near	high	8
Southwest	high	low	far	low	12
Southwest	high	low	far	middle	3
South	middle	high	middle	middle	4
South	low	high	middle	high	2
South	low	high	middle	middle	6
Northwest	middle	low	far	low	8
Northwest	middle	low	far	middle	2
Northwest	high	low	far	low	5
Middle	middle	high	middle	middle	5
Middle	low	high	middle	middle	6
Northeast	low	high	middle	middle	9
Northeast	low	high	near	high	1
Northeast	middle	low	far	low	3
North to east	low	high	near	high	8
North to east	low	high	near	middle	2
North	middle	middle	middle	middle	7
North	middle	middle	far	middle	3

is the average of the results by several soft divisions. The computational cost is apparently reduced after the division, and the internal relationship is much reflected.

6.4 KNOWLEDGE DISCOVERY STATE SPACE

As we all know, to switch up and down to different granularities is a powerful ability of human thinking in problem solving. The process of human cognition and thinking actually is the transformation process of concepts at different granularities and levels, i.e., the transition of discovery state from one relatively stable state to another.

Data mining is the simulation of human cognition and thinking. The data in a specific problem or environment is the accumulation of quantitative states, from which, however, regularity and order may be hidden. By means of data mining, we can discover the regularity, order, correlation, and deviation embedded in the disordered, irregular data, and further achieve the data induction and integration at different abstract levels, such as the micro-level, middle-level, and macro-level. Currently, there are two primary issues in the research of data mining. First, how to formally describe the transformation of discovery states from data to concept, and then to rules in human cognition. Secondly how to formally describe the induction and reduction process of knowledge from the fine to the rough granularity. These issues are the fundamental problems in AI research as well.

For the above problems, we can refer to the multiscale, multilevel, and multi-granularity properties of physical spaces to give the basic idea of the discovery state space in data mining, i.e., the discovery state space also is a multiscale, multilevel, and multigranularity state space, in which each state is representative of a relatively stable knowledge formation in the process of data mining, and the overall data mining process corresponds to a transformation from one state space to others. Thus, it is necessary to make clear first the means of raw state space, feature space, and concept space.

6.4.1 THREE KINDS OF STATE SPACES

Raw data space is a space domain to analyze the raw data set. It is the initial space of data mining, as the basis of knowledge discovery. For a given raw data set with m objects, in which each object can be a tuple or record in a database, let $x_1, x_2, \ldots, x_n$ be the measure values of the n attributes of each object. Since the measure values belong to the same object, they should be considered as a whole and be abstract as an n-dimensional vector $x = (x_1, x_2, \ldots, x_n)^T$. Thus, all possible values of vector x can construct an n-dimensional raw data space, denoted as Ω^n and each object can be mapped as a data point in space. The distribution of m objects in this n-dimensional data space can exactly reflect the whole properties of the raw data set.

Considering that the raw data space usually has noisy, error, redundant, or even false data, it will be difficult to obtain a satisfactory result to directly mine in raw data space. More importantly, are these n properties equally important for the knowledge to be discovered? Are there any noisy and redundant properties? All these problems obviously will significantly affect the final result, so space transformation or compression of the raw data space is required. With the precondition of retaining significant data information, the objects in raw data space are mapped as the data points in lower-dimensional or higher-dimensional space, which can better reflect the intrinsic property of raw data distribution in some aspects. Mining in feature space can improve the correctness and understandability of the discovery operation effectively as well as the performance of the data mining process. As a result, in practice, data mining usually takes feature space as the working space, and raw data space is only used to generate interesting feature spaces by means of space transformation.

Concept, as the basic unit of cognition, is measured by granularity. For each attribute or dimension of feature space, all simple concepts covering the whole attribute can be raised to form a larger concept at higher granularity. The relationship of concepts in different dimensions further form the concept space and the relationship always can be represented as a space state or knowledge state. Since simple concepts in the same attribute category can be expressed at different granularities, the relationship of concepts in different dimensions and granularities form different states in concept space, i.e., multiple knowledge states.

The transformations from raw data space to feature data space and then to concept space actually accomplish the significant data reduction stage, and thereafter we no longer have to care about the distribution of raw data.

6.4.2 STATE SPACE TRANSFORMATION

Obviously, there are two kinds of state space transformations in data mining: the transformation from raw data space to feature data space, and the transformation from feature data space to concept space, as illustrated in Figure 6.22.

Particularly, in case the quality of raw data is good enough, there can be direct transformation from raw data space to concept space. According to the demand for interactive mining, it is also possible to transform from concept space back to raw data space or feature space.

The transformation from raw data space to feature space is mainly involved with feature extraction and selection, also called "dimensional reduction," which means that, without loss of significant information, the high-dimensional data is transformed into a low-dimensional feature space, that is the most representative of the structure of data distribution. Common dimensional reduction approaches include principle component analysis (PCA), singular value decomposition (SVD), and multidimensional scaling (MDS), etc. The basic idea of the above dimensional reduction approaches is to extract subspace by coordinate transformation in which the data has better distribution property. Besides, considering that large data sets in practical applications usually include many noisy features, the selection of feature subset is also an effective approach of dimensional reduction. Nevertheless, it is explicit that the mapping from data space to feature space is essentially a one-to-multiple mapping. Therefore, different dimensional reduction approaches will generate different feature spaces, and consequently result in different concept spaces and discovering different knowledge states. Of course, this is not contradictory with the mechanism of human cognition, since feature selection forms different views of knowledge discovery, just as the projections of light from different angles onto the same object can display different scenes, although they have their own blind areas.

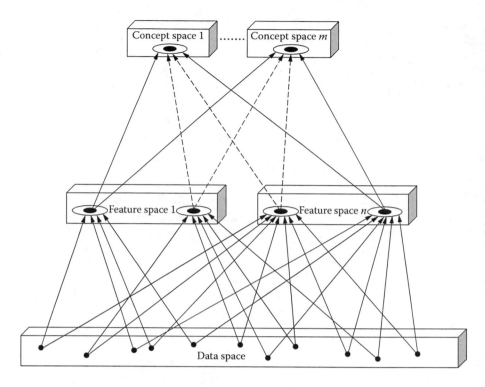

FIGURE 6.22 State space transformations.

The transformation from feature space to concept space is usually related to three issues: the discretization of continuous attribute and the formation of concept and pan concept tree, clustering and classification, and concept association in different attribute categories at different granularities. The first issue can be dealt with by the cloud model, which has been mentioned in Section 6.3. Second, clustering and classification is a fundamental problem in all data mining approaches, and even can be considered as a basic problem of the whole science, which will be discussed in detail in Chapter 7. As for the third issue, there are numerous concept associations in different attribute categories at different granularities, which usually is closely related to the discovery tasks, user background knowledge and related commonsense knowledge. Because of the fact that data mining is application-oriented, the discovered results may be rubbish knowledge, e.g., the association of diaper and beer, or well-known commonsense knowledge, if there are not any constraints given before. The valuable knowledge is always obtained by interactive exploration and verification during the process of data mining, which involves both human and machine.

In conclusion, inspired by the state space and state transformation in physics, we form the framework of discovery state space and space transformation, in which data field and cloud model have become important tools.

6.4.3 MAJOR OPERATIONS IN STATE SPACE TRANSFORMATION

Rather than focusing on the strategy of deductive logic in previous AI research, the physical approach for knowledge discovery with uncertainty focuses on the knowledge extraction process from the individual to the common, and from the sensational to the rational. This approach takes induction as essence, discovery state space as the framework, and data field and cloud model as significant tools. By applying various approaches including induction, analogy, association, false proof, and deduction, it discovers knowledge from the database, and verifies the discovered knowledge again in the database. Here we set up the general framework of the knowledge generation system based on relational database by means of discovery state space.[14]

Figure 6.23 demonstrates the framework of knowledge generation system. For a given discovery task, the system first analyzes the task, searches the database according to the data dictionary, and collects and preprocesses the related data. The preprocessed data will be transformed into discovery state space, i.e., transformations from raw data space to feature data space and from feature data space to concept space. In this step, the data is reduced and the concept associations are discovered. The concept associations in different attribute categories and at different granularities will be induced into the natural states in concept space, i.e., the knowledge states. Considering the uncertainty in knowledge discovery due to the incomplete induction, cloud model may be used to generate appropriate linguistic values and form the qualitative representation of the discovered knowledge, in which the uncertainty in discovered knowledge can be described. Furthermore, the discovered knowledge can be verified by means of false proof and deduction. The proved knowledge or rules can also be transformed into quantitative data by cloud model, and a virtual database

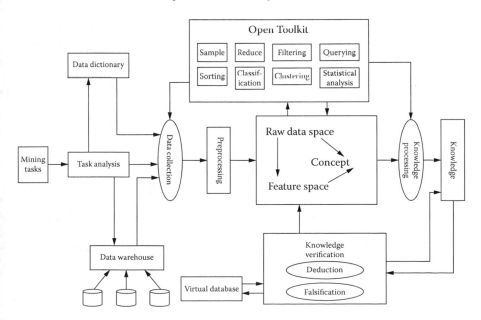

FIGURE 6.23 A framework of knowledge generation system based on relational databases.

can be constructed for further comparison and learning. On the other hand, the verification result may be exploited to modify the strategy or mechanism of space transformation in discovery state space, and regenerate new knowledge.

During the implementation, we emphasize the interactive process by human and machine, as well as the visualization for interacting. Rather than unsupervised discovery or supervised discovery with fixed mode, we consider the relationship between human and machine as a partnership during the process of knowledge discovery. The user's commonsense and background knowledge are combined in the interactive process, and the relationship between data and concepts is illustrated in way of a picture, chart, and field. Moreover, the object-oriented technology, various developed tools, and open toolbox are also compatible methods in data mining.

REFERENCES

1. Zezong Xi, *The Five Major Milestones of Human Cognitive Evolution*, Tsinghua University Press, Beijing, 2000.
2. Deyi Li, Wenyan Gan, and Luying Liu, Artificial Intelligence and Cognitive Physics, In: *Proceedings of the 10th Annual Conference of Chinese Association of Artificial Intelligence (CAAI-10)*, Guangzhou, China, 2003.
3. Yizhang Chen, The Strategy of the Brain Science Research, In: Tao Zhang, ed., *The Frontier and Future of Science*, pp. 36–47, Science Press, Beijing, 1998.
4. Friederich Engels, *Dialectics of Nature*, People's Publishing House, Beijing, 1971.
5. Wenyan Gan, Study on Clustering Problem for Data Mining Foundations, Ph.D. thesis, PLA University of Science and Technology, Nanjing, 2003.
6. Huijun L., Face Recognition Based on Data Field, Master's degree thesis, PLA University of Science and Technology, Nanjing, 2002.
7. Wenyan Gan and Deyi Li, Optimal choice of parameters for a density-based clustering algorithm, In: *The 19th International Conference on Rough Sets, Fuzzy Sets, Data Mining and Granular Computing (RSFDGrC 2003)*, Chongqing, China, 2003.
8. Wenyan Gan and Deyi Li, Hierarchical clustering based on kernel density estimation, *Journal of System Simulation*, Vol. 2, pp. 302–306, 2004.
9. S. Guha, R. Rastogi, and K. Shim, CURE: an efficient clustering algorithm for large databases, In: *Proceedings of the 1998 ACM SIGMOD International Conference on Management of Data*, Seattle, WA, 1998.
10. Rong Jiang, Deyi Li, and Jianhua Fan, Automatic generation of pan-concept-tree on numerical data, *Chinese Journal of Computers*, Vol. 23, No. 5, pp. 471–477, 2000.
11. Rong Jiang, Research and Applications of Data Mining in Time Sequence, Ph.D. thesis, PLA University of Science and Technology, Nanjing, 2000.
12. Yi Du, Research and Applications of Association Rules in Data Mining, Ph.D. thesis, PLA University of Science and Technology, Nanjing, 2000.
13. Kaichang Di, The Theory and Methods of Spatial Data Mining and Knowledge Discovery, Ph.D. thesis, Wuhan Technical University of Surveying and Mapping, Wuhan, 1999.
14. Deyi Li, The discovery state space theory, *Mini-Micro Systems*, Vol. 15, No. 11, pp. 1–6, 1994.

7 Data Mining for Discovering Knowledge with Uncertainty

In the cognitive physics approach, a concept is represented in terms of a physical atom model, the interactions between objects are expressed by means of field, and the hierarchical structure is represented by means of granularity. Meanwhile, the state transformation in the discovery state space is applied to carry out the induction and reduction from original data space to feature space and further to concept space. In concept space, the natural states, which are multiscaled and multigranular, correspond to multiple knowledge states, i.e., the knowledge and mode to be discovered.

Of course, the idea above only gives out the basic framework of data mining, and the methodologies and tools should be studied in more details. In this process, it is extremely necessary to understand the multiple kinds of uncertainties in data mining.

7.1 UNCERTAINTY IN DATA MINING

7.1.1 DATA MINING AND KNOWLEDGE DISCOVERY

Data mining, as commonly understood, is the process of extracting hidden information and knowledge that are previously unknown and potentially useful, out of a large quantity of data that is incomplete, fuzzy, and noisy. The original data is considered as the source of knowledge, like mining in mineral stones. The original data may be structural, such as the data in relational database, it may be semi-structural, such as text, graph and image data, and it may even be of different structures. The methodologies in knowledge discovery can be either mathematical or nonmathematical, and they can be either deduction or induction. The discovered knowledge may be applied to information management, query optimization, decision support, and process control, etc., and it can be used for data self-maintenance as well.

It is necessary to point out that all the discovered knowledge is relative, confined by some specific preconditions and constraints and oriented to some specific fields. Data mining is also a repeatedly interactive process between human and machine. Based on the discovery task and a user's background knowledge, the user will conduct research on data to adopt and design appropriate mining tools at first step for automatic knowledge extraction. Thereafter, the data will be modified and the mining tools will be adjusted according to the mining result, so as to obtain better or different results. These two steps will iterate until the satisfactory results are generated. In general, the process of data mining and knowledge discovery consists of the following basic steps:

1. The description of discovery task: describes and determines the mining task according to the background knowledge of the user and the data property of the application field.
2. Data collection: selects all the data set related to the discovery task.
3. Data preprocessing: checks the integrity and consistency of the data, filters out noise, corrects the mistake, recovers the lost data, and transforms the data, including a large quantity of attributes or features, to a low-dimensional space, which is the most representative of the internal relationship within the data.
4. Data mining: designs and adopts effective data mining algorithms and develops implementation according to the discovery task.
5. Explanation and evaluation: explains the discovered knowledge and its correctness, verifies and evaluates the effectiveness of the knowledge, the consistency with the initial data, and the novelty for the user.

Of all the five steps, data mining is the most important and significant step. Through 10 years of research, although a lot of effective methodologies and tools in data mining have been developed, such as recursive analysis, discriminate analysis, learning from demonstration, genetic algorithm, neural networks, multidimensional data analysis, and attribute-oriented inductive method, etc., there is still a large gap between the performance of the existing methodologies and the expectation of the public, i.e., the expectation of automation and intelligentization in the data mining process, and the expectation of objectiveness, preciseness, and invariance of the discovered knowledge. There are many reasons for this gap; however, one significant reason lies in that people have neglected the uncertainty in the process of data mining and the uncertainty of the discovered knowledge.

7.1.2 Uncertainty in Data Mining Process

The majority of data mining tasks are oriented to some specific field for application. In the description and determination of a mining task, the specialized knowledge and background are required for the users. For example, according to his or her background and experience, the user can preset a group of variables or relational forms as the initial assumption for the unknown relationship in data mining, so that the efficiency in the mining process is enhanced. Due to the fact that the common-sense knowledge and the background knowledge of the user are uncertain, the initial description of the task contains uncertainty as well.

In the data collection step, different users may be interested in the knowledge in different hierarchies and of different sorts. It is difficult to determine which original data should be collected. Even for the same user, the collection of necessary data is not fixed because the category and property of the knowledge to be discovered are unforeseeable.

In the data preprocessing step, the handling of null data, measurement error, and noisy data is influential to the eventual result as well. The subsequent data mining process is essentially an exploratory data analysis process, whose only purpose is to discover the hidden knowledge and patterns within data. If the preprocess technique cannot obtain high quality data, the old adage "garbage-in-garbage-out" applies. Moreover, in the large-scale practical data set, there exist a lot of trivial or redundant features, which will reduce the effectiveness, correctness, and understandability of the mining result. Uncertainties exist in the way to recover the lost data, correct errors, filter out noises, and select the subset of significant features. Uncertainties are inevitable, especially in the case where the property of the knowledge to be discovered is unknown.

A key step in data mining is to design, adopt, and implement effective algorithms based on the mining task. Generally speaking, the majority of data mining algorithms are based on methodologies of machining learning, pattern recognition, statistical analysis, and so on. Extraction of knowledge and patterns is conducted from different perspectives. When the user is not clear on the properties of the knowledge that he/she is interested in, the adoption of mining algorithms will be uncertain. With the development in technologies of databases and networks, the gap between the abilities of data collection, organization and storage, and the ability of data analysis is gradually enlarged. It may be true that the data set itself is not valuable in the original state, and the knowledge extracted from the data and implemented in practice is something valuable. However, the scale and dimensions of the data is overwhelmingly large for the majority of mining algorithms nowadays. In the extreme case, either the spatial cost or the temporal cost will make infeasible the mining in the giant data set. The effective reduction approach is only operated on the sample set, but uncertainty is introduced due to the fact that different sampling methods will end up with different sample sets. Moreover, the majority of mining algorithms present demand for preset parameters by the user, and the effectiveness of the mining result is largely dependent on the valid initialization of the parameters. However, in applications, the data set is usually giant, and the distributive features are unknown, so it is extremely difficult to preset parameters by the user. One practical way is to select some parameters based on the user's understanding of the task and his/her limited background knowledge. Consequentially, the mining result will be uncertain.

The eventual aim of data mining is to provide the user with novel, potentially useful knowledge and modes. Obviously, it is significant for the user to understand and evaluate the acquired knowledge quickly and precisely. It is shown by the research in cognitive psychology that neither a long numerical result nor a too concise inductive knowledge will be acceptable for the user. As a result, it is necessary to properly induce and reduce the acquired knowledge, and describe it in the way that can be easily understood, such as visualized method and natural language expression. It is true that the internal relationship in the data is expressed and directed in the visualized method; however, in the application of high-dimensional knowledge expressions, it cannot be employed. The other approach, the natural language method, is familiar to humans because it is the accustomed way of thinking. The fundamental unit in this method is linguistic value, related to the qualitative concept, which is the basic unit in human thought. Due to the fact that there are internal uncertainties in the qualitative concepts, the main problem in the knowledge explanation by means of natural languages lies in the way to describe the uncertainties in qualitative concepts and how to implement the uncertainty transformation from quantitative data to qualitative concepts. Moreover, there should be a balance between the parsimony and the preciseness of the mining result. Many objective measurements for evaluation have been proposed, such as the evaluation of compactness and divisibility measure of the clustered knowledge, and the evaluation of support and confidence in association knowledge; however, the evaluation criteria, such as novelty and the ability for implementation, depend greatly on the background knowledge and the degree to which the user is interested in such knowledge. As a result, the step of knowledge explanation and evaluation includes uncertainties as well.

7.1.3 Uncertainty in Discovered Knowledge

In fact, there are uncertainties not only in the process of data mining, but also in the discovered knowledge. The research subjects in data mining are mainly the knowledge of intercommunity and the knowledge of outlier hidden in a large quantity of data. They consist of the following types:

1. Generalization: the general description knowledge representative of the class features. It detects the characterizing and generalized knowledge at the middle scale and macro-scale level, based on the micro-feature of the data. It is also the recapitulation, refinement, and abstraction of the data.
2. Classification and clustering: reflects the convergent mode or classifies all the objects according to its attributes. Classification is applied to describe the known data classes or models (functions) of concepts, so as to classify the objects with unknown class index by the known models. Clustering knowledge is the descriptive knowledge that divides a group of data into a series of meaningful subsets according to the attributes.
3. Association: reflects the dependence between one event and another, and it is also called "dependency relationship."
4. Prediction: predicts the data in the future, based on past and current data. This can be considered as the association with temporal information as the key attribute.
5. Outlier: describes the difference and some exceptions, revealing the exceptional phenomena, such as special samples deviated from the standard type, or the deviated value other than the clustered classes, etc.

Although different features exist within the aforementioned types of knowledge, there is an internal relationship as well. For instance, classification and clustering is the precondition for the detection of generalization, association, and outlier in a data mining system. It may realize the effective generalization and description. A more important aspect is that after partition of a similar subset, if data mining tools, such as attribute-oriented induction, are applied, significant rules and modes can be detected based on classification and clustering. Moreover, classification and clustering are widely applied in the detection of association and serial knowledge.

Many association knowledge discovery systems employ classification and clustering for the fundamental tasks, such as the discretization of numerical attributes, automatic generation of conceptual hierarchies, and searching of association rules. Consequently, data mining is substantially the cognitive process in which knowledge of intercommunity and outlier is extracted from one common data source. Knowledge of intercommunity and outlier are relative because the knowledge of intercommunity in one granular level may turn to be the knowledge of outlier in another granular level, and vice versa. In conclusion, the discovered knowledge is of relativity.

7.2 CLASSIFICATION AND CLUSTERING WITH UNCERTAINTY

Classification and clustering is one of the most fundamental and most significant activities in the human social, producing, and research activities. A basic ability for humans to understand the world is to distinguish different objects and classify them according to the similarities within them.

Classification is to induce the connotation of the concept according to its given extension, i.e., to describe and distinguish the models or the classification functions so as to classify objects with unknown class index by means of these models and functions. The induced models and functions are based on the analysis of the training data set with known class indices, so it is a supervised learning method.

As a supervised learning method, classification contains uncertainties. There are occasions that the object to be classified is adjacent to the center of two classes. Besides, if the number of training data is not large enough, the learning result will probably not be reflective of the overall structure of the data set. Hence, there will be a lot of uncertain problems in the classification of new data.

Clustering is very different from classification in that it acquires neither connotation nor extension of the concept. The number and structure of the classes are not predetermined as well. This approach is also called "unsupervised learning." Clustering detects the structure of the class according to the distributive features. The given objects of extension will converge to the connotation of the related concept to minimize the similarity between classes and maximize the similarity within each class.

Compared with classification, the problem of clustering involves more uncertainties. For a given data set, the number of clustering classes and the center of each class are dependent not only on the distribution of data, but also on the application background and objectives of clustering. According to the research in cognitive psychology, people would like to divide the data into 7 ± 2 classes at a certain level. If there are too many or too few classes, the granularity will be modified, and clustering will be redone at a higher or lower level. So the clustering result is uncertain, and the word "correctness" is not strictly applicable in clustering. Moreover, generally there is no training set and class index in clustering tasks. Every existing object contributes to the clustering result. Hence, clustering is more complex, more uncertain than classification, and it turns out to be an active and challenging research direction.

7.2.1 CLOUD CLASSIFICATION

Many classification approaches have been proposed for classification in data mining, such as decision tree induction, Bayes classification, neural networks, genetic algorithm, and so on. Within them, decision tree induction is the most classical approach.

Based on the training set, decision tree induction induces the classification rules in the form of decision tree from a group of samples which have been already classified. In detail, this approach is top-down recursive. The attribute values in the internal nodes are compared, and according to the different attribute values, the downward branch at that particular node will be determined. Conclusion will be drawn at the leaf node. In a decision tree, leaf nodes represent the classes to be classified into, non-leaf nodes represent the test attribute or the attribute group, and the path from the root to a leaf node corresponds to a classification rule. The merit of this approach is that users wouldn't need too much background knowledge, so it is widely employed in fields of medicine, gaming, and business. And it even becomes the foundation of some induction systems of business rules.

A. The limitation of commonly used approaches based on decision tree induction, such as ID3.

In the approach of decision tree induction, ID3 is the most representative algorithm.[1] According to this algorithm, the complexity of the decision tree is greatly related to the information content that it conveys. For minimization of the test number, the decision tree is constructed by heuristic approach based on information theory, i.e., at each non-leaf node, to select the attribute with the highest information gain as the test attribute for the current node. This approach can minimize the average test number for classifying one object. In the end, a simple tree though not the simplest, will be generated.

In ID3, the key of tree construction lies in the measurement of information gain of the tested attribute. Let D be a data set containing n data objects. Assume that there are m distinct classes $C_i(i = 1, 2,...,m)$. Let n_i be the object number in the class C_i. Then the average information content for classifying a given object can be computed as

$$I(n_1,n_2,...,n_m) = -\sum_{i=1}^{m} p_i\log_2(p_i)$$

where, $p_i = n_i/n$ represents the probability of the case that an arbitrary object belongs to the class C_i.

Let A be the attribute chosen as the test attribute, and $\{a_1,a_2,...,a_k\}$ be k distinct values of A. The data set D can be divided into k subsets $S_i(i = 1,2,...,k)$ according to A, and S_i only contains the objects where $A = a_i$. Let $s_{ij}(i = 1, 2,...,m, j = 1, 2,...,k)$ be the number of samples inclusive of C_i in the subset S_j. Then after the classification base on A, the average information content for classifying a given object can be computed by

$$E(A) = -\sum_{j=1}^{k} \frac{s_{1j} + s_{2j} + \cdots + s_{mj}}{n} I(s_{1j}, s_{2j},...,s_{mj})$$

where $I(s_{1i}, s_{2i},...,s_{mi}) = -\sum_{i=1}^{m} p_{ij}\log_2(p_{ij})$ and $p_{ij} = s_{ij}/|S_j|$, $|S_j| = s_{1j} + s_{2j} + \cdots + s_{mj}$.

Based on this, the information gain on the attribute A is

$$\text{Gain}(A) = I(n_1, n_2, \ldots, n_m) - E(A)$$

Once the information gains are obtained for all the attributes, the algorithm will select the attribute with the highest gain as the test attribute for the current node, create one branch for every value of the attribute, and divide the data set accordingly. The algorithm operates recursively until all the data is classified or no attribute is left for data separation. Here we provide the concrete algorithm for decision tree generation according to a given training set.

Algorithm 7.1 Generate_DecisionTree

Input: training data set represented by discrete attribute: *samples*; set of candidates attribute: *attribute_list*
Output: a decision tree: *decision_tree*
Steps:

BEGIN

Create the current node N;

If (*attribute_list* is non empty) and (*samples* is non empty)

{

If(*samples* $\subseteq$ class C)

Return N as a leaf node, and denote it as class C;

End if

Select the attribute *test_attribute* with the highest information gain in *attribute_list* to denote the node N;

For every attribute value a in *test_attribute*

{

Create a branch with condition *test_attribute* = a from the node N;

attribute_list = *attribute_list*/{*test_attribute*};

//*s* is a partition of samples, i.e. the subset of samples with *test_attribute* = a

$s = \{x \in samples | x.test\_attribute = a\}$;

Generate_DecisionTree(*s*, *attribute_list*);

}

}

Else

Return N as a leaf node, and index it as the class with the largest sample number in the original training set.

End if

END

The limitation of this algorithm is that in the construction of the tree, all the attributes are required to be either category attribute or discrete attribute. However, in a practical data base there are large quantities of numerical attributes. A major challenge to ID3 and the related algorithms lies in the way to extend the tree-representative classification rules to those numerical attributes. Improved algorithms such as C4.5/C5.0 introduce interval approach to divide the continuous attributes,[2] so as to extend the classified attribute to numerical attributes. However, there are still problems in such a method with the most critical being the compulsory partition neglecting the internal feature of data distribution.

Here we illustrate the decision tree by inductive learning on the test data, called "sonar.data," using C5.0 algorithm. sonar.data is a data set of sonar signals[3] from Rulequest Research Center. It consists of 200 samples, 60 numerical attributes in [0, 1]. They are classified into two classes: rock sonar signals (R) and mental cylinder sonar signals (M). From the decision tree by the algorithm and the inductive rules, it can be seen that there are compulsory partition points, such as 0.168, 0.0392, etc., the structure of the decision tree is complicated, and the inductive rules are highly intricate. Thus it is difficult to be implemented in real application.

```
C5.0 INDUCTION SYSTEM [Release 1.10]

------------------------------------------------------------

Read 200 cases (60 attributes) from sonar.data


Decision tree:

------------------------------------------------------------

a10 <= 0.168:

:... a00 > 0.0392: M (7.0/1.0)

:      a00 <= 0.0392:

:      :...a03 <= 0.0539: R (58.0/2.0)

:            a03 > 0.0539:

:                :...a46 <= 0.0949: R (3.0)

:                     a46 > 0.0949: M (6.0)

a10 > 0.168:

:...a44 > 0.2611: M (34.0)

      a44 <= 0.2611: ….

   :  ….

------------------------------------------------------------
```

```
Extracted rules:

-----------------------------------------------

Rule 1:  (cover 6)

             a00  <=  0.0392

             a03  >  0.0539

             a10  <=  0.168

             a46  >  0.0949

   -> class  M   [0.875]


Rule 2:  (cover 7)

             a00  >  0.0392

             a10  <=  0.168

   -> class  M   [0.778]


Rule 3:  (cover 126)

             a10  >  0.168

   -> class  M   [0.703]
   :
```

B.   Cloud classification

The decision tree can be constructed by means of cloud-based approach[4] to solve problems in the aforementioned method. As a first step, classification complexity (*CC*) is introduced to measure the complexity in a classification problem.

Let *D* be a data set containing *n* attributes $A_i (i = 1, 2,...,n)$, and $|A_i|$ be the number of values which A_i can be in the universal set. The classification complexity is

$$CC = \prod_{i=1}^{n} |A_i|$$

If there is a numerical attribute taking continuous values, *CC* will be infinity. Obviously for a classification problem with infinite classification complexity, the unique solution is to discretize the continuous attribute and transform it into a classification problem with low complexity, which is described by category attributes.

According to the discussion in Chapter 6, Section 6.3.1, the width and number of subsets are given subjectively in traditional discretization approaches, e.g., interval method. The distributive situation is not considered, and the uncertainties in the extraction of qualitative concepts from continuous data are not reflected either. While in the discretization process by cloud transformation, a series of basic concepts represented by clouds can be automatically generated according to the distribution of data values. In this way, the universal set is divided "softly," and the result can be more similar to the construction way in human thinking. Thus the uncertainties within the transformation from quantitative values to qualitative concepts are reflected.

Cloud classification employs the concept of climbing-up technology based on pan concept tree so as to reduce the classification complexity. There are four basic steps:

1. Discretize each numerical attribute by means of cloud transformation algorithm to generate a series of basic concepts expressed by clouds.
2. According to the number of concepts instructed by the user, climb up each basic concept of numerical attribute to an appropriate conceptual level.
3. Based on the obtained concept set, softly divide the original value of each numerical attribute by means of maximum determination approach.
4. Construct the decision tree expressed in linguistic value according to ID3 algorithm.

Step 1 is referred to in Chapter 6, Section 6.3.1, and steps 2, 3, and 4 are demonstrated as follows.

Algorithm 7.2 CloudClassifier

Input: training data set D

attribute set *attribute_list* consisting $A_i(i = 1, 2,...,n)$

$C^1,... C^i,...$ //C^i is the basic concept set of numerical attribute A_i

$num^1,... num^i,...$ //num^i is the concept number of the numerical attribute A_i instructed by the user.

Output: a decision tree: *decision_tree*

Steps:

BEGIN

$D' = D$;

For each numerical attribute $A_i \in$ *attribute_list*

{

//Conceptually raise each attribute according to the concept number instructed by the user

$C^i = $ ConceptRise1(C^i, num^i);

}

//Scan the data set D', and extend the attribute value by means of maximum determination according to the concept set of the numerical attributes;

For each tuple t in D'

{

For each numerical attribute A_i in *attribute_list*

$A_i = \text{CloudMap}(A_i, C^i, 1)$;

}

decision_tree = Generate_DecisionTree(D', *attribute_list*);

END

C. Comparison of experimental results

The test is conducted on the data in sonar.data by the cloud classification, with a program implemented by Visual Basic. The result is shown as follows, within which each numerical attribute is divided into five qualitative concepts.

```
CloudClassifier Discovery Results

-----------------------------------------------------

Read 200 cases (60 attributes) from sonar.data


Decision tree:

------------------------------

a10 <= Normal

:... a00 > Very Small

:      a00 <- Very Small

:      :...a03 <=Small

:            a03 > Small

:                  :...a46 <= Small

:                        a46 > Small

a10 > Normal.......


Extracted rules:

Rule 1: (cover 8)
```

```
          a00 <= Very Small
          a03 > Small
          a10 <= Normal
          a46 > Small
      -> class M
```

```
  Rule 2: (cover 5)
            a00 > Very Small
            a10 <= Normal
      ->    class M   [0.778]
```

```
  Rule 3: (cover 20)
            a16 > Large
            a22 <= Very Large
            a40 <= Large
            a50 <= Very Small
      ->    class R
```

```
  :
```

```
  Rule 8: (cover 4)
            a24 <= Very Large
            a26 > Very Large
            a49 <= Very Small
            a50 > Very Small
      ->    class R
```

Obviously, the non-leaf nodes in the decision tree constructed by cloud classification are denoted by the linguistic values in expressions of clouds, and within them "very large," "large," "normal," "small," and "very small" are the five linguistic values. The inducted classification rules are relatively understandable. For evaluation of correctness and robustness of the decision tree constructed by cloud classification, we classify 1,000 new samples in sonar.data by C5.0 and CloudClassifier separately. Tables 7.1 and 7.2 illustrate the classification result.

TABLE 7.1
Classification Result with C5.0

Classification Result	Sample Number of Sonar Signal in Rock	Sample Number of Sonar Signal in Metal	Sample Number of False Classification
Class 1	12	654	12
Class 2	323	11	11
Total	335	665	23

It can been seen that the correctness of the decision tree constructed by cloud classification is higher. The combination of the cloud approach and the traditional classification approach may form a novel and more powerful classification approach.

7.2.2 CLUSTERING BASED ON DATA FIELD

Usually the clustering problem in data mining is motivated by efficiently processing large scale data sets. There are many urgent research problems, such as extendibility of clustering algorithms, clustering of complex shape, clustering in high-dimensional space, and expressions of the clustering result. A lot of clustering methods have been proposed up until now.

A. The limitation of classical clustering algorithms

Regarding the difference in the similarity measure and the evaluation criteria of clustering, the classical clustering approaches may be divided into partitioning methods, hierarchical methods, density-based methods, and grid-based methods, etc.

Let D be a data set including n objects, the basic thought in partitioning methods is as follows. For a given cluster number k and a distance-based object function F, divide the data set into k classes so as to optimize the fitness function. The clustering problem turns to be a searching problem that will optimize the fitness function in the giant solution space, if an appropriate fitness function is introduced to evaluate the clustering effectiveness. Due to the fact that optimization of the fitness function is substantially an NP (Non-deterministic Polynomial) complete problem, it is definitely

TABLE 7.2
Classification Result with CloudClassifier

Classification Result	Sample Number of Sonar Signal in Rock	Sample Number of Sonar Signal in Metal	Sample Number of False Classification
Class 1	6	660	6
Class 2	329	5	5
Total	335	665	11

infeasible to try every solution. Hence the local search-based recursive relocation approach is commonly employed. The merit of this approach is that it is simple and at least a local optimum will be guaranteed. However, it has the following short-comings as well:

1. The comparison between the convergent clustering result and the optimal clustering result (the global optimum of F) cannot be foreseen.
2. The convergent result will be affected by the initialization. Thus, although the partitioning method is simple, the clustering result is not satisfactory and there exists a so-called "bias toward spherical clusters," It is sensitive to noise and input sequence, and the cluster number has to be preinstructed by the user. Classical algorithms in this approach include K-means,[5] K-mediods,[6] CLARA,[7] and CLARANS,[7] etc.

The basic thought in a hierarchical method is to recursively group or separate the data, and divide the data set into nesting hierarchy-like structures or cluster spectrums. Its main merit is that the preinstructed cluster number is not required, and the multi-hierarchical clustering structure can be obtained at different granularities. Nevertheless, the temporal expense in computation is high, a terminating condition must be instructed by the user, and the step of grouping/separation of a class may not be cancelled once done. As a result, the false combination/splitting will lead to clustering result with low quality. Moreover, traditional hierarchical clustering algorithms, such as single-link and complete-link, employ chain distance to measure the similarity between classes, and the result will involve "bias toward spherical clusters" or "chain phenomenon." In the improved hierarchical algorithms, multiple clustering technologies are integrated to effectively enhance clustering quality and algorithm performance, but clustering results seriously depend on proper initialization. The classical algorithms involve BIRCH,[8] CURE,[9] ROCK,[10] and Chameleon,[11] etc.

A density-based method is proposed for data clustering with complex shapes. Each cluster corresponds to a relative dense region in the data distribution. Clustering is to separate the high-density connected regions that are isolated by low-density regions. In low-density region, noise and outlier data are inevitable. The main merit of this approach is that it can detect the cluster of an arbitrary shape with arbitrary scale, and it is able to deal with huge noise and outlier data. However, effectiveness of global density estimation depends on elaborate selection of some density parameters, and an appropriate noise threshold set by the user is required for the density based clustering expression, so the clustering quality is highly dependent on the selected parameters by the user. The classical algorithms of this sort contain DBSCAN,[12] OPTICS,[13] and DENCLUE,[14] etc.

A grid-based method takes clustering analysis by means of spatial partition. It divides the space into a finite number of grid units, generates a grid structure, and implements all the clustering operations on the grid network. Its main merit is that the processing time is independent on the number of objects, and it has good efficiency as well as extendability. Nevertheless, the clustering quality is dependent on the quantitative scale in grid partition. STING,[15] WaveCluster,[16] CLIQUE,[17] MAFIA,[18] and OptiGrid[19] are its representatives.

Through the analysis and comparison of the classical clustering algorithms, it can be seen that the main problems in the current clustering algorithms are as follows:

1. In real applications, the feature of data distribution is unforeseeable ahead of clustering analysis. The cluster might be spherical, slim, concave, nested, hollow, or in other arbitrarily complex shape and structure. Hence, the clustering algorithm should be able to detect the clusters in arbitrary shape, size, and density.
2. Almost all the clustering algorithms contain the parameters instructed by the user, such as the cluster number, density parameter, and noise threshold in the density-based method, and so on. These parameters determine the clustering result to a large extent. However, in real applications, the selection of optimized parameters depends on the concrete features of data distribution, in case there is not enough prior knowledge for the user except the huge data volume with high dimension, so it will be extremely difficult to set appropriate parameters.
3. Generally speaking, there exist thousands of features or properties in large-scale relational databases and transaction databases, while the classical clustering algorithms are mainly confined to low dimensional data set. The data distribution in high dimension is usually sparse and asymmetric, so the traditional algorithms will not be capable of dealing with high-dimensional problems to some extent. As a result, the clustering problem in high dimension is a challenge in the current research.
4. For applications with data mining, the information to be processed by clustering analysis is usually tremendous, and sometimes it will even reach tera- or petabytes. The operational time in dealing with such giant database is required to be predictable and acceptable by the user, so the temporal complexity usually may not be tolerable if it is exponential-like.
5. In a real database, there are large quantities of noise and outlier data. In some specific applications, it is more meaningful to detect exceptions than clusters, for example the detection of hostile behavior in E-commence can reduce the economical loss effectively. Consequently the ability of noise and outlier recognition is required for the clustering algorithm.

Moreover, there are problems in the understandability of clustering results, and the clustering ability in unstructured complex data, etc.

We propose a clustering method based on a data field to tackle these problems. It starts from the discovery state space, introduces the data field for description of the interaction and spatial distribution of the data objects, and implements the hierarchical partition based on the naturally nested structure of the equipotential lines/surfaces in the data potential field, and the self-organized feature in the data field.

B. Hierarchical clustering based on data potential field

In the detection of clustering knowledge, hierarchical clustering and density clustering are two important methods. The main advantage of the former lies in the resulting multi-hierarchy clustering structure at different granularities. The main advantage of the latter is that it is able to detect clusters in arbitrary shape and is also insensitive to noise. Thus the combination of their merits to generate clustering modes at different hierarchies has been a popular research topic.

Based on the topological structure of the data potential field, a hierarchical clustering algorithm based on the topology of the potential field[20] has been proposed. Its basic idea is to describe the interaction and spatial distribution of the data objects by means of data potential field, and treat the data objects circumscribed by each equipotential line/surface as a natural cluster, and consider the nested structure, consisting of distinct equipotential lines/surfaces, as the cluster spectrum. In this way, the clustering at different hierarchies can be carried out. Because of the fact that when the integral of the unit potential function is finite, the difference between the potential function of the data field and the probability density function will be a normalization constant. The nested topological structure formed by equipotential lines or surfaces can be view as the hierarchical partition of data in different densities. Consequently, this approach combines the merits of hierarchical clustering and density clustering. Before the detailed illustration on the hierarchical clustering algorithm based on the potential field topology, let's introduce a generalized density clustering algorithm DENCLUE.

1. The basic idea in DENCLUE

DENCLUE is a generalized clustering algorithm based on kernel density estimation. By means of different kernel functions, this algorithm can sum up density clustering algorithms such as DBSCAN, and by adjusting the window width σ of the kernel function, it can also reveal the internal hierarchical structure in data distribution.

Let $D = \{x_1, x_2, \ldots, x_n\}$ be a data set consisting of n objects in space Ω, DENCLUE algorithm can be described as follows:

a. The kernel estimation on global density function. $\forall x \in \Omega$, the probability density function can be estimated as

$$f^D(x) = \frac{1}{n} \sum_{i=1}^{n} K\left(\frac{x - x_i}{\sigma}\right)$$

where $K(x)$ is the kernel function, which is usually a symmetric density function with one peak at the origin, e.g., Gaussian function, square wave function, etc. σ is the window width of the kernel function.

b. Density attractor and density attraction. Given a local maximum point x^* of the global density function, for an arbitrary $x \in \Omega$, if there exists a point set $x_0, x_1, \ldots, x_k$ so that $x_0 = x, x_k = x^*$ and $x_i \ (0 < i < k)$ lies in the gradient direction of x_{i-1}, then x is attracted in density by x^* and x^* is a density attractor of x.

If the kernel function $K(x)$ is continuous and differentiable at each point, the climbing method based on gradient can be employed to search for density attractors.

c. Center-based clustering. With a given density attractor x^*, if there exists a subset $C \subseteq D$ so that for $\forall x \in C$, x is attracted in density by x^* and $f^D(x^*) \geq \xi$ (ξ is a preset noise threshold), then C is the cluster with x^* as the center.

d. Clustering with an arbitrary shape. Let X be a set consisting of density attractors. If there exists a subset $C \subseteq D$ satisfying:

$\forall x \in C$, there exists a density attractor $x^* \in X$ so that x is attracted in density by x^* and $f^D(x^*) \geq \xi$;
$\forall x_i^*, x_j^* \in X$ ($i \neq j$), there exists a path $P \subset \Omega$ from x_i^* to x_j^*, which satisfies condition that $\forall y \in P$, $f^D(y) \geq \xi$. C is called the cluster of an arbitrary shape determined by X.

Obviously, there are two key parameters to be preset in the algorithm: the window width σ and density threshold ξ. The selection of σ is influential to the estimation of the global density function, and consequently affects the number of density attractors or the number of clusters. Let σ_{max} be the maximized σ when $f^D(x)$ contains only one density attractor (the local maximum point), and σ_{min} be the minimized σ when $f^D(x)$ contains n density attractors. This algorithm believes that each value in the largest domain $[\sigma_{min}, \sigma_{max}]$ of σ corresponds to the clustering result of the original data at different hierarchies. When $\sigma = \sigma_{min}$, each object will turn into one cluster so that the clustering result consists of n clusters with one object each. As σ increases, the number of density attractors will reduce, which corresponds to the clustering result at a higher hierarchy. When $\sigma = \sigma_{max}$, all the objects will join one cluster. In this way, the user can acquire the natural hierarchical structure in clusters by means of σ adjustment in $[\sigma_{min}, \sigma_{max}]$. As for the optimal selection of σ, this algorithm believes that any σ in the largest subset $I \subset [\sigma_{min}, \sigma_{max}]$, which can stabilize the number of clusters, corresponds to a reasonable clustering result. Once σ is set, the algorithm can determine the final clustering result by introducing the global noise threshold ξ, and consequently divides the data set by the hierarchical clustering for various σ.

After analysis of the hierarchical clustering idea above, we find a substantial problem, that is whether each σ in the $[\sigma_{min}, \sigma_{max}]$ is corresponding to the internal hierarchy of the data distribution. As we know, during the hierarchical clustering process, the membership relation of the object cannot change once it is determined. Besides, it is impossible to exchange objects between clusters either. In DENCLUE algorithm, the definition of a cluster is based on the density attractor, and the combination of clusters is realized by that of the density attractors as well. Because the density attractor corresponds to the local maximum point of the global density function, and $\nabla f^D(x) = 0$, there are two traditional combination modes for the density attractors when σ increases, i.e., combination of saddle points and combination of degenerated saddle points. In the first combination mode, two density attractors will be combined smoothly into a new density attractor. In the second mode, one of the density attractors will disappear and consequently the data objects belonging to this attractor will be attracted by other different clusters. This means that the membership relation will be changed. Obviously it disobeys the fundamental idea in the hierarchical clustering method. Moreover, if the value of σ indeed reflects the internal hierarchical structure of data distribution, the number of density attractors or the number of clusters ought to be a monotonical decreasing function in terms of σ. Nevertheless, the monotony cannot be guaranteed even in a simple two-dimensional case. In conclusion, the window width σ does not correspond to the hierarchical structure in data distribution.[21]

Once σ is determined, the clustering result will only correspond to a certain density hierarchy by introducing the global noise threshold ξ. The algorithm must collect a group of appropriate noise thresholds to generate clustering results at different density hierarchies. Certainly, it is not feasible to set these thresholds manually by the user.

2. Hierarchical clustering based on the topology of the potential field

The idea in the hierarchical clustering based on the topology of the potential field is to optimally select the influence factor σ for generation of potential field distribution in the first step. Thereafter, the data objects contained in each equipotential line/surface are treated as a natural cluster, and the nested structures consisting of different equipotential lines/surfaces are treated as the cluster spectrum. In this way, clustering at different hierarchies is realized. When the integral of unit potential function is finite, the difference between the potential function and the probability density function will be only one normalization constant. The data objects contained in each equipotential line/surface actually corresponds to a relatively dense cluster, and the nested structure can be considered as the clustering partition at different density hierarchies.

Let's investigate the distribution of equipotential lines in the data field generated by 390 data points in a two-dimensional space with equal mass, as shown in Figure 7.1(a). The equipotential lines for a group of appropriately selected potential values are clustering naturally with the dense region of data as their centers. When $\psi = 0.0678$, all the data will cluster into A, B, C, D, and E in hierarchy 1 automatically. As ψ decreases, data clusters closer to each other will be combined, for example clusters A and B form spectrum AB at hierarchy 2 and clusters D and E form spectrum DE at hierarchy 3. When $\psi = 0.0085$, all the data clusters are combined into one at hierarchy 5, which is the largest spectrum ABCDE. The resulting natural spectrum graph is illustrated in Figure 7.1(b).

In the implementation, with the consideration that local maximum points could be regarded as some "virtual field sources," all the data objects are convergent by self-organization due to the attraction by their own "virtual field sources." Local maximum points can be considered as cluster centers, which form the initial partition. Thereafter, these initial clusters are combined based on regular saddle point iteration between two local maximum points, and consequentially the clusters at different hierarchies are generated.

In the process to determine local maximum points and saddle points in the potential field distribution, the algorithm first searches all the critical points satisfying $\nabla f^D(x) = 0$ by means of interval analysis that is linearly convergent. Thereafter, it classifies the critical points according to the eigenvalues of the Hesse matrix $\nabla^2 f^D(x)$. For a given critical point x, let $l_1 \leq l_2 \leq \ldots \leq l_d$ be the d eigenvalues of the Hesse matrix $\nabla^2 f^D(x)$, where $d \geq 2$ is the dimension of the space. If $l_d < 0$, x is a local maximum point in the potential field distribution; if $l_1 > 0$, x is a local minimum point in the potential field distribution; if $l_1, l_2, \ldots, l_d \neq 0$ and $n_p, n_q \geq 1$

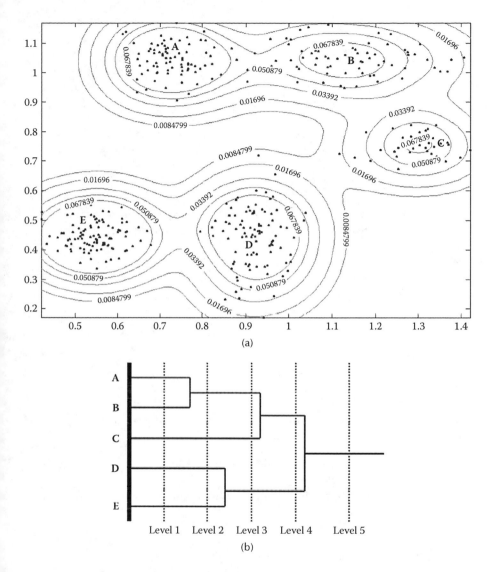

FIGURE 7.1 The equipotential line distribution and cluster spectrum of a two-dimensional data potential field. (a) Equipotential line graph and (b) cluster spectrum.

(n_p is the number of positive eigenvalues, and n_q is the number of negative eigenvalues), x is a saddle point in the potential field.

3. Algorithm description

Let $D = \{x_1, x_2,...,x_n\}$ be a data set inclusive of n objects in a known space $\Omega \subseteq \mathbf{R}^d$. There are five steps in the hierarchical clustering algorithm based on the topology of the potential field:

1. Randomly select $n_{sample} \ll n$ samples from D to optimally estimate the influence factor σ.
2. Apply grid partition with quantitative scale $\sqrt{2}\sigma$ on the smallest subspace $X = [X_1^l, X_1^h] \times \cdots \times [X_d^l, X_d^h] \subseteq \Omega$, which includes all the data points. Then construct a B$^+$ tree structure to store the information such as the key values of every nonempty grid unit, the object number n_C in grid unit, and the object mean $x_C = \frac{1}{n_C} \sum_{x \in C} x$.
3. Search all of the topological critical points in the potential field within the space X, and determine local maximum points and saddle points according to the eigenvalues of the Hesse matrix.
4. Generate the initial partition with the local maximum points of the potential field as the cluster centers.
5. Combine the initial clusters iteratively based on the regular saddle points of the potential function, and obtain clustering results at different hierarchies.

Algorithm 7.3 Hierarchical clustering based on the topology of the potential field, PField_Clustering algorithm

Input: data set $D = \{x_1, x_2, \ldots, x_n\}$
       sample number n_{sample}
       noise threshold ξ
Output: the hierarchical partition $\{\Pi_0, \Pi_1, \ldots, \Pi_k\}$
Steps:

1. Select n_{sample} samples randomly to construct the sample data set *SampleSet*
2. //Optimization of the influence factor σ

$$\sigma = \text{Optimal\_Sigma}(SampleSet)$$

3. //Apply grid partition on the space and construct an index tree

$$Map = \text{CreateMap}(D, \sigma)$$

4. //Search in the topological critical points

$$CriticalPoints = \text{Search\_CtiticalPoints}(Map, \sigma)$$

5. Set *MaxPoints* as the set of local maximum points, and *SadPoints* as the set of saddle points.
6. //Initially divide the data according to the set of local maximum points

$$\Pi_0 = \text{Initialization\_Partition}(Map, D, MaxPoints, \sigma, \xi)$$

7. //Combine the initial clusters iteratively according to the set of saddle points

$$[\Pi_1, \ldots, \Pi_k] = \text{Saddle\_Merge}(Map, \Pi_0, MaxPoints, SadPoints, \sigma, \xi)$$

There are two parameters in the algorithm above: random sample number n_{sample} and noise threshold ξ. The sample number is usually set as $n_{sample} = [\alpha \cdot n]$, $\alpha \geq 0.05$, while the noise threshold ξ is applied to judge whether the initial clusters are meaningful. Because the final clustering result is determined by the regular saddle points in the potential field, ξ, which is in a relatively stable domain, will not affect the clustering result. If noise data are not included in the data set D, the value domain of ξ will be $[0, \min_{x^* \in \text{MaxPoints}} \varphi(x^*)]$, and usually let $\xi = 0$. Let $\|D_{noise}\|$ be the size of noise data set, if noise data are included in D, then $c \leq \xi < \min_{x^* \in A} \varphi(x^*)$, where A is the set of local maximum points generated by the non-noisy data, and c is equivalent to the potential value generated by $\|D_{noise}\|$ noise data with uniform distribution, i.e., $c = \varphi_{D_{noise}}(x)$.

4. Performance analysis of the algorithm

With a given sample volume $n_{sample} \ll n$, the time complexity in the optimization of σ is $O(n_{sample}^2)$. The time complexity in the one-round scanning of the data set, application of grid partition in the space, and B$^+$ tree construction, is $O(n + n_{grid} \cdot \log(n_{grid}))$, where n_{grid} is the number of nonempty grid and $n_{grid} \ll n$. The time complexity in the topologically critical points searching and the initial partition on the data is $O(n \cdot \log(n_{grid}))$. Let n_{saddle} be the number of regular saddle points, and obviously $n_{saddle} \ll n$. The time complexity of the iterative combination of the initial clusters is $O(n_{saddle} \cdot \log(n_{grid}))$. Hence the overall time complexity of this algorithm is $O(n_{sampe}^2 + n + (n_{grid} + n + n_{saddle}) \cdot \log(n_{grid}))$. Apparently, when n is huge, the time complexity will approach $O(n \cdot \log(n_{grid}))$, that the performance and efficiency of this algorithm is similar to that of DENCLUE.

5. Comparison of experimental results

Now let's verify the effectiveness of the hierarchical clustering algorithm based on the topology of the potential field by two simulation data sets and one practical data set. The program implemented in MATLAB® 6.1 and runs on a PC.

Experiment 1

Figure 7.2 shows the test data (all the data have been normalized). Within them, Dataset1 contains 3,200 data points and the clusters appear as five spherical and ellipsoidal shapes with different sizes and densities. Dataset2 is obtained from literature (reference 11). It contains 10,000 data points, and 9 clusters with different shapes, sizes, and density are included together with some linear noise and uniform noise. The compared algorithm in the experiment is DENCLUE algorithm.

Figure 7.3 illustrates the clustering results in Dataset1 by DENCLUE algorithm (σ is set to the optimal value 0.117). Obviously, clustering results will be highly dependent on ξ. But no matter how ξ is adjusted, DENCLUE algorithm cannot extract correctly the five natural clusters from the data.

Figure 7.4 demonstrates the clustering results in Dataset1 and Dataset2 by the hierarchical clustering algorithm based on the topology of the potential field. The sampling rate $\alpha = 10\%$, and the number of clusters are set as $k = 5, k = 9$, respectively. Obviously, this algorithm is able to reveal the natural clustering feature in the data distribution, detect clusters in different shapes, sizes, and densities, and filter out

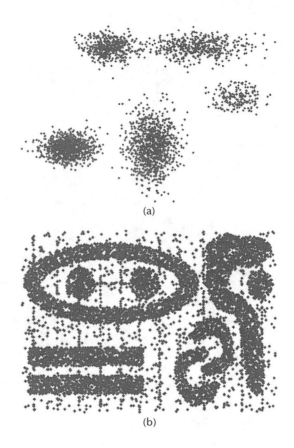

(a)

(b)

FIGURE 7.2   Data sets to be tested. (a) Dataset1: 3,200 data points and (b) Dataset2: 10,000 data points.

noise data effectively. The clustering result remains stable and independent of the careful parameter selections of the users.

Experiment 2

The tested set is the famous Iris data, which is treated as a standard test set for evaluation on the performance of supervised or unsupervised learning algorithms. The published Iris data by Fischer in 1936 contained the features of three plants, i.e., Setosa, Versicolour, and Virginica. For each kind, he selected 50 samples and measured the length of sepal (X_1), the width of sepal (X_2), the length of petal (X_3), and the width of petal (X_4). Table 7.3 shows the sample data.

Considering that the properties X_3 and X_4 are two significant features of the Iris data set,[22,23] the data is projected to the feature subspace spanned by X_3 and X_4 for visualization, as shown in Figure 7.5.

It can be noticed from Figure 7.5 that there is one group of data that has good separability, while the other two kinds are weak in this aspect. After analysis on

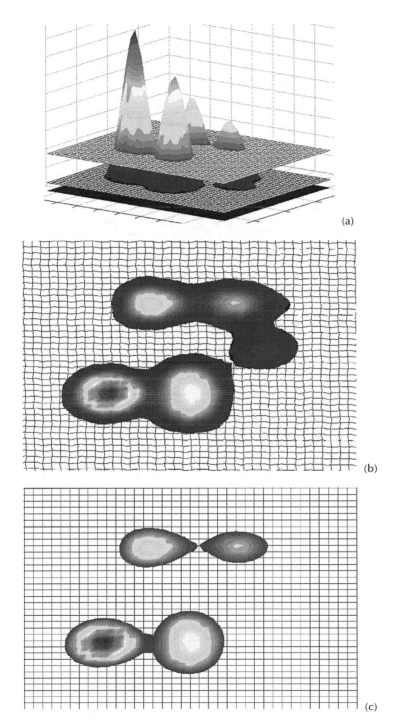

FIGURE 7.3 The clustering results in Dataset1 by DENCLUE algorithm. (a) Clustering result with σ=0.117, (b) clustering result with ξ= 0.282, and (c) clustering result with ξ= 0.402.

(a)

(b)

FIGURE 7.4 The clustering results in Dataset1 and Dataset2 by PField_clustering algorithm. (a) Clustering result in Dataset1 with k=5, ξ=0 and (b) clustering result in Dataset2 with k=9, ξ=0.015.

clustering of Iris data by means of PField-Clustering algorithm, the result is shown in Table 7.4 with $k = 3$ and $\xi = 0$. The clustering performs best in the $X_3 - X_4$ subspace, and the false classification number is 4. When clustering is conducted in a higher-dimensional space, the performance becomes worse, mainly due to the introduction of insignificant features with weak separability. Actually, those insignificant or noisy

TABLE 7.3
Iris Data Set

Index	Iris Setosa				Iris Versicolour				Iris Virginica			
	X_1	X_2	X_3	X_4	X_1	X_2	X_3	X_4	X_1	X_2	X_3	X_4
1	5.1	3.5	1.4	0.2	7.0	3.2	4.7	1.4	6.3	3.3	6.0	2.5
2	4.9	3.0	1.4	0.2	6.4	3.2	4.5	1.5	5.8	2.7	5.1	1.9
⋮	⋮	⋮	⋮	⋮	⋮	⋮	⋮	⋮	⋮	⋮	⋮	⋮
50	5.0	3.3	1.4	0.2	5.7	2.8	4.1	1.3	5.9	3.0	5.1	1.8

Note: unit of X is cm.

features are not only helpless to show the clustering structure, but also make the data distribution confusing as well as reduce the efficiency of the clustering algorithm and the effectiveness of the clustering result. Hence, only the significant features should be selected to uncover the underlying clustering structure of data, rather than "the max the better".

Figure 7.6 illustrates the comparison of clustering results among the PField_Clustering algorithm and other clustering methods. If only the significant attributes X_3 and X_4 are selected, the numbers of false classifications via SVM algorithm,[24] information theory method,[25] and SPC algorithm[26] are 4, 5, and 15, respectively. As the number of attributes grows, the false classification rates of the four algorithms all increase. Generally speaking, the clustering quality of PField_Clustering algorithm is better, and there are some shortcomings in this algorithm as well. The major one lies in the introduction of B+, which is to enhance the searching efficiency in the adjacent objects in order to improve the computational complexity in the potential function. However, the searching efficiency on B+ tree will substantially decrease as the spatial dimension rises. Usually it is not suitable to conduct data clustering with a dimension exceeding 20. As a result, a dynamic clustering based on data force fields is necessary for the clustering problem in high dimension.

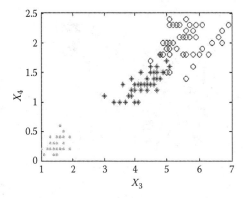

FIGURE 7.5 The projected distribution of the Iris data on the feature subspace spanned by X_3 and X_4.

TABLE 7.4
The Clustering Result in Iris Data Set by PField_Clustering Algorithm

Selected Properties	σ	Number of False Classification
X_3, X_4	0.054	4
X_2, X_3, X_4	0.06	6
X_1, X_2, X_3, X_4	0.83	14

C. Dynamic clustering based on data force fields

The idea of dynamic clustering was first proposed by W. E. Wright in his gravitational clustering algorithm[27] in 1977. In this algorithm, every point in the space is regarded as a point with unit mass. According to Newton's law of universal gravitation, the objects will converge to the center due to the gravitational effect. This algorithm iteratively simulates the motion of the objects and investigates all the possible combinations. The main points include:

1. The calculation of the new position of an object should take into consideration the interaction of all current objects.
2. When two objects are close enough, one object can be eliminated, but the mass of the other will increase accordingly.
3. The motion distance in each iteration cannot exceed δ.
4. The algorithm will terminate when all the objects are combined to be one.

Actually, this method, which describes the interactions between objects in terms of gravity, corresponds to the description by long-range field. Because the clustering feature in data distribution cannot be apparently revealed by long-range field, this algorithm is accompanied with bias toward spherical clusters[28] and cannot deal with

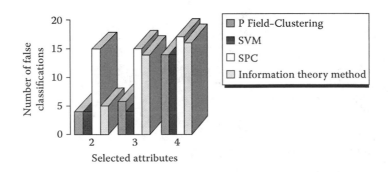

FIGURE 7.6 The comparison on the clustering results among PField_Clustering algorithm and other clustering algorithms.

noisy data effectively. Moreover, the convergency of this algorithm is weak as well, with $O(n^2)$ at least, as the time complexity.

Oyan et al. [28] introduce a high-order gravity formula to tackle problems of bias toward spherical clusters and convergency in Wright algorithm. The interactive gravity between two objects is expressed by

$$F_g = \frac{C_g \times M_1 \times M_2}{r^k}$$

where M_1 and M_2 are masses of the two data objects, r is the distance between them, and C_g is the gravitational constant.

Because the high-order gravity formula is a description of short-range field on the interaction between data, the improved gravitational clustering algorithm is able to relieve the "bias toward spherical clusters" relatively. One one hand, the work of Oyan et al. strengthens our belief in cognitive physics, but on the other hand, it brings forth a problem that the selection of distance exponent k depends on the concrete distribution of the data, so improvement is required for the algorithm. Meanwhile, Oyan et al. introduce the concept of "air friction" to guarantee the convergency of the algorithm. The air friction, consuming the total energy in the system, is expressed by $F_r = C_r \times v^2$, where C_r is the air frictional coefficient. Although the introduction of air friction can guarantee that all the objects will be convergent to one cluster, it can hardly improve the algorithm performance substantially and the time complexity is till $O(n^2)$. Moreover, the introduction of new parameters, such as air frictional coefficient C_r, distance exponent k and object density D, will reduce the applicability and make it inapplicable to large scaled real data set.

1. The idea of dynamic clustering based on data force fields

The basic idea of dynamic clustering based on data force fields is to describe interactions of objects by data fields, and cluster the objects via simulation of their motion in the data force field. Without the effect from external forces, the objects will be attracted by each other and converge; when two of them meet or are close enough, they will be combined into a new object, the mass and momentum of which are the sums of the former; the object combination in the simulation can be regarded as the cluster combination in the hierarchical clustering process, i.e., the subclusters are gradually combined into a new cluster at higher hierarchies with larger granularities; the algorithm is operated iteratively until all the object clusters go into one group.

It is not necessarily true that the more the initial cluster number in the human cognition process is, the better the clustering result will be. Classically, people are interested in hierarchical structures with at most tens of initial clusters. Hence, rather than displaying all the interactions and motions between all the objects, we conduct simplified estimation on the object masses in the beginning to obtain a few kernel objects with non-zero mass, thereafter generate the initial clusters with the kernel objects as their representatives, and finally combine the kernel objects iteratively to implement the hierarchical clustering.

a. Simplified estimation of object masses

Let $D = \{x_1, x_2, \ldots, x_n\}$ be a data set with n objects in the space $\Omega \subseteq \mathbf{R}^p$. The potential function of its data field is

$$\varphi(x) = \sum_{i=1}^{n} \left(m_i \times e^{-\left(\frac{\|x - x_i\|}{\sigma}\right)^2} \right)$$

If the masses, $m_1, m_2, \ldots, m_n$, may not be equal, they can be regarded as a group of functions in terms of the spatial position $x_1, x_2, \ldots, x_n$. Once the overall distribution is obtained, the masses can be optimally estimated via minimizing a certain error criteria related to partition function $\varphi(x)$ and the density function of the overall distribution. In detail, let $x_1, x_2, \ldots, x_n$ be n simple samples from a continuous d-dimensional set, and $p(x)$ be the overall density. When σ is fixed, we can minimize the criteria of squared integral of the error, i.e.,

$$\min J = \min_{\{m_i\}} \int_{\Omega} \left(\frac{\varphi(x)}{(\sqrt{\pi}\sigma)^d} - p(x) \right)^2 dx \tag{7.1}$$

Expand this formula and obtain

$$\min J = \min_{\{m_i\}} \int_{\Omega} \left(\frac{\varphi^2(x)}{(\sqrt{\pi}\sigma)^{2d}} - \frac{2p(x) \cdot \varphi(x)}{(\sqrt{\pi}\sigma)^d} + p^2(x) \right) dx \tag{7.2}$$

Obviously, $\int_{\Omega} p^2(x) dx$ is independent on $m_1, m_2, \ldots, m_n$, so the objective function can be simplified to

$$\min J = \min_{\{m_i\}} \left(\int_{\Omega} \frac{\varphi^2(x)}{2(\sqrt{\pi}\sigma)^d} dx - \int_{\Omega} \varphi(x) p(x) dx \right) \tag{7.3}$$

Within this formula, $\int_{\Omega} \varphi(x) p(x) dx$ is the mathematical expectation of $\varphi(x)$, which can be approximated by the mean of the n independently selected sample function, i.e.,

$$\min J = \min_{\{m_i\}} \left(\frac{1}{2(\sqrt{\pi}\sigma)^d} \int_{\Omega} \varphi^2(x) dx - \frac{1}{n} \sum_{j=1}^{n} \varphi(x_j) \right) \tag{7.4}$$

Substituting $\varphi(x) = \sum_{i=1}^{n}\left(m_i \times e^{-\left(\frac{\|x-x_i\|}{\sigma}\right)^2}\right)$ into Equation 7.4, we can obtain

$$\min J = \min_{\{m_i\}}\left(\frac{1}{2 \cdot (\sqrt{2})^d}\sum_{i=1}^{n}\sum_{j=1}^{n}m_i \times m_j \times e^{-\left(\frac{\|x_i-x_j\|}{\sqrt{2}\sigma}\right)^2} - \frac{1}{n}\sum_{i=1}^{n}\sum_{j=1}^{n}m_i \times e^{-\left(\frac{\|x_i-x_j\|}{\sigma}\right)^2}\right) \quad (7.5)$$

Apparently, this is a classical constrained quadratic programming problem. The constraints are $\sum_{i=1}^{n}m_i = 1$ and $\forall i, m_i \geq 0$. A group of optimal estimation on masses can be obtained through optimal solution, denoted as $m_1^*, m_2^*, \ldots, m_n^*$. Analyze this optimization problem qualitatively, and one can obtain the necessary and sufficient condition to minimize the objective function

$$\frac{\partial J}{\partial m_i}\bigg|_{i=1,2,\ldots,n} = \frac{1}{(\sqrt{2})^d}\sum_{j=1}^{n}m_j \times e^{-\left(\frac{\|x_i-x_j\|}{\sqrt{2}\sigma}\right)^2} - \frac{1}{n}\sum_{j=1}^{n}e^{-\left(\frac{\|x_i-x_j\|}{\sigma}\right)^2} = 0 \quad (7.6)$$

Substituting Equation 7.6 into Equation 7.5, we can obtain

$$\min J = -\frac{1}{2(\sqrt{2})^d}\sum_{i=1}^{n}\sum_{j=1}^{n}m_i \times m_j \times e^{-\left(\frac{\|x_i-x_j\|}{\sqrt{2}\sigma}\right)^2} \quad (7.7)$$

i.e., the minimization of the objective function J is equivalent to the maximization of

$$\sum_{i=1}^{n}\sum_{j=1}^{n}m_i \times m_j \times e^{-\left(\frac{\|x_i-x_j\|}{\sqrt{2}\sigma}\right)^2}$$

As $m_1, m_2, \ldots, m_n$ satisfy the normalization condition, the maximization of

$$\sum_{i=1}^{n}\sum_{j=1}^{n}m_i \times m_j \times e^{-\left(\frac{\|x_i-x_j\|}{\sqrt{2}\sigma}\right)^2}$$

can be implemented by attaching large masses to a few adjacent objects. The optimization result of the objective function is that a few objects in dense regions obtain relatively large masses, while those objects far away have relatively small masses or zero masses.

We estimate the masses of 1,200 data points in a two-dimensional data field based on the above method (with influence factor $\sigma = 0.078$). Figure 7.7 shows the estimation result, in which 71 points with non-zero masses are denoted by red points. Apparently, all those points with non-zero masses are allocated in the relatively

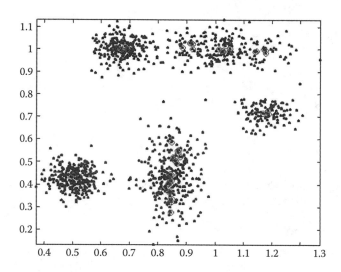

FIGURE 7.7 Simplified estimation on the object masses in the data field ($\sigma = 0.078$).

dense region, and their number is greatly less than the number of data points in the original data set.

We regard the data objects with non-zero masses as the representatives in the data field, and investigate the distributions of equipotential fields generated by the representative set and the original data set, as shown in Figure 7.8. The two potential fields are distributed similarly, i.e., the data field of a few kernel objects can approximate the data field generated by the original data set; in other words, the distribution of data fields is mainly dependent on the interactions among the kernel objects, while the effects of the other objects with small mass are minor.

There have been many standard algorithms to solve the constrained quadratic programming in Equation 7.5. The most frequently used algorithm is to introduce a group of nominal variables $\alpha_1, \alpha_2, \ldots, \alpha_n$, let $m_i = \frac{e^{\alpha_i}}{\sum_{j=1}^{n} e^{\alpha_j}}$, $i = 1, 2, \ldots, n$, and simplify the constrained quadratic programming problem into a nonlinear optimization problem without constraints, followed by the conjugate gradient method to solve it.[29] The conjugate gradient method has linear convergent speed, but the optimization result is dependent on the initial point selection. In this book, we apply the sequential minimal optimization (SMO) method.[30] Its time complexity is $O(n^2)$, but the optimization result is independent of the initial point selection and has good robustness.

In real applications, the algorithm with time complexity $O(n^2)$ is not applicable to a large-scale data base, so we employ a random sampling approach with sample volume $n_{sample} \ll n$ in order to reduce the computational cost. Usually the minimal sampling rate is recommended as no less than 5%.[9]

Let $D_{core} = \{x_i \in D \mid m_i^* > 0, i = 1, 2, \ldots, n\}$ be the representative set after optimization. The potential and field strength vector of an arbitrary point in the simplified data field is

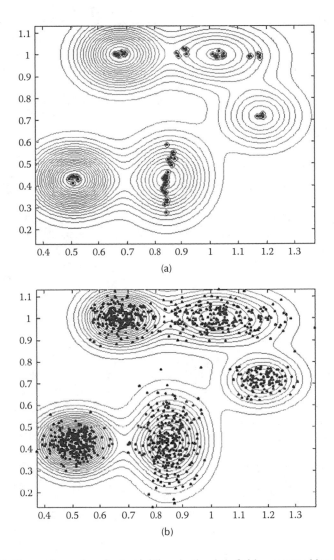

FIGURE 7.8 Comparison of equipotential lines in the data fields generated by the representative set and the original data set. (a) The distribution of equipotential lines in the data field generated by the representative sets and (b) the distribution of equipotential lines in the data field generated by the original data set.

$$\varphi(x) = \varphi_{D_{core}}(x) = \sum_{x_i \in D_{core}} \left(m_i^* \times e^{-\left(\frac{\|x - x_i\|}{\sigma} \right)^2} \right) \qquad (7.8)$$

$$F(x) = \sum_{x_i \in D_{core}} \left(m_i^* \cdot (x_i - x) \cdot e^{-\left(\frac{\|x - x_i\|}{\sigma} \right)^2} \right) \qquad (7.9)$$

b. Initial cluster partition based on representatives

As the distribution of a data field is determined by the interactions in a few representatives with relatively large masses located in dense regions, we regard those
representatives as the cluster representatives in the initial partition. Those objects
attracted by the same representative are considered one data cluster. Thus we can
obtain the definition of central cluster based on representatives.

Definition 7.1

*Let $x^* \in D_{core}$ and m^* be a representative and its mass, respectively. If there exists a
subset $C \subseteq D$, so that $\forall x \in C$, exists a point sequence $x_0 = x, x_1, \ldots, x_k \in \Omega$, satisfying
$\|x_k - x^*\| < 0.705\sigma \cdot m^*$ and x_i be on the gradient direction of x_{i-1} ($0 < i < k$), then
C is the cluster of with representative x^*.*

The central cluster based on representatives actually regards the representatives
with non-zero masses as the cluster centers and partitions the data via motion
simulation of the other data objects in the data field. In the implementation, the
maximum distance from each object $x \in D$ to the data set D_{core}, so as to filter noise
effectively. If $\max_{x^* \in D_{core}} \|x^* - x\| > 3\sigma$, which means there is no representative in
the 3σ neighborhood of the location for this object, it will be regarded as a noise
point and filtered out. For the non-noise data object we classify it into one kernel
object via climbing method instructed by the field strength direction. Once the initial
partition is done, the iterative simulation on the interactions and motions of representatives will function to implement the combination of initial clusters.

c. Dynamic clustering of the representatives

The clustering via the simulation of interactions and motions in the representatives
is essentially the investigation on all the possible cluster combinations through the
iterative simulation of the motions in a short time interval $[t, t + \Delta t]$ by each representative. Let $m_i^*(t)$ denote the mass of the representative $x_i^* \in D_{core}$ at time t,
and $x_i^*(t)$ denote the position vector, $i = 1, 2, \ldots, |D_{core}|$. In case the external forces are
eliminated, the field force on the object is

$$F^{(t)}(x_i^*) = m_i^*(t) \cdot \sum_{x_j^* \in D_{core}} \left(m_j^*(t) \cdot \left(x_j^*(t) - x_i^*(t) \right) \cdot e^{-\left(\frac{\|x_j^*(t) - x_i^*(t)\|}{\sigma} \right)^2} \right) \tag{7.10}$$

According to Newton's second law, fundamental law of dynamics, the instanta-
neous acceleration vector of the representative x_i^* is

$$a^{(t)}(x_i^*) = \frac{F^{(t)}(x_i^*)}{m_i^*(t)} = \sum_{x_j^* \in D_{core}} \left(m_j^*(t) \cdot (x_j^*(t) - x_i^*(t)) \cdot e^{-\left(\frac{\|x_j^*(t) - x_i^*(t)\|}{\sigma} \right)^2} \right) \tag{7.11}$$

If Δt is small enough, the motion of each representative is approximately uniformly variable motion in the interval $[t, t + \Delta t]$. Let $v^{(t)}(x_i^*)$ be the velocity vector of the representative x_i^* at the time t. The position vector and velocity vector at time Δt is approximately

$$x_i^*(t + \Delta t) = x_i^*(t) + v^{(t)}(x_i^*) \times \Delta t + \frac{1}{2} a^{(t)}(x_i^*) \times \Delta t^2 \qquad (7.12)$$

$$v^{(t + \Delta t)}(x_i^*) = v^{(t)}(x_i^*) + a^{(t)}(x_i^*) \times \Delta t \qquad (7.13)$$

When the two objects meet or the distance between them is $\|x_i^*(t) - x_j^*(t)\| \le 0.705\sigma \cdot (m_i^*(t) + m_j^*(t))$, they will be combined into a new object denoted as x_{new}^*. According to the law of conservation of momentum, the mass, position, and velocity vectors of the new object can be calculated as

$$m_{new}^*(t) = m_i^*(t) + m_j^*(t) \qquad (7.14)$$

$$x_{new}^*(t) = \frac{m_i^*(t) \cdot x_i^*(t) + m_j^*(t) \cdot x_j^*(t)}{m_i^*(t) + m_j^*(t)} \qquad (7.15)$$

$$v^{(t)}(x_{new}^*) = \frac{m_i^*(t) \cdot v^{(t)}(x_i^*) + m_j^*(t) \cdot v^{(t)}(x_j^*)}{m_i^*(t) + m_j^*(t)} \qquad (7.16)$$

The algorithm is operated recursively until all of the objects are combined into one or a terminating condition instructed by the user is satisfied.

In the aforementioned dynamic clustering process, as the number of remaining objects decreases, the masses of representatives will increase gradually, and the inertia keeping the motion trend at the initial time become increasingly stronger. As a result, it may cause a convergency problem similar to the one in the Wright algorithm. To guarantee the final convergency, we simply fix the initial velocity vector of objects to 0, and derive the simplified position vector formula as

$$x_i^*(t + \Delta t) = x_i^*(t) + \frac{1}{2} a^{(t)}(x_i^*) \times \Delta t^2 \qquad (7.17)$$

That means the position vector of the representative at time $t + \Delta t$ is only dependent on the position and velocity at time t and iteration interval Δt.

As for the selection of Δt, an adaptive method is adopted in this book. Before each iteration, we calculate the minimum distance between representatives $\min\_dist = \min_{i \neq j} \|x_i^*(t) - x_j^*(t)\|$, and the maximum acceleration $\max\_a = \max_i \|a^{(t)}(x_i^*)\|$. Thereafter, set $\Delta t = \frac{1}{f}(\sqrt{\frac{2\min\_dist}{\max\_a}})$, where f is a constant standing for time resolution, which is 100 here.

2. Algorithm description

Let $D = \{x_1, x_2, \ldots, x_n\}$ be a data set containing n objects in the space $\Omega \subseteq \mathbf{R}^d$. There are four basic steps in the dynamic clustering algorithm based on data force fields:

1. Optimization of the influence factor σ
2. Simplified estimation of the object quality
3. Initial partition on the data based on representatives
4. Iterative simulation on the interactions and motions of representatives to realize the hierarchical combination of the initial clusters

Here we provide the detailed algorithm description.

Algorithm 7.4 Dynamic clustering algorithm based on data force fields (abbreviated as data-field clustering)

Input: data set D, sample number n_{sample}
Output: hierarchical partition of the data $\{\Pi_0, \Pi_1, \ldots, \Pi_k\}$
Steps:

1. Select n_{sample} samples randomly to construct a sample data set *SampleSet*
2. //Optimization of σ

$$\sigma = Optimal\_Sigma(SampleSet)$$

3. //Simplified estimation of the object mass

$$M = Estimate\_Mass(SampleSet, \sigma)$$

4. Let $D_{core} = \{x \in D | Mass(x) > 0\}$
5. //Initial partition of the data

$$\Pi_0 = Initialize\_Partition\ (D, D_{core}, M, \sigma)$$

6. //Cluster combination

$$[\Pi_1, \ldots, \Pi_k] = Dynamic\_Merge(\Pi_0, D_{core}, M, \sigma)$$

3. Algorithm performance

The performance of this algorithm can be analyzed as follows. Fix the sample volume $n_{sample} \ll n$, the time complexity of σ optimization and simplified estimation on the mass is $O(n_{sample}{}^2)$. If the representative number is n_{core}, $n_{core} \ll n_{sample}$, the complexity of initial partition is $O(n_{core} * n)$. Let N_i be the number of remaining objects after the ith ($i = 0, 1, \ldots, p$) combination, where $N_0 = n_{core}$, $N_p = 1$. The time complexity of iterative combination is $C \cdot \sum_{i=0}^{p-1} N_i^2$, and the average time complexity is

$$E\left(\sum_{i=0}^{p-1}\left(C \cdot N_i^2\right)\right) = C \cdot \sum_{i=0}^{p-1} E\left(N_i^2\right) \leq C \cdot n_{core} \cdot \sum_{i=0}^{p-1} E(N_i)$$

where C is a constant. Let $q = \max_{i \in (0,p)}(\frac{E(N_{i+1})}{E(N_i)})$, $0 < q < 1$, then $E(N_i) \le (n_{core} \cdot q^i)$. We can obtain $E(N_i) \le (n_{core} \cdot q^i)$, so $\sum_{i=0}^{p-1} E(N_i) \le \frac{n_{core}}{1-q}$, i.e., the average temporal complexity of the iterative combination of representatives is $O(\frac{C \cdot n_{core}^2}{1-q})$. As a result, the total temporal complexity is $O(n_{sample}^2 + n \cdot n_{core} + \frac{C \cdot n_{core}^2}{1-q})$. Obviously, when $n_{sample} \ll n$, the temporal complexity of this system is approximately linear, i.e., $O(n)$.

4. Experimental results and comparison

Here we verify the performance and effectiveness of the dynamic clustering algorithm based on data fields via two simulation data sets. All the programs are coded in MATLAB 6.1 and run on a PC.

Experiment 1

Figure 7.9(a) shows the data set Dataset1.[28] There are 400 data points in this set. The clustering results from the Wright algorithm and dynamic clustering algorithm based on data force fields are illustrated in Figure 7.10. Obviously, bias toward spherical clusters is inevitable in the Wright algorithm. However, the clustering

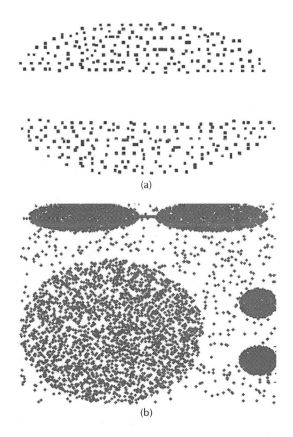

(a)

(b)

FIGURE 7.9 Two data sets to be tested for the dynamic clustering based on data force fields. (a) Dataset1: 400 points and (b) Dataset2: 8,000 points.

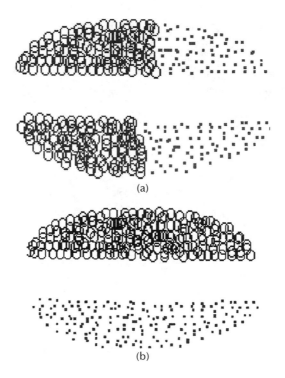

FIGURE 7.10 Comparison of the clustering results with Dataset1. (a) Wright clustering ($k = 2$, $\delta = 1$) and (b)Data-field clustering ($k = 2$).

quality is higher by the dynamic clustering algorithm, as the clustering feature is revealed correctly.

Experiment 2

Figure 7.9(b) shows the data set Dataset2.[9] It contains 10^5 data points, including five clusters of different shapes, sizes, and densities together with some uniformly distributed noise. In the experiment, we select 8,000 data points randomly, and employ different algorithms, i.e., the improved hierarchical clustering algorithms BIRCH and CURE, the popular K-mean algorithm, and the dynamic clustering algorithm based on data force fields. Figure 7.11 demonstrates the results. Obviously, spherical basis exists in BIRCH and K-means. CURE can discover the correct clustering structure in the distribution if appropriate parameters are selected, but it cannot effectively deal with the noise data. Comparatively, the dynamic clustering algorithm based on data force fields has merits, such as satisfactory clustering quality, effective processing of noise data, and independence of the elaborate selection on parameters by the user. We further our investigation on the extendability of the dynamic clustering utilizing Dataset2. Figure 7.12 shows the test result. Apparently, this algorithm is extendable, as the operational time is approximately linear to the size of the data set.

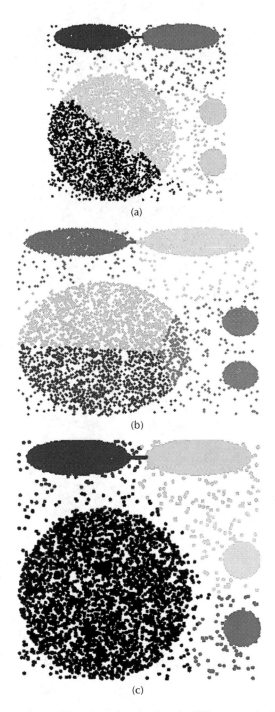

(a)

(b)

(c)

FIGURE 7.11 Comparison of the clustering results via different methods. (a) BIRCH ($k = 5$), (b) K-means ($k = 5$), (c) CURE ($k = 5$, $\alpha = 0.3$, number of representatives = 10), and (d) data-field clustering ($k = 5$).

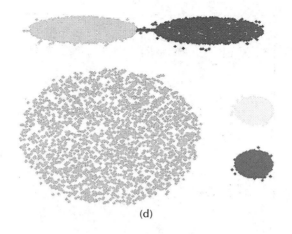

(d)

FIGURE 7.11 (Continued)

7.2.3 OUTLIER DETECTION AND DISCOVERY BASED ON DATA FIELD

As mentioned earlier in this chapter, classification and clustering are mainly utilized in data mining to discover classical grouping features, while small groups or points deviating from the classical patterns are regarded as noises and filtered out. However, the noise for one person may turn up to be the signal for another. Filtering of outlier points or abnormal patterns will probably lose some significant information or

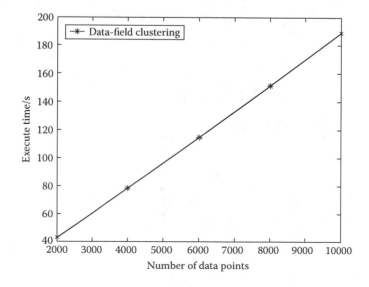

FIGURE 7.12 Extendability experiment of data-field clustering on different-scale data sets.

knowledge. In other words, outlier points themselves might be valuable. For examples, in cheating detection, outlier points can reveal behaviors of cheating, and in market analysis, deviant points may be related to consumption behaviors by costumers who are either extremely rich or extremely poor. Thus, the discovery of outlier points or outlier knowledge has been a significant and interesting direction in data mining.

A. Limitation of classical methods to discover outlier points

Once the data set containing n objects and the expected number k of outlier points is instructed, the problem of outlier point discovery can be described as to find the k objects, which are the most abnormal or the most inconsistent compared with the remaining data. Obviously, it is essential in the definition of "abnormal" and "inconsistent." Based on the different definitions of outlier points, common detection methods are generally divided into statistical methods, distance-based methods, and outlier-based methods, etc.[31,32]

In statistical methods, the data set is assumed to obey some probability distribution, followed by a discordancy test to determine the outlier data. Its main problem lies in that the majority of assumption test aim at a single attribute, while many mining tasks require the discovery of outlier points to be conducted in multiple attributes. Besides, distributive parameters should be known beforehand; however, in reality, the data distribution is probably unknown. Moreover, this method will be helpless if the data are distributed in such a way that it cannot be described by any standard distribution.

In the distance-based method, outlier points are regarded as the objects without enough neighbors, which are defined based on the distance to the given object. Compared to the statistical method, this one extends the idea of a discordancy test in multiple standard distributions, and avoids the large computational expense inevitable in the discordancy test. Nevertheless, this approach requires two parameters to be presented by the user: neighborhood radius r for the definition of neighbors and the outlier point threshold p. Searching for appropriate values of these parameters is tentative, especially when the user is not clear about the internal features of the data distribution. Thus, this approach has limitation in applications.

The outlier-based method imitates the human thinking pattern. By means of observing main features of an object group, we determine the outlier points that are apparently different from others. For example, in a large-scale multidimensional database, if the unit value of a cube is extremely different from the expectation according to the statistical model, it can be regarded as a outlier point. The advantage of this method comes from its high effectiveness. The time complexity is usually $O(n)$, where n is the object number. However, because data features are unknown beforehand, the definition of outlier function is complex. Moreover, this method is not applicable to outlier points with different dimensions in multiple concept hierarchies.

B. Outlier point detection algorithm based on data field

A outlier point detection algorithm[32] based on data field is proposed to tackle the problems in common outlier detection method. Suppose that a data set contains n

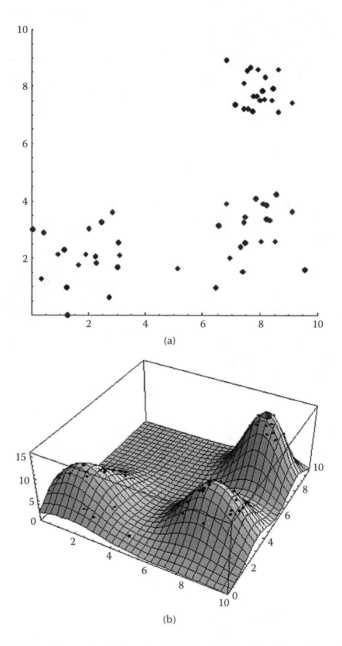

FIGURE 7.13 A two-dimensional data set and the distribution of its three-dimensional potential field.

objects, and the number of expected outlier points is k. First, data potential field is introduced to describe the interactions and spatial distribution of all the data objects. The objects in dense regions will obtain higher potentials, and those in sparse regions will have lower potentials, as shown in Figure 7.13. Second, all objects will be ranked based on the potential values according to their positions. Finally, the k objects with the least potentials will be selected as the outlier points.

The algorithm is illustrated below.

Algorithm 7.5 Outlier point detection algorithm based on data fields

Input: data set $D = \{x_1, x_2, \ldots, x_n\}$, the number of outlier points k, sample number n_{sample}

Output: k outlier points

Steps:

1. Select n_{sample} samples randomly to construct a data set *SampleSet*
2. //Optimize the influence factor σ
   σ = Optimal_Sigma(*SampleSet*)
3. //Employ grid partition of the space and construct an index tree
   Map = CreateMap(D, σ)
4. Compute the object potentials, and rank them ascendingly according to the potential values
5. Output the first k objects as the outlier points

There are two parameters in this algorithm: the expected number of outlier points k and the random sampling parameter n_{sample} for σ optimization. Within them, $n_{sample} \ll n$. If n is huge, $n_{sample} = [\alpha \cdot n]$, where $\alpha \geq 0.05$.

C.   Algorithm performance analysis

With a fixed sample volume $n_{sample} \ll n$, the time complexity of σ optimization is $O(n_{sample}^2)$. The time complexity in the one-round scanning of the data set, application of grid partition in the space, and B$^+$ tree construction, is $O(n + n_{grid} \cdot \log(n_{grid}))$, where n_{grid} is the number of nonempty grid and $n_{grid} \ll n$. The time spent on potential computation for an arbitrary object is equivalent to the average time spent in searching on the B$^+$ tree. As result, the total time complexity of this algorithm is $O(n_{sample}^2 + n + n_{grid} \log(n_{grid}) + n \log(n_{grid}))$. When n is huge, it will approximate $O(n \cdot \log(n_{grid}))$.

D.   Experimental results and analysis

Here, we apply the outlier point detection algorithm based on data field to the face recognition problem in access control systems. Outlier points, i.e., strangers' faces, are expected to be recognized by this algorithm.

The program is coded in MATLAB 6.1 and runs on a PC. Japanese female facial expression database[33] (JAFFE) is adopted for tested data, which consists of 213 frontal facial gray-level images for 10 people. The size of an original image is 256 × 256 in pixels, and the intensity of each pixel has 256 levels. Figure 7.14 illustrates 10 facial images from JAFFE, in which 7 are from the same person KA and the other 3 are outlier images from KR, YM, and NA.

In the test, the original images are normalized via preprocessing. Rotation, cutting, and scaling are applied to each image to eliminate the disturbance from

KA. DI3. 44   KA. SU3. 38   KA. FE2. 46   KA. AN2. 40   KA. NE2. 27

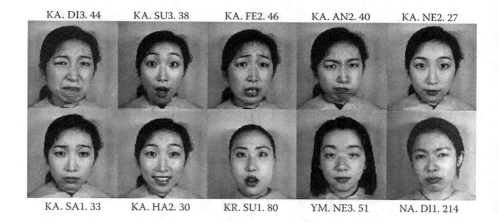

KA. SA1. 33   KA. HA2. 30   KR. SU1. 80   YM. NE3. 51   NA. DI1. 214

FIGURE 7.14 Facial images adopted for the outlier detection experiment.

hairs, background, and illumination. After preprocessing, we obtain standard facial images with 128×128 pixels, in which the locations of the two eyes are fixed, as shown in Figure 7.15. For convenience, we index each facial image by a letter within A–J. A–G stand for KA, and H, I, and J stand for KR, YM, and NA, respectively.

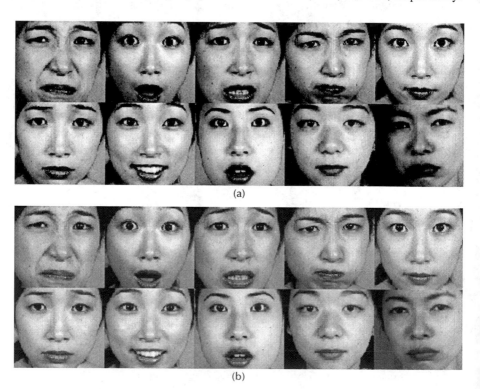

(a)

(b)

FIGURE 7.15 Standard facial images after preprocessing.

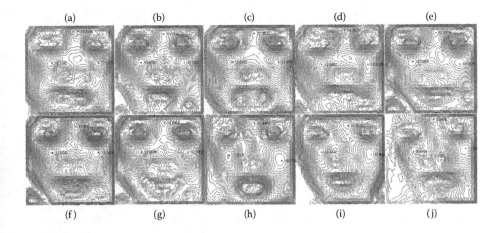

FIGURE 7.16 Distribution of equipotential lines in standard facial images.

Each pixel in the image is regarded as one data object in the two-dimensional space, and its intensity is normalized into the interval [0, 1] and regarded as the data object mass. In this way, interactions of all the pixels build up a data field. Figure 7.16 shows the equipotential lines of the data fields. Apparently, regions with higher potentials are located in areas with larger intensities, such as cheek, forehead, top of nose, etc. In other words, the distribution of the potential field can apparently reveal such facial areas as cheek, forehead, top of nose, and so on.

In the distribution, each local maximum point contains the influence of all the neighboring pixels. The local maximum points and their positions can be considered as logic features of the facial image. The facial data field can be projected into the feature space spanned by these logic features, as shown in Figure 7.17.

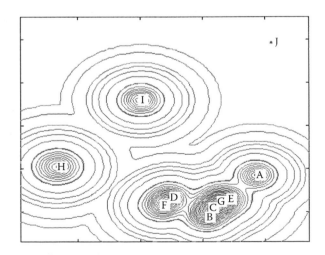

FIGURE 7.17 The second-order data field generated in the new feature space.

In the new feature space, each face is projected to a data point, and the interactions in all the data points form the second-order data field, in which outlier features are contained. As the result of outlier point detection algorithm based on data field, ranked defiant points are NA.DI1.214(J), YM.NE3.51(I), and KR.SU1.80(H). In this way, the algorithm detects the three strangers' faces.

7.3 DISCOVERY OF ASSOCIATION RULES WITH UNCERTAINTY

Association knowledge, as a significant type of knowledge in data mining, was proposed by R. Agrawal in the research on the database for supermarkets[34] in order to describe the dependent relation between attributes. It is also known as "association rules." One classical example is that "90 percent of customers will purchase milk together with bread and butter." It is valuable to discover all the similar association rules for sales strategy planning in marketing. With this information, the sellers may sell different kinds of goods in bundles, or distribute these goods together to stimulate consumption and increase the sales income. Association rules have been widely applied to lots of fields; for instance, doctors may discover common characteristics of patients with the same disease from thousands of clinical histories, so as to help cure the disease.

7.3.1 RECONSIDERATION OF THE TRADITIONAL ASSOCIATION RULES

Let $I = \{i_1, i_2, \ldots, i_m\}$ be an item set containing m distinct items, and $T = \{t_1, t_2, \ldots, t_n\}$ be a transaction database, in which every transaction $t_j \in T$ is a set composed of a group of items in I, i.e., $t_j \subseteq I$. An association rule is an implication in the form

$$X \rightarrow Y$$

where $X \subseteq I$, $Y \subseteq I$, and $X \cap Y = \varnothing$. If the ratio for inclusion of $X \cup Y$ by T is denoted a sup, the rule $X \rightarrow Y$ is said to have sup as support in T. If the ratio for inclusion of Y by the events which include X is $conf$, the rule $X \rightarrow Y$ is said to be satisfied in T with $conf$ as confidence, i.e.,

$$conf = \frac{\sup(X \cup Y)}{\sup(X)} \times 100\%$$

where support represents the emergence frequency of the rule in the event database, and confidence stands for the degree to which the rule is believable.

In general, people are favorable to those association rules with high support and strong confidence, which are also called "strong association rules." The basic task of data mining for the association rules is to discover strong association rules in the large-scale database. It essentially involves the following two basic steps:

1. To search for frequent item sets, i.e., to discover those item sets from the event database T with sup larger than the threshold $minsup$, which are set by the user.
2. To utilize the frequent item set for generation of association rules with $conf$ no less than the threshold $minconf$ presented by the user.

In these steps, it is determined by the preset thresholds whether the association rules have high support and strong confidence.

It is easy to implement step 2 by algorithms.[31] With a given frequent item set A, one scanning in the database is sufficient to assess whether all the nonempty subset a in A satisfy the precondition, i.e., $\frac{\sup(A)}{\sup(a)}$ is no less than confidence instructed by the user. Thereafter, we can obtain all the association rules in the form $a \rightarrow (A - a)$. Hence, the overall performance of the association rule mining is determined by the first step, in which the critical issue is how to effectively search for the frequent item set in the large-scale database. Let I be an item set containing m distinct items. The number of all the possible item combinations is $2^m - 1$, so when m becomes huge, it is impossible to search for the frequent item set by visiting all the possible combinations. As a solution, Apriori algorithm[35] is usually adopted. In fact, the majority of common association rule mining algorithms are based on the Apriori algorithm.

Apriori algorithm is mainly based on a anti-monotonic assumption: if the item set $X \subseteq I$ is a frequent item set, then all of their non-empty subsets are frequent item set; and if X is non-frequent, then all of its hyper-sets are non-frequent. According to this assumption, Apriori algorithm compresses the searching space via an iterative method, which is to search for the frequent item set by means of the candidate item set. First, it determines a one dimensional frequent item set L_1, which consists of the items with $sup > minsup$. Second, it generates the two-dimensional candidate item set based on L_1, and detects all the two-dimensional frequent item sets, denoted as L_2. Thereafter, the algorithm iterates for every hierarchy until no more frequent item set can be detected. Let L_{k-1} ($k = 1, 2,...,m$) be a $k - 1$ dimensional frequent item set. The k-dimensional candidate item set C_k is a hyper-set of L_{k-1}. All the k-dimensional frequent item set is included in C_k. As a result, the algorithm can effectively eliminate the nonfrequent item set in C_k and generate L_k, so as to search for the higher dimensional frequent item set. The algorithm is described below.

Algorithm 7.6 Discovery of frequent item set (Apriori)

Input: the transaction database T, support threshold $minsup$
Output: the frequent item set L in T
Steps:

BEGIN

//Scan the whole transaction database T, calculate the support number for each item, and compute its support. Put into L_1 the set containing the item with support no less than $minsup$

L_1 = find_frequent_1-itemsets(T)

//Iteratively combine the item sets in L_1, and search for the frequent item set

for ($k = 2$; $L_{k-1} \neq \emptyset$; k++){

//Combine the $k - 1$-frequent item set in $L_k - 1$, and generate the set C_k of candidate item sets.

C_k=apriori_gen(L_{k-1}; $minsup$)

//Scan the database

for each transaction $t \in T$ {

//Find all the possibly included candidate item sets for each transaction in the database, and store these candidate item sets into C_t

$C_t = \text{subset}(C_k, t)$

//Increase the counter for each candidate item set in C_t by 1

for each candidate $c \in C_t$

c.counter ++

}

//Put those candidate sets which satisfy threshold condition into L_k

$L_k = \{c \in C_k|\ c.\text{count} \geq minsup\}$

}

return $L = \cup_k L_k$

END

It can be seen from the analysis that this algorithm can effectively solve the frequent item set searching problem in a large-scale database by utilizing anti-monotonicity. However, this algorithm is aiming at the transaction database with Boolean values, and support and confidence threshold is required in advance. Thus there are several limitations in the application of association rule mining:

1. The support and confidence threshold are usually precise values in the present applications of association rule mining. For example, user will set $minsup = 32\%$, $minconf = 81\%$. Those item sets with support no less than 32% are frequent item sets and are able to generate association rules; however, only those rules with confidence no less than 81% are strong association rules, which are the association rules meaningful to the user. Nevertheless, this demand in precise thresholding will not only challenge the user by accurate threshold selection, but also deviate the qualitative thinking pattern of humans. Does it mean that those rules with $conf = 80.9\%$ are definitely meaningless if $minconf = 81\%$?

2. In the large database, there exist numerical attributes ubiquitously other than Boolean and category attributes, e.g., people's income, age, geographical location, etc. For such kind of database, transformation from numerical attributes to Boolean attributes is a prerequisite, and thereafter Apriori algorithm and other improved algorithms can be employed for association rules mining. But in this transformation, there may exist the following problems.[36] If the partition interval is too narrow, support in the item set containing this interval will be low, and consequently the number of frequent sets will be small. On the other hand, if the partition interval is too

large, confidence of the rule containing this interval will be small, and consequently the number of generated rules will be small and the information content in the rule will be reduced accordingly. Hence the challenging problem in the association rule mining on numerical attributes arises in the valid and effective partition on the universal set of the numerical attributes, so as to reflect the distributive feature of the attributes.

7.3.2 ASSOCIATION RULE MINING AND FORECASTING

Uncertainties exist in human thinking, so it is more natural to describe support and confidence by qualitative linguistic values such as "very low," "low," "medium," "high," and "very high," rather than by precise quantitative values. The key problem still lies in the way to implement the uncertainty transformation between qualitative linguistic values and quantitative numerical values. For the partition of a numerical attribute domain, the transformation from quantitative expression to qualitative description is an applicable approach, which can reflect uncertainties in human thinking as well as the distributive feature of the attribute value in the domain.

Association knowledge mining algorithm based on cloud models[37] is proposed to conquer the limitation stated above. At this moment, cloud models are utilized to represent support and confidence qualitatively. The forward cloud generator is employed to realize the transformation from qualitative linguistic values to quantitative numerical values. The cloud transformation is applied to divide the numerical attribute domain into some qualitative concepts expressed in clouds so as to discretize numerical attributes. This way, the previous Apriori algorithm could be implemented for association rule mining on various kinds of data in the large-scale database.

The knowledge granularity in the to-be-discovered association rule is usually reflected by the user-set number of qualitative concepts on the related attributes.[38] In general, the larger the granularity, the fewer the number of concepts, and the more macro the discovered association knowledge is. Association knowledge mining algorithm based on cloud models is demonstrated below.

Algorithm 7.7 CloudAssociationRules

Input: relation database RDB
        attribute set $P = \{P_1, P_2,\ldots, P_m\}$
        minsup(Ex_1, En_1, He_1)
        minconf(Ex_2, En_2, He_2)
Output: association rules satisfying both the support and confidence
Steps:

BEGIN

    //Apply cloud transformation on each numerical attribute and obtain the qualitative concepts, the number of which is preset by the user

    for each Attribute P_i in RDB do

        if the domain of P_i is numerical

            {

//Require the user to input the expected number of qualitative concepts "n"

Ask(n);

//Divide the attribute P_i by cloud transformation, obtain n qualitative concepts and their numerical characters, and store them in the set C_{pi}

$C_{pi} = $ Cloudtransform(P_i)

}

//Express the numerical attributes by qualitative concepts
for each tuple t in RDB, do

for $i = 1$ to m do

{

if $t[i]$ is numerical, then

//Substitute the precise numerical value to a qualitative concept via maximum determination

$t[i] = $ CloudMap($t[i]$, C_{pi}, 1)

}

Transform the relational database RDB into the transaction database T, the attributes in which are the set of all the attribute values in RDB

$L_1 = $ find_frequent_1-itemsets(T)

for ($k = 2$; $L_{k-1} \neq \varnothing$; k++)

{

//Generate support by cloud generators randomly

$minsup = $ CG(Ex_1, En_1, He_1)

//Combine the $k - 1$ frequent item set in L_{k-1}, and obtain the candidate item set C_k

$C_k = $ apriori_gen(L_{k-1}; $minsup$)

//Scan the database

for each transaction $t \in T$

for each candidate $c \in C_k$ do

if $c \subseteq t$ then c.count++

//Put the candidate set satisfying $minsup$ into L_k

$L_k = \{c \in C_k | \ c.\text{count} \geq minsup\}$

$$L = \cup_k L_k;$$

}

for each frequent itemset l_k in L, $k \geq 2$

genrules(l_k, l_k)

End

procedure genrules(l_k: frequent k-itemset, x_m: frequent m-itemset)

$X = \{(m-1)\text{-itemsets } x_{m-1} | x_{m-1} \in x_m\}$

//Generate confidence by cloud generator randomly

$minconf = CG(Ex_2, En_2, He_2)$

for each x_{m-1} in X {

conf = support(l_k)/support(x_{m-1})

if (conf $\geq$ minconf) then {

print the rule "$x_{m-1} \Rightarrow (l_k - x_{m-1})$"

with support = support(l_k), confidence=conf

if ($m - 1 > 1$) then

//Set x_{m-1} as the precondition in the rule, and continuously generate association rules

genrules(l_k, x_{m-1})

}

}

It can be seen that, the obtained qualitative concepts after discretization via cloud transformation are reflective of actual distribution of the attribute values. Due to the fact that a qualitative concept has an obscure boundary, the obtained association rules will be more in accordance with the human thinking pattern. By means of concept climb-up process, association rules in different hierarchies will be generated. Moreover, the threshold will be "soft," and has obtain boundary, rather than a fixed quantitative value. The user can obtain several mining results with uncertainties through the association rule mining procedure based on soft thresholds.

Let's consider the spatial database on Chinese geography and economy, which is discussed in Chapter 6, Section 6.1. CloudAssociationRules algorithm is adopted for association rule mining on the numerical attributes.[39,40] After the cloud transformation on the numerical attributes in Table 6.1, the category attribute can be obtained, as shown in Table 6.3. According to the requirement by CloudAssociationRules, it is further transformed into a Boolean database as illustrated in Table 7.5. SE, SW, S, NW, Md, NE, E2N, N, H, M, L, F, and Nr stand for southeast, southwest, south,

TABLE 7.5
Boolean Database after Being Transformed

Location								Altitude			Road Net Density			Distance from Sea			Annual Income		
SE	SW	S	NW	Md	NE	E2N	N	H	M	L	H	L	M	Nr	F	M	H	M	L
1	0	0	0	0	0	0	0	0	1	0	1	0	0	1	0	0	1	0	0
1	0	0	0	0	0	0	0	0	1	0	1	0	0	1	0	0	0	1	0
1	0	0	0	0	0	0	0	0	0	1	1	0	0	1	0	0	1	0	0
0	1	0	0	0	0	0	0	1	0	0	0	1	0	0	1	0	0	0	1
0	1	0	0	0	0	0	0	1	0	0	0	1	0	0	1	0	0	1	0
0	0	1	0	0	0	0	0	0	1	0	1	0	0	0	0	1	0	1	0
0	0	1	0	0	0	0	0	0	0	1	1	0	0	0	0	1	1	0	0
0	0	1	0	0	0	0	0	0	0	1	1	0	0	0	0	1	0	1	0
0	0	0	1	0	0	0	0	0	1	0	0	1	0	0	1	0	0	0	1
0	0	0	1	0	0	0	0	0	1	0	0	1	0	0	1	0	0	1	0
0	0	0	1	0	0	0	0	1	0	0	0	1	0	0	1	0	0	0	1
0	0	0	0	1	0	0	0	0	1	0	1	0	0	0	0	1	0	1	0
0	0	0	0	1	0	0	0	0	0	1	1	0	0	0	0	1	0	1	0
0	0	0	0	0	1	0	0	0	0	1	1	0	0	0	0	1	0	1	0
0	0	0	0	0	1	0	0	0	0	1	1	0	0	1	0	0	1	0	0
0	0	0	0	0	1	0	0	0	1	0	0	1	0	0	1	0	0	0	1
0	0	0	0	0	0	1	0	0	0	1	1	0	0	1	0	0	1	0	0
0	0	0	0	0	0	1	0	0	0	1	1	0	0	1	0	0	0	1	0
0	0	0	0	0	0	0	1	0	1	0	0	0	1	0	0	1	0	1	0
0	0	0	0	0	0	0	1	0	1	0	0	0	1	0	1	0	0	1	0
...	...	...	...	...	...	...	...	...	...	...	...	...	...	...	...	...	...	...	...

northwest, middle, northeast, east to north, north, high, middle, low, far, and near, respectively.

If the softened support threshold is low (0.06, 0.01, 0.0005), and the softened threshold of confidence is high (0.75, 0.08, 0.0005), then eight frequent 4-item sets can be obtained by CloudAssociationRules algorithm. If the conjunction of three attributes: "geometric location," "road net density," and "distance from sea" are selected as the rule precondition, and "annual income" is the postcondition, in the level of a certain conceptual granularity, then eight association rules satisfying the threshold of confidence can be generated, as below. Figure 7.18, which is not a map, illustrates the visualized rules.

Rule 1: If the location is "southeast," the road net density is "high," and the distance from the sea is "near," then the annual income per capita is "high."

Rule 2: If the location is "east to north," the road net density is "high," and the distance from the sea is "near," then the annual income per capita is "high."

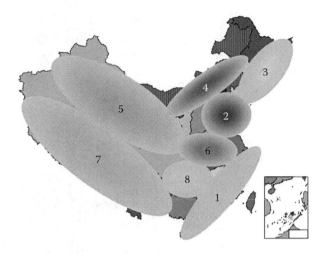

FIGURE 7.18 Association rules on the annual income per capita (1–8).

Rule 3: If the location is "northeast," the road net density is "high," and the distance from the sea is "medium," then the annual income per capita is "medium."

Rule 4: If the location is "north," the road net density is "medium," and the distance from the sea is "medium," then the annual income per capita is "medium."

Rule 5: If the location is "northwest," the road net density is "low," and the distance from the sea is "far," then the annual income per capita is "low."

Rule 6: If the location is "middle," the road net density is "high," and the distance from the sea is "medium," then the annual income per capita is "medium."

Rule 7: If the location is "southwest," the road net density is "low," and the distance from the sea is "far," then the annual income per capita is "low."

Rule 8: If the location is "south," the road net density is "high," and the distance from the sea is "medium," then the annual income per capita is "medium."

As the intermediate result of the above rules, the frequent two-item set and the frequent three-item set are obtained. For instance the rules below illustrate the relations between road net density and altitude, together with geographical location. The visualized representation is shown in Figure 7.19, which is not a map.

Rule 1: If the altitude is "low," then the road net density is "high."

Rule 2: If the altitude is "high," then the road net density is "low."

Rule 3: If the altitude is "medium" and the location is "northwest," then the road net density is "low."

Rule 4: If the altitude is "medium" and the location is "north," then the road net density is "medium."

For discovery of association rules in different granularities, we can ascend or descend concepts' level. For examples, to combine "northwest" and

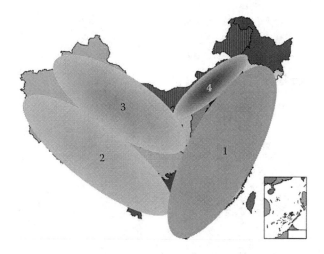

FIGURE 7.19 Association rules on the road net density.

"southwest" to "west," and to combine "south" and "middle" to "middle south." By this means, the eight rules in Figure 7.18 are reduced to six (shown in Figure 7.20, which is not a map). Rules 1, 2, 3, and 4 remain the same, while rules 5 and 7 are combined into a new rule indexed as 5, and rules 6 and 8 are combined into a new rule indexed as 6.

Rule 5: If the location is "west," the road net density is "low," and the distance to sea is "far," then the annual income per capita is "low."

Rule 6: If the location is "middle south," the road net density is "high," and the distance to sea is "medium," then the annual income per capita is "medium."

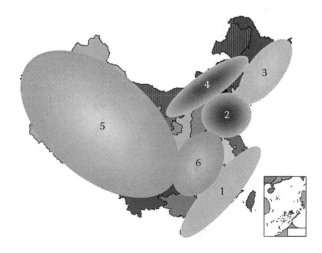

FIGURE 7.20 More abstract association rules on the annual income per capita.

From the aforementioned experiment, it can be seen that the support and confidence described by qualitative linguistic values can simulate the uncertainties in human thinking, and make the discovered association knowledge robust and easy to understand. The idea of conceptual granularity and concept cross-layer jumping method by the cloud model can effectively realize the granularity computation in discovery of association knowledge. Moreover, the association rule mining method based on the combination of the cloud model and Apriori algorithm does not only enhance the understandability of the association knowledge of numerical attributes, but strengthens and extends the effectiveness and applicability of Apriori algorithm.

7.4 TIME SERIES DATA MINING AND FORECASTING

The data mining technologies discussed above deal with static data, which is independent of the time attribute. However, there exist a large number of complex time series data in real applications, such as telephone records, credit card trading, stocks trading, video streaming data, Web logs, monthly rain quantity of a certain region, railway passenger flow volume, etc. It is also a significant and popular research topic to extract the predictive information and knowledge out of a large quantity of time series data.

Time series data mining (TSDM), is to extract the time-related information and knowledge based on the variation trend and feature of the time series data, so as to predict and control the future motion. The presently applied time series data mining methods include similarity search, periodic pattern discovery, sequential pattern discovery, and time series prediction, etc. In applications, people do not only wish to discover knowledge reflecting internal features and developing regularities, e.g., periodic patterns and sequential ones, but also hope to utilize this knowledge to predict the developing trend of a related event. As a result, time series prediction has become the main objective in TSDM.

Time series prediction, also known as trend analysis, is to analyze time series data $\{x_1,..., x_t,...,x_n\}$, where n is the length of the series and x_t is the sampled value at time t, so as to predict the future series $\{x_{n+1}, x_{n+2},...\}$. Due to the variety, continuity, time-variance, and orderliness of time series data, there are great challenges in time series prediction. For example, time series data are generally a giant quantity of continuous data, so the cost for random access is huge. Besides, variation with time is fast as well, so the response should almost be in time. Moreover, time series data are mainly at a low level and contain multiple attributes, so the ability for multidimensional analysis and processing is required.

Up until now, many time series prediction methods have been proposed, such as classical mathematical analysis, neural network method, and machine learning method, etc.

Since 1968, when George Box and Gwilym M. Jenkins proposed the Box-Jenkins modeling theory for time series analysis, the classical mathematical analysis method has been developed rapidly. Time series prediction is performed by establishing random models, e.g., auto-regressive model (AR), auto-regressive moving average model (ARMA), and auto-regressive integrated moving average model (ARIMA), and it is applied into fields of financial analysis and market analysis successfully. However, the random modeling can only express effectively the time series with finite length, and the model resulting from data insertion will be unable to explain the data. Moreover, the classical data analysis method is only applicable to static time series, and it provides directly the precise prediction value and its confidence interval, so the understandability of the time series knowledge is poor.

The neural network method establishes a prediction model with a neural network by training on a period of past data, so as to make prediction. These kinds of methods have been widely applied to water demand,[41] prediction of the financial trend,[42] prediction of solar activities,[43] and so on. In real applications, due to the fact that many time series data are not static but inclusive of time-variant feature parameters and distributions, it is impossible to conduct the prediction by establishing a single prediction model. Drossu proposed a precise retraining method based on statistics, in which the model would be retrained for new weights if the present model did not fit current data. Meanwhile, they discussed the way to estimate the initial weights in each layer of the neural network via statistical model, so as to design and train the neural network faster and more effectively, and applied it to time series prediction.

In the past, machine learning methods were frequently applied to static problems. Recently, this type of methods also are applied to solve the problems involving the time attribute. For instance, R. Boné introduced the finite state machines or automata theory for time series prediction. The basic idea is to dicretize the time series into some finite alphabet and, by using techniques from the theory of finite automata, build a finite automation to recognize the suffixes of any given texts with a certain length. This approach had been applied successfully for the prediction of sunspot activity. Besides, Dieterich and Michalski utilized the machine learning method to establish a system for prediction of the series in the poker game Eleusis.[44]

Although the methods of data analysis, neural network, and machine learning all have their merits, the majority belongs to the precise quantitative method for time series, i.e., to establish the mathematical model, neural network model, or automatic machine model by means of feature extraction or parameter training, for prediction. The selection of model structures and parameters is not tightly related to the knowledge, so it is difficult to be understood by the user. Meanwhile, these methods in majority provide one or a series of data or numerical interval(s) as the prediction result. The quantitative result is usually weak and not understandable. Besides, the majority of these methods neglect an important factor in time series data, i.e., the time granularity problem. If the time granularity is too small, the algorithm will be trapped by the details, and the data variation will become too big to be predicted. If the time granularity is too large, the important or even determinative knowledge will probably be lost. The data with different time granularities will have different functions in time series prediction.

In order to tackle the problems above, time series prediction mechanism based on cloud models is proposed.[45] With cloud models as the basis for knowledge expression, it introduces two kinds of predictive knowledge: quasiperiodic variant regulation and current trend, and it synthesizes predictive knowledge with two distinct granularities for implementation of time series prediction in different hierarchies.

7.4.1 Time Series Data Mining Based on Cloud Models

A. Cloud-based expression on predicted knowledge[46,47,48]

Let D: $\{(t_i,b_i) \mid 0 \le i <T\}$ be a given time series data set, where t_i is a certain time of the numerical attribute A, and b_i is the value of the numerical attribute A at time t_i. $b_i<b_j$ is satisfied if and only if $i < j$. Our objective is to predict the value of b_l at future time t_l.

The first step that leads to accomplishing this objective is to discover the variation regulation from the database D. Hence, the main problem lies in the expression of knowledge.

1. Expression of knowledge with semiperiodic regulation

In nature and human society, many behaviors occur according to a certain natural temporal interval, such as year, month, week, or day, etc. They are to some extent periodic. However in reality, there exist many uncertain factors affecting these behaviors. It is impossible to completely reveal these factors. If we emphasize too much these precise details, we will lose track of the overall regulation of the time series. For example, temperature in the summer is generally high, but it does not exclude some cool days. As a qualitative–quantitative transformation, the cloud model can reflect the overall regulation via its numerical characteristics, as well as the irregular details via the deviation of cloud drops.

2. Expression of knowledge on the current trend

In the time series prediction, the current time series state should be paid more attention to, aside from the long-term regularity. Although the knowledge with quasiperiodic regulation reflects the overall variation trend of the time series, any object or event changes gradually with relative stability and is more affected by the current state. Thus the expression of knowledge on the current trend and its function for prediction becomes significantly influential. The current trend is subject to the variant regulation of the current data, and its knowledge expression should be uncertain, so it is natural to represent the main stream and its uncertainties by means of expectation, entropy, and hyper-entropy in the cloud model.

B. Cloud-based time series prediction

Let T be the length of quasiperiod of the time series. There exist an integer k and time $t_c \in [0,T]$, satisfying $t_l = t_c + k*T$. The time series data $D\{(t_i,b_i) \mid 0 \le i < l\}$ can be divided into the history data set HD and the current data set CD as below:

$$HD = \{(t_i, b_i) \mid t_0 \le t_i < k*T\}$$

$$CD = \{(t_i, b_i) \mid k*T \le t_i < t_l\}$$

Those qualitative rule sets for prediction can be discovered based on the data in *HD*, as below:

$$A_1 \rightarrow B_1$$

$$A_2 \rightarrow B_2$$

$$\vdots$$

$$A_m \rightarrow B_m$$

The quasiperiodic regulation expressed by qualitative rules is reflective of historical and global knowledge, and acts as the foundation of prediction. A_i, which reflects different time granularities, is a time-related linguistic value expressed by the cloud model. B_i is a quasiperiodic regulation expressed by cloud model.

According to the data distribution in *CD*, we can utilize the backward cloud generator to obtain the current trend that is the current cloud model *CCM*. The knowledge expressed by *CCM* represents the recent and local predictive knowledge.

Here we emphasize the way to implement the prediction mechanism on the time series via synthesizing these two sorts of knowledge.

Step 1. Activate one rule $A_i \rightarrow B_i$ in the qualitative rule set. First, with a given time t_i', we adopt the maximum determination (please refer to Algorithm 6.5) to activate one rule in the qualitative rule set as the quasiperiodic regulation. If $A_i \rightarrow B_i$ is activated, then the postcondition B_i is called as a "historical cloud," which acts as the fundamental predictive knowledge.

Step 2. Generate the predictive cloud S_t by synthesizing the historical cloud B_i and the current cloud *CCM*. According to Chapter 6, Section 6.3, we utilize cloud combination algorithm to synthesize B_i and *CCM* for S_t.

Step 3. Obtain the prediction result based on the new predictive rule $A_i \rightarrow S_t$. We construct a new qualitative rule $A_i \rightarrow S_t$, activate this rule for multiple times, and obtain prediction results with different uncertainties, which are provided to the user as a set.

7.4.2 STOCK DATA FORECASTING

We will discuss the example of stock prediction for further illustration on the aforementioned prediction mechanism. The stock market varies almost unpredictably. Aside of experience-based analysis, technical analysis is also required for prediction. Based on the past and current situations, data analysis and logical reasoning are employed to induce some classical regulation for the prediction of future trends. There have been a number of stock analysis software in the world, such as "Qianlong," which is a dynamic analysis system and "Investor," which is a consultant analysis and decision system on finance and stocks. They are mainly analysis software providing the functions of multiple technical parameters calculation and historical curve plotting. They have user friendly interfaces, and are applicable. Nevertheless, they cannot provide prediction information in general.

In technical analysis, K line prediction describes the gaming record in the stock market by visualized graphs. It is able to reveal the strength of the stock trend, as well as the balance variation between the buyer and the seller, so as to help the user predict the future market.[49,50] However, faced with the huge K line data, people prefer to obtain qualitative descriptions, especially the combination pattern of the current K lines as well as its usage in practice.[51-53] Nowadays, there have been some software with K line prediction, e.g., "Analyzer" stocks analyzing software, etc.[54] However, they mainly adopt the traditional interval partition method, i.e., classification according to the variation range between the closing price and the opening price. This partition is subjective and short of a uniform standard. Fixed partition to the interval will lead to false judgments on some critical states.

Cloud-based method for soft partition on the stocks data transforms the stocks data into discrete qualitative concepts via cloud transformation. It establishes the classical K line pattern database and forms qualitative rule sets describing quasiperiodic regulations. Thereafter, it utilizes the current trend of stocks to predict the K line by matching, and meanwhile, it combines the analysis on the matched amount and matched price to predict the suitable time for purchasing or selling.

A. Cloud-based description on K line data

In the K line analysis on stocks, a single K line and the relation between two K lines are sufficient to describe the complete pattern in all the K lines. A single K line is composed of an entity and two shadow lines, as shown in Figure 7.21.

The entity is the rectangle generated by the opening price (OPEN) and closing price (CLOSE), and its main features include "red/black" and length. The shadow lines include an upper shadow line between the highest price (HIGH) and the upper edge of the entity, and a lower shadow line between the lower edge of the entity and the lowest price (LOW). The main features of the shadow lines include the length relation between the two shadow lines, together with whether the shadow line length is zero. As for single K lines, there is a difference in their size as well as in their color (red/black.) The size of a K line refers to the length of the entity part in the K line, and it can be measured by the following price fluctuating index (PFI):

$$PFI = \frac{CLOSE - OPEN}{OPEN} \times 100\%$$

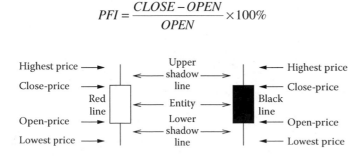

FIGURE 7.21 The K line graph.

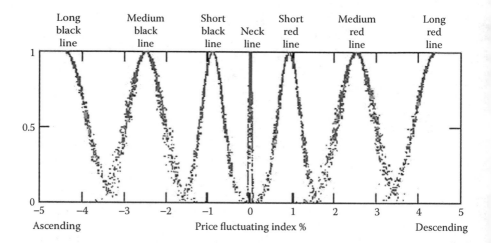

FIGURE 7.22 The cloud model expression of the graphic entity in a single *K* line.

Regarding PFI as an attribute value, we can establish cloud models for seven qualitative concepts accordingly, so as to represent the "red/black" and size of the graphic entity in a single *K* line. By this means, we implement soft classification on the entity sorts, as demonstrated in Figure 7.22.

Based on the existence of the upper/lower shadow lines and their lengths, single *K* lines can be categorized into two large classes and six small classes, as shown in Table 7.6.

In the Table 7.6, the existence and the length of shadow lines are both relative and qualitative. We can establish linguistic values constructed by cloud models to represent the lengths of the shadow lines. In classification of shadow lines, we introduce "soft zero" to imitate the uncertainty in human decision. The algorithm is illustrated below. "Soft zero" is a qualitative concept with 0 as the expectation, considerably small numbers as the entropy and the hyper-entropy. Its quantitative value is little random.

TABLE 7.6
The Classes of Shadow Lines

	Marubozu K Line			Shadow K Line		
Classes	All bald K line	Black Marubozu	Red Marubozu	Shadows with equal lengths	Shadows with the lower longer	Shadows with the upper longer
Definition	With only the entity but not shadow lines	With only the entity and the lower shadow line, but not the upper one	With only the entity and the upper shadow line, but not the lower one	With the two shadow lines equally long approximately	With the lower shadow line longer than the upper one	With the upper shadow line longer than the lower one

Algorithm 7.8 The shadow line classification algorithm

Input: *OPEN*; //the opening price
              CLOSE; //The closing price
              HIGH; //The highest price
              LOW; //The lowest price
              ZERO. //The soft zero
Output: *kind*. //The kind of shadow line
Step:

BEGIN

    //Computing the length of the upper shadow line

    length_high=HIGH–MAX(*OPEN,CLOSE*);

    //Computing the length of the lower shadow line

    length_low=MIN(*OPEN,CLOSE*)–*LOW*;

    //Generating the soft zero

    zero=get_zero(*ZERO*);

    IF |*length_high*|<|*zero*| THEN

            IF |*length_ low* |<|*zero*| THEN

                    kind = all bald K line;

            ELSE *kind* = bareheaded K line;

    ELSE

            IF |*length_low*| < |*zero*| THEN

                    kind = barefooted K line;

            ELSE

                    {

            //Computing the difference between the lengths of the upper and
lower shadow lines

                    length = length_high - length_low;

                    SWITCH length

                        {

                        CASE *length* ≥ |*zero*| : *kind* = the length of the upper shadow line;

                        CASE *length* ≤ -|*zero*| : *kind* = the length of the lower shadow line;

                        OTHERWISE : *kind* = the length of either one of the two
shadow lines;

                        }

                    }

    OUTPUT(kind);

END

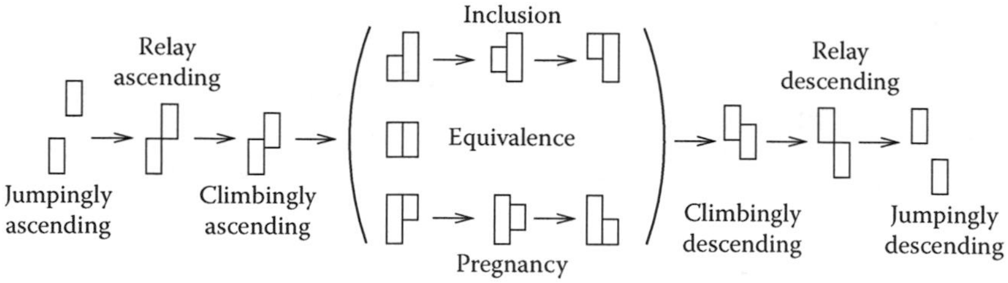

FIGURE 7.23 The relationship between two K lines.

Although a single K line is reflective of the current comparison between the two competitive sides, it is not sufficient to represent the trend in stock markets, neither can it act as the basis for prediction. The relation among multiple K lines should be considered for stocks prediction. By means of investigating the relationship between two K lines in the traditional K line pattern, the relational graph as shown in Figure 7.23 can be extracted. It can be seen that the transition within the states is continuous, the difference between the states is vague, and no clear boundary can be extracted.

For further description of the relationship between two K lines, relative fluctuating relation (RFR) and relative fluctuating index (RFI) can be adopted. RFR consists of ascending, staying, and descending, related to the left, middle, and right parts in Figure 7.23. In these three fluctuating relations, RFI can be defined as shown in Table 7.7, where max_1 and max_2 are the upper edges of the two K line entities, respectively, while min_1 and min_2 are their lower edges. Qualitative concept sets can be established to divide softly the fluctuating index in each fluctuate relation, so as to distinguish the mini-classes inside.

Based on RFI, we construct clouds to represent qualitative concepts, e.g., "jump-up ascending," "relay ascending," "climb-up ascending," "inclusion," "equivalence," "pregnancy," "slide-down descending," "relay descending," and "jump-down descending." The RFI concept of staying is a soft zero. Those with positive RFIs are ascending, and those with negative ones are descending, respectively. The variation in the absolute value of RFI is representative of the gradual change of all kinds of mini-states. For instance, for the descending state, the formula

$$\frac{min_1 - max_2}{(max_1 - min_1) + (max_2 - min_2)}$$

TABLE 7.7
RFR and RFI

RFR	Ascending	Descending	Staying
Judgment Conditions	$max_2 > max_1$ $min_2 > min_1$	$max_2 < max_1$ $min_2 < min_1$	Otherwise
RFI	$\frac{min_2 - max_1}{(max_1 - min_1) + (max_2 - min_2)}$	$\frac{min_1 - max_2}{(max_1 - min_1) + (max_2 - min_2)}$	$\frac{(max_2 - max_1) + (min_1 - min_2)}{(max_1 - min_1) + (max_2 - min_2)}$

can be utilized to calculate RFI. The increase in the absolute value of RFI reveals the increase of the descending trend, i.e., slide-down descending motion is gradually turned into jump-up descending motion.

B. Prediction mechanism based on the cloud *K* line

1. Establishing the pattern database of traditional K line combination

By means of the cloud method, we can encode the single K pattern and the relationship pattern between two K lines, and each concept can be allocated one code. In this way, we can implement the symbolic representation of the K line graph. Let Σ, Ψ and Γ be the symbol sets descriptive of the entity pattern, and the shadow line pattern of the single K line, and the relationship pattern between the K lines, respectively. The combination pattern of K lines can be defined by a quadruple sequence:

$$\{(S_1, KIND_1, LR_1, FR_1), (S_2, KIND_2, LR_2, FR_2), \ldots\ldots, (S_n, KIND_n, LR_n, FR_n)\}$$

where n is the number of K lines included in the pattern, $S_i \in \Sigma$ is entity pattern of the ith single K line, $KIND_i \in \Psi$ is the shadow line pattern of the ith single K line, $LR_i \in \Gamma$ is the relationship pattern between this K line and the previous one, and $FR_i \in \Gamma$ is the relationship pattern between this K line and the first one.

The practical K line pattern can be expressed by one or multiple symbol sequences, based on the definition above. The existing practical K line patterns can be organized by alphabetical order to form a practical K line pattern database. Besides, the corresponding practice meanings (e.g., purchasing and sale) are linked to the patterns for K line prediction.

2. Recognition of the traditional K line combination pattern

Based on KMP linear matching algorithm proposed by D. E. Knuth, J. H. Morris, and V. R. Pratt, the K line combination pattern in the symbolized stocks data can be recognized in real time, and the K line prediction can be done thereafter.

By means of failure function f, KMP algorithm can determine the maximum length of the first true subsequence, which is self-matching. When a certain matching is unsuccessful, the value of failure function will help determine the position at which the next matching begins. Let $Q = \{q_1 q_2 \ldots q_m\}$ and $P = \{p_1 p_2 \ldots p_n\}$ be the text sequence and the pattern sequence, respectively, and $m \gg n$. Let k be the maximum length of the subsequence in the text sequence, which matches the pattern sequence of the first time, and j be the subscript of the last letter in the matching subsequence in the text sequence. Define failure function as

$$f(j) = k$$

If there is no subsequence matching the pattern sequence, $k = 0$.

This algorithm computes the failure function f iteratively, and outputs a set of non-negative integers, i.e., index $= \{0, 1, 2, \ldots\}$ to represent the matching situation of the pattern sequence and the text sequence. Yang and Ma can be referred to for details on this algorithm.[50]

In the procedure of real time encoding on the K line data, S_i, $KIND_i$, LR_i and FR_i in each K line pattern correspond to several different qualitative concepts, so there will be multiple combined coding. For different qualitative concepts, the value of K line pattern will have different certainty degrees, and hence the degree of reliability for the recognized pattern will be different as well. Based on this, we introduce a quinary sequence of the stocks data

$$\{(S_1, KIND_1, LR_1, FR_1, Certainty_1),......, (S_i, KIND_i, LR_i, FR_i,$$
$$Certainty_i),......\} \ (i = 1,2,...,n)$$

where *Certainty$_i$* is the degree of reliability on the possible patterns of the current K line graph described by means of $(S_i, KIND_i, LR_i, FR_i)$.

Cloud-based K line prediction algorithms[55,56] can be developed based on the analysis above. The triple element group Match_State=(dic_pattern_point, first_Kline, reliability) records the prediction result. The dic_pattern_point is the pointer of the matching pattern in the traditional K line combination pattern database, first_Kline is the first K line data value in the K line data for pattern matching, and reliability is the accumulated degree of reliability for pattern matching.

Algorithm 7.9 Cloud-based K line prediction

Input: //K line data (*OPEN, CLOSE, HIGH, LOW*)
        K_line
        //the traditional K line pattern database
        DICTIONARY;
        //the pointer of the matching pattern in the traditional K line combined pattern database
        dic_pattern _point (*pattern$_i$*, first_Kline(*S,KIND,LR,FR*), *meaning*)
Output: //signals of purchasing and sale, and the evaluation of its prediction effect
        (*forecast_result, forecast_effect*)
Steps:

BEGIN

    Match_State={(dic_pattern_point, (0,0,0,0), 1)}

    //i is the time coordinate

    For ($i = 0$, $i < \infty$)

    {

    Forecast = $\varnothing$;

    //Encode the size of the entity

     S = K_concept_detect (*K_line$_i$*);

    //Encode the kind of shadow line

KIND = KIND_concept_detect(K_line_i);

//Encode the relation between the neighboring entities.

LR = RELATION_concept_detect (K_line_{i-1}, K_line_i);

For ((S and *KIND* and *LR*)∈ Match_State. first_Kline)

    {

    //Encode the relation with the first K line

    FR_i = RELATION_concept_detect (*firstK_line_i*, K_line_i);

    //Combine the 4 parameters and encode the K line data

    $data_i$ = combination (S_i, $KIND_i$, LR_i, FR_i);

    while (each element (S, *KIND*, *LR*, *FR*, certainty)∈ $data_i$)

        {

        //Recognize the traditional K line combination pattern by linearly matching algorithm

            index = Pattern_Match (*K_line*, dic_pattern_point (*pattern_i*))

            first_Kline = *Match_State. first_Kline*

            //Calculate the degree of reliability for the recognized pattern

            reliability = calculate (*certainty*);

            //Match the state set

            Forecast = *Forecast* ∪ (*index*, *first_Kline*, *reliability*);

        }

    //Adopt the pattern with the highest degree of reliability

    forecast = select{*element*|*element*∈ *Forecast*∧

    element.reliability = MAX (*Forecast,reliability*)}

    //Evaluate the degree of reliability

    effect = evaluation (*forecast.reliability*);

    //Output the practical meaning of this pattern and the evaluation result on the prediction effect

    OUTPUT (*forecast.index.meaning, effect*);

    }

  }

END

C. Examples on *K* line prediction

Here we test the purchasing point predicted by "morning star" via the cloud-based prediction method. "Morning star," which reflects the reversely rising, is a famous combination of multiple *K* lines. It is composed of three *K* lines. The first one is a medium or long black line, the second is probably a black or red line with a short entity jump-up descending, and the third is a red line above medium red line or more, which is inserted into the first black line. The internal mechanism is that in the descending case, if there is stable evidence after accelerated descending, this will be the signal of reversely rising. The first medium or long black line reflects the accelerated descending, the jump-up descending in the second *K* line indicates the further accelerated descending, the small entity reflects the balance of gaming and the stable state after ascending, and the third line, which is a medium or long red line, shows the settlement of multiple strengths and the reverse ascending from the bottom.

The test regards the maximum profit in 10 days as the criteria of whether it is profitable, and also as the criteria of whether the predicted signal for purchasing point is successful. For instance, after the recognition of a certain traditional pattern and the command of purchasing, the system purchase at the opening price of the following day. If the maximum profit over 10 days reaches 10% or above, the purchasing signal will be deemed successful.

First, "Analyzer" from Huitianqi (Shenzhen) Computer Co. Ltd., is utilized to analyze the pattern on "morning star" through the *K* line data of the stock 000017 "ST China A" from March 31, 1992 to March 21, 2000. There are all-together 6 pattern signals, including 3 success signals, and 3 failure signals, as shown in Table 7.8. The purchasing price is the opening price of the next period in recognition, the selling price is the highest price within the 10 days, and the profit is the maximum profit (including the commission fee) over the 10 days.

The cloud-based prediction method is able to detect the pattern in the critical state and prevent from omitting effective patterns. For example in the *K* line graph of 000017 "ST China A" from November 7, 1996 to November 11, 1996, the closing price of the first black line and the opening price of the second red line are both 7.80, so the relation between the two is relay descending according to traditional interval partition, rather than jump-down descending. But if we express the stocks data based on the cloud, the relation between the two can be either relay descending

---

TABLE 7.8
Recognition of "morning star" by "Analyzer"

Index	Pattern Time	Purchasing	Selling	Profit (%)	Successful?
1	1992.11.16/11.17/11.18	8.91	12.38	38.95	√
2	1994.05.11/05.12/05.13	5.61	5.68	1.25	×
3	1994.07.28/07.29/08.01	4.00	5.15	28.75	√
4	1996.05.02/05.03/05.06	3.65	5.10	39.73	√
5	1997.08.12/08.13/08.14	8.50	8.60	1.18	×
6	1998.08.17/08.18/08.19	5.35	5.82	8.79	×

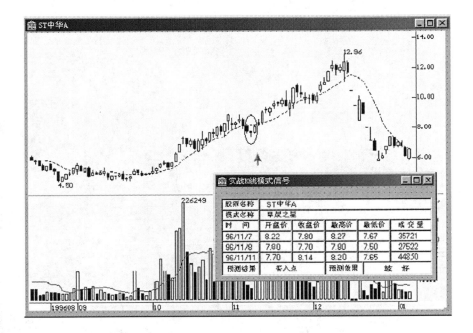

FIGURE 7.24 Recognition of "morning star" and prediction of purchasing point based on the cloud.

or jump-down descending, with the only difference in the degree of certainty on these qualitative concepts. Although the degree of certainty on jump-down descending through this set of data combination is lower than the one on the relay descending, the data combination fits the other conditions in the "morning star" pattern well, so the final evaluation on the prediction effect is still good. This signal predicts the purchasing point successfully, as shown in Figure 7.24. The ellipse points out the recognized pattern and the arrows indicate the purchasing point. The prediction effect is the reliability evaluation on the predicted result.

Although the cloud-based prediction method increases the number of recognized patterns, it includes some false signals as well. After the analysis on the data from March 31, 1992 to March 21, 2000, 13 "morning star" pattern signals are detected, including 8 success signals and 5 failure signals. As a further analysis, the position of purchasing signal should be the low price shortly after the descending stops. As this is at the bottom of the process stopping the descending, this low price should not be apparently lower than the recent lowest point. Figure 7.25 illustrates the successfully eliminated purchasing signal via bottom control strategy. When the additional technology is utilized to detect the false signal, the ellipse becomes dashed, the arrow is hollow, and the prediction effect is "exclusive."

If we further adopt the bottom control strategy and predict the purchasing point of 000017 "ST China A" once more, we can obtain 8 purchasing signals, exclusive of 4 false purchasing signals in the original predicted results. Seven successful purchasing points are detected, together with only 1 failure signal, and the success rate is enhanced to 87.5%, as shown in Table 7.9. The "exclusive effect" is the effect

FIGURE 7.25 Exclusion of false purchasing signal with the "morning star" pattern via bottom control strategy.

TABLE 7.9
Recognition of "morning star" by the Cloud Method

Index	Pattern Time	Purchasing Price	Selling Price	Profit (%)	Successful?	Exclusive Effect of Failure Signal
1	1992.11.16/11.17/11.18	8.91	12.38	38.95	√	Not excluded
2	1993.05.10/05.11/05.12	14.24	15.11	6.11	×	Excluded
3	1993.09.15/09.16/09.20	9.01	9.38	4.11	×	Excluded
4	1994.01.31/02.01/02.02	6.14	7.41	20.68	√	Not excluded
5	1994.05.11/05.12/05.13	5.61	5.68	1.25	×	Excluded
6	1994.05.17/05.18/05.19	5.46	5.51	0.92	×	Not excluded
7	1994.07.28/07.29/08.01	4.00	5.15	28.75	√	Not excluded
8	1996.05.02/05.03/05.06	3.65	5.10	39.73	√	Not excluded
9	1996.07.01/07.02/07.03	4.05	5.30	30.86	√	Not excluded
10	1996.11.07/11.08/11.11	8.38	10.75	28.28	√	Not excluded
11	1997.04.10/04.11/04.14	9.48	11.32	19.41	√	Excluded
12	1998.08.17/08.18/08.19	5.35	5.82	8.79	×	Excluded
13	1999.12.24/12.27/12.28	5.29	5.95	12.48	√	Not excluded

of purchasing point prediction by further bottom control strategy to exclude the false signal.

The basic expressions in stock markets are the match amount and the match price. The historical and current match amounts and prices can reveal the past and current market behaviors, respectively. Hence, it is possible to combine the analysis on the relationship between the match amount and price based on recognition of traditional K line patterns, so as to improve the prediction accuracy on the purchasing and selling points.

Let's consider the case of selling point prediction on "three consecutive red lines." The emergence of three consecutive red lines is a traditional K line form of the selling signal, indicating the approaching of the three red optimal selling points. It is composed of three consecutive medium or big red lines, and the three red lines show the shape of relay or jump-up ascending. This pattern reveals the fact that although the buyer's strength is significantly high and has achieved the peak point, it will drop after this pattern, and so the holder should decide to sell the stock.

We take the data of 000001 "Shenzhen Development A" from January 1994 to January 2000 as the tested data. The criterion for loss is that the maximum loss within 10 days exceeds 10%. The evaluation for the prediction signal of selling point is based on this criterion. There are all together 6 pattern signals, including 3 success signals and 3 failure signals (success rate of 50%), after the analysis by "Analyzer," as shown in Figure 7.26. However, if the cloud-based prediction is adopted, 9 pattern

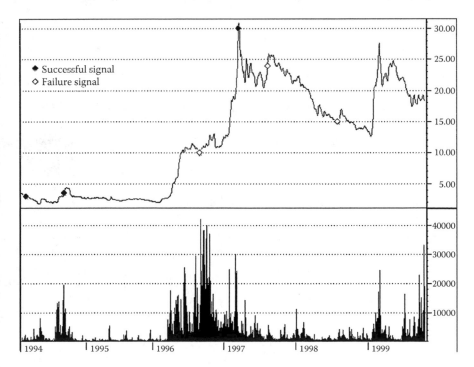

FIGURE 7.26 Prediction of the three consecutive "yang" line patterns via "Analyzer."

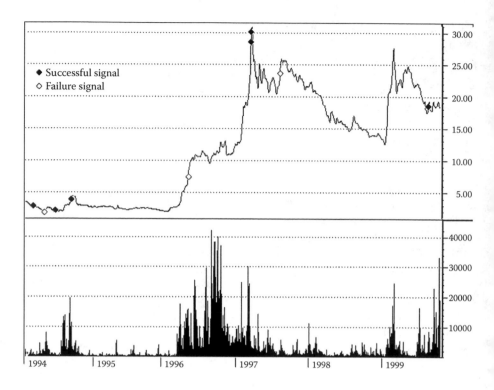

FIGURE 7.27 Prediction of the three consecutive "yang" line patterns via cloud model.

signals can be detected, including 6 success signals and 3 failure signals (success rate of 66.67%), as shown in Figure 7.27.

To improve the prediction reliability, we can further analyze the pattern meanings. In the ascending process of "three consecutive red lines," it is indicated that the buyer's strength has achieved the peak point and will turn to dropping. By statistical analysis of the amount–price relation in the emergence of "three consecutive red lines," we discover that if the trading volume is not rising along with rising price, it indicates a sell signal, which means that the stock market will be in a downtrend. If we add match amount and match price control strategy and predict the "Shenzhen Development A" by the cloud method again, we can exclude the failure signal effectively. Seven signals will be detected, including 6 success signals and 1 failure signal (success rate of 85.56%), as shown in Figure 7.28.

From the aforementioned examples of data mining for stocks, it can be seen that in the process of time series data mining, the cloud method may effectively reveal the critical state in applications of either the qualitative concept description or the expression of time series knowledge, which is complex and uncertain. It can improve the accuracy in time series prediction as well. Thus, quantitative methods have been severely challenged.

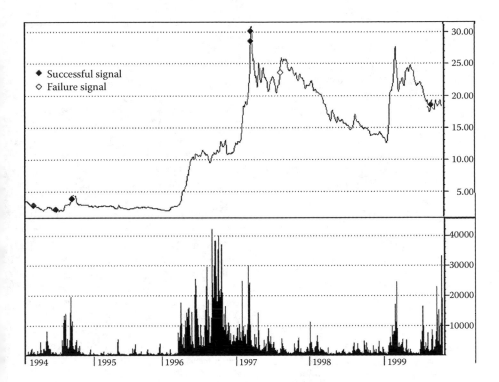

FIGURE 7.28 Prediction of the three consecutive "yang" line patterns with consideration of amount–price relation.

REFERENCES

1. J. R. Quinlan, Induction of decision trees, *Machine Learning*, No. 1, pp. 81–106, 1986.
2. J. R. Quinlan, *C4.5: Programs for Machine Learning*, Morgan Kaufmann, San Mateo, CA, 1993.
3. Data set of sonar signals. *http://www.rulequest.com.*
4. Jianhua Fan, Data Mining Techniques Based on Cloud Theory and Their Applications in C4ISR Systems, Ph.D. thesis, Nanjing Communications Engineering Institute, Nanjing, 1999.
5. R. Duda and P. Hart, *Pattern Classification and Scene Analysis*, John Wiley & Sons, New York, 1973.
6. K. L. Kaufman, P. J. Rousseeuw, *Finding Groups in Data: An Introduction to Cluster Analysis*, John Wiley & Sons, New York, 1990.
7. R. Ng and J. Han, Efficient and effective clustering methods for spatial data mining, In: *Proceedings of the 20th International Conference on Very Large Databases*, Santiago, Chile, 1994.
8. T. Zhang, R. Ramakrishnman, and M. Linvy, BIRCH: an efficient method for very large databases, In: *Proceedings of ACM SIGMOD International Conference on Management of Data*, Montreal, Canada, 1996.

9. S. Guha, R. Rasogi, and K. Shim, CURE: an efficient clustering algorithm for large databases, In: *Proceedings of the 1998 ACM SIGMOD International Conference on Management of Data*, Seattle, Washington, 1998.

10. S. Guha, R. Rasogi, and K. Shim, ROCK: a robust clustering algorithm for categorical attributes, In: *Proceedings of the 15th International Conference on Data Engineering*, Sydney, Australia, 1999.

11. K. George, E. H. Han, and V. Kumar, CHAMELEON: a hierarchical clustering algorithm using dynamic modeling, *IEEE computer*, Vol. 27, No. 3, pp. 329–341, 1999.

12. M. Ester, H. P. Kriegel, and J. Sander, A density-based algorithm for discovering clusters in large spatial databases with noise, In: *Proceedings of the 2nd International Conference on Knowledge Discovery and Data Mining*, Portland, Oregon, 1996.

13. M. Ankerst, M. Breunig, H. P. Kriegel et al., OPTICS: ordering points to identify the clustering structure, In: *Proceedings of 7th ACM SIGMOD International Conference on Management of Data*, Philadelphia, 1999.

14. A. Hinneburg and D. A. Keim, An efficient approach to clustering in large multimedia databases with noise, In: *Proceedings of the 4th International Conference on Knowledge Discovery and Data Mining*, New York, 1998.

15. W. Wang, J. Yang, and R. Muntz, STING: a statistical information grid approach to spatial data mining, In: *Proceedings of the 23rd International Conference on Very Large Databases*, Athens, Greece, 1997.

16. G. Sheikholeslami, S. Chatterjee, and A. Zhang, WaveCluster: a multi-resolution clustering approach for very large spatial databases, In: *Proceedings of the 24th International Conference on Very Large Databases*, New York, 1998.

17. R. Agrawal, J. Gehrke, D. Gunopolos et al., Automatic subspace clustering of high-dimensional data for data mining application, In: *Proceedings of ACM SIGMOD International Conference on Management of Data*, Seattle, Washington, 1998.

18. H. Nagesh, S. Goil, and A. Choudhary, MAFIA: efficient and scalable subspace clustering for very large data sets. In: *Technical Report CPDC-TR-9906-010, Center for Parallel and Distributed Computing*, Evanston: Northwestern University, 1999.

19. A. Hinneburg and D. A. Keim, Optimal grid-clustering: towards breaking the curse of dimensionality in high-dimensional clustering, In: *Proceedings of 25th International Conference on Very Large Databases*, Edinburgh, 1999.

20. Wenyan Gan, Study on Clustering Problem for Data Mining Foundations, Ph.D. thesis, PLA University of Science and Technology, Nanjing, 2003.

21. Wenyan Gan and Deyi Li, Optimal Choice of Parameters for a Density-based Clustering Algorithm. In: *The 19th International Conference on Rough Sets, Fuzzy Sets, Data Mining and Granular Computing (RSFDGrC'2003)*, Chongqing, 2003.

22. I. Kononenko, Estimating attributes: analysis and extension of RELIEF, In: *Proceedings of the 7th European Conference on Machine Learning*, Catania, Italy, 1994.

23. H. Liu and R. Setiono, Chi2: Feature selection and discretization of numeric attributes, In: *Proceedings of the 7th IEEE International Conference on Tools with Artificial Intelligence*, Herndon, Virginia, 1995.

24. A. Ben-Hur, D. Horn, H. T. Siegelmamm et al., A support vector clustering method, In: *Proceedings of the 15th International Conference on Pattern Recognition*, Barcelona, Spain, 2000.

25. N. Tishby and N. Slonim, Data clustering by Markovian relaxation and the information bottle-neck method, *Advances in Neural Information Processing Systems*, No. 13, pp. 640–646, 2000.

26. M. Blatt, S. Wiseman, and E. Domany, Data clustering using a model granular magnet, *Neural Computation*, No. 9, pp. 1804–1842, 1997.
27. W. E. Wright, Gravitational Clustering, *Pattern Recognition*, No. 9, pp. 151–166, 1977.
28. Y. J. Oyang, C. Y. Chen, and T. W. Yang, A study on the hierarchical data clustering algorithm based on gravity theory, In: *European Conference on Principles of Data Mining and Knowledge Discovery*, Freiburg, Germany, 2001.
29. Yi Xue, *Optimization Theory and Approaches*, Beijing University of Technology Press, Beijing, 2001.
30. S. Bernhard, C. P. Hohn, A. T. Hohn et al., Estimating the support of a high-dimensional distribution, *Neural Computation*, Vol. 13, No. 7, pp. 1443–1471, 2001.
31. Jiawei Han and Micheline Kamber, *Data Mining: Concepts and Techniques*, Morgan Kaufmann, San Francisco, 2000.
32. L. Huijun, Face Recognition Based on Data Field, Master's degree thesis, PLA University of Science and Technology, Nanjing, 2002.
33. Michael J. Lyons, Shigeru Akamatsu, Miyuki Kamachi et al., Coding Facial Expressions with Gabor Wavelets, In: *Proceedings of the 3rd IEEE International Conference on Automatic Face and Gesture Recognition*, Nara, Japan, 1998.
34. R. Agrawal, T. Imielinske, and A. Swami, Mining association rules between sets of items in large databases, In: *Proceedings of the ACM SIGMOD International Conference on the Management of Data*, Washington, D.C., 1993.
35. R. Agrawal and R. Srikant, Fast algorithms for mining association rules, In: *Proceedings of the 1994 International Conference on Very Large Databases*, Santiago, Chile, 1994.
36. R. Srikant and R. Agrawal, Mining quantitative association rules in large relational tables. In: *Proceedings of the 1996 ACM SIGMOD International Conference on Management of Data*, pp. 1–12, ACM Press, Montreal, Quebec, Canada, 1996.
37. Yi Du, Zilin Song, and Deyi Li, Mining Association Rules Based on Cloud Model, *Journal of PLA University of Science and Technology*, Vol. 1, No. 1, pp. 29–35, 2000.
38. Yi Du, Research and Applications of Association Rules in Data Mining, Ph.D. thesis, PLA University of Science and Technology, Nanjing, 2000.
39. Deyi Li, Kaichang Di, Deren Li et al., Mining association rules with linguistic cloud models, *Journal of Software*, Vol. 11, No. 2, pp. 143–158, 2000.
40. Kaichang Di, The Theory and Methods of Spatial Data Mining and Knowledge Discovery, Ph.D. thesis, Wuhan Technical University of Surveying and Mapping, Wuhan, 1999.
41. S. Canu, R. Sobral, and R. Lengelle, Formal neural network as an adaptive model for water demand, In: *Proceedings of the International Neural Network Conference (INNC)*, Paris, 1990.
42. A. Varfis and C. Versino, Univariate economic time-series forecasting by connectionist methods, In: *Proceedings of the International Neural Network Conference (INNC)*, Paris, 1990.
43. F. Fessant, S. Bengio, and D. Collobert, On the prediction of solar activity using different neural network models, www.syntim.inria.fr/fractales.
44. T. G. Dietterich and R. S. Michalski, Learning to Predict Sequences. In: R. S. Michalski, J. G. Carbonell, and T. M. Mitchell, eds., *Machine Learning: An Artificial Intelligence Approach (Volume 2)*, pp. 63–106, Morgan Kaufmann, Los Altos, 1986.
45. Rong Jiang, Deyi Li, and Hui Chen, Time-series prediction based on cloud model, *Journal of PLA University of Science and Technology*, Vol. 1, No. 5, pp. 13–18, 2000.
46. Fan Yang, Ye Wang, and Deyi Li, Cloud prediction based on time granularity, In: *Proceedings of the 5th Pacific-Asia Conference on Knowledge Discovery and Data Mining*, Hong Kong, 2001.

47. Rong Jiang and Deyi Li, Similarity search in time series based on shape representation, *Computer Research and Development*, Vol. 37, No. 5, pp. 601–608, 2000.
48. Rong Jiang and Deyi Li, Time-series prediction with cloud models in DMKD, In: *Proceedings of the 3rd Pacific-Asia Conference on Knowledge Discovery and Data Mining*, Beijing, 1999.
49. Zhen Wu, *Stocks in Graph*, Reformation Press, Beijing, 1999.
50. Dasheng Yang and Jingwen Ma, *Approaches for Stock Prediction*, Guangdong Economy Publishing House, Huiyang, 1999.
51. Zhangzhe Li, *A Few Techniques in Stocks*, Reformation Press, Beijing, 1999.
52. Beijing Jin Hong En Corporation, *Master in Stocks*, Tsinghua University Press, Beijing, 1999.
53. Jügong Wang, *Fluctuation and Common Prediction in Stocks*, Economic Management Press, Beijing, 1997.
54. Feng Xue, *Practical Techniques in Stocks Analysis*, Guangdong Economy Publishing House, Huiyang, 1999.
55. Rong Jiang, Research and Applications of Data Mining in Time Sequence, Ph.D. thesis, PLA University of Science and Technology, Nanjing, 2000.
56. Fan Yang, Cloud-based Prediction Approach in Time Series, Master's degree thesis, PLA University of Science and Technology, Nanjing, 2001.

8 Reasoning and Control of Qualitative Knowledge

Human intelligence with uncertainty reflects human adaptability to the uncertain environment. People have been utilizing three classical experiments to simulate this kind of uncertain intelligence: chess playing between human and computer, the soccer match between robots, and the inverted pendulum. During the past 50 years, artificial intelligence (AI) has made great progress in the symbolic theorem proving and logic reasoning, resulting in defeating Kasparov by the computer "Deep Blue." The robot soccer match also reflects the progress in uncertain processing related to computer vision, planning, cooperation, and control. In the control of an inverted pendulum, which is a classical research topic in automatic control, the balance and robustness are regarded as the effective way to evaluate intelligent control. This is another important content in the research of AI with uncertainty. In this chapter, we plan to utilize the reasoning and control by qualitative knowledge rather than through the precise mathematical model of the plant, and implement stable control by qualitative rule controller reflecting the control experience by human natural language.

8.1 QUALITATIVE RULE CONSTRUCTION BY CLOUD

The cloud-based qualitative knowledge reasoning regards the concept as the fundamental expression, discovers qualitative knowledge from database, and constructs rule generators. The rule database is composed of multiple qualitative rules. Once a specific condition is input into the system to activate multiple qualitative rules, the reasoning and control with uncertainty will be implemented by the reasoning engine. Knowledge is generally the inter-relation between concepts. In the control field, the rules, such as "perception–action," are usually adopted to express the logic cause–result relations. The precondition, i.e., perception, can be composed of one or multiple conditions, and the postcondition of the rule, i.e., the action, represents the concrete control behavior. The concepts of both precondition and postcondition can be of uncertainty.

8.1.1 Precondition Cloud Generator and Postcondition Cloud Generator

The cloud-based qualitative rule generator is combined by precondition cloud generator and postcondition cloud generator.

According to the mathematical property of cloud, aforementioned in Chapter 5, Section 5.4, we can see that the qualitative concept C can be expressed by the normal cloud $C(Ex, En, He)$ in the universal set U. The distribution of the cloud drop in U has expectation Ex and variance $En^2 + He^2$.

Suppose there is a rule

$$\text{if } A \text{ then } B$$

where A and B correspond to the concepts C_1 and C_2 in the universal sets U_1 and U_2, respectively.

Let a be a certain point in U_1, the distribution of certainty degree of the case that a belongs to C_1 can be generated by cloud generator, which is called a "precondition cloud generator," as shown in Figure 8.1(a). Let μ, $\mu \in [0, 1]$ be a certainty degree, the distribution of drops on the concept C_2 in U_2, which satisfies this certainty degree, can be generated by cloud generator, called "postcondition cloud generator," as shown in Figure 8.1(b).

U_1 and U_2 can be either one-dimensional or multidimensional. Generally, the postcondition cloud generator is one-dimensional, and the precondition cloud generator can be multidimensional by combination of several one-dimensional precondition cloud generators.

The algorithm of the one-dimensional precondition cloud generator is illustrated below.[1,2]

Algorithm 8.1 One-dimensional precondition cloud generator

Input: the numerical characteristics of the qualitative concept C_1 (expectation Ex, entropy En, hyper-entropy He, a specific value a)
Output: the cloud drop corresponding to the specific value a and its certainty degree μ

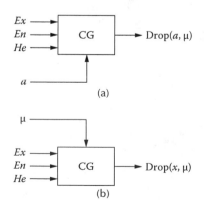

FIGURE 8.1 One-dimensional (a) precondition cloud generator and (b) postcondition cloud generator.

Steps:

BEGIN

$En' = \text{NORM}(En, He^2);$

$\mu = e^{\frac{-(a-Ex)^2}{2(En')^2}};$

OUTPUT $drop\,(a, \mu);$

END

The specific value a and the certainty degree μ, which is generated by the precondition cloud generator, construct the joint distribution (a, μ), as shown in Figure 8.2(a). All cloud drops are distributed in the line $x = a$.

The algorithm of the postcondition cloud generator is provided below.[1,2]

Algorithm 8.2 Postcondition cloud generator

Input: the numerical characteristics of the qualitative concept C_2 (expectation Ex, entropy En, hyper-entropy He, certainty degree μ)
Output: the cloud drop b with certainty degree μ

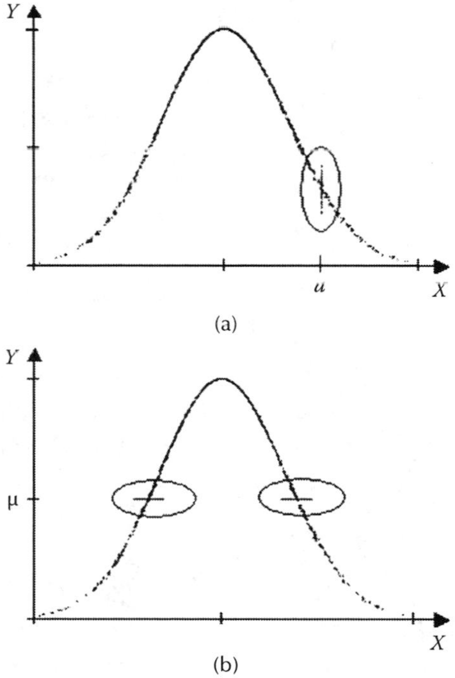

(a)

(b)

FIGURE 8.2 The joint distribution of cloud drops. (a) The cloud drop distribution of the precondition cloud generator and (b) the cloud drop distribution of the postcondition cloud generator.

Steps:

BEGIN

$En' = \text{NORM}(En, He^2)$;

$b = Ex \pm En'\sqrt{-2\ln\mu}$;

OUTPUT $drop$ (b, μ);

END

The specific certainty degree μ and the drop b which is produced by postcondition cloud generator construct the joint distribution (b, μ) as shown in Figure 8.2(b). All the drops are in the same line $y = \mu$. According to the discussion in Chapter 5, Section 5.4, the drops satisfy the two normal distributions with expectation $EX = Ex + \sqrt{-2\ln\mu}\,En$ and variance $DX = -2He^2\ln\mu$, and expectation $EX = Ex - \sqrt{-2\ln\mu}\,En$ and variance $DX = -2He^2\ln\mu$, respectively.

8.1.2 RULE GENERATOR

The single-condition–single-rule can be expressed by

If A then B

where A and B are qualitative concepts. For example, in the rule "if the altitude is high, then the population density is low," A represents the concept of "high altitude," and B represents the concept of "low population density." If we combine one precondition cloud generator and one postcondition cloud generator, as shown in Figure 8.3, we can obtain a single conditional rule, called single-condition–single-rule generator.

Algorithm 8.3 Single-condition–single-rule generator

Input: the qualitative concept $C_1(Ex_A, En_A, He_A)$ of the precondition A
the qualitative concept $C_2(Ex_B, En_B, He_B)$ of the postcondition B
a specific value a in the universal set U_1 of the precondition
Output: the cloud drop b in the universal set U_2 of the postcondition, and its certainty degree μ

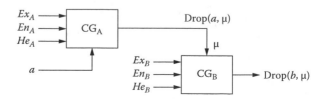

FIGURE 8.3 Single-condition–single-rule generator.

Steps:

BEGIN

//Generate a normally random number En'_A with expectation En_A and deviation He_A^2.

$$En'_A = \text{NORM}(En_A, He_A^2)$$

$$\mu = e^{-\frac{(a - Ex_A)^2}{2En'^2_A}}$$

//Generate a normally random number En'_B with expectation En_B and deviation He_B^2.

$$En'_B = \text{NORM}(En_B, He_B^2);$$

//If the input activates the rising edge of the precondition, then the postcondition is also at its rising condition, and vice versa.

if $a < Ex$ then

$$b = Ex_B - \sqrt{-2\ln(\mu)}\,En'_B$$

else

$$b = Ex_B + \sqrt{-2\ln(\mu)}\,En'_B \ ;$$

OUTPUT(b, μ);

END

In the single-condition–single-rule generator, if a specific input a in the universal set U_1 of the precondition activates CG_A, it will generate a certainty degree μ randomly. This value reveals the activation strength on the qualitative rule by a, and it acts as the input for the postcondition cloud generator to generate drop(b, μ) randomly. If a activates the rising edge of the precondition, then the output b by the rule generator corresponds to the rising edge of the postcondition, and vice versa.

Uncertainty is contained in this algorithm. For a certain input a in U_1, it cannot output a certain b. The certainty degree μ randomly generated by CG_A transits the uncertainty in U_1 to U_2. CG_B outputs a random cloud drop–drops (b, μ) under the control of μ, so the drop b is also uncertain. In this way, uncertainty is transited in the reasoning process by rule generators.

For the research in multicondition–single-rule generator, we first discuss the construction of double-condition–single-rule generator.

The double-condition–single-rule can be expressed visually by

$$\text{If } A_1, A_2 \text{ then } B$$

For example, the qualitative rule "if temperature is high and pressure is high, then the speed is fast" reflects the relation of three qualitative concepts in the domains of temperature, pressure, and speed, i.e., A_1 = "high," A_2 = "high," and B = "fast."

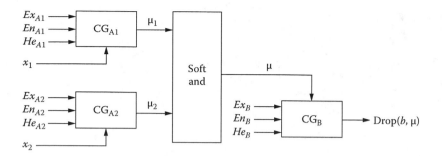

FIGURE 8.4 The double-condition–single-rule generator.

Two precondition cloud generators and one postcondition cloud generator can be connected according to Figure 8.4 so as to construct a double-condition rule, called a double-condition–single-rule generator.

The precondition includes the "and" relation of two qualitative concepts, and this relation is hidden in the expression by natural language. A_1, A_2, and B correspond to the concepts C_{A_1}, C_{A_2}, and C_B in U_{A_1}, U_{A_2}, and U_B, respectively. The degrees of "and" between μ_1 and μ_2 are not stated clearly in logic. Hence, we can introduce a new concept, i.e., "soft and," to implement the generation of μ from μ_1 and μ_2 and construct a double-condition–single-rule generator.

We regard "soft and" as a qualitative concept, expressed by a two-dimensional normal cloud $C(1, Enx, Hex, 1, Eny, Hey)$. The universal sets of the two dimensions correspond to the value domains of the certainty degrees μ_1 and μ_2, and they are both in [0, 1]. The expectation of the drops (x, y) after quantitative transformation by "soft and" is (1, 1). At this point, the certainty degree μ is strictly 1, and so the "soft and" is equivalent to logic "and." The certainty degrees of the cloud drops in other positions are less than 1. This shows the uncertainty of "and," which is the special property of "soft and." The farther the distance from the cloud drop to the expectation point, the less the certainty degree μ.[3]

Enx, Eny, Hex, and *Hey* can be adopted as the adjustment parameters for the degree of "soft and." When $Enx = Eny = 0$ and $Hex = Hey = 0$, "soft and" will be degenerated to logic "and." In the definition of "soft and," the output cloud drop and its joint distribution (x, y, μ) are meaningful only with x and y in [0, 1]. Thus, the cloud graph of the joint distribution looks like a quarter of a hill, as illustrated in Figure 8.5.

Compared with the selection of $\min\{\mu_1, \mu_2\}$ from the fuzzy set as the strength of postcondition activation, it is more adaptable to adopt the quantitative transformation of "soft and" by cloud model.

The multicondition–single-rule generator can be constructed by expansion of the method utilized in the double-condition–single-rule generator.

The single-condition–single-rule and multicondition–single-rule generated above can be stored in the rule database for further reasoning and control of the qualitative knowledge.

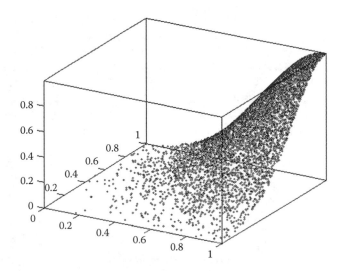

FIGURE 8.5 The quantitative transformation of the qualitative concept "soft and."

8.1.3 FROM CASES TO RULE GENERATION

In the practice of reasoning and qualitative control, it is impossible to obtain a precise model of the plant. However, usually there exist a large quantity of data containing the precise output activated by the precise input, based on practical manipulation. This information constructs classical cases, such as:

"If the temperature is 50°F and the pressure is 40 Pa, then the speed is 40 r/s."

"If the temperature is 55°F and the pressure is 60 Pa, then the speed is 60 r/s."

"If the temperature is 70°F and the pressure is 80 Pa, then the speed is 90 r/s."

"If the temperature is 90°F and the pressure is 90 Pa, then the speed is 100 r/s."

⋮

⋮

The word "classical" emphasizes that these cases are the templates that must be obeyed.

The number of these cases and their data distribution are reflective of the key control point in reasoning and control, and they also represent the turning point in the nonlinear relationship between input and output. It might be true that this nonlinear relationship can hardly be expressed in terms of mathematical func-tions, but people can realize reasoning by means of comparison within these classical cases. This is the case-based reasoning (CBR).[4] Its main idea is that with a given input, it searches for and matches the case in the case database, and generates the output. It usually happens that the complete matching with a classical case is not possible, so modification is required for the output. The shortcoming of this approach lies in that the control of some key points cannot cover all the possible occasions. To tackle this problem, cloud transformation and backward cloud generator can be employed to abstract the precise cases for qualitative concepts expressed by linguistic values, and thereafter construct qualitative rules to provide a reasoning mechanism. In these qualitative rules, each linguistic value can be expressed by the three numerical characteristics of the cloud model, the semantic meaning of which is irrelevant.

Once these qualitative rules are obtained, the output with uncertainty can be generated through reasoning mechanism after the new input.

8.2 QUALITATIVE CONTROL MECHANISM

In this section, the cloud-based qualitative control method, the classical fuzzy control method, and the probability control method are compared to illustrate the qualitative control mechanism of the cloud-based method. All these three methods are utilized to solve the uncertainty problems in the control process.

8.2.1 FUZZY, PROBABILITY, AND CLOUD CONTROL METHODS

For convenience, we first provide a classical case by the fuzzy control method and the probability control method.[5-7] This is a control problem on motor speed based on temperature variation. There is a rule database consisting of five qualitative rules as below:

If the temperature is "cold," then adjust the motor speed to "stop."

If the temperature is "cool," then adjust the motor speed to "slow."

If the temperature is "just right," then adjust the motor speed to "medium."

If the temperature is "warm," then adjust the motor speed to "fast."

If the temperature is "hot," then adjust the motor speed to "blast."

It should be noticed that in the five qualitative rules above, the variables in the precondition and the postcondition are natural linguistic values rather than precise numbers. What will be the output of a precise temperature such as 68°F?

Fuzzy control constructs rule database by fuzzy rules. If the input condition is determined, it calculates the membership degree of this input to all the qualitative concepts in the precondition, and regards this as the strength to activate the postcondition. If there are multiple rules activated simultaneously, the reasoning engine will be enabled for a certain output.

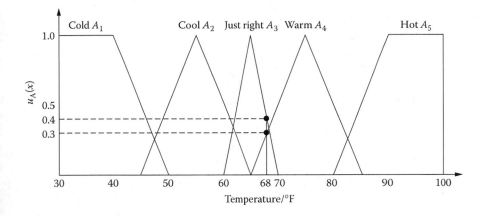

FIGURE 8.6 Membership function of the qualitative concepts in the precondition.

In this example, the control mechanism of fuzzy control is like this:

1. Assume that the membership functions of the five qualitative concepts in the precondition are triangle shaped functions in the temperature domain, as shown in Figure 8.6. They can be expressed in mathematics as follows:

$$\mu_{cold}(x) = \begin{cases} 1 & x \in [30,40] \\ 1 - \dfrac{x-40}{50-40} & x \in [40,50] \\ 0 & otherwise \end{cases}$$

$$\mu_{cool}(x) = \begin{cases} \dfrac{x-45}{55-45} & x \in [45,55] \\ 1 - \dfrac{x-55}{65-55} & x \in [55,60] \\ 0 & otherwise \end{cases}$$

$$\mu_{justright}(x) = \begin{cases} \dfrac{x-60}{65-60} & x \in [60,65] \\ 1 - \dfrac{x-65}{70-65} & x \in [65,70] \\ 0 & otherwise \end{cases}$$

$$\mu_{warm}(x) = \begin{cases} \dfrac{x-65}{75-65} & x \in [65,75] \\ 1 - \dfrac{x-75}{85-75} & x \in [75,85] \\ 0 & \text{otherwise} \end{cases}$$

$$\mu_{hot}(x) = \begin{cases} \dfrac{x-80}{90-80} & x \in [80,90] \\ 1 & x \in [90,100] \\ 0 & \text{otherwise} \end{cases}$$

The membership functions of the five qualitative concepts in the postcondition are also defined as triangle shaped functions in speed domain, as shown in Figure 8.7. They are expressed in mathematics below.

$$\mu_{stop}(z) = \begin{cases} 1 - \dfrac{z}{30} & \delta \in [0,30] \\ 0 & \text{otherwise} \end{cases}$$

$$\mu_{slow}(z) = \begin{cases} \dfrac{z-10}{30-10} & \delta \in [10,30] \\ 1 - \dfrac{z-30}{50-30} & \delta \in [30,50] \\ 0 & \text{otherwise} \end{cases}$$

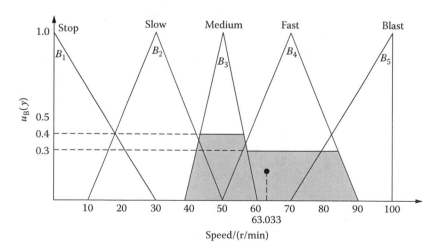

FIGURE 8.7 The Mamdani fuzzy control method.

$$\mu_{medium}(z) = \begin{cases} \dfrac{z-40}{50-40} & \delta \in [40,50] \\[2mm] 1 - \dfrac{z-50}{60-50} & \delta \in [50,60] \\[2mm] 0 & otherwise \end{cases}$$

$$\mu_{fast}(z) = \begin{cases} \dfrac{z-50}{70-50} & \delta \in [50,70] \\[2mm] 1 - \dfrac{z-70}{90-70} & \delta \in [70,90] \\[2mm] 0 & otherwise \end{cases}$$

$$\mu_{blast}(z) = \begin{cases} \dfrac{z-70}{100-70} & \delta \in [70,100] \\[2mm] 0 & otherwise \end{cases}$$

If there is a precise input t in the temperature domain, the method calculates the membership degrees to the five qualitative concepts for each of the five fuzzy rules.

2. If there is only one positive membership degree μ_i, the ith rule is activated with strength μ_i, and the program goes to step 3. If there is more than one positive membership degree, μ_i, and μ_{i+1}, the ith and $i +$ 1th rules are activated with strengths μ_i and μ_{i+1}, respectively, and the program goes to step 4.

3. If there is only one activated rule, the program directly cuts the membership function of the postcondition by μ_i, and obtain the precise output according to the criteria that if it is on the rising/dropping edge the corresponding rising/dropping edge will be activated.

4. If there are multiactivated rules, the Mamdani fuzzy control method (product–sum–gravity methods)[8] will be utilized. The multiactivation strength will be applied to cut the postcondition of the related rules to obtain the overlapping of several trapeziums. Thereafter, the center of area (COA) will be calculated to generate the precise output.

In this example, when a precise temperature $t = 68°F$ is input to the system, the 3rd and 4th rules will be activated, with activation strengths 0.4 and 0.3, as illustrated in Figure 8.6.

Thereafter, the membership functions of the postcondition are cut by the two activation strengths, as shown in Figure 8.7. By means of Mamdani fuzzy control method, the COA of the shadow area, which is the sum of the reaction area of the two rules, will be calculated for the precise output of the reasoning.

$$COA = \frac{\int_{-\infty}^{\infty} y \times \mu_B(y) dy}{\int_{-\infty}^{\infty} \mu_B(y) dy} = \frac{942.35}{14.95} = 63.033 \text{ r/min}$$

In other words, when the input temperature is 68°F, the motor speed will be 63.033 r/min by the fuzzy controller.

The probability control method constructs the rule database by rules together with probability. Its control mechanism is below:

1. Define the conditional probability distribution functions of the five qualitative concepts in the precondition as

$$P_1[cold \mid x] = \begin{cases} 1 & x \in [30,45] \\ (50-x)/5 & x \in [45,50] \\ 0 & otherwise \end{cases}$$

$$P_2[cool \mid x] = \begin{cases} (x-45)/5 & x \in [45,50] \\ 1 & x \in [50,60] \\ (65-x)/5 & x \in [60,65] \\ 0 & otherwise \end{cases}$$

$$P_3[justright \mid x] = \begin{cases} (x-60)/5 & x \in [60,65] \\ (70-x)/5 & x \in [65,70] \\ 0 & otherwise \end{cases}$$

$$P_4[warm \mid x] = \begin{cases} (x-65)/5 & x \in [65,50] \\ 1 & x \in [70,80] \\ (85-x)/5 & x \in [80,85] \\ 0 & otherwise \end{cases}$$

$$P_5[hot \mid x] = \begin{cases} (x-80)/5 & x \in [80,85] \\ 1 & x \in [65,70] \\ 0 & otherwise \end{cases}$$

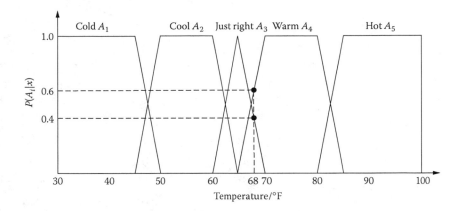

FIGURE 8.8 The probability density functions of the qualitative concepts in the precondition.

From the definition above, it can be seen that the sum of the probabilities of the event that an arbitrary point belongs to one of the five concepts should be 1. The probability density functions of the precondition are illustrated in Figure 8.8.

Meanwhile, define the probability density functions (Figure 8.9) of the five qualitative concepts in the postcondition by the formulas below.

$$f_1(z) = \begin{cases} (30-z)/450 & z \in [0,30] \\ 0 & otherwise \end{cases}$$

$$f_2(z) = \begin{cases} (z-10)/400 & z \in [10,30] \\ (50-z)/400 & z \in [30,50] \\ 0 & otherwise \end{cases}$$

$$f_3(z) = \begin{cases} (z-40)/100 & z \in [40,50] \\ (60-z)/100 & z \in [50,60] \\ 0 & otherwise \end{cases}$$

$$f_4(z) = \begin{cases} (z-50)/400 & z \in [50,70] \\ (90-z)/400 & z \in [70,90] \\ 0 & otherwise \end{cases}$$

$$f_5(z) = \begin{cases} (z-70)/450 & z \in [70,100] \\ 0 & otherwise \end{cases}$$

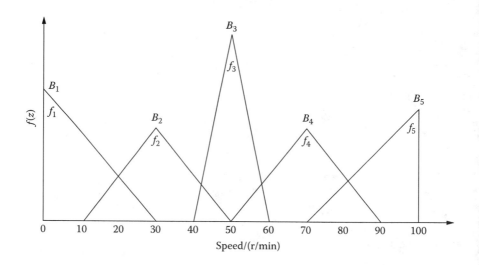

FIGURE 8.9 The probability density functions of the qualitative concepts in the postcondition.

2. Once a temperature t is input into the system, calculate the five conditional probability density functions of the qualitative concepts for each probability rule, and obtain p_1, p_2, p_3, p_4, p_5.
3. The output, i.e., the motor speed, is a random value z with probability density function

$$f(z) = p_1 \times f_1(z) + p_2 \times f_2(z) + p_3 \times f_3(z) + p_4 \times f_4(z) + p_5 \times f_5(z)$$

When a precise input $t = 68°F$ is exerted on the system, all the other conditional probabilities are 0, except $p[\text{"just right"}|68°F] = 0.4$ and $p[\text{"warm"}|68°F] = 0.3$. Because the expectations of $f_3(z)$ and $f_4(z)$ are 50 r/min and 70 r/min, respectively, the expectation of the output motor speed is

$$\text{MEAN}(z) = 0 + 0 + 0.4 \times 50 + 0.3 \times 70 + 0 = 62 \text{ r/min}$$

For the same input temperature $t = 68°F$, the motor speed obtained by the fuzzy control method is constantly 63.033 r/min, while the expectation of speed by the probability control method is 62 r/min.

After the introduction of fuzzy control and probability control, it is necessary to describe the reasoning mechanism of the cloud-based rule generator in detail.

For easy comparison with the aforementioned two methods, the cloud of the five qualitative concepts in temperature domain is expressed below:

$$C_{A_1} = \begin{cases} 1 & x \in [30, 40] \\ C(30, 20/3, 0.05) & otherwise \end{cases}$$

$$C_{A_2} = C(55, 10/3, 0.05)$$

$$C_{A_3} = C(65, 5/3, 0.05)$$

$$C_{A_4} = C(75, 10/3, 0.05)$$

$$C_{A_5} = \begin{cases} C(90, 10/3, 0.05) & otherwise \\ 1 & x \in [90, 100] \end{cases}$$

The joint distribution between the cloud drops of the five qualitative concepts in the precondition and their certainty degrees are shown in Figure 8.10.

Similarly the clouds for the five qualitative concepts of the postcondition are expressed below.

$$C_{B_1} = C(0, 10, 0.05)$$

$$C_{B_2} = C(30, 20/3, 0.05)$$

$$C_{B_3} = C(50, 10/3, 0.05)$$

$$C_{B_4} = C(70, 20/3, 0.05)$$

$$C_{B_5} = C(100, 10, 0.02)$$

The joint distribution between the cloud drops of the five qualitative concepts in the postcondition and their certainty degrees are shown in Figure 8.11.

When there is a precise input t in the temperature domain, we calculate its certainty degrees to the five qualitative concepts in the preconditions of each of the five cloud rules.

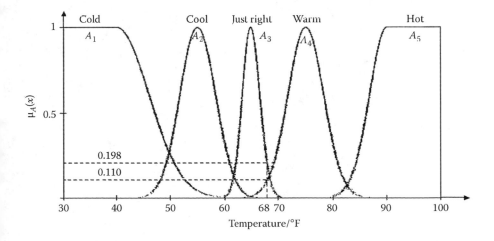

FIGURE 8.10 The cloud graph of the qualitative concepts in the precondition.

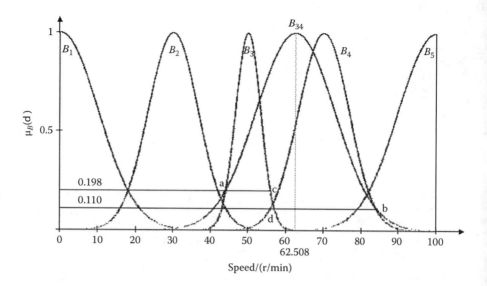

FIGURE 8.11 The cloud graph of the qualitative concepts in the postcondition and the virtual cloud.

If there is only one positive certainty degree μ_i, then the ith rule will be activated with activation strength of μ_i, and the output will be generated directly by the single-rule generator.

If there is more than one positive certainty degree, we assume they are μ_i and μ_{i+1}. Then the ith and $i + 1$th rules will be activated with strengths of μ_i and μ_{i+1}, respectively. The output will be constructed by means of virtual cloud.

In this example, when $t = 68°F$ is input to the system, the 3rd and 4th rules are activated with strengths 0.198 and 0.110, as shown in Figure 8.10.

Four cloud drops will be generated after the activation on the postcondition by these two degrees of uncertainty, as shown in Figure 8.11. The two cloud drops at the two sides are selected to construct a virtual concept $C_{B_{34}}$, which is expressed by the cloud as well. The formation of the virtual cloud is as follows.

Let $B_{34}(Ex, En, He)$ be a virtual cloud with the same shape. It covers the two drops $a(x_1, \mu_1)$ and $b(x_2, \mu_2)$. Set $He = 0$ temporarily, as we have only the position of the two drops at this time. Through the geometrical method, the expectation and the entropy of the virtual cloud B_{34} can be calculated as

$$Ex = \frac{x_1\sqrt{-2\ln(\mu_2)} + x_2\sqrt{-2\ln(\mu_1)}}{\sqrt{-2\ln(\mu_1)} + \sqrt{-2\ln(\mu_2)}}$$

$$En = \frac{x_2 - x_1}{\sqrt{-2\ln(\mu_1)} + \sqrt{-2\ln(\mu_2)}}$$

If there are more cloud drops (x_1, μ_1), $(x_2, \mu_2), \ldots$, (x_n, μ_n), the backward cloud generator can produce the expectation, entropy, as well as the hyper-entropy of the virtual cloud.

In this example, the expectation of the virtual concept $C_{B_{34}}$ is $Ex = 62.508$ r/min, which is the output of the motor speed.

The similar method can be utilized to obtain the motor speed for different input temperatures.

Comparing these three control mechanisms, we notice that in the fuzzy control method a certain membership function is required, and the motor speed is constant for the same input temperature. By contrast, in the probability control and cloud-based control the outputs are uncertain each time but, in the same overall variation trend as the fuzzy control method, as shown in Figure 8.12. The cloud-based method has avoided the strict requirement in the probability method that the probability density functions of "stop," "slow," "medium," "fast," and "blast" should be given. The description for these linguistic values is similar to the description for the temperature values, e.g., "cold," "cool," "just right," "warm," and "hot". They are expressed in terms of expectation, entropy, and hyper-entropy, and are more understandable.

8.2.2 Theoretic Explanation of Mamdani Fuzzy Control Method

In fuzzy control, the Mamdani method is applied ubiquitously. It adopts the computation method of "product–sum–gravity" when multiple rules are activated

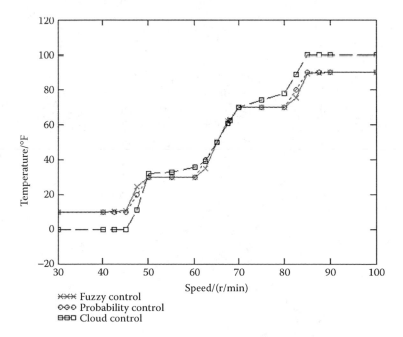

×××× Fuzzy control
◇◇◇ Probability control
◻◻◻ Cloud control

FIGURE 8.12 The corresponding relation between input and output by different control methods.

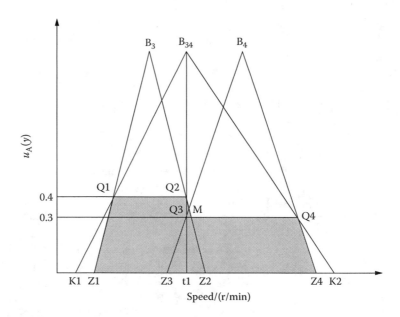

FIGURE 8.13 Explanation of the Mamdani method by the cloud-based method.

simultaneously, but the theoretical explanation is not provided in literature. According to the idea of cloud-based control, we attempt to give a theoretical explanation of the Mamdani method.

We can still use Figure 8.7 as an example. When two rules are activated simultaneously, the two adjacent activated concepts can be utilized to construct a new virtual concept, the central value of which corresponds to the output value. It can be proved that this central value is the gravity value by the Mamdani control method.[9] For simplicity, we substitute the normal cloud with the simple triangular cloud, as shown in Figure 8.13. B_{34} is the new virtual concept formed after the activation of B_3 and B_4.

Because

$$Area|_{\Delta B_3 Q_1 Q_2} = Area|_{\Delta B_{34} Q_1 Q_2}$$

$$Area|_{\Delta B_4 Q_3 Q_4} = Area|_{\Delta B_{34} Q_3 Q_4}$$

$$Area|_{\Delta Q_1 K_1 Z_1} \approx Area|_{\Delta Q_2 T_1 Z_2}$$

$$Area|_{\Delta Q_3 Z_3 T_1} \approx Area|_{\Delta Q_4 Z_4 K_2}$$

so,

$$COA|_{Polygon Q_1 Z_1 Z_4 Q_4 M Q_2} \approx COA|_{\Delta B_{34} K_1 K_2}$$

The sum of the areas of B_3 and B_4 approximates the area of B_{34}, so the horizontal coordinate of the part in shadow is the same as the expectation of the virtual concept B_{34}.

When the normal cloud is applied to represent the qualitative concept in the rule, a similar conclusion can be obtained. In this way, we illustrate the theoretical explanation of the Mamdani control method by the concept of virtual cloud. The Mamdani method contains the virtual concept generated by the concepts in the two activated rules.

8.3   INVERTED PENDULUM — AN EXAMPLE OF INTELLIGENT CONTROL WITH UNCERTAINTY

The reasoning and control based on qualitative knowledge have been widely applied in areas of expert system, decision support, etc. They can be utilized in the field of automatic control as well.

The most common point of creatures, nature, and man-made systems lies in the fact that they all realize system stabilization by feedback. In the development of science and technology, which has lasted for more than 3,000 years, humans have designed numerous systems based on feedback control. The great process of civilization has been witnessed by numerous examples, such as the ancient timer and dams, the swing clock, the telescope in medieval times, the stream machine in the industrial revolution, airplanes, automobiles, telephones, analog computers, radars, satellites, missiles, digital computers, and space shuttles. All these well-known inventions directly promote and develop the technology of automatic control.

8.3.1   INVERTED PENDULUM SYSTEM AND ITS CONTROL

In the development of automatic control theory and technology, the correctness of a certain theory is usually verified through the control of a classical plant by a controller designed according to this theory. The inverted pendulum is one of such plants with long-term popularity. The research can be conducted on a lot of control theories and methods, such as PID (Proportional-Integral-Derivative) control, adaptive control, state feedback control, neural network control, fuzzy control, etc. As a result, for a brand new control method, if people cannot strictly prove it at the theoretical level, they can verify the correctness and applicability physically by the inverted pendulum.

What is an inverted pendulum then? There are players in the circus who push up long bars on their heads, with heavy objects on the end of the bar. It can be abstractly considered as an unstable pendulum which is inverted, i.e., the gravity center is higher than the supporting point. It can gain good stability by the intuitive and qualitative control methods according to a human player.

People have tried for a long time to quantitatively describe this complex, structurally variant, and nonlinear system by precise mathematical approaches. Nevertheless, it is too difficult. It has been decades since people have regarded the inverted pendulum as the "pearl on the crown"[10] pursued by any automation researcher.

The research of inverted pendulum is also valuable for engineering. The standing and walking of robots is similar to a double link inverted pendulum system. It is more than 30 years ago that the first robot was created in the United States; however, the key technology in the robot — walking — remains a challenging problem. The trembling in the reconnaissance satellite will affect the image quality tremendously, so automatic stabilization is required to eliminate the trembling. Flexible rocket (multistage rocket) is invented to prevent the breaking of the single-stage rocket at the turning, and consequently the attitude control of this system can refer to the research in the multistage inverted pendulum.

In conclusion, research on the inverted pendulum is of practical value. In the past few decades, there have been hundreds of papers[11–19] on the inverted pendulum by scholars from the United States, Japan, Hong Kong, Canada, Sweden, Norway, etc. There have been inspiring products in the research of the single, double, and triple one-dimensional inverted pendulums, and the single- and double-link inverted pendulums in a plane. There have been some research products in national universities and institutions in China as well.[20–31] Presently, it has become a common educational tool in automation.

8.3.2 Inverted Pendulum Qualitative Control Mechanism

We start at the single-link inverted pendulum, as shown in Figure 8.14. The inverted pendulum L_1 is equivalent to the bar played in the circus, and the car is equivalent to the player. The pendulum and the car are connected by a nonfrictional rotational potentiometer. The external force F on the car and the moved distance x is equivalent to the manipulation of the player. θ is the angle from the vertical line to the pendulum, and it is defined as positive if the pendulum is on the right. This angle can be measured by the potentiometer. The origin of the moved distance is in the middle of the track. x is defined as positive if it is on the right of the origin.

The control objective of a single-link inverted pendulum is to stabilize the inverted pendulum, i.e., $\theta \approx 0$ and $x \approx 0$, by the appropriate controlling forces in the track with finite length even after disturbance.

It can be seen that the force transition between the pendulum and the car is a "coupling" relation, which transits the external force F on the car to the inverted pendulum and makes it stable. Combined with human intuition, it is easy to conduct qualitative analysis for a qualitative physical model of the single-link inverted pendulum system.[32,33]

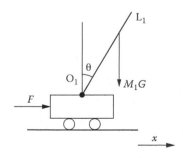

FIGURE 8.14 The illustration graph of a single-link inverted pendulum.

If there is no external force F, once the pendulum tilts to the left, the gravitational moment on the pendulum will make the tilting to the left in acceleration, and the car will move to the right. Once the pendulum tilts to the right, it will speed up such movement and the car will move the left.

If the external force F is to the right, the car will obtain a moving trend to the right, and the pendulum will gain the trend of tilting to the left. If F is to the left, the car will gain the trend of moving to the left, and the pendulum will be likely to tilt to the right.

The system of double-link inverted pendulum has one pendulum added to the single-link inverted pendulum. One rotational potentiometer of the same model is connected between the two pendulums to measure the second angle. It is more difficult to control this system than the single one. However, the control mechanism is similar, with the only difference being the compulsory force on the first pendulum is exerted by the car, while the compulsory force on the second pendulum is exerted by F' through the first one. In this way, F' is an indirect controlling force on the second pendulum, and thus the control on the second pendulum by the car is indirect.

Figure 8.15 shows the double-link inverted pendulum. θ_2 is the angle from the extended line of the first pendulum and the second pendulum, and clockwise direction is positive. The definition of θ_2 here is different from other literature (θ_2 is the angle from the vertical line to the second pendulum in other literature), so that the measured value can be directly revealed for convenience in analysis.

The control objective in the double-link inverted pendulum system is to control the car appropriately to stabilize the second pendulum without divergent oscillation and pose the car at $x \approx 0$, even after disturbance.

In the qualitative analysis of this system, we can easily associate it with two occasions. In the first, a circus player steps on board with a rolling ball under it. He has to swing his upper body to keep his balance, so the lower part can be considered as the first pendulum and the upper part as the second one. However, the actuating force on the upper part is exerted by the waist, which corresponds to assembling a motor between the first and second pendulums. Thus it is different from the inverted pendulum system. The other case is to put erect two wooden bars connected by a rotational link. It is extremely difficult, as the controller has

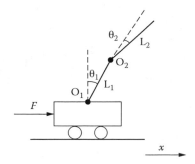

FIGURE 8.15 The illustration graph of a double-link inverted pendulum.

to concentrate on the upper pendulum and manipulate the lower bar accordingly. This occasion is similar to the inverted pendulum system discussed here. If the connection between the lower bar and the palm is not guaranteed, the delay of the controlling force will be more severe. Combined with the practical human controlling experience, it is not difficult to obtain the qualitative physical model of a double-link inverted pendulum system.

Assume no external force F is exerted onto the system. Under the function of the gravitational moment of the pendulum, if the upper pendulum L_2 tilts to the right, O_2 will move to the left, and thus L_1 will tilt to the left by a certain angle, so the car will move to the right. All the motion will be opposite if the initial tilting is opposite.

If an external force F is exerted to the left, L_1 will tilt to the right, and the point O_2 will move to the right, and consequently L_1 will move to the left.

In summary, once L_2 tilts a little, the car will exert an indirect force F' at the point O_2 through L_1, and this force will keep L_2 back to the dynamically stable position. This is the basic mechanism for the car to control the double-link inverted pendulum.

8.3.3 Cloud Control Policy of Triple-Link Inverted Pendulum

The triple-link inverted pendulum is the system with an additional pendulum added to the double-link inverted pendulum, as shown in Figure 8.16. The rotational potentiometer to measure the third angle is the same kind as the other two. It is aimed to keep the pendulums in stable states for a long time by the motion of the car, even with disturbance.

Such an inverted pendulum is nonlinear, and all physical systems are nonlinear to a certain extent. Conventional nonlinear control schemes often require a prior knowledge on mathematical structure and accurate parameters, which are usually not accessible. For example, according to control theory, the mathematical model for the pendulum can be constructed using Lagrange method under some assumptions.[15]

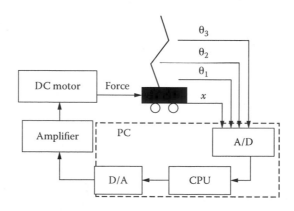

FIGURE 8.16 The experimental block graph of a triple-link inverted pendulum.

The nonlinear system equation resulting from the Lagrange method can then be written in the following form:

$$\frac{d}{dt}\left(\frac{\partial T}{\partial \dot{q}_j}\right) - \frac{\partial T}{\partial q_j} + \frac{\partial V}{\partial q_j} + \frac{\partial D}{\partial \dot{q}_j} = Uj + Fj \quad (j = 1,2,3,4)$$

$$q = [x \quad \theta_1 \quad \theta_2 \quad \theta_3]^T$$

$$F_j = -sign(q_j)u_j N_j$$

$$U = [Ks \quad U \quad 0 \quad 0 \quad 0]^T$$

where u (in volts) is the control input from the computer to the analog amplifier, Ks (in N/V) is the overall electronic systems input conversion gain and Fj is the coulomb friction term in the jth coordinate direction.

The nonlinear system equation resulting from the Lagrange method can then be written in the following form. To find a stabilizing controller for the pendulum, the equation of motion has to be linearized about the vertical position. The linearized model, which then becomes the basic foundation for all stabilization methodologies, is represented in state space form as follows.

$$\mathbf{F(q)\ \ddot{q} + G(q,\dot{q})\dot{q} + H(q) = L(q,u)}$$

As a matter of fact, a physical multilink inverted pendulum is a multivariate, nonlinear, fast-reaction and unstable system with a lot of uncertainties in the environment. There is no accurate mathematical model to fully describe it. However, human experts in theses cases may well achieve the control by control rules which are squeezed out from their long experience and represented by intuitive natural language. The natural languages play a very important role in representing the uncertainty in human control and reasoning.[34-36]

A. Qualitative analysis of the triple-link inverted pendulum system

Figure 8.17 is the illustration graph of a triple-link inverted pendulum system, which is obviously a tightly coupled system. There are eight state variables for representation of the system. The control objective can be expressed visually by $\theta_1 \approx 0$, $\theta_2 \approx 0$, $\theta_3 \approx 0$, $x \approx 0$.

x: the position of the car on the track
$\dot{x}$: the velocity of the car
θ_1: the tilting angle of the first pendulum with respect to the vertical direction
θ_2: the tilting angle of the second pendulum with respect to the first pendulum
θ_3: the tilting angle of the third pendulum with respect to the second pendulum
$\dot{\theta}_1, \dot{\theta}_2, \dot{\theta}_3$: the angular velocity of the first, second and third pendulum

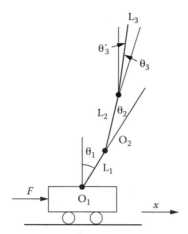

FIGURE 8.17 The illustration graph of a triple-link inverted pendulum.

After simple analysis on the triple-link inverted pendulum system, we can obtain the following qualitative conclusions:

1. If θ_1, θ_2, and θ_3 are initialized as zero and the gravitational moment of L_1, L_2, and L_3 are neglected, the force F to the right will make the first pendulum tilt to the left, i.e., the position of O_1 will move to the right, O_2 to the left, and O_3 to the right. Similarly, if the force is in the direction to the left, all the processes will be in the opposite direction.

2. θ_1 and θ_2 are initialized as zero and F is neglected. If the third pendulum tilts to the right, its motion will be accelerated by its gravitational moment, and consequently the second pendulum will tilt to the left and the first one to the right, i.e., O_3 will move to the left, O_2 to the right, O_1 to the left and the car to the left. The interaction from the upper pendulum to the lower one and the gravitational function of the lower pendulum itself will accelerate the variation. Similarly, if the third pendulum tilts to the left, the process will be opposite.

3. θ_1 and θ_3 are initialized as zero and F is neglected. If the second pendulum tilts to the right, the gravity of the third pendulum, together with the gravitational moment of the first pendulum, will further the motion of the second one. The first and third pendulums will tilt to the left, i.e., O_2 will move to the left, O_3 to the right, O_1 to the right, and the car to the right. The gravitational interaction from the upper pendulum to the lower one, together with the gravitational moment of the lower pendulum itself, will accelerate the variation. Similarly, if the second pendulum tilts to the left, the process will be opposite.

4. θ_2 and θ_3 are initialized as zero and F are neglected. If the first pendulum tilts to the right, the gravities of the upper pendulums together with the gravitational moment of itself will further the motion to the right. Meanwhile, the third pendulum will move to the right, the second to the left,

i.e., O_3 will move to the left, O_2 to the right, O_1 to the left, and the car to the left. The gravitational interaction from the upper pendulum to the lower one, together with the gravitational moment of the lower pendulum itself, will accelerate the variation. Similarly, if the first pendulum tilts to the left, the process will be opposite.

Obviously, the force F is directly exerted on the car, and transited to L_3 through L_1 and L_2 by means of coupling. Hence, it can be seen that for stabilization, it should be first achieved that $\theta_3 = 0$, then the second pendulum should be stabilized ($\theta_2 = 0$), followed by the stabilization of the lowest pendulum, i.e., $\theta_1 = 0$, and finally the stabilization of the car ($x = 0$) will be considered. As a result, the third pendulum can be regarded as the most significant one. The parameters of its rule generator should be most important, and those of the second and third pendulums and the car will be in a descending order.

Finally, it is necessary to discuss the relation of differential control D ($\dot{\theta}_1$, $\dot{\theta}_2$, $\dot{\theta}_3$, $\dot{x}$) and the proportional control $P(\theta_1, \theta_2, \theta_3, x)$. In the system, the advantage of proportional control is its immediate reaction once an error exists; however, if the plant is self-stable, there will be a static error. The differential control is sensitive to the variation trend of the error, and the reactive response can be speeded up to reduce the overshooting and increase the stability. Nevertheless, it is also sensitive to noise, which will reduce the system stability. Hence it is required to select appropriate proportional control to reduce the error and choose proper differential control to enhance the stability. The relation between these two will be more important than the internal relation of either one.

After analysis, the signals in this system can be ranked according to the descending order in the significance as follows:

$$\theta_3, \dot{\theta}_3, \theta_2, \dot{\theta}_2, \theta_1, \dot{\theta}_1, x, \dot{x}$$

Based on this, we design the cloud controller, in which the cloud-based rule generator is utilized to control the signals above.

B. The cloud controller of the triple-link inverted pendulum system

The cloud controller (Figure 8.18) mainly employs the cloud generator to control various signals in the triple-link inverted pendulum system. The design of this controller involves several aspects:

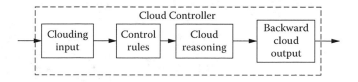

FIGURE 8.18 Theoretical block chart of the cloud controller.

1. Determine the input and output variables of the cloud controller.
2. Design the control rules of the controller, including the number of rules and the contents of the rules.
3. Select the cloud types for expression of the preconditions and the post-conditions of the rules.
4. Select the universal sets of the input and output variables of the cloud controller, and determine the parameters of the cloud controller, such as the quantitative factor, the three numerical characteristics of the cloud, etc.
5. Program the algorithm for the cloud controller.
6. Select the sampling time of the cloud controller algorithm appropriately.

Within the six steps, the key one is the design of control rules, which consists of three parts: selection of the linguistic value set to describe the input/output linguistic variables, definition of the ranges of each linguistic value, and establishment of the control rules of the cloud controller. The rules of the cloud controller are generally reflected by a group of qualitative rules containing qualitative concepts.

In real applications, due to the fact that people are accustomed to dividing the events into two categories, we can describe the input/output states in the cloud controller by the words "large" and "small." Considering the zero state of the variable, there are altogether five qualitative concepts, i.e., negatively large, negatively small, zero, positively small, positively large. Based on this, five concepts can be defined for each input/output variable in the construction of cloud rule generator. The concrete control rules of the triple-link inverted pendulum are illustrated as below, and the parameter set of the qualitative concepts in the rules is shown in Table 8.1.

The rules set $RS(\theta_3)$ of the tilting angle of the third pendulum θ_3:

If the tilting angle θ_3 is positively large, then the output force F of the motor will be positively large.
If the tilting angle θ_3 is positively small, then the output force F of the motor will be positively small.
If the tilting angle θ_3 is zero, then the output force F of the motor will be zero.
If the tilting angle θ_3 is negatively small, then the output force F of the motor will be negatively small.
If the tilting angle θ_3 is negatively large, then the output force F of the motor will be negatively large.

The rules set $RS(\theta_2)$ of the tilting angle of the second pendulum θ_2:

If the tilting angle θ_2 is positively large, then the output force F of the motor will be negatively large.
If the tilting angle θ_2 is positively small, then the output force F of the motor will be negatively small.
If the tilting angle θ_2 is zero, then the output force F of the motor will be zero.
If the tilting angle θ_2 is negatively small, then the output force F of the motor will be positively small.

TABLE 8.1
The Parameter Set of the Qualitative Concepts in the Rule Generators for a Triple-Link Inverted Pendulum System

Precondition	Negatively Large	Negatively Small	Zero	Positively Small	Positively Large
RS(θ_1)	(−150, 31, 0.059, 1)	(−57, 19, 0.04, 0)	(0, 11.4, 0.0256, 0)	(57, 19, 0.04, 0)	(150, 31, 0.059, 2)
RS($\dot{\theta}_1$)	(−550, 30, 0.03, 1)	(−209, 6903, 0.02, 0)	(0, 42, 0.0128, 0)	(209, 69.3, 0.02, 0)	(550, 30, 0.03, 2)
RS(θ_2)	(−500, 103.5, 0.044, 1)	(−190, 63, 0.03, 0)	(0, 38, 0.0192, 0)	(190, 63, 0.03, 0)	(500, 103.5, 0.044, 2)
RS($\dot{\theta}_2$)	(−700, 145, 0.06, 1)	(−266, 88, 0.033, 0)	(0, 53.2, 0.0224, 0)	(266, 88, 0.033, 0)	(700, 145, 0.06, 20)
RS(θ_3)	(−800, 166, 0.044, 1)	(−304, 101, 0.03, 0)	(0, 60.8, 0.0192, 0)	(304, 101, 0.03, 0)	(800, 166, 0.044, 2)
RS($\dot{\theta}_3$)	(−850, 176, 0.06, 1)	(−323, 107, 0.033, 0)	(0, 640, 0.0224, 0)	(323, 107, 0.033, 0)	(850, 176, 0.06, 2)
Postcondition	(−100, 20.7, 0.023, 1)	(−38, 12.6, 0.015, 0)	(0, 7.6, 0.01, 0)	(38, 12.6, 0.015, 0)	(100, 20.7, 0.023, 2)

If the tilting angle θ_2 is negatively large, then the output force F of the motor will be positively large.

The rules set $RS(\theta_1)$ of the tilting angle of the second pendulum θ_1:

If the tilting angle θ_1 is positively large, then the output force F of the motor will be positively large.
If the tilting angle θ_1 is positively small, then the output force F of the motor will be positively small.
If the tilting angle θ_1 is zero, then the output force F of the motor will be zero.
If the tilting angle θ_1 is negatively small, then the output force F of the motor will be negatively small.
If the tilting angle θ_1 is negatively large, then the output force F of the motor will be negatively large.

The rule set $RS(x)$ of the car displacement x:

If the car displacement x is positively large, then the output force F of the motor will be negatively large.
If the car displacement x is positively small, then the output force F of the motor will be negatively small.
If the car displacement x is zero, then the output force F of the motor will be zero.
If the car displacement x is negatively small, then the output force F of the motor will be positively small.
If the car displacement x is negatively large, then the output force F of the motor will be positively large.

The rule set $RS(\dot{\theta}_3)$ of the angular velocity $\dot{\theta}_3$ of the third pendulum:

If the angular velocity $\dot{\theta}_3$ is positively large, then the output force F of the motor will be positively large.
If the angular velocity $\dot{\theta}_3$ is positively small, then the output force F of the motor will be positively small.
If the angular velocity $\dot{\theta}_3$ is zero, then the output force F of the motor will be zero.
If the angular velocity $\dot{\theta}_3$ is negatively small, then the output force F of the motor will be negatively small.
If the angular velocity $\dot{\theta}_3$ is negatively large, then the output force F of the motor will be negatively large.

The rule set $RS(\dot{\theta}_2)$ of the angular velocity $\dot{\theta}_2$ of the second pendulum:

If the angular velocity $\dot{\theta}_2$ is positively large, then the output force F of the motor will be negatively large.
If the angular velocity $\dot{\theta}_2$ is positively small, then the output force F of the motor will be negatively small.

If the angular velocity $\dot{\theta}_2$ is zero, then the output force F of the motor will be zero.

If the angular velocity $\dot{\theta}_2$ is negatively small, then the output force F of the motor will be positively small.

If the angular velocity $\dot{\theta}_2$ is negatively large, then the output force F of the motor will be positively large.

The rule set RS($\dot{\theta}_1$) of the angular velocity $\dot{\theta}_1$ of the second pendulum:

If the angular velocity $\dot{\theta}_1$ is positively large, then the output force F of the motor will be positively large.

If the angular velocity $\dot{\theta}_1$ is positively small, then the output force F of the motor will be positively small.

If the angular velocity $\dot{\theta}_1$ is zero, then the output force F of the motor will be zero.

If the angular velocity $\dot{\theta}_1$ is negatively small, then the output force F of the motor will be negatively small.

If the angular velocity $\dot{\theta}_1$ is negatively large, then the output force F of the motor will be negatively large.

The rule set RS($\dot{x}$) of the car velocity $\dot{x}$:

If the car velocity $\dot{x}$ is positively large, then the output force F of the motor will be positively large.

If the car velocity $\dot{x}$ is positively small, then the output force F of the motor will be positively small.

If the car velocity $\dot{x}$ is zero, then the output force F of the motor will be zero.

If the car velocity $\dot{x}$ is negatively small, then the output force F of the motor will be negatively small.

If the car velocity $\dot{x}$ is negatively large, then the output force F of the motor will be negatively large.

In Table 8.1, the two qualitative concepts "positively large" and "negatively large" are expressed by half-normal clouds, and the other three are expressed by normal clouds.

Figure 8.19 demonstrates the control flowchart of the triple-link inverted pendulum. It can be seen that five rule controllers on eight signals are utilized, including the three tilt angles (θ_3, θ_2, θ_1), their differentials ($\dot{\theta}_3$, $\dot{\theta}_2$, $\dot{\theta}_1$), the displacement of the car x, and the speed of the car $\dot{x}$. According to the significance order of these signals, which has been discussed before, we have to set some signals with high priority and control them once they exceed the range. In the experiment, five rule controllers control the pendulum sequentially according to their priorities by means of "soft zero," which is a normally random number with expectation zero and entropy En. In the control, it will vary each time. According to the judgment conditions in the five rule controllers, there will be related "soft zeros" SZ_{θ_3}, SZ_{θ_2}, SZ_{θ_1}, SZ_x, $SZ_{\dot{\theta}_3}$, $SZ_{\dot{\theta}_2}$, $SZ_{\dot{\theta}_1}$, $SZ_{\dot{x}}$, the entropies of which effectively determine the probabilities

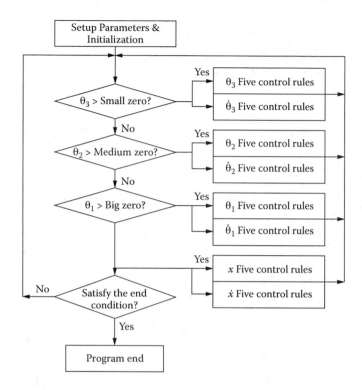

FIGURE 8.19 Control flowchart of the triple-link inverted pendulum.

of entrance into the related rule controller. The range and probability of the "soft zero" will vary according to different entropies. These "soft zeros" may be classified into "big zero," "medium zero," and "small zero" based on their values. Consequently, the transition between the rule controllers can be realized by the values of the "soft zeros."

We have implemented effective control on a triple-link inverted pendulum via the cloud control method. The eight signals of the triple-link inverted pendulums are illustrated in Figure 8.20. Figure 8.21 shows the graph of the triple-link inverted pendulum[37] demonstrated in IFAC'99 in July 1999, in Beijing. In the demonstration, the system has excellent stability, even in the case where a bunch of flowers or disturbance of knocking are added into the system.

8.3.4 BALANCING PATTERNS OF AN INVERTED PENDULUM

In the inverted pendulum system, the rotational potentiometers are joints. Although they are frictionless, the difference in agility of the joints will result in different dynamical stability of the system under control. The discussion of the dynamically stable attitudes in this problem will benefit the other research, such as the multistage flexible rocket.

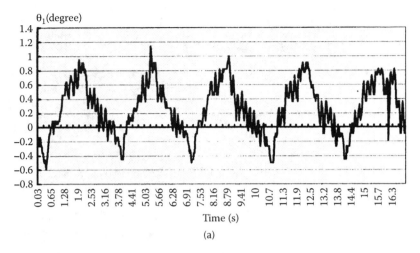

(a)

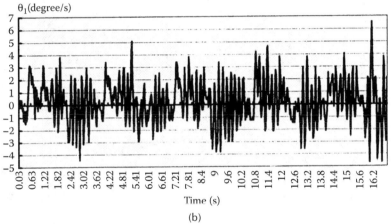

(b)

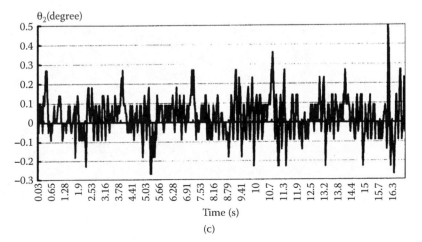

(c)

FIGURE 8.20 Eight signals of the triple-link inverted pendulum.

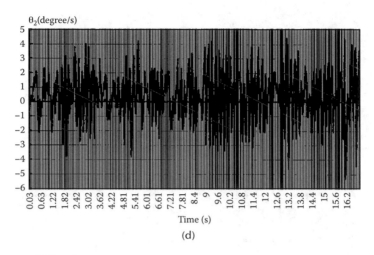

(d)

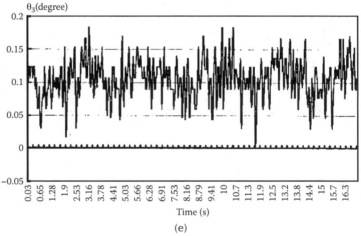

(e)

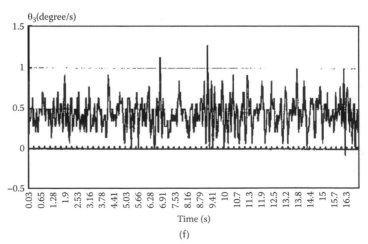

(f)

FIGURE 8.20 (Continued).

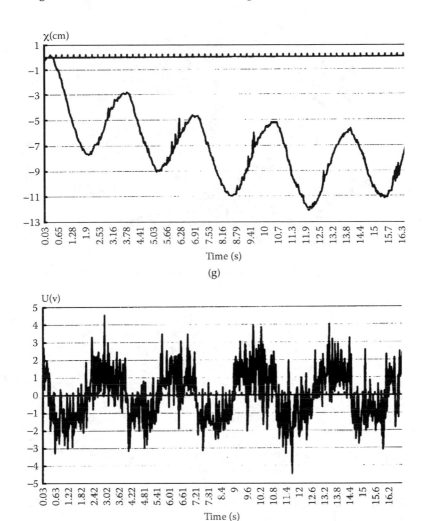

FIGURE 8.20 (Continued).

Definition 8.1 Association degree[38]

The association degree ρ between the pendulums, which is the measurement of the coupling between the two pendulums, is defined as

$$\rho_n = 1 - \frac{|\theta_n|}{90°}$$

where θ_n is the measured angle of the nth pendulum ($n = 1, 2, \ldots$), ρ_1 is the association degree of the first pendulum and the car, ρ_n is the association degree of the $n - 1$th and nth pendulum.

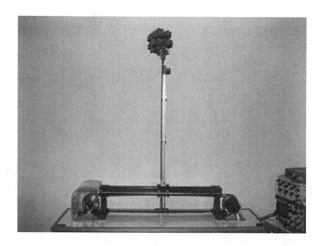

FIGURE 8.21 The robust experiment of the triple-link inverted pendulum.

When ρ_n approaches 1, the association degree of the corresponding pendulums becomes large, which means that the coupling between the two adjacent pendulums is so tight that they move like one pendulum. When ρ_n approaches 0, the association degree is small, resulting in weak coupling so that the swing amplitude of the lower pendulum is apparently greater than that of the upper one.

1. Balancing patterns of the single-link inverted pendulum

We still consider the example of bar erection by a circus player. He can concentrate on the bar on his shoulder, and move his shoulder once any tilting occurs. He can either move until the tilting increases to some extent. Thus, we can come up with two kinds of balancing patterns for a single-link inverted pendulum system. From one perspective, it has only one association degree ρ_1, which takes the value in "large" and "small," so this single-link inverted pendulum system has two balancing patterns: large ρ_1 and small ρ_1.

    a. Balancing pattern 1: large ρ_1, as shown in Figure 8.22. At this time, the association between the first pendulum and the car is large. The pendulum erects on the car, and the car moves slowly on the track with small displacement.

    b. Balancing pattern 2: small ρ_1, as shown in Figure 8.23. At this time, the association between the first pendulum and the car is small. The car moves back and forth regularly on the track with large displacement.

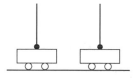

FIGURE 8.22 Balancing pattern 1 of the single-link inverted pendulum (large ρ_1).

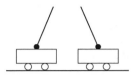

FIGURE 8.23 Balancing pattern 2 of the single-link inverted pendulum (small ρ_1).

2. Balancing patterns of the double-link inverted pendulum

There are two association degrees, i.e., ρ_1 and ρ_2, in a double-link inverted pendulum system. If each of the two association degrees can take either "large" or "small," there will be four combinations, i.e., large ρ_1 with large ρ_2, small ρ_1 with relatively large ρ_2, small ρ_1 with small ρ_2, and large ρ_1 with relatively small ρ_2.

The fourth state "large ρ_1 with relatively small ρ_2" is an unstable state, as shown in Figure 8.24. When the second pendulum tilts to the right, θ_2 and $\dot{\theta}_2$ will increase. At this time, the O_2 will move to the right to try to keep the pendulum stable, resulting in the left motion of the car. Consequently θ_1 and $\dot{\theta}_1$ will increase positively. In order to guarantee the stability of the first pendulum, the motor should be controlled for larger force to the right. In this process, the car has to adjust the control on O_1 before it is able to control O_2, so the motion of the car cannot be stabilized. As a result, there is no balancing pattern with large ρ_1 and relatively small ρ_2. It can be concluded that in any circumstance, ρ_2 should be greater than ρ_1. In an n link inverted pendulum system, there in no state of large ρ_{n-1} with relatively small ρ_n, large ρ_{n-2} with relatively small ρ_{n-1},..., and large ρ_1 with relatively small ρ_2. Thus, there are altogether three classical balancing patterns of the double-link inverted pendulum system.

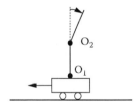

FIGURE 8.24 Double-link inverted pendulum that is unstable (large ρ_1 with relatively small ρ_2).

a. Balancing pattern 1: large ρ_1 with large ρ_2, as shown in Figure 8.25. The association degrees between the first and the second pendulums are relatively large, so they erect on the car, which moves slowly back and forth with small displacement.

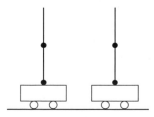

FIGURE 8.25 Balancing pattern 1 of the double-link inverted pendulum (large ρ_1 with large ρ_2).

b. Balancing pattern 2: small ρ_1 with relatively large ρ_2, as shown in Figure 8.26. In this case, the association degree between the first and the second pendulums is large, while that between the first pendulum and the car is relatively small. As a result, the system looks like one pendulum tilting back and forth apparently to keep balance.

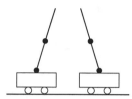

FIGURE 8.26 Balancing pattern 2 of the double-link inverted pendulum (small ρ_1 with relatively large ρ_2).

c. Balancing pattern 3: small ρ_1 with small ρ_2, as shown in Figure 8.27. In this case, the association degrees between the two pendulums and that between the first pendulum and the car are small; however, because ρ_2 is greater than ρ_1, the displacement of the car is large. As a result, the system looks like the first pendulum swings apparently to keep balance, while the second one remains erect.

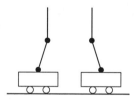

FIGURE 8.27 Balancing pattern 3 of the double-link inverted pendulum (small ρ_1 with small ρ_2).

3. Balancing patterns of the triple-link inverted pendulum

There are three association degrees (ρ_1, ρ_2, ρ_3) in the triple-link inverted pendulum system, and each association degree can be either "large" or "small," so there are all-together eight combinations:

    i. large ρ_1, large ρ_2, with large ρ_3
    ii. small ρ_1, large ρ_2, with large ρ_3
   iii. large ρ_1, small ρ_2, with large ρ_3
   iv. small ρ_1, small ρ_2, with large ρ_3
    v. large ρ_1, large ρ_2, with small ρ_3
   vi. small ρ_1, large ρ_2, with small ρ_3
  vii. large ρ_1, small ρ_2, with small ρ_3
 viii. small ρ_1, small ρ_2, with small ρ_3

According to the analysis of the double-link inverted pendulum, the association degree of the upper pendulums must be greater than the lower pendulums so as to keep the balance. This rule is still applicable to the triple-link inverted pendulum system, so the possible balancing patterns are (i), (ii), (iv), and (viii).

a. Balancing pattern 1: large ρ_1, large ρ_2, with large ρ_3, as shown in Figure 8.28. In this case, the three association degrees are all large, and the displacement of the car is small. Hence, the system looks like an erect single-link inverted pendulum.

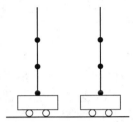

FIGURE 8.28 Balancing pattern 1 of a triple-link inverted pendulum (large ρ_1, large ρ_2, with large ρ_3).

b. Balancing pattern 2: small ρ_1, large ρ_2, with large ρ_3, as shown in Figure 8.29. In this case the association degree between the car and the first pendulum is small, while those between the pendulums are large. The displacement of the car is large. The system looks like a single-link pendulum swinging apparently.

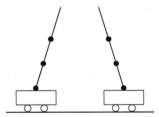

FIGURE 8.29 Balancing pattern 2 of a triple-link inverted pendulum (small ρ_1, large ρ_2, with large ρ_3).

c. Balancing pattern 3: small ρ_1, small ρ_2, with large ρ_3, as shown in Figure 8.30. In this case, the two lower association degrees are small, while the upper one is large. The displacement of the car is large. The upper two pendulums erect all through the process, while the first pendulum swings apparently.

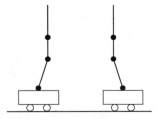

FIGURE 8.30 Balancing pattern 3 of a triple-link inverted pendulum (small ρ_1, small ρ_2, with large ρ_3).

d. Balancing pattern 4: small ρ_1, small ρ_2, with small ρ_3, as shown in Figure 8.31. In this case, all the connections in the joints are soft, so the amplitude of the system is relatively large and the swinging frequency is relatively slow.

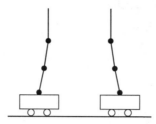

FIGURE 8.31 Balancing pattern 4 of a triple-link inverted pendulum (small ρ_1, small ρ_2, with small ρ_3).

Figure 8.32 demonstrates the periodic variation of a triple-link inverted pendulum which is in the fourth balancing pattern. The attitudes are different at different times. The angles between the pendulums vary according to time; however, in any circumstance the lower association degree is greater than the upper one so as to keep balance.

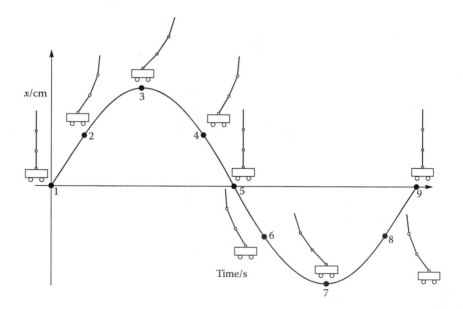

FIGURE 8.32 The periodic variation of the pendulum in the fourth balancing pattern.

Figure 8.33 shows the relation between the displacement of the car and the time for the four classical balancing patterns. The amplitudes and periods are distinct in different patterns.

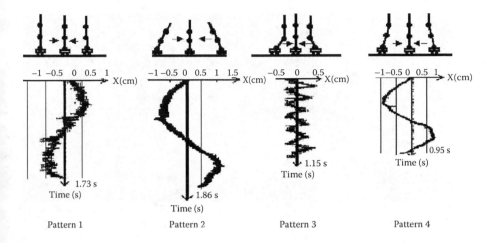

FIGURE 8.33 The relation curves between the car displacement and the time for a triple-link inverted pendulum in different balancing patterns.

For balancing the triple link inverted pendulum, the controlling force F on the car is

$$F = F_1 + F_2 + F_3$$

where F_1, F_2 and F_3 are the controlling forces for the first, second and third pendulums, generated by the rule sets $RS(\theta_1)$ and $RS(\dot{\theta}_1)$, $RS(\theta_2)$ and $RS(\dot{\theta}_2)$, $RS(\theta_3)$ and $RS(\dot{\theta}_3)$, respectively. The association degrees ρ_1, ρ_2, and ρ_3 can be changed by modification of the cloud parameters in $RS(\theta_1)$, $RS(\dot{\theta}_1)$, $RS(\theta_2)$, $RS(\dot{\theta}_2)$, $RS(\theta_3)$, and $RS(\dot{\theta}_3)$. By this means, the four classical balancing patterns can be constructed.

Figure 8.34 records the dynamically switching curve in the process pattern 1 $\rightarrow$ pattern 2 $\rightarrow$ pattern 3 $\rightarrow$ pattern 4.

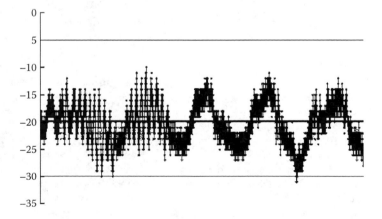

FIGURE 8.34 The dynamically switching curve between different balancing patterns of the triple-link inverted pendulum.

It is of great significance to conduct the induction and research on the balancing patterns of the inverted pendulums. By means of modification of the cloud parameters, the motor voltage can be adjusted so as to control the attitude of the system. It provides a possible solution for operational attitude setting of the plant in applications. Meanwhile the research in balancing patterns has deepened the exploiture in the cloud, and broadened the cloud application.

As a conclusion, the reasoning and control based on qualitative knowledge are important tools in intelligent control, as well as the significant part in the research on AI with uncertainty. We have introduced the cloud-based uncertain reasoning and control mechanism and solved the stabilization problem in the triple-inverted pendulum system, which is a classical problem in intelligent control. The cloud-based mechanism is explicit and direct, exclusive of complex reasoning and computation. Hence it can simulate the uncertainty in human thinking activities, and it is of applicable values as well.

REFERENCES

1. Kaichang Di, The Theory and Methods of Spatial Data Mining and Knowledge Discovery, Ph.D. thesis, Wuhan Technical University of Surveying and Mapping, Wuhan, 1999.
2. Yi Du, Research and Applications of Association Rules in Data Mining, Ph.D. thesis, PLA University of Science and Technology, Nanjing, 2000.
3. Deyi Li, Yi Du, Guoding Yin et al., Commonsense knowledge modeling, *16th World Computer Congress 2000*, Beijing, 2000.
4. C. S. Roger and B. L. David, Creativity and learning in a case-based explainer, *AI*, Vol. 40, No. 1–3: 353–385, 1989.
5. B. Kosko, *Fuzzy Thinking, the New Science of Fuzzy Logic*, Hyperion, New York, 1993.
6. M. Laviolette, A probabilistic and statistical view of fuzzy methods, *Technometrics*, Vol. 37, No. 3: 249–266, 1995.
7. A. Kandel, A. Martins, and R. Pacheco, Discussion: on the very real distinction between fuzzy and statistical methods, *Technometrics*, Vol. 37, No. 3: 276–281, 1995.
8. M. Mizumoto, Fuzzy controls under product-sum-gravity methods and new fuzzy control methods, in: A. Kandel and G. Langholz, eds., *Fuzzy Control Systems*, CRC Press, London, pp. 276–294, 1993.
9. Deyi Li, Uncertainty reasoning based on cloud models in controllers, *Computers and Mathematics with Applications*, Elsevier Science, Vol. 35, No. 3: 99–123, 1998.
10. F. Schaefer and H. Cannon, On the control of unstable mechanical systems, *3rd International Federation of Automatic Control World Congress*, London, 1966.
11. C. Anderson, Learning to control an inverted pendulum using neural network, *IEEE Control Systems Magazine*, Vol. 4, pp. 31–36, 1989.
12. J. Eker and K. J. Åström, A nonlinear observer for the inverted pendulum, *Proceedings of the 18th IEEE Conference on Control Applications*, Dearborn, Michigan, 1996.
13. T. Yamakawa, Stabilization of inverted pendulum by a high-speed fuzzy logic controller hardware system, *Fuzzy Sets and Systems*, Vol. 32, pp. 161–180, 1989.
14. D. Saez and A. Cipriano, Design of fuzzy model based predictive controllers and its application to an inverted pendulum, *Fuzzy — IEEE'97*, pp. 915–919, 1997.

15. L. Chen and R. Smith, Closed-loop model validation for an inverted pendulum experiment via a linear matrix inequality approach, *Proceedings of the 36th Conference on Decision and Control*, San Diego, California, 1997.

16. K. Furuta and M. Yamakita, Swing-up control of inverted pendulum using pseudo-state feedback, *Journal of Systems and Control Engineering*, Vol. 206, pp. 263–269, 1992.

17. H. Meier, Z. Farwig, and H. Unbehauen, Discrete computer control of a triple-inverted pendulum, *Optimal Control Applications and Methods*, Vol. 11, No. 1: 157–171, 1990.

18. K. G. Eltohamy and C. Kao, Real time stabilization of a triple linked inverted pendulum using single control input, *IEE Proceedings Control Theory Applications*, Vol. 144, No. 5: 498–504, 1997.

19. H. Zhang, X. Ma, and P. Wang, Design fuzzy controllers for complex systems with an application to 3-stage inverted pendulums, *Information Science*, Vol. 72, pp. 271–284, 1993.

20. Guangxiong Wang, Jing Zhang, and Jingquan Zhu, Output feedback control of inverted pendulum: fragility and robustness, *Electric Machine and Control*, Vol. 6, No. 3: 221–223, 2002.

21. Naiyao Zhang, C. Ebert, R. Belschner et al., Fuzzy cascade control of an inverted pendulum, *Control and Decision*, Vol. 11, No.1: 85–88, 1996.

22. Jiangbin Zhu and Jianiang Yi, Swing up control of double inverted pendulum, *Journal of System Simulation*, Vol. 15, No. 7: 1043–1046, 2003.

23. Fuyan Cheng, Guomin Zhong, and Youshan Li, A parameter fuzzy controller for a double inverted pendulum, *Information and Control*, Vol. 24, No. 3: 189–192, 1995.

24. Dongjun Zhang, Shuang Cong, Zexiang Li et al., Study and realization of rotary double inverted-pendulum control, *Information and Control*, Vol. 24, No. 3: 189–192, 1995.

25. Hongwei Yao, Xiaorong Mei, Zhenqiang Yang et al., Analysis and design of a double inverted pendulum based on fuzzy dynamic fuzzy model, *Control Theory and Applications*, Vol. 18, No. 2: 224–227, 2001.

26. Feizhou Zhang, Weiji Chen, and Chengzhi Shen, Research on mechanism of imitating human intelligent control triple inverted pendulum, *Journal of Beijing University of Aeronautics and Astronautics*, Vol. 25, No. 2: 151–155, 1999.

27. Jianfu Cao and Fumin Cao, The robust stability analysis of a balanced inverted pendulum, *Control Theory and Applications*, Vol. 16, No. 4: 611–614, 1999.

28. Jianqiang Yi, Stabilization control of parallel-type double inverted pendulum system, *Control and Decision*, Vol. 18, No. 4: 504–506, 2003.

29. Hongxing Li, Zhihong Miao, and Jiayin Wang, Adaptive fuzzy control with variant universal set on a quadric inverted pendulum, *Science in China (E Edition)*, Vol. 32, No. 1: 65–75, 2002.

30. Jun Xiao, Shi Zhang, and Xinhe Xu, Fuzzy control of the four level inverted pendulum system, *Journal of System Simulation*, Vol. 13, No. 6: 752–755, 2001.

31. Jun Cheng, Yong Wang, Nanchen Huang et al., A computer control for ARM-driven inverted pendulum, *Electric Machines and Control*, Vol. 5, No. 4: 277–280, 2001.

32. Hui Chen, Qualitative Quantitative Transforming Model and Its Application, Master's degree thesis, PLA University of Science and Technology, Nanjing, 1999.

33. Ning Zhou, Cloud Model and Its Application in Intelligent Control, Master's degree thesis, PLA University of Science and Technology, Nanjing, 2000.

34. Feizhou Zhang, Yuezu Fan, Deyi Li et al., Intelligent control based on the membership cloud generators, *Acta Aeronautica ET Astronautica Sinica*, Vol. 20, No. 1: 89–92, 1999.

35. Hui Chen, Deyi Li, Chengzhi Shen et al., A clouds model applied to controlling inverted pendulum, *Journal of Computer Research and Development*, Vol. 36, No. 10: 1180–1187, 1999.

36. Feizhou Zhang, Yuezu Fan, Chengzhi Shen et al., Intelligent control inverted pendulum with cloud model, *Control Theory and Applications*, Vol. 17, No. 4: 519–524, 2000.

37. Li Deyi, Chen Hui, Fan Jianhua et al., A Novel Qualitative Control Method to Inverted Pendulum Systems, *14th International Federation of Automatic Control World Congress*, Beijing, 1999.

38. Deyi Li, The cloud control method and balancing patterns of triple link inverted pendulum systems, *The Chinese Engineering Science*, Vol. 1, No. 2: 41–46, 1999.

9 A New Direction for AI with Uncertainty

Looking back at the development of artificial intelligence (AI), although astonishing achievements have been made, is it still far from human expectations and has a long way to go, especially on the processing ability of the uncertainty problem.

It took a long time for computer science to break away from electronics. Similarly, it also took a long time for software to break away from computer science. Needless to say, knowledge science will take a long time to break away from software. The nature of the computer is to materialize the Turing computer model into a Von Neumann architecture by using electric or optical components as the smallest units. Although information technology and computer networks are developing more and more rapidly, the present theory and structure of the computer, which is based on the binary system, has not changed greatly. We eagerly expect the birth of new types of computers, such as the quantum computer. With the development of software technology and engineering, people expect more hardware-independent software systems. Programming, once a branch of computing mathematics, has always been thought of as a very high degree of mental labor. The first operation system was just a boot program to coordinate the computing unit, the memory unit and the I/O (Input/Output) unit. But now, it has become the basic computer software, which people are trying their best to separate from the manufacturing and production of the computer. The technology of multilayer software platforms and tools has made it possible for the software to be independent of programming when it is being designed. Furthermore, it is unnecessary for people to understand the architecture and the operating system of the computer. That is to say, the computer is more and more convenient for human–computer interaction and is increasingly coming closer to the thinking habits and processing methods of human beings. However, the intelligent behaviors to be implemented through software design and programming such as reasoning, decision making, learning, interacting, etc. are still interwoven with the software itself. So, people hope to separate the knowledge hidden in the software from software design and the actual implementation. This tendency has called for new requirements for AI, an important one of which is the representation of uncertainty knowledge.

A natural tendency for human beings is to search for the answer to a problem using familiar ways. When a new area of knowledge is involved, people are always inclined to apply the familiar knowledge they have already acquired to tackle the new area. However, we will always meet with some insurmountable obstacles, so it is necessary to find and establish new theories and methods applicable to the new area.

315

For the past decade or so, we have done some research around the uncertainty in AI with the support from the National Natural Science Foundation, Hi-Tech Research and Development Program of China (863 Program), the National Basic Research Program (973 Program) and the National Defense Pre-Research Foundation of China.[1-13] Such studies seem to be integrated into an organic whole, unifying many local but important results into a satisfactory structure, which shows how uncertainty in intelligence has expanded and generalized the traditional discipline of AI.

This chapter is a brief introduction to the present research we are doing and the future research we are going after, both of which reflect the research direction of uncertainty in AI.

9.1 COMPUTING WITH WORDS

"Computing," in its traditional sense, involves for the most part computation of numbers and symbols. However, in the past three decades, the term has taken on a much broader meaning. For example, in many colleges and universities, the original name "computer department" has been changed to "department of computing." Now image processing, planning, and optimizing, decision support and knowledge discovery are all regarded as computing. In contrast, humans employ language in thinking, decision making, and reasoning. And they are better suited at utilizing concept and language value for computation and reasoning. In 1965, after L. A. Zadeh proposed the concept of fuzzy set, there appeared quite a few methods of fuzzy set calculation and fuzzy number operation. In 1996, Zadeh further presented his idea of "computing with words"[14]; a way in which concepts, linguistic values or words, instead of numerical values, are used for computation and reasoning. It lays more emphasis on the role of natural human language played in human intelligence and focuses more on the method of dealing with uncertainty in concepts, linguistic value, and words.

"Computing with words" put forward by Zadeh is mainly based on uncertainty processing of fuzzy sets. The cloud model is a way of expressing randomness in natural linguistic values, fuzziness, and their correlation. In short, it is the model of the uncertainty transition between qualitative concept and quantitative description. Naturally, it is a research study direction to study computing with words based on the cloud model.

Computing with words by using the cloud model includes algebra operations, logic operations, and mood operations. The result of the cloud computing can be taken as a new word of a certain granularity, i.e., a subconcept or a composite concept.

The following basic rules are the "computing with words" based on the cloud model:

1. Algebra Operations

In a certain domain U, there are two clouds $C_1(Ex_1, En_1, He_1)$, $C_2(Ex_2, En_2, He_2)$. The computing result of C_1 and C_2 is $C(Ex, En, He)$. The algebra operations of C_1 and C_2 can be defined as follows:[15]

Addition

$$Ex = Ex_1 + Ex_2$$

$$En = \sqrt{En_1^2 + En_2^2}$$

$$He = \sqrt{He_1^2 + He_2^2}$$

Subtraction

$$Ex = Ex_1 - Ex_2$$

$$En = \sqrt{En_1^2 + En_2^2}$$

$$He = \sqrt{He_1^2 + He_2^2}$$

Multiplication

$$Ex = Ex_1 Ex_2$$

$$En = |Ex_1 Ex_2| \times \sqrt{\left(\frac{En_1}{Ex_1}\right)^2 + \left(\frac{En_2}{Ex_2}\right)^2}$$

$$He = |Ex_1 Ex_2| \times \sqrt{\left(\frac{He_1}{Ex_1}\right)^2 + \left(\frac{He_2}{Ex_2}\right)^2}$$

Division

$$Ex = \frac{Ex_1}{Ex_2}$$

$$En = \left|\frac{Ex_1}{Ex_2}\right| \times \sqrt{\left(\frac{En_1}{Ex_1}\right)^2 + \left(\frac{En_2}{Ex_2}\right)^2}$$

$$He = \left|\frac{Ex_1}{Ex_2}\right| \times \sqrt{\left(\frac{He_1}{Ex_1}\right)^2 + \left(\frac{He_2}{Ex_2}\right)^2}$$

It is meaningful that only the concepts mentioned by upward computing belong to one domain. When the entropy and the hyper-entropy of a cloud are zeroes, the algebra operations become the computing between cloud and accurate value.

The algebra operations of cloud have the following characteristics:

a. Addition and multiplication are satisfied with commutative law and associative law:
   Commutative laws: $A + B = B + A$, $AB = BA$.
   Associative laws: $(A + B) + C = A + (B + C)$, $(AB)C = A(BC)$.

b. Generally speaking, the algebra operations of cloud add the uncertainty. However, addition and subtraction between cloud and accurate value do not change the uncertainty. So we cannot get $C - B = A$ from $A + B = C$; $AB = C$ cannot infer $C \div B = A$.

2. Logical Operations

Given $A(Ex_A, En_A, He_A)$, $B(Ex_B, En_B, He_B)$ in domain U. The logical operation between A and B, traditionally including EQUAL, INCLUDE, AND, OR and NOT, can be separately defined as follows:
   a. *A* EQUALS *B*:

$$A = B \Leftrightarrow (Ex_A = Ex_B) \wedge (En_A = En_B) \wedge (He_A = He_B)$$

   b. *A* INCLUDES *B*:

$$A \supseteq B \Leftrightarrow [(Ex_A - 3En_A) \le (Ex_B - 3En_B)] \wedge [(Ex_B + 3En_B) \le (Ex_A + 3En_A)]$$

   c. *A* AND *B*: There are three cases

If $|(Ex_A - Ex_B)| \ge |3(En_A + En_B)|$, the computing result is null.

If $|(Ex_A - Ex_B)| < |3(En_A + En_B)|$, A excluding B, furthermore $Ex_A \ge Ex_B$, the result is

$$C = A \cap B \Leftrightarrow$$

$$Ex_C \approx \frac{1}{2} |(Ex_A - 3En_A) + (Ex_B + 3En_B)|$$

$$En_C \approx \frac{1}{6} |(Ex_B + 3En_B) - (Ex_A - 3En_A)|$$

$$He_C = \max(He_A, He_B)$$

If $A \supseteq B$ or $B \subseteq A$, then the result is

$$C = \begin{cases} A & A \subseteq B \\ B & A \supseteq B \end{cases}$$

d. A OR B: If $A \cap B \neq \varnothing$, while $Ex_A \leq Ex_B$, the result is

$$C = A \cup B \Leftrightarrow$$

$$Ex_C = \frac{1}{2}(Ex_A - 3En_A + En_B + 3En_B)$$

$$En_C = En_A + En_B$$

$$He_C = \max(He_A + He_B)$$

e. A NOT: there are two cases
If A is a half-cloud, then the result is a half-cloud, namely

$$C = \bar{A} \Leftrightarrow$$

$$Ex_C \approx \min(U) \text{ or } \max(U)$$

$$En_C \approx \frac{1}{3}(U - 3En_B)$$

$$He_C \approx He_A$$

If A is an integrated cloud, then the result is composed of two half-clouds, namely

$$C = \bar{A} \Leftrightarrow \qquad\qquad C = \bar{A} \Leftrightarrow$$

$$Ex_C \approx \min(U) \qquad\qquad Ex_C \approx \max(U)$$

$$En_C \approx \frac{1}{3}[Ex_A - \min(U)] \qquad En_C \approx \frac{1}{3}[\max(U) - Ex_A]$$

$$He_C \approx He_A \qquad\qquad He_C \approx He_A$$

The cloud computing mentioned above can be expanded to logical operations of multiple clouds.

The logical operations have the following characteristics:

Idempotent laws: $A \cup A = A, \quad A \cap A = A$
Commutative laws: $A \cup B = B \cup A, \quad A \cap B = B \cap A$
Associative laws: $(A \cup B) \cup C = A \cup (B \cup C), \quad (A \cap B) \cap C = A \cap (B \cap C)$
Absorption laws: $(A \cap B) \cup A = A, \quad (A \cup B) \cap A = A$
Distributive laws: $A \cap (B \cup C) = (A \cap B) \cup (A \cap C), \quad A \cup (B \cap C) = (A \cup B) \cap (A \cup C)$
Laws of identity: $A \cup U = U \quad A \cap U = A, \quad A \cup \varnothing = A, \quad A \cap \varnothing = \varnothing$
Complementary law: $\bar{\bar{A}} = A$
Cloud's logic operation does not satisfy the law of excluded middle, namely

$$A \cup \bar{A} \neq U, \quad A \cap \bar{A} \neq \varnothing$$

The upward logical operations are only used in the same universal domain. To the logical operations in different domains, it can be done with the help of related concepts of "AND", "OR", etc. to build "SOFT AND," "SOFT OR" cloud model to realize soft computing.

3. Mood Operations

Mood operations, which are used to represent the affirmative degree of the linguistic value, can be classified into strengthened mood and softened mood operations. The basic idea is that strengthened mood decreases the entropy and hyper-entropy of linguistic value; softened mood increases the entropy and hyper-entropy of linguistic value; increased or decreased amplitudes can be determined by virtue of golden section ($k = \frac{\sqrt{5}-1}{2} = 0.618$), etc.

Given cloud $C(Ex, En, He)$ in domain U, suppose $C'(Ex', En', He')$ is the result of the mood operations, then we can define:

Strengthening mood ($0 < k < 1$)

$$En' = kEn \quad He' = kHe \quad Ex' = \begin{cases} Ex, & \text{when C is an integrated cloud} \\ Ex + \sqrt{-2\ln k}\, En' & \text{when C is a half-rising cloud} \\ Ex - \sqrt{-2\ln k}\, En' & \text{when C is a half-falling cloud} \end{cases}$$

Weakening mood ($0 < k < 1$)

$$En' = \frac{En}{k} \quad He' = \frac{He}{k} \quad Ex' = \begin{cases} Ex, & \text{when C is an integrated cloud} \\ Ex - \sqrt{-2\ln k}\, En & \text{when C is a half-rising cloud} \\ Ex + \sqrt{-2\ln k}\, En & \text{when C is a half-falling cloud} \end{cases}$$

A linguistic value can be recovered to the original value by strengthening following softening. The cloud mood operations can be used many times to generate a series of linguistic values with different moods.

It is necessary to point out that the definition of cloud computing is closely related to the application. The cloud computing laws defined above are appropriate in some applications, but to other applications, new laws should be involved. Nevertheless, the cloud model could be the point of departure for natural language computation, since it represents concepts or linguistic values drawn from a natural language.

9.2 STUDY OF COGNITIVE PHYSICS

9.2.1 EXTENSION OF CLOUD MODEL

So far, through using the cloud model to describe concepts and express the linguistic value of language, this book has solved the problem of formalization expression of uncertainty knowledge dealing with randomness, fuzziness, and correlation. But in both uncertainty knowledge and intelligence, many concepts are composite and involve many domains. If they are to be represented by cloud model, their expectations are difficult to be expressed by simple numerical values. Maybe a group of parameters are needed. Moreover, the cloud drops made by the cloud generator are not just points in the universal domain, but complicated topological structures. That is why we proposed the idea of extended cloud.

In Chapter 4, we discussed that fractal is an important phenomenon of uncertainty. Fractal geometry is an important tool with which to study a chaos phenomenon. In nature, among the nonlinear complex phenomena there exist some self-similar or scale-free features, which are simple but important. Many natural plant patterns are fractal. With the development of computer graphics, people can simulate various types of living organisms. Self-similarity supplies a theoretical basis for the computer simulation of fractal graphs. With the help of the extended cloud generator and simple functional iteration, the fractal phenomenon in nature, such as excursion or variation of some uncertain plants, can be better simulated.

The main idea of the extended cloud model is to extend the expectation, one of the original digital features, to a parameter set or a rule set, still called expectation, and extend the effect of the other two features, entropy and hyper-entropy, to the whole parameter set or rule set. The cloud thus produced is called "extended cloud."

Next we will give an example of the fractal growth of a tree in nature. The extended cloud is used to simulate the uncertainty of the growing process.

Given the original data set,

$$\{\alpha, \beta, LB, RB\}$$

Where, α is the left deflection angle; β is the right deflection angle; LB is the left length; RB is the right length; $0 \leq LB$; $RB \leq 1$.

Suppose the primary tree length is L, then the fractal tree will grow up with the following rule R:

a. Begin from the top of the tree, left α, draw the left branch 1: $L \times LB$, right β, draw the right branch 2: $L \times RB$.
b. From the top of branch 1, left $\alpha + \alpha$, draw the left branch 3: $L \times LB \times LB$, right $\beta + \beta$, draw the right branch 4: $L \times RB \times RB$. From the top of branch 2, left $\alpha + \alpha$, draw the left branch 5: $L \times LB \times LB$, right $\beta + \beta$, draw the right branch 6: $L \times RB \times RB$.

$\vdots$
$\vdots$

Continue this cycle iteratively till the Mth step. The $2^{M+1} - 1$ short lines will build a binary tree, named "fractal tree."

If the expectation of the cloud model is $\{\alpha = \beta = 40°LB = RB = 0.7\}$, by virtue of the normal cloud generator, cloud drops with different shapes can be obtained.

That is random variation tree. Suppose

$$\alpha' = CG(40°, 0.05, 0.001, 5)$$

$$\beta' = CG(40°, 0.05, 0.001, 5)$$

$$LB' = CG(0.7, 0.1, 0.01, 5)$$

$$RB' = CG(0.7, 0.1, 0.01, 5)$$

The generated five parameter sets $\{\alpha', \beta', LB', RB'\}$ will produce the variation tree by the rule R just like Figure 9.1 is showing.

Transfer the rule R to R' as follows:

a. $\alpha_1 = CG(40°, 0.05, 0.001, 1)$, $\beta_1 = CG(40°, 0.05, 0.001, 1)$, $LB_1 = CG(0.7, 0.1, 0.01, 1)$, $RB_1 = CG(0.7, 0.1, 0.01, 1)$

From the top of the tree, left α_1, draw the left branch 1: $L \times LB_1$, right β_1, draw the right branch 2: $L \times RB_1$.

b. $\alpha_2 = CG(40°, 0.05, 0.001, 1)$, $\beta_2 = CG(40°, 0.05, 0.001, 1)$, $LB_2 = CG(0.7, 0.1, 0.01, 1)$, $RB_2 = CG(0.7, 0.1, 0.01, 1)$.

From the top of branch 1, left $\alpha_1 + \alpha_2$, draw the left branch 3: $L \times LB_1 \times LB_2$, right $\beta_1 + \beta_2$, draw the right branch 4: $L \times RB_1 \times RB_2$. From the top of branch 2, left $\alpha_1 + \alpha_2$, draw the left branch 5: $L \times LB_1 \times LB_2$, right $\beta_1 + \beta_2$, draw the right branch 6: $L \times RB_1 \times RB_2$.

$$\vdots$$

Continue this cycle iteratively to the Mth step. The $2^{M+1} - 1$ short lines will build a fractal tree.

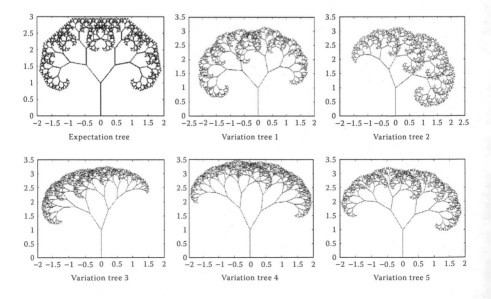

FIGURE 9.1 Simulating plant variation in virtue of extended cloud effect on parameter set.

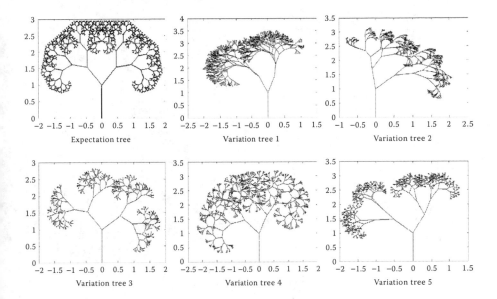

FIGURE 9.2 Simulating plant variation in virtue of extended cloud effect on rule set.

Then we will get the variation trees showed in Figure 9.2.

Of course we can simulate the variation of the plants with extended cloud action on the parameter set or the rule set. We can image the group of cloud drops, i.e., the various variation trees will be more rich and colorful.

Another way to extend the cloud model is to find a proper cloud drop from the group of cloud drops generated by the extended cloud as a new expectation and produce a new generation of drops from which to find another drop that is to be the next expectation. Continue the cycle to simulate the evaluation and variation in natural circumstances from generation to generation. Figure 9.3 illustrates this idea with a fractal tree, where the expectation of the next generation comes from the cloud drop of the previous generation.

Integrating cloud model and fractal further reveals the randomness included in the self-similarity of complex events, demonstrating the diversity of uncertainty. And the expectation of the extended cloud reflects the regularity hidden in the uncertain phenomenon. In different application backgrounds, the expectation of cloud has different implications. For instance, it can be the topology features of networks (as shown in Figure 9.4), the physiognomy features of the terrains, or the genetical features of the races, etc. The parameter set and the rule set can be changed to simulate a different uncertain phenomenon. In fact, the current research of certainty is far from being enough and much remains to be done.

9.2.2 Dynamic Data Field

In Chapter 6, we referred to the field in physics that describes the interaction between the objects in order to describe formally human cognitive and thinking processes

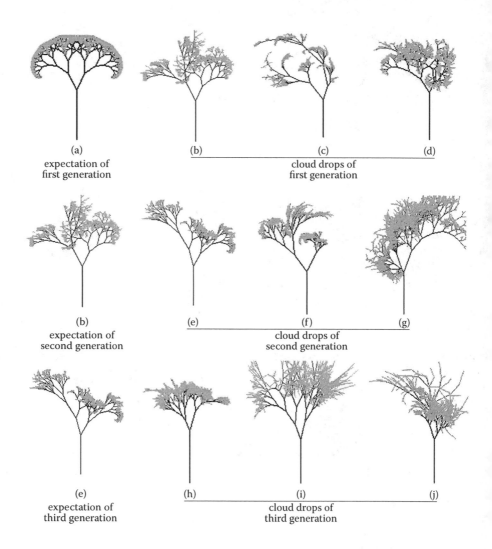

(a)
expectation of
first generation

(b)   (c)   (d)
cloud drops of
first generation

(b)
expectation of
second generation

(e)   (f)   (g)
cloud drops of
second generation

(e)
expectation of
third generation

(h)   (i)   (j)
cloud drops of
third generation

FIGURE 9.3 Simulating the variation of plants in virtue of extended cloud.

from data to information to knowledge, and thus establish the cognitive fields in a discovery state space, by which the processes of human memorization and thought can be represented and dealt with in a visualized way.

All the data fields discussed so far in this book only concern static data that is independent with time, and the corresponding fields are stabilized active fields. However, all things in the objective world are constantly moving and changing, be it tiny like a cell or a molecule, or colossal like a star or even the whole universe. If continuity and irreversibility in the process of the movements of matter are taken into accounts, the hypothesis of static field obviously seems too simple and can hardly satisfy the requirements of all uncertainty knowledge discovery. Taking human memory as an example, it is an important link in human cognitive activities.

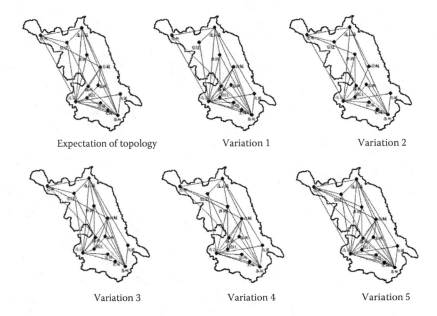

| Expectation of topology | Variation 1 | Variation 2 |

| Variation 3 | Variation 4 | Variation 5 |

FIGURE 9.4 Simulating the variation of network topology in virtue of extended cloud.

With the passing of time, however, it will gradually fade away or even fail entirely. In contrast, with continued repetition and enhancement, it will be renewed to last for a long period of time. As a matter of fact, from the perspective of the human cognitive process, time is a very important concept. Therefore, it is necessary to introduce the time property into the data field, or in other words, let the data field become "alive."

Talking about dynamic data fields, two factors should be taken into account: the quality of the object will vary with time and the location of the object will change with time due to interaction of the objects or the impact of outside forces. As for the dynamic data field produced only by the quality change of the object, its potential function can be inferred directly from the potential energy function of the static data field:

$$\varphi(x) = \sum_{i=1}^{n} \varphi_i(x) = \sum_{i=1}^{n} \left(m_i(t) \times e^{-\left(\frac{\|x - x_i\|}{\sigma}\right)2} \right)$$

where $m_i(t)$ is the quality of the object $i(i = 1,2,\dots,n)$ at time t.

For example, according to the statistics of the total number of severe acute respiratory syndrome (SARS) patients sampled from all the provinces throughout China in 2003, if we take each province as a data object and the number of SARS patients spotted in the province as the quality of the object, then we can use the dynamic data fields to formalize a distribution map of SARS preventive focus areas across the country. From the map we can see the shift of preventive focus areas with the passing of time. Figure 9.5 (sketch map, not a map) shows samplings of the

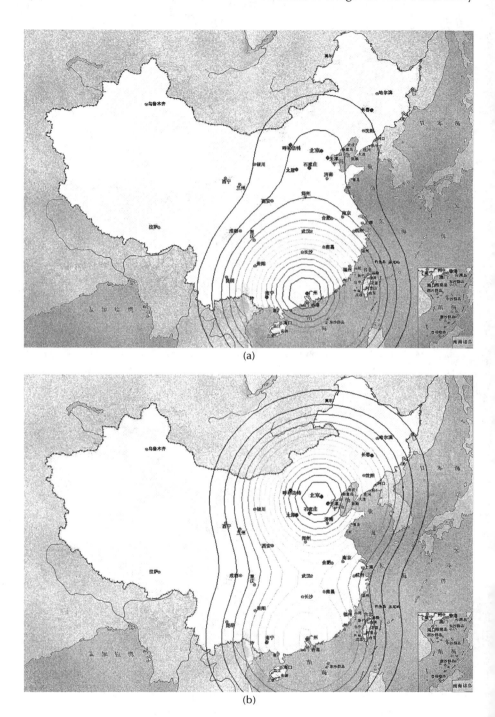

FIGURE 9.5 SARS prevention focus at different periods and the variation of its distribution.

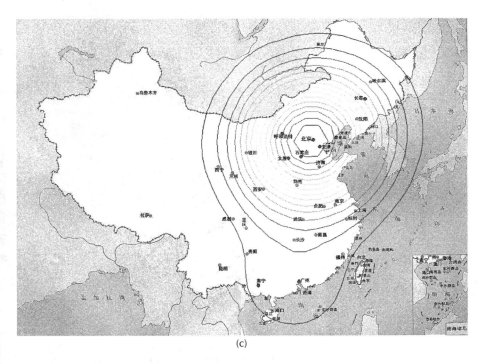

(c)

FIGURE 9.5 (Continued)

dynamic data field at three different times. It is easy to see the shift of SARS preventive focus areas from Guang Dong to Beijing.

In a dynamic data field resulting from the displacement of the object, the potential energy function can be expressed as:

$$\varphi(x) = \sum_{i=1}^{n} \varphi_i(x) = \sum_{i=1}^{n}\left(m_i \times e^{-\left(\frac{\|x - x_i(t)\|}{\sigma}\right)^2} \right)$$

where $x_i(t)$ is the spatial position of the object $i(i = 1,2,\ldots,n)$ at time t.

Figure 9.6 shows samples of dynamic fields that were produced by seven moving objects at different times in space. It can be seen from the sketches that without outside forces taking part, the objects move toward each other due to mutual attraction and gradually converge, and redistribution of dynamic fields occurs accordingly.

In actual practice, the quality and position of the objects in dynamic fields often change simultaneously, leading to more complicated changes in the field. To look into this kind of complicated dynamic data fields, more effective field analysis techniques are needed. And much remains to be done in using the Fourier transform as reference, wavelet transform, and time-varying of quantum physics field analysis.

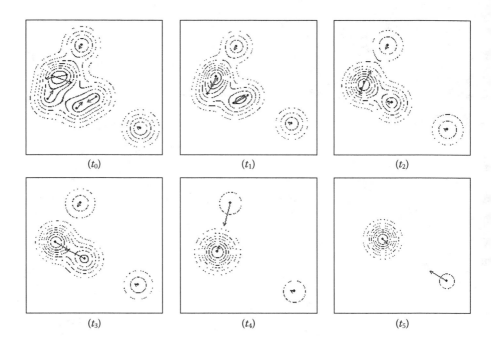

FIGURE 9.6 Samples of dynamic fields at different times.

9.3 COMPLEX NETWORKS WITH SMALL WORLD AND SCALE-FREE MODELS

Mathematics deals with laws and characteristics within the abstraction in number and shape of widely different things in the objective world. The theory of random graphs has been used to make historic contributions to the research of complex networks. Now, "small world" and "scale-free" networks have pushed the research to a new high.

On the mathematical side of networks, we are only concerned with whether there is a connection between the nodes rather than their locations and shape of the links. The organization of locations of the nodes and the specific shapes of the links is often referred to as "network topology." Let's take the Internet as an example where routers can be seen as nodes, while optical fibers as connections. On the WWW, clients/servers can be taken as nodes, while requests/answers as connections. In aviation networks, airports can be regarded as nodes, while airlines as connections. Networks are pervasive. The numerous phenomena in the real world can be described by networks, such as inter-relationships of humans, semantic connections of words, brain structures of living organisms, ecosystems, food-chain structures and various political, economic, and social relations.

Then what topological structures should be used to abstract all these real network systems? Scientists used to believe that the relations between all the elements of real systems could be represented by some regular structures, i.e., regular graph. In the late 1950s, famous mathematicians P. Erdös and A. Rényi put forward the random graph model, laying the theoretical foundation for the research of complex networks.[16] In this model, whether there is a link to connect two nodes is not certain and it is decided by a probability. So they are called "random networks." In the following forty years, random graphs were always used as basic models with which to study complex networks. Only in recent years have scientists found out that a large number of real networks like the Internet, power grids, and virus propagation networks have statistics characteristics and they are all different from both regular networks and random networks. Scientists call them complex networks, to which no precise definition has been given yet. They are so called probably because they are a topological abstraction from a huge number of real complex systems. Besides, they seem more complicated than regular networks and random networks. Even today, there is no simple and acknowledged way to construct a complex network that completely matches features of real network systems.

In 1998, D. J. Watts and S. H. Strongatz published a paper in *Nature* in which the small world model was introduced to describe the transformation of a completely regular network to a completely random network.[17] The small world network not only has the clustering feature like a regular network, but also has a relatively short average path length like a random network. The shortcuts between different clusters make the average diameters of the network relatively small, hence the name "small world." In a paper published in *Science* in 1999, A. L. Barabási and R. Albert pointed out that the degree distribution in many real complex networks take a power-law form.[18] As power-law distribution has no characteristic length, such a network is called a "scale-free network." In this kind of network, nodes cluster to form individual communities. If random nodes in the network are attacked, it has strong robustness against failure. But if important nodes with high connectivity are deliberately attacked, this network will be very weak. The coexistence of robustness and weakness is a basic characteristic of a scale-free network.

The two ground-breaking creations have triggered strong interest in the research of complex networks and have drawn considerable attention from experts of various areas such as mathematics, physics, computer science, biology, sociology and economics, enabling the study of complex networks to embody not only mathematics and engineering, but also physics, biology, social science, and many other disciplines.

9.3.1 Regularity of Uncertainty in Complex Networks

The Internet, WWW, human relations network, large-scale power grid, brain neural network, and all kinds of metabolism networks are real examples of complex networks. Those complex networks are on a large scale. They have not only thousands or millions of nodes, but also the complex connections among nodes will become very complicated, according to the dynamically increasing or decreasing nodes. There are also many uncertain phenomena. To measure the uncertainty of complex networks, three parameters are used: degree distribution, clustering coefficient, and average distance. They are the key elements in studying complex networks.

Definition 9.1 Degree

The degree of the node i is the number of links associated with this node in the topology.

Definition 9.2 Degree distribution P(k)

The probability that the degree of an arbitrary node is k.

Definition 9.3 Average distance L

The minimum distance from one node to another is the minimum number of links between these two nodes. The average (expectation) of the minimum distances between any two nodes is called the "average distance of the network."

Definition 9.4 Clustering coefficient C

For a given node i, the nodes directly connected with i are the neighbors of i. If the node i has k neighbors, these neighbors can have C_k^2 links theoretically. If the number of links within these neighbors is m, the clustering coefficient of the node i is defined as $C_i = m_i/C_k^2$. The average of all nodes' clustering coefficients is called the "clustering coefficient of the network."

Figure 9.7 is a connection of five nodes. To node i: Figure 9.7(a) is a star distribution of which the clustering coefficient C_i is 0; Figure 9.7(b) shows that $C_i = 2/3$; Figure 9.7(b) shows that C_i is 1. And in this case, node i has the best clustering feature. In the star connection showed in Figure 9.7(a), because the clustering coefficient of each node equals 1, the clustering coefficient of the star network is $\frac{n-1}{n}$, in which n is the quality of nodes and it will approach 1 when n is very large. The clustering coefficient of the complete connection showed in Figure 9.7(c) equals 1. Compared with (a), (c) has a better clustering feature. So the definition of network clustering coefficient here should be further discussed.

In a regular graph, every node has the same degree distribution — δ distribution — which has the large clustering coefficient and long average distance. Erdös and Rényi introduced probability theory to graph theory and proposed the random graph model. The most classical random graph model is the ER random graph model, which is a G (n, p) binomial random graph named after the initials of the two author's first

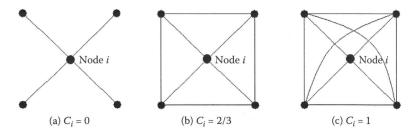

(a) $C_i = 0$ (b) $C_i = 2/3$ (c) $C_i = 1$

FIGURE 9.7 Clustering feature of node i reflected by the clustering coefficient. (a) $C_i = 0$, (b) $C_i = 2/3$, and (c) $C_i = 1$.

names. In the ER random graph, n is the number of nodes, and p is the connection probability among nodes. The connections of different nodes are independent. There is no repeated connection. Random graphs have small clustering coefficients and short average distance. Its degree distribution obeys Poisson distribution. Within the random graph, although the connections between nodes are random, the final network is highly "democratic." The degrees of most nodes will become almost the same. Nodes having very high or low degrees than the normal nodes are very rare.

The difference between a regular graph and random graph can be described by their clustering coefficient and average distance. One characteristic of a regular network is that it has large clustering coefficient and long average distance, while a characteristic of a random graph is that it has small clustering coefficient and short average distance. Then, is there a network with large clustering coefficient and small average distance? Yes, the answer is small world model discovered by Watts and Strogatz,[17] or the WS model named after them.

Early in 1965, Zipf had found there is an idempotent law in linguistics. In 1999, Barabási and Albert found the degree distribution of complex networks also obeys power law distribution $P(k) = ck^{-\gamma}$, where γ is independent with the scale of the networks, so it is called "scale-free network," namely BA model. Scale-free networks are controlled by only a few high-degree key nodes (such as Yahoo!® and Google™). Most other nodes are very small. Table 9.1 shows the difference represented by the degree distribution, average distance, clustering coefficient of ER random graph, small world network, scale-free network, and complex networks of the real world.

Because of the uncertainty of complex networks of the real world, there is little mathematic meaning in random graph, small world network, and scale-free network in the real world and there is no strict boundary among the network topology models. For example, the classical random graph degree distribution is binomial. When node quantity n is very large, binomial distribution can be simulated by poisson distribution whose limit distribution is normal distribution. What is the mechanism from normal to power law to star-layered structure and finally to absolute star structure? To degree distribution, the transform of these distributions means the evolving from average to concentration. Regular graphs are absolute average, but star structures with only one center are the extreme case of degree distributions. Figure 9.8 shows their transform.

TABLE 9.1
The Difference between Different Networks

Network Property	ER Random Graph	Small World Network	Scale-Free Network	Complex Networks of the Real world
Degree distribution	Poisson distribution	Poisson distribution	Power law distribution	Power law distribution
Average distance	short	short	short	short
Clustering coefficient	small	large	large	large

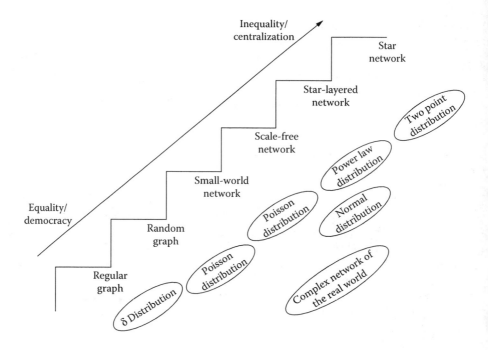

FIGURE 9.8 The transform of degree distribution.

In the real world, many complex networks have the features of small world and scale-free ones. Many scientists believe that some common rules are hidden in the external uncertainty and variety of the networks that seem to be both independent and unrelated, such as Internet, human brain, and creature groups. Complex systems, any giant systems, or microsystems may have the same structure. Limited by some basic rules, these structures and rules may be very simple, and they may be equally adapted to cells, computers, languages, and societies. Acknowledging these rules will greatly change our understanding of the subject and object worlds.

9.3.2 SCALE-FREE NETWORKS GENERATION

Simulating complex networks topology of the real world by computer is the basis of complex network knowledge representation. How to produce the network topology of those that have small-world or scale-free features? This is the question that scientists in different disciplines are asking.

The WS model gives us a way to realize small world features. It randomly and repeatedly modifies the connections of regular network to make it possess large clustering coefficient and small average distance at the same time. The modification is that for all the connections of each nodes, disconnect a node with the probability $p(0 < p < 1)$, then connect it to a new node that is selected from the remaining ones randomly. If the selected node is already connected, select another node to connect it again. The produced network will have large clustering coefficient and small average distance at the same time, namely the features of small world.

The BA model gives us a mechanism to realize scale-free networks. Barabási and Albert point out two main reasons for real systems producing scale-free network by self-organizing: networks expand continuously by the addition of new nodes and new nodes attach preferentially to nodes that are already well connected.[18] The reason complex networks have scale-free power distribution is that many increasing natural or social phenomena have the characters of gradually growing up and preferential adhering.

Algorithm 9.1 Small World Generator Algorithm

Input: regular graph of N nodes. The degree of each nodes is K, probability $p(0 < p < 1)$
Output: small world network topology of N nodes
Steps:

1. To a certain node, break each of its connections by probability p. If the connection is broken, the node connects to another node randomly which has no connection to it.
2. Return to step 1, until we have visited every node in the network.

It can be proved that, compared with regular graphs, the numbers of nodes and connections do not increase. The generated network has smaller average distance and larger clustering coefficient, namely small world features.

For visualizing representation, the capital cities of the provinces or those important cities in China are regarded as nodes, which are sorted by their developed economy and displayed according to the geography locations. Given the initial topology structure as Figure 9.9(a) (sketch map, not a map) has shown, initial state is $N = 34$, $K = 4$, $p = 0.2$, the generated small world network topology can be represented as Figure 9.9(b).

There are many methods to generate a scale-free network, here are the two common algorithms:

Algorithm 9.2 Scale-free Network Generator Algorithm 1

Input: two separated nodes, with the same probability $q(1/2 < q < 1)$
Output: scale-free network topology
Steps:

1. Decide whether to add a node by probability $1 - q$.
2. Select two disjunct nodes from present ones arbitrarily. Decide whether to add a connection by probability q.
3. Return to step 1, until enough nodes are generated.

It can be proved that the degree distribution obeys power distribution; its exponent is:

$$\gamma = 1 + 1/q$$

For $q \rightarrow 1$, there is $\gamma \rightarrow 2$; for $q \rightarrow 1/2$, there is $\gamma \rightarrow 3$, so $2 < \gamma < 3$.

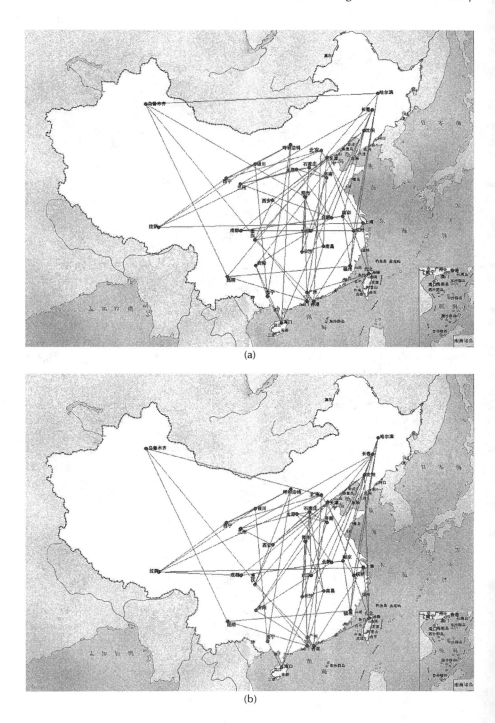

FIGURE 9.9 (a) Initial network topology and (b) small world network topology.

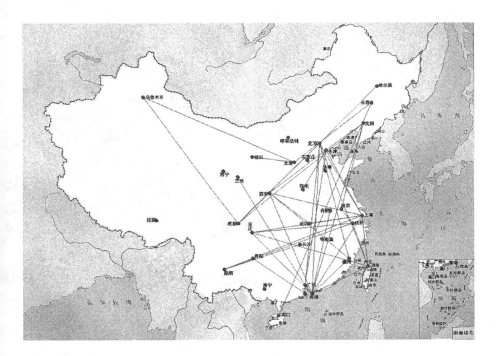

FIGURE 9.10 Scale-free network with $2 < \gamma < 3(q = 0.6)$.

$2 < \gamma < 3$ scale-free networks generated by Algorithm 9.2 can be represented by the former visualization method, the result diagram is shown in Figure 9.10 (sketch map, not a map).

Algorithm 9.3 Scale-Free Network Generator Algorithm 2

Input: N nodes with different connection degrees, parameter $K(K \leq N)$
Output: scale-free network topology
Steps:
1. Add a new node.
2. Begin from the new node, connect K nodes with K connections, the node choosing probability is proportional to its degree.
3. Return to step 1, until enough nodes are generated.

It can be proved that the degree distribution of the network obeys power distribution with the exponent $\gamma = 3$. Here γ is independent of the selection of the initial condition N, K. Figure 9.11 (It is not a map) is the topology diagram generated by Algorithm 9.3. Figure 9.11(a) is the initial state, in which $N = 5$, $K = 1$. First, we will rank the capitals of each province and the key cities by their developed economy. Then add the nodes by the rank. Last, a topology diagram as in Figure 9.11(b) with 34 nodes can be generated.

Considering the nodes can either increase or decrease, we propose another kind of scale-free network generator algorithm.

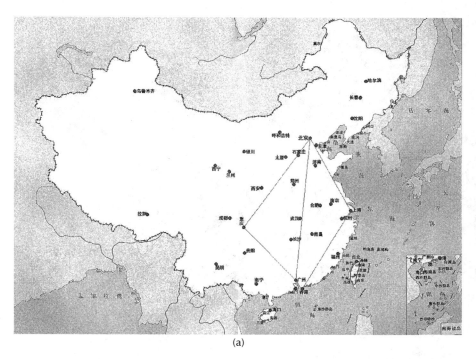

(a)

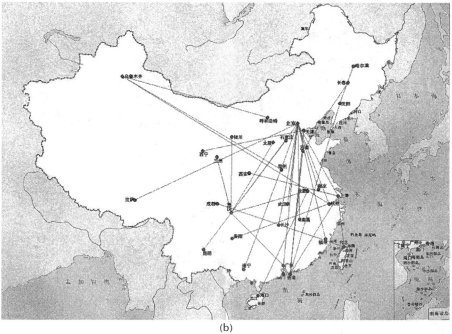

(b)

FIGURE 9.11 Scale-free network topology with γ = 3. (a) Initial network topology and (b) scale-free network topology.

Algorithm 9.4 Scale-Free Network Generator Algorithm 3

Input: N nodes with different connection degrees, parameter $K(K \le N)$
   Node growing increase probability p and decline probability q $(q<<p)$
Output: scale-free network topology
Steps:

1. Add a new node with probability p.
2. Begin from the new node, connect K nodes with K connections, the node choosing probability is proportional to its degree.
3. Delete the node and its connections with probability q. If yes, the probability to delete the node is inversely proportional to its degree.
4. Return to step 1 until enough nodes are generated.

Figure 9.12 is the topology diagram generated by Algorithm 9.4. The initial state is $N = 5$, $K = 1$. The probability of node growing increase is $p = 0.8$. The probability of node decline is $q = 0.05$. First, we will rank the capitals of each province and the key cities by their economic development. We then add the nodes by their rank. After taking 58 iterations, the network topology diagram can be generated as in Figure 9.12(b).

The upward four network topology generators can simulate the generation of small world network and scale-free network, respectively, and transform from small-scale networks to complex networks.

Because of the scale-free feature of most real complex networks, its nature is independent of the scale. So, for a network having millions of nodes, we can discover its nature by studying its thousands of nodes. How to use data fields to simplify and make abstract the complex networks to small-scale networks, while keeping their natural features, such as small-world effect and scale-free features, is the emphasis of our future work.

Small world and scale-free features are the abstraction of the nature complex networks. Actually, not all kinds of networks strictly obey the same power distribution. So, it is difficult to master the standard of "small" average distance and "large" clustering coefficient of small-world features. For instance, to the Internet, different scales have different power exponents. The fluctuation of such power exponents may be limited, so can we imitate the idea of normal cloud generator widening the request of normal distribution to construct power cloud generator to widen power distribution request so as to study the uncertainty in complex networks? Conversely, if different random states of one complex network are acknowledged, can we imitate the idea of reversed normal cloud generator to find the rules in complex networks?

In Chapter 4, it is mentioned that for all human languages, whatever the frequencies of character, word, and sentence, their statistical features obey Zipf law to a certain extent. In this issue, the power distribution of complex networks can be used to understand the natural languages. Probably building a Zipf cloud generator is necessary. It would become a challenging topic in the AI area.[19]

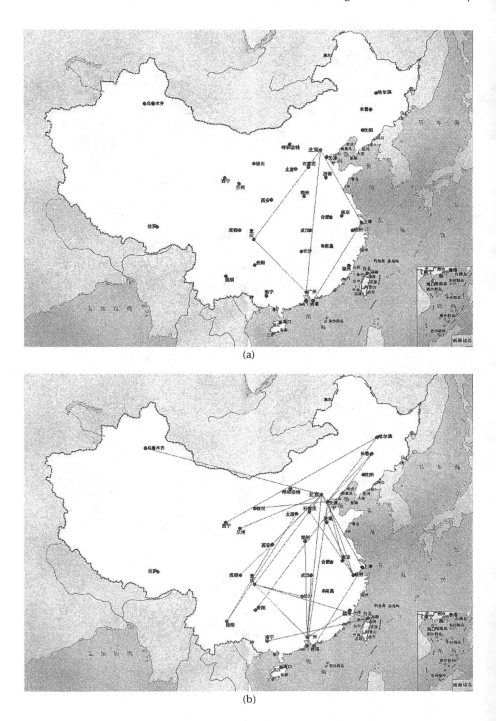

FIGURE 9.12 (a) Initial network topology and (b) scale-free network topology.

9.3.3 APPLICATIONS OF DATA FIELD THEORY TO NETWORKED INTELLIGENCE

Graph theory studies real networks by virtue of abstracting objects to nodes, and relations to links. The main concern is the topology structure of the network, not the location, quality, and features of the connection, and distance between nodes, etc. But in real networks, nodes and links have physical meaning. So it is not proper to treat all the nodes or links the same. For example, in urban traffic networks, road levels and city scales are different. In human relations networks, influence of individuals is dependent on relations, whether they are close or distant. If neglecting such differences in abstracting all the objects and relations, the result will not be good.

In complex networks of the real world, especially next generation network (NGN), besides nodes and links, there are many important elements that should be taken into account, such as distance, rate of flow, bandwidth, computing resource, communication resource, software resource, memory resource, management and control of the information resource, coexistence of grid computing and peer-to-peer computing. Orderliness in randomness, certainty in uncertainty, cooperativeness in competition, etc. should be found. In a word, it is far from enough to study real networks only by nodes and links.

It will be a new train of thought in formulating some important elements as nodes and links. For example, the mass of nodes can be used to represent the city scale of the traffic networks, the throughput of nodes in information network, point rate in the WWW, and the individual reputation in human relation networks. The distance between nodes or length of the connections can represent the geography relations between the cities in the traffic networks, bandwidth of information networks, linked number between hypertext in WWW, and closeness in human relation networks.

Hence, it will be a good attempt to extend the network topology research method, which has been used to deal with nodes and links to nodes, links, between-ness, distance, and mass.

In Figure 9.5, the spreading state of the SARS virus is represented by a network, in which cities are nodes while spread paths are links. Obviously, the cities' number of patients and the distance between cities will affect virus transmission greatly. We employ city patient number as the quality of the node, geography distance between cities as the distance of the node or the length of the connection. Then with dynamic data field idea, potential function $V_p = m(t)e^{-\frac{r^2}{2B^2}}$ is introduced, in which r is the distance from P to O reflecting the geography distance between cities in this case, $m(t)$ is the quality of the node at time t reflecting the patient number of the city, and B is the radiation factor. By these means, the spread of the SARS virus can be well simulated.

Furthermore, if the four elements — nodes, quality of nodes, links, and distance — are not enough, more elements can be involved into studying complex networks. This is the research direction in the future.

9.4 LONG WAY TO GO FOR AI WITH UNCERTAINTY

9.4.1 Limitations of Cognitive Physics Methodology

Although many scholars always admit that all human efforts are restricted by limited and uncertain knowledge, yet it is not until recently that people have accepted the theory of uncertainty. For example, the uncertainty theory has been effectively used in finance for profitability analysis of the stock exchange market and financial risk evaluation. The same applies to the research of AI with uncertainty.

The process of research into AI with uncertainty is actually a process of continuous improvement and a process of negation of the negation. For instance, at an earlier stage, based on Zadeh's concept of "degree of membership" and "membership function," the concept of "membership function cluster" was proposed. Later, the concept developed into "membership cloud," then into the cloud model and further into the extended cloud. Let's look at another example. Cognitive physics, which uses for reference the idea of the atom model and the field, regard the cognitive process of the human brain as a transformation from initial data field to characteristic data field and further to the concept space. These ways of approaching problems are not without limits.

Let's take cloud computing as an example. Following the construction of a normal cloud model, the natural research direction is cloud computing, including algebra operations, logic operations and even synthetic cloud, geometrical cloud, and virtual cloud. When defining various kinds of algorithms, people tend to slip into the pitfall of defining for the sake of definition, trying to seek after formal perfection. Then does the so-called perfection in mathematical forms have any real meaning? Doesn't it go against the objective of AI research with uncertainty?

Take another example from the research of cognitive physics. Since human subjective cognition is considered as the reflection of the objective world, basic approaches of physics can be used as reference. Yet, none of the disciplines are as closely linked as AI and philosophy. The concept of cognitive physics might be challenged by philosophy. Whether it is the objective world or the subjective knowledge, the analytical method or the deductive method, or reversion theory or holism, they are all processes in search for truth. And we are so happy about being involved in it.

9.4.2 Divergences from Daniel, the Nobel Economics Prize Winner

On the frontiers of science and technology research today, many disciplines are interwoven, resulting in astonishing accomplishments. For his contributions to decision making with uncertainty, professor Daniel Kahneman was awarded the Nobel Prize of Economics in 2002. This is a good example of innovation based on discipline crossing.

Although Kahneman is a professor of psychology, having been working on behavioral science and cognitive science for a long time, he was awarded the Nobel Prize of Economics. His most important achievements are in his research into human decision making under uncertainty situations, showing how human decision making behaviors deviate systematically from standard predicted results following economic theories. He has proved that under uncertain situations, since people's judgment tends to abide by the law of "small numbers" based on "small samples" they have taken, or because they blindly believe the familiar information they have easily obtained and the preciseness of their subjective probability, they will deviate systematically from the basic probability theory in decision making. Besides, he has discovered that when making decisions under uncertainty situations, people seem to depend on the differences between result and expectation rather than the result itself. In other words, people have usually had a reference in mind before comparing the difference with the reference. For example, if a worker gets a pay raise of $100, he may feel that it is nothing to be happy about. But if his salary is reduced by $100, he may feel quite unhappy. From this we can see that the same 100 dollars is not the same in value in people's minds. Kahneman has revealed the cause and nature of rational deviation in decision making under uncertainty conditions, and points out that the irrationality of deviation from traditional models is rule-abiding and predictable. Although people's economic behaviors do not conform to strict theoretical hypothesis, they are not random and erroneous.

It is easy to associate Kahneman with Herbert Simon, a famous American computer scientist and psychologist, who is not only the founder of AI and cognitive science, winning the Turing award in 1975, but has also made remarkable breakthroughs in economic theory, winning the Nobel Prize of Economics in 1973. His theory of "bounded rationality" deals with decision making process within economic organizations. He believes that in decision making, people cannot have all the information needed, and so they can only make satisfactory rather than optimal decisions.

The contributions to the research of uncertainty AI made by Kahneman and Simon are quite inspiring. In this pluralized modern society, disciplines of various fields in natural science are intercrossed. There is also a tendency of intercrossing natural science with social science. This tendency can be said to be characteristic of our time. AI takes on the simulation of human intellectual activities as its research objective. In the simulation of thinking, perception, instinct, sudden awakening, imagination, innovation, prediction, adaption and coordination of the human brain, there remains much to be done. When tackling uncertainty problems, the human brain does not always do it "by the rule" or "by the theorem," neither does it do it by precise mathematical analysis and calculation. Besides, preferential attachment is natural and inevitable in decision making. There are many problems that are difficult to the computer but easy to the human brain. Things like memory, thinking, imagination, and sensitivity that form the physiological basis are far from being explored. It is too early to expect the machine to be capable of having intelligence with uncertainty like humans and of simulating completely human intelligence, sensitivity, and behaviors.

The endless quest of AI for decision making and human thinking from deterministic AI to AI with uncertainty decides that AI is to be intercrossed with computing science, information science, mathematics, life science, brain science, cognitive science, psychology, and philosophy. Maybe, aesthetics will also be involved.

Both the aesthetic appraisal of great works of art and the understanding of great sciences take wisdom and intelligence. Science and art both seek generalization, great depth and meaningfulness; both seek the true and the beautiful. This is where the charm of basic research and intercrossed research lies. It is a great pleasure to appreciate the splendid views offered by the convergence of different disciplines and the convergence of science and art. Let both poets and scientists keep a pure heart. Let us, together with the readers, make joint efforts and encourage each other.

Thank you for finishing reading the book. You are welcome to visit the authors' Web site www.thss.tsinghua.edu.cn/ldy/index_ldy.asp and contribute your comments on it.

REFERENCES

1. Changyu Liu, Deyi Li, and Lili Pan, Uncertain Knowledge Representation Based on Cloud Model. *Computer Engineering and Applications*, No. 2: 32–35, 2004.
2. Deyi Li, Yi Du, and Rong Jiang, Cloud Model and Its Application to Data Mining. In: *Proceedings of the International Conference on Engineering Technological Science (ICET'2000)*, Beijing, 2000.
3. Deyi Li, Xuemei Shi, and M. M. Gupta, Soft Inference Mechanism Based on Cloud Models. In: *Proceedings of the 1st International Workshop on Logic Programming and Soft Computing: Theory and Applications*, Bonn, Germany, 1996.
4. Deyi Li, Jiawei Han, and Xuemei Shi, Knowledge Representation and Discovery Based on Linguistic Models. In: Lu H. J., Motoda H., eds., *KDD: Techniques and Applications*, pp. 3–20, World Scientific Press, Singapore, 1997.
5. Shuliang Wang, Deren Li, Wenzhong Shi et al., Cloud Model-Based Spatial Data Mining. *Geographical Information Science*, Vol. 9, No. 2: 67–78, 2003.
6. Shuliang Wang, Wenzhong Shi, Deyi Li et al., A Method of Spatial Data Mining Dealing with Randomness and Fuzziness. In: *Proceedings of the 2nd International Symposium on Spatial Data Quality*, Hong Kong, 2003.
7. Shuliang Wang, Deren Li, Wenzhong Shi et al., Rough Spatial Description. *International Archives of Photogrammetry and Remote Sensing*, Vol. 13, No. 2: 503–509, 2002.
8. Yang Fan, Ye Wang, and Deyi Li, Cloud Prediction Based on Time Granularity. In: *The 5th Pacific-Asia Conference on Knowledge Discovery and Data Mining*, Hong Kong, 2001.
9. Shi Xuemei, Chung Chan Man, and Li Deyi, An Adaptable Linguistic Mining Approach for the Volatile Stock Market Data. In: *Proceedings of PAKDD99*, Beijing, 1999.
10. Jianhua Fan and Deyi Li, Mining Classifications Knowledge Based on Cloud Models. In: *Proceedings of PAKDD99*, Beijing, 1999.
11. Deyi Li, D. W. Cheung, Xuemei Shi et al., Uncertainty Reasoning Based on Cloud Models In Controllers. *Computers and Mathematics with Applications*, Vol. 35, No. 3: 99–123, 1998.
12. Deyi Li, Knowledge Representation in KDD Based on Linguistic Atoms. *Journal of Computer Science and Technology*, Vol. 12, No. 6: 481–496, 1997.
13. Jianhua Fan and Deyi Li, An Overview of Data Mining and Knowledge Discovery. *Journal of Computer Science and Technology*, Vol. 13, No. 4: 348–368, 1998.
14. L. A. Zadeh, Fuzzy Logic = Computing with Words. *IEEE Transactions on Fuzzy Systems*, Vol. 4, No. 1: 103–111, 1996.

15. Kaichang Di, The Theory and Methods of Spatial Data Mining and Knowledge Discovery, Ph.D. thesis, Wuhan Technical University of Surveying and Mapping, Wuhan, 1999.
16. P. Erdös and A. Rényi, On The Evolution of Random Graphs. *Publication of Mathematical Institute of the Hungarian Academy of Sciences*, No. 5: 17–61, 1960.
17. D. J. Watts and S. H. Strogatz, Collective Dynamics of Small World Networks, *Nature*, No. 393: 440–442, 1998.
18. A. L. Barabási and R. Albert, Emergence of Scaling in Random Networks, *Science*, Vol. 286: 509–512, 1999.
19. Deyi Li, Changyu Liu, and Yi Du, Artificial Intelligence with Uncertainty, *Journal of Software*, Vol.15, No.11: 1583–1594, 2004.

Research Foundation Support

The research projects in this book were supported by the following National Research Foundations:

1. National Natural Science Foundation of China
   * Research of Knowledge Discovery in Database, 1993–1995, No. 69272031
   * Qualitative Control Mechanism and Implement of Triple Link Inverted Pendulum Systems, 1998–2000, No. 69775016
   * The Methodology Research of Knowledge Representation and Knowledge Discovery in Data Mining, 2000–2002, No. 69975024
   * Study on Data Mining Foundations, 2004–2006, No. 60375016
   * Recognition Theory of Unnormal Knowledge, 2004–2007, No. 60496323
2. National Basic Research Program of China (973 Program)
   * Theory and Methodology Research of Data Mining and Knowledge Discovery, 1999–2003, No. G1998030508-4
   * Common Foundations of Advanced Design for Large-Scale Application Software System: Theory and Methodology Research of Intelligent Design, 2004–2008, No. 2004CB719401
3. The National Hi-Tech Research and Development Program of China (863 Program)
   * The Methodology and Applications of Knowledge Discovery, 1998–2000, No. 863-306-ZT06-07-02
4. Defense Advance Research Project of China
   * 1999–2001, No. 99J6.5.1-JB0203
   * 2004–2006, No. 51406020304HK01

Related National Patents in this book:

* Membership Cloud Generator and the Controller Composed by It. No. ZL95103696.3
* Controllable Method and Equipment of Communication Jamming. No. 200310102119.1 (Proposal)
* A Embedding and Extraction Method of Digital Watermarking to Relational Database. 200310117358.4 (Proposal)
* A Management Method of Relational Database with Digital Watermarking. 200310122488.7 (Proposal)

Index

A

Absorption laws, 319
Abstract concepts, 110
Abstract languages, 52
Accuracy, unity with fuzziness, 48, 49
Addition, natural language operations, 317, 318
Agile production, 12
AI methodologies, 21
  behaviorism, 35–38
  connectionism, 30–35
  summary, 38–39
  symbolism, 21–29
AI research perspectives, 109
AI technology, impacts on society, 12–13
AI with uncertainty
  current shortcomings of, 340–341
  new directions for, 315–316
  perspectives on study of, 107–112
Algebra operations, computing with words, 316–318
Algorithm concepts, 22
Algorithms
  Apriori algorithm for association rule discovery, 245–246
  backward normal CG with certainty degree in MATLAB®, 128–129
  backward normal CG with certainty degree in VC++®, 129–130
  backward normal CG without certainty degree in MATLAB, 130
  backward normal CG without certainty degree in VC++, 131
  Cloud-based K line prediction algorithm, 262–263
  CloudAssociationRules algorithm, 247–249
  CloudClassifier algorithm, 210–211
  CloudClassifier experimental results, 211–212
  CloudMap algorithm, 193
  Cloudtransform algorithm, 184–185
  ConceptRise1 algorithm, 189–190
  ConceptRise2 algorithm, 191
  1D normal CG in MATLAB, 119–120
  1D normal CG in VC++, 120–122
  data-field clustering algorithm, 234
  decision tree algorithm example, 208–209
  Generate_DecisionTree algorithm, 207
  optimization algorithm of influence coefficient, 175, 177
  outlier detection algorithm, 241
  PField_Clustering algorithm, 220–221
  scale-free network generator algorithm, 333, 335, 337
  shadow line classification algorithm, 259
  small-world generator algorithm, 333
Analyzer software, 264
AND operations, natural language based, 318
Animal languages, 51
Annual income per capita, 250
  association rules on, 251, 252
Approximation error function, 186
Approximation partition, 83
Approximation space, 82
Apriori algorithm, for association rule discovery, 245–246
Argonne National Laboratory, 11
ARPANET, 13
Art, relationship to science, 50, 341–342
Artificial intelligence
  50-year history, 1
  coinage of term, 2
  crosstrends with brain science and cognitive science, 15–18
  Dartmouth Symposium origins, 1–4
  defined, 1
  early development and growth, 3–4
  future goals, 4–8
  influence of brain science, 15–17
  information age developments, 12–15
  lack of unified theoretical system, 39
  mathematical foundation, 61
  and philosophy, 340
  prior achievements, 8–12
  research perspectives, 107–112
Artificial life, 7–8
Artificial neural networks (ANNs), 3, 109
  and connectionism, 21
  early developments in, 30
  mathematical description, 32
Association degree
  in double-link inverted pendulum system, 307, 308
  in inverted pendulum systems, 305

Association rules, 205
  on annual income per capita, 251, 252
  Apriori algorithm, 245–246
  Boolean database after transformation, 250
  in data mining, 204
  data mining and forecasting, 247–253
  discovering with uncertainty, 244–253
  emergence frequency of, 244
  mining for Chinese geography and economy
    database, 249–253
  reconsideration of traditional, 244–247
  on road net density, 252
Associative laws, 318, 319
Associative memory, in Hopfield neural networks,
  33
Associativity laws, 77
Atom models, concept expression through, 154
Atoms
  as basic element of proportional calculus, 25
  as irreducible propositions, 24
Attribute table, after soft division, 195
Attribute values, location in conceptual levels,
  192
Auto-regressive model, of TSDM, 253
Automatic climbing-up, 188
Automatic stabilization, 292
Average distance, in complex networks, 329, 330
Axiomization, and probability, 63
Axons, 31

B

Back propagation (BP), of multilayered
  networks, 3
Back-propagation neural network model, 34–35
  mechanism chart, 35
Backward cloud generator, 115, 125–128, 289
  abstracting precise cases with, 280
  with certainty degree in MATLAB, 128–129
  with certainty degree in VC++, 129–130
  precision analysis of, 132–133
  in shooting competition model, 137
  without certainty degree in MATLAB, 130
  without certainty degree in VC++, 131
Balance, 90
Balance points, 33
Balancing patterns
  application significance, 312
  and association degree, 305
  double-link inverted pendulum, 307–308
  of inverted pendulum, 302, 305–312
  periodic variation of pendulum in, 310
  relation curves, car displacement and time, 311
  single-link inverted pendulum, 306, 307
  triple-link inverted pendulum, 309–310

Bald Man puzzle, 48
Bayes classification, 206
Bayes' theorem, 62
  axiomization definition of probability, 63
  conditional probability and, 64–65
  relationship and logical operation of random
    events, 62
Behaviorism methodology, 21, 35, 39
  birth and development, 35–36
  and intelligent control, 37–38
  and robot control, 36–37
  three periods of, 36
Bell membership function, 78, 146, 147
  MSE of, 147
  pervasiveness of, 145–148
Bernoulli's law of large numbers, 61
Biometric school, of human intelligence research,
  108
BIRCH clustering algorithm, 214, 236
  experimental results, 237
Bohr, Niels
  complementary principle, 45
  conflict with Albert Einstein, 43
Boltzmann formula, 75
Boundary set, 77
Brain science, 107
  and AI, 15
  influence on AI, 15–17
  information processing mechanisms in, 154
  Nobel Prize winners, 16
  and self-cognition in terms of field, 155

C

Car displacement, 311
  in triple-link inverted pendulum system, 311
Case-based reasoning (CBR), 280
Cauchy membership function, 78, 146
Center-based clustering, 216
Central cluster, defined based on representatives,
  232
Central limit theorem, 71–72, 145
Cerf, Vinton G., 13
Certainty degree, 287, 288
  statistical analysis of cloud drops', 140–142
Chaos, 89–90
  basic characteristics, 90–91
  edge of, 7
  geometric characteristics, 93–94
  strange attractions of, 92–93
Chaos theory, 45
Chaotic attractors, 92
Character recognition, 9
Chess playing, 5–6, 178
  intelligent control experiments, 273

Chinese Academy of Engineering, xiii
Chinese Association of Artificial Intelligence, xiii
Chinese character recognition technology, 9
Chinese characters, relationship to pictures, 51
Chinese geography/economy
    association rule mining for, 249–253
    attribute table after soft division, 195
    Boolean database, 250
    database of, 194
    numerical characteristics of 2D cloud model
        representing location, 195
Chinese Institute of Electronics, xiii
Church's thesis, 21
Ci Hai, 54
Classical control theory, 36
Classical probability, 62
Classification, 198
    comparison of experimental results,
        211–213
    in data mining, 204
    as prerequisite for association rules, 204
    with uncertainty, 205
Classification complexity (CC), 209
Climbing-up strategy, 188, 190
    in association rule mining, 249
    in model of visual perception, 188–196
CLIQUE clustering algorithm, 214
Cloud, 199
    circle representation, 114
    and cloud drop, 112–113
    3D representation, 114
    expectation curves, 142–143
    gray-level representation, 114
    mathematical properties of, 138–143
    numerical characteristics, 113–115
    significance of normal, 148–150
Cloud-based K line prediction, 262–263
Cloud-based rule generator, reasoning
    mechanism, 286–289
Cloud classification, 206, 209–211
    experimental results comparison, 211–213
    limitation of common decision tree approaches,
        206–207
Cloud clustering, 115
Cloud computation, 115
Cloud control, 115, 286–289
    control rules with, 298
    input and output variables, 298
    similarities to uncertainty in human thinking,
        312
    of triple-link inverted pendulum, 297–302
Cloud drops, 112–113
    contributions to concepts, 123
    in fractal tree variations, 323
    joint distribution, 275, 287

statistical analysis of certainty degree, 140–142
statistical distribution analysis, 138–139
Cloud generator, 118
    backward cloud generator, 125–128
    and contributions of cloud drops to concepts,
        123
    forward cloud generator, 118–122
Cloud graph
    of qualitative concepts in postcondition, 288
    of qualitative concepts in precondition, 287
    visualization approaches, 114, 138
Cloud K line, prediction mechanism based on,
    261–263
Cloud models, xii, 107, 154
    2D, 118
    data distribution function based on, 186
    entropy in, 114–115
    expected values in, 114–115
    extension of, 320–323
    failure to satisfy law of excluded middle, 319
    as fundamental model of concept, 157
    as fuzziness compensated by randomness, 133
    generating linguistic values using, 199
    hyper-entropy in, 114–115
    multidimensionality of, 116–117
    normal cloud generator, 118–138
    pervasiveness of, 144–150
    as point of departure for natural language
        computation, 320
    prediction of consecutive yang line patterns
        using, 268
    for qualitative rule construction, 273–280
    as randomness compensated by fuzziness, 133
    representing concepts with, 112–117
    of shooting competition, 134–138
    for time series data mining, 255–256
    types of, 115–117
    understanding lunar calendar solar terms with,
        124–125
    understanding normal, 133–138
Cloud reasoning, 115
Cloud transformation, 183
    in data mining, 183
CloudAssociationRules algorithm, 247–249
CloudClassifier algorithm, 210–211
    experimental results, 211–213
CloudMap algorithm, 193
Cloudtransform algorithm, 184–185
Clustering, 198
    with arbitrary shapes, 217
    based on data fields, 213
    center-based, 216
    in complex networks, 330
    in data mining, 204
    density-based method for complex shapes, 214

dynamic based on data force fields, 226–238
grid-based method, 214
limitation of classical algorithms, 213–215
as prerequisite for association rules, 204
results with DENCLUE algorithm, 223
results with PField-Clustering algorithm, 224
with uncertainty, 205
Clustering algorithms
hierarchical with basis in data potential fields,
215–226
limitations of classical, 213–215
Clustering coefficient, 329, 331
in scale-free networks generation, 332
Cognition, 49
as symbol processing, 23
Cognitive learning, 17
Cognitive physics, 154
challenges from philosophy, 340
cloud model extension, 320–323
concepts as atom models in, 201
and dynamic data fields, 323–328
knowledge discovery through, 153
limitations for AI with uncertainty, 340
Cognitive psychology, 17, 107
Cognitive science
and AI, 15
influence on AI, 17
and similarity between perception and objective
events, 153
Cognitive systems, robotic research and, 37
Combinatorial optimization problems, 34
Combined cloud model, 115, 117
Commonsense knowledge
common understanding about, 54–55
relationship to local cultures/customs, 56
relativity of, 55–56
repeatability and preciseness, 149
uncertainties in, 54
vs. professional knowledge, 55–56
Commutative laws, 62, 77, 318, 319
Competition, cooperativeness within, 339
Complement, 77, 80
Complementary laws, 77, 319
Complex networks
differences between ER Random, Small World,
Scale-Free, 331
real-world, 331
regularity of uncertainty in, 329–332
scale-free feature of, 337
scale-free networks generation, 332–338
with small-world and scale-free models,
328–329
Composition, 80
Computational cognition, 22, 23
Computers, thinking in natural languages, 54

Computing with words, 150, 316
algebra operations, 316–318
logical operations, 318–320
mood operations, 320
Concave/convex membership function, 78, 145
Concept association, 198
Concept hierarchy, 182
uncertainty in, 182–196
Concept on U, 83
Concept space, 196
Concept trees, 182
non-fixed structure of, 183
ConceptRise1 algorithm, 189–190
ConceptRise2 algorithm, 191
Concepts
as atom models in cognitive physics, 201
as basic model of natural language, 154
constructing at different abstraction levels, 187
contributions of cloud drops to, 123
expressing with atom models, 154
importance in natural language, 110
measuring by granularity, 197
and nouns, 52
qualitative nature of, 112
randomness and fuzziness relationships in,
110–112
randomness in, 53
relationships between, 52
representing with cloud models, 112–117
Conceptual granularity, for climbing-up, 188
Confidence level, 78, 132, 253
in association rule mining, 246
Conflict, 58
Conflict resolution, in expert systems, 28–29
Connection degrees, in scale-free networks, 335
Connectionism methodology, 21, 30, 39
back-propagation neural network model,
34–35
birth and development, 30
and Hopfield neural network model, 33–34
strategy and technical characteristics, 30–33
Connotation, 52
Conservative fields, 159
potential as function of position, 160
Constrained quadratic programming problem, 230
Continuous data, discretization of, 183–186
Control methods
cloud generator, 286–289
fuzzy control, 280–284
input-output relations by various, 289
of inverted pendulum system, 291–292
probability density function, 284–286
Control rules, design for triple-link inverted
pendulum, 298
Control theory approach, to AI research, 109

Convergence
   in classification, 214
   in dynamic systems, 44
   and hierarchical clustering, 218
   in Wright algorithm, 227
Coulomb's law, 155, 158
Credibility, of expert systems, 29
Credit card fraud detection systems, 12
Cross-layer thinking, 157
CS5.0 algorithm, 208
CURE clustering algorithm, 236
Current trend, knowledge expression based on,
      254, 255

D

Dartmouth Symposium, 1
   interdisciplinary communication at, 1–2
Data, vs. knowledge in AI technology, 14–15
Data collection, in data mining, 202
Data distribution
   based on cloud model, 186
   experimental, 185
   unforeseeability in clustering analysis, 215
Data distribution function, 186, 187
Data-field clustering algorithm, 234
   comparison with BIRCH clustering, 237
   experimental results, 236
   extendability of, 237, 238
Data fields, xii, 155–156, 199
   application to networked intelligence, 339
   clustering based on, 213
   comparison of equipotential lines generated in,
      231
   comparison of functional forms, 162
   data force lines in, 171
   dynamic, 323–328
   equipotential plot example, 156
   facial expressions generated from, 180
   influence factor and, 172–177
   modeling object interactions with, 155–156
   nonlinear transformation of facial, 180
   optimization of field function, 172–177
   outlier detection and discovery based on,
      238–244
   from physical fields to, 158–160
   plot of force lines for 2D, 172
   plot of force lines for 3D, 173
   potential fields and force fields, 160–172
   simplified estimation of object masses
      in, 230
   and visual thinking simulation, 178–181
Data force fields, 171
   associated vector intensity functions, 170
   for 2D data field, 172

   for 3D data field, 173
   dynamic clustering based on, 226–227,
      227–233
Data mining, 11, 14, 60
   balancing parsimony and preciseness
      in, 204
   and cloud transformation, 183
   defined, 201
   in feature space, 197
   and knowledge discovery, 201–202
   physical methods for, xii
   as recursive interactive process, 201
   as simulation of human cognition and thinking,
      196
   for time series data, 253–269
   uncertainty in, 201–205, 202–204
Data points, relationship among, 160
Data potential fields, effect on distribution, 163
Data preprocessing, in data mining, 202
Data reduction/abstraction, 157, 199
Data restoration, back propagation in, 35
Database applications, 14
De Moivre-Laplace theorem, 72
De Morgan's laws, 77
Decision making
   deviations from probability theory, 341
   under uncertainty conditions, 340–341
   use of language in, 316
Decision tree induction, 206
   with ID3, 206–207
   limitations of common approaches to
      classification, 206–207
   non-leaf nodes in, 212
Decomposition theorem, and expanded principle,
      78–79
Deep Blue, 178, 273
   rivalry with Kasparov, 5–6
Deep Thought, 6
Defense Advance Research Project (China), 345
Definable set of R, 83
Degree distribution, 329
   in complex networks, 330
   transform of, 332
DENCLUE algorithm, 216–218
   clustering results with, 223
DENDRAL expert system, 10
Dendrites, 31
Density attractor, 216
Density clustering, 215
Deterministic science, 43–44
Differential control, of triple-link inverted
      pendulum, 297
Dimensional reduction, 197
Dinosaur extinction, 46
Discretization approaches, 183

Distributed information storage, in neural networks, 32
Distributed smart robots, 12
Distribution maps, SARS preventive focus, 325–327
Distributive laws, 319
Distributivity laws, 77
Disturbance, 58
Divergent oscillation, in double-link inverted pendulum, 293
Division, natural language operations, 317
Document mining, 11
Domestic appliances, AI automation of, 12
Double-condition-single-rule generator, 277, 278
Double-link inverted pendulum, 293
    balancing patterns, 307–308
    similiarities to standing/walking of robots, 291
    unstable, 307
Down continuity, 81
Du, Yi, xiii
Dynamic clustering, 236
    algorithm description, 234
    algorithm performance, 234–235
    based on data force fields, 226–227, 227–233
    comparison of results with BIRCH and data-field clustering, 237
    experimental results and comparison, 235–236
    initial cluster partition based on representatives, 232
    of representative data, 232–233
    simplified estimation of object masses in data field, 230
    test data sets for, 235
Dynamic data fields, 323–328, 325

E

Efficiency, improvement through fuzziness, 47
Egypt, historical origins of AI in, 1
Einstein, Albert
    conflict with Niels Bohr, 43
    definition of entropy, 75
Electric brain, 6
Electrical potential, 159
Electromagnetic force, 155
Electronic entropy, 75
Electrostatic fields, 159
Energy function, in neural networks, 33, 34
English words, relationships to symbols, 51
Entropy, 74–76, 132, 139, 154, 173, 258, 289
    in backward cloud model, 133
    in cloud drop distribution, 138
    in cloud models, 114–115
    decrease with strengthened mood, 320
    as granularity of concepts, 157

increased with softened mood, 320
    as measure of uncertainty about potential field distribution, 173
EQUAL operations, natural language-based, 318
Equipotential plot, 166
    of data fields, 156
    distribution of, 218, 230
    in generated data lines, 231
    for hierarchical clustering, 219
    for potential field of single data object, 167
Equipotential surfaces, for 3D potential field, 168
Equivalence relations, 82
ER random graph networks, 330, 331
Error correction learning, 34
Error estimation, in backward cloud generator, 132
Error feedback propagation, 34
Error threshold, 185
Eurasian Academy of Sciences, xiii
Evolvement processes, 91
Expectation, 139, 144, 154, 289
    differences from result, 341
    extending, 321
    as kernel of concepts, 157
    of normal cloud, 142–143
    in orthogonal direction, 143
    in perpendicular direction, 143
Expected value, in cloud models, 114–115
Experimental results
    C5.0, 213
    CloudClassifier algorithm, 211–213, 213
    dynamic clustering, 235–236
    hierarchical clustering algorithm, 221–226
    outlier detection algorithms, 241–244
Expert systems
    DENDRAL, 10
    and symbolism methodology, 28–29
Expertise enlargement, flexibility in, 29
Exponential potential, 160
Extended cloud models
    simulating network topology variations with, 325
    simulating plant variation with, 320–323
Extension, uncertainty of, 52
External sets, 77

F

Facial data fields
    feature extraction using, 181
    nonlinear transformation of, 180
Facial expressions
    distribution of equipotential lines, 243
    generating from raw images based on data fields, 180

images for outlier detection experiment, 242
second-order data field in new feature space, 243
standard facial images after preprocessing, 242
Facial recognition, 9
False classification, 225
in stock market analysis, 265
Fault tolerance, in neural networks, 33
Feature extraction, 180
of facial image, 181
Feature points, number of, 181
Feature space, 196
transformation to concept space, 197, 198
Feedback control, system stabilization by, 291
Feigenbaum, Mitchell Jay, 89
Feigenbaum constant, 89, 91
Fermi theory, 155
Field strength, and object distances, 166
Fifth Generation Computer experiment, 3
use of PROLOG for, 27
Finance sector, AI applications, 12
Financial analysis, TSDM in, 253
Fingerprint recognition, 9
Force fields, of data, 160–172
Forecasting
association rules, 247–253
time series data mining for, 253–269
Forgetting, 59
Forward cloud generator, 115, 118–119
in association rule mining, 247
one-dimensional normal CG in MATLAB, 119–120
one-dimensional normal CG in VC++, 120–122
two-dimensional forward normal, 121–122
Four fundamental forces, 155
Fourier transform, 94, 183
and dynamic data fields, 327
Fractal
geometric characteristics, 93–94
as uncertainty phenomenon, 321
Fractal geometry, 94
Fractal trees, 321–324
Frequency approach, 62
Frequency distribution function, 185
Frequent item sets, 245
searching for, 244
Friendliness, of expert systems, 29
Function approximation, back propagation in, 35
Functional forms, for data field potentials, 162
Fuzziness, 47–48
and accuracy, 49
beauty of, 49–50
objectivity of, 48–49
prohibition in concept trees, 182
relationship to randomness in concepts, 110–112, 144
in sensation words, 53
in shooting competition, 137
Fuzzy control, 37, 280–284, 286
Fuzzy logic, 48
Fuzzy mapping, 79
Fuzzy relation, 79–80
confirming membership of, 80
Fuzzy rules, 280
Fuzzy set theory, 76, 150
decomposition theorem and expanded principle, 78–79
fuzzy relation, 79–80
membership degree and membership function, 76–78, 111
possibility measure, 81
and uncertainty processing, 316
Fuzzy theory, and cloud models of shooting competition, 135

G

Gamma membership function, 77, 145
Garbage-in-garbage-out, applicability to data mining, 203
Gaussian functions, 165
Gaussian kernel, 96, 97
Gaussian potential, 160, 161
Generalization, in data mining, 204
Generate_DecisionTree algorithm, 207
code example, 208–209
Genetic variation, 46
Gesture language recognition, 9
Go matches, 178
Golden section search method, 175
Granularity, 88
in association rule mining, 247
describing knowledge hierarchies with, 156–158
and entropy, 157
of knowledge, 84
in knowledge discovery, 186
measuring concepts by, 197
relationship to rough set, 87
and super/subsystems, 156–157
switching among different levels of, 157, 196
in time series data problems, 254
Gravitational force, 155
in triple-link inverted pendulum, 296
Grid research, 14

H

Half-cloud model, 115, 116, 117, 319, 320
Hardware-independent software systems, 315
Heisenberg, Werner, uncertainty principle
 of, 45
Heuristic search techniques, 2
 in chess playing, 6
Hi-Tech Research and Development Program
 (China), 316
Hierarchical clustering
 algorithm description, 219–221
 algorithm performance analysis, 221
 based on data potential fields, 215–220
 comparison of experimental results,
  221–226
 equipotential line distribution and cluster
  spectrum, 219
 PField_Clustering algorithm, 220–221
 testing data sets, 222
Hierarchy
 in cognitive development, 157
 of concepts, and uncertainty, 182–196
 describing with granularity, 156–158
 as granularity in cognitive physics, 201
 in structure of matter, 153
 universality in natural phenomena, 156
High-order gravity formula, 227
Hopfield Neural Network, 3, 30
 and connectionism methodology, 33–34
Human brain
 ability to grasp fuzzy concepts, 50
 handling of uncertainty, xi
 working mechanism of, xi
Human intelligence research, 39
 basis in mathematics and computer
  architecture, 108
 multiple perspectives, 107–109
 and natural language, 109
 with uncertainty, 273
Human-machine interactions, 315
 in climbing-up, 188
 in Go matches, 178
 as partnership during knowledge discovery
  process, 200
 recursive in data mining, 201
HWPen, 9
Hyper-entropy, 154, 258, 289
 in backward cloud model, 133
 in cloud models, 114–115
 decrease with strengthened mood, 320
 increased with softened mood, 320
 as psychological power in shooting
  competition, 148
Hyperplane function, 97, 98

I

ID3, limitations in classification, 206–207
Idempotent laws, 77, 319, 331
Identity recognition, 9
Image matching techniques, 9
Image mining, 11
Image recognition, 9
Impermanence, of knowledge, 58–60
Imprecise category, and rough set, 82–84
INCLUDE operations, natural language-based,
 318
Inclusion, 80
Incompleteness, of knowledge, 57
Incompleteness theorem, 57
Incoordination, of knowledge, 58
Indiscernibility relation, 82, 85
Industrial robotics, 11, 36
Inevitable phenomena, 62
Inference engines, 28
Influence coefficient, 161, 175
 optimization algorithm, 175, 177
 optimization of, 176
 and optimization of data field function,
  172–177
 potential force fields and variance of, 174
 selecting in hierarchical clustering, 218
Information Age developments, 12
 AI technology impacts, 12–13
 from data to knowledge, 14–15
 intelligent grid, 13–14
 World Wide Web, 13–14
Information content, classifying with decision tree
 induction, 206–207
Information deluge, xi
Information entropy, 75
Information gain, in decision tree induction, 207
Inner randomness, 91
Input feed-forward propagation, 34
Intelligent control, and behaviorism, 37–38
Intelligent design, 12
Intelligent grid, 13–14
Intelligent robots, 36
Interdisciplinary approach, 341–342
 at Dartmouth Symposium, 1–2
 future breakthroughs, 18
Intermittent chaos, 91
International Joint Conference on AI (UCAI), 3
International Journal of AI, 3
Internet development, 13
Intersection, 77, 80
Intuitionist computability, 21
Inverted pendulum control system, 36, 38
 applications, 291–292
 balancing patterns, 302–312

cloud control policy for triple-link inverted pendulum, 294–302
double-link inverted pendulum, 293
as example of intelligent control with uncertainty, 291
qualitative control mechanism, 292–294
single-link inverted pendulum, 292
Iris recognition, 9
Iris test data set, 222, 225
hierarchical clustering with, 222–226
projected distribution on feature subspace, 225
result with PField_Clustering algorithm, 226
Irrotational fields, 158

J

Jinshi and Juren, 56
Joint probability density function, 142
Journal of the American Statistical Association, 100
Junior knowledge, 83

K

K line data
cloud-based description on, 257–261
cloud model expression of graphic entity, 258
K line graph, 257
recognition of traditional combination pattern, 261–263
relationship between two K lines, 260
Kahneman, Daniel, 340, 341
Karush-Kuhn-Tucker (KKT) condition, 99
Kasparov, Garry, 178, 273
rivalry with Deep Blue, 5–6
KDD Gold Cup award, 11
Kernel functions, 94–97
kernel density estimation, 169
support vector machine, 97–100
Khinchine's law of large numbers, 71
Knowledge
granularity of, 84, 87
impermanence of, 58–60
incompleteness of, 57–58
incoordination of, 58
language as carrier of, 51–52
metabolism of, 58
uncertainties of, 57
Knowledge accumulation, through written languages, 52
Knowledge discovery, xii
cognitive physics methods, 153
and data mining, 201–202
in data mining, 186
data mining for, 201

human-machine partnerships in, 200
in relational databases, 155–156
uncertainty in, 204–205
Knowledge discovery in database (KDD), 11, 15
Knowledge discovery state space, 196–200
Knowledge engineering, 14–15
historical achievements, 10–11
Knowledge expression
based on current trend, 255
with semiperiodic regulation, 255
Knowledge generation system, based on relational databases, 199
Knowledge hierarchy
describing with granularity, 156–158
relationship to concept granularity, 182
Knowledge inference, 39
Knowledge representation, xi, 39
Knowledge uncertainties, 43
in commonsense knowledge, 54–56
and fuzziness, 47–50
impermanence of knowledge, 58–60
incompleteness of knowledge, 57–58
incoordination of knowledge, 58
in natural languages, 51–54
and randomness, 43–47

L

Lagrangian multipliers, 98
and control of triple-link inverted pendulum, 294
nonlinear system equation with, 295
Language. *See also* Natural language
as carrier of human knowledge, 43, 51–52
use in thinking, decision making, and reasoning, 316
Law of excluded middle, 319
Laws of identity, 77, 319
Laws of large numbers, 70–71
Learning
in neural networks, 33
three types of, 17
Levy-Lindeberg theorem, 71
Li, Deyi, xiii
Li-Yorke theorem, 90
Life, origin of, 46
Life science, 108
Lindeberg theorem, 72
Linear membership function, 77, 145
Linguistic values
in mood operations, 320
vs. mathematical symbols, 110
LISP. *See* List processing language
List processing language (LISP), 26
Local instability, 91

Local maximum points, in hierarchical clustering, 218
Location, numerical characteristics of 2D cloud model representing, 195
Logic programming languages, 3, 26–28, 108
Logic Theorist, 2
Logical operations, computing with words, 318–320
Logical school, 178
  of human intelligence research, 108
Long-range field, description by, 226
Lunar calendar, understanding with cloud models, 124–125
Lyapurov exponents, 92

M

Machine learning
  approach to TSDM, 254
  and data mining, 203
Machine theorem proof, 5
Machine vs. human, in chess playing, 6
MAFIA clustering algorithm, 214
Magnanimous data, 15
Mamdani fuzzy control method, 282
  explanation by cloud-based method, 290
  theoretical explanation, 289–291
Match amount/match price, in stock market analysis, 267
Matching, in rule choice and execution, 28
Mathematical approach, 178
  to AI research, 109
Mathematical expectation, 66, 67
  in cloud models, 115
Mathematical foundation
  chaos and fractal, 89–94
  fuzzy set theory, 76–81
  kernel functions and principal curves, 94–104
  probability theory, 61–76
  rough set theory, 81–82
Mathematical theorem proof, 2
MATLAB, 235
  backward normal CG with certainty degree in, 128–129
  backward normal CG without certainty degree in, 130
  1D normal cloud generator in, 119–120
Maximum determination, 193, 194
  theoretical chart of, 192
McCarthy, John, 1, 2, 26
  as father of AI, 2
Mean squared errors (MSE), 147
Measure entropy, 92, 93

Median granularities, 87
Medical expert systems, 10
Membership cloud, 340
Membership degree, 76–78, 136, 154, 159, 340
  and attribute value conceptual levels, 192
  via maximum/random determination, 193
  of Youth, 111
Membership function, 76–78, 77, 79, 115, 150, 340
  2D, 136
  with fuzzy control, 281
  in fuzzy sets, 111, 289
  pervasiveness of bell, 145–148
  of qualitative concepts in postcondition, 282
  of qualitative concepts in precondition, 281
Membership function cluster, 340
Membership relation, 86
  among concepts on different hierarchies, 182
Memory
  as retention of perceptions, 17
  role of time in, 325
  as storage of human knowledge, 59
Mercer kernels, 96, 97
Mercer theorem, 95, 97, 99
Methodologies. See AI methodologies
Minimization problems, optimal choice of influence coefficient, 175
Minsky, Marvin, 1, 2
Mobile entropy, 75
Modern control theory, 36
Monotone nondecreasing, 66
Monotonicity, 81
Mood operations, computing with words, 320
Morning star
  exclusion of false purchasing signal with bottom control strategy, 266
  recognition and cloud-based prediction of purchasing point, 265
  recognition by Analyzer, 264
  recognition by cloud method, 266
Motor speed, with fuzzy control method, 289
Mountain-shaped membership function, 78, 146, 147
Movement states, 90
Multi-input/multi-output problems, 36
Multicondition-single-rule generator, 277, 278
Multidimensional normal distribution, 69–70
Multidimensional scaling (MDS), 197
Multilayered networks, back propagation algorithm, 3
Multiplication, natural language operations, 317, 318
MYCIN medical expert system, 10

N

Nanjing Institute of Communication Engineering, xiii
National Basic Research Program (China), 316, 345
National Defense Pre-Research Foundation (China), 316
National Hi-Tech Research and Development Program (China), 345
National Natural Science Foundation (China), xiii, 316, 345
Natural language, 316. *See also* Language
  approach to AI research, 109
  as carrier of human knowledge, xi, 51–52
  cloud model as bridge between AI and, 107
  as embodiment of human intelligence, 109
  evaluating shooting competition with, 137
  importance of concepts in, 110
  uncertainties in, 51, 52–54
  use in data mining, 203
Natural language understanding, 10
Natural reasoning, 54
Nature
  fuzziness in, 49
  randomness inherent in, 45
Network convergence, 33
Network topology, 328
  initial *vs.* scale-free, 336, 338
  initial *vs.* small world, 334
  scale-free example, 335
  simulating variation with extended cloud model, 325
Networked intelligence, applications of data field theory to, 339
Neural network approach
  to AI research, 109
  to TSDM, 253, 254
Neural network simulator, 2
Neural networks (NNs), 3
  China's first conference on, 30
  technical characteristics, 32–33
Neural science, 107
Neurobiologists, Nobel Prize winners, 16
Neurons, 31
Newell, Allen, 2, 23
Newtonian mechanics, deterministic science and, 43–44
Newton's law of universal gravitation, 155, 158, 226
Newton's second law, 232
Next generation network (NGN), 339
Nobel Prize winners, 16
  Daniel Kahneman, 340, 341

Noise
  and clustering analysis, 215
  global threshold, 218
Nondeterministic Polynomial, 30, 213
Nonlinear mapping, 96
  of facial data fields, 180
Nonparametric density estimation, 166
Nonprocedural program execution, in expert systems, 29
Normal cloud
  expectation curves, 142–143, 144
  mathematical properties, 138–143
  pervasiveness of, 144–150
  significance of, 148–150
  as weakened normal distribution, 149
Normal cloud generator, 118. *See also* Cloud generator
Normal cloud model, understanding, 133–138
Normal distribution, 67, 148
  in cloud models, 118
  definition and properties, 67–68
  multidimensional, 69–70
  pervasiveness of, 144–145
NOT operations, natural language-based, 319
Nouns, and concepts, 52
Nuclear-like potential functions, 161, 163, 165, 169

O

Object distances, 166
Object interactions
  data field models of, 155–156
  as data fields in cognitive physics, 201
  in dynamic data fields, 323–324
On-line analysis, 12
One-dimensional normal distribution, 69
One-dimensional precondition cloud generator, 274–275
One-dimensional principal component, 101
Opportunity, as low-probability event, 47
OptiGrid clustering algorithm, 214
OR operations, natural language-based, 319
Oral language, 51
Outlier detection, 204
  algorithm for, 241
  algorithm performance analysis, 241
  approximation to human thinking patterns, 239
  based on data fields, 238–239, 239–241
  and clustering analysis, 215
  2D data set and 3D potential field for, 240
  distribution of equipotential lines in facial images, 243
  experimental results and analysis, 241–244

limitations of classical methods, 239
    second-order data field for, 243
Outlier points
    discovering in multiple attributes, 239
    value of, 239

P

Pan concept tree, 198
    continuous granularities in, 188
    leaf nodes of, 188
Paradox, 48
Parallel processing, in neural networks, 32
Parameter set, simulating plant variation with
        extended cloud effect on, 322
Parzen window, 139
Patents, authors', 345
Pattern recognition
    back propagation in, 35
    and data mining, 203
    historical achievements, 8–9
    in stock market analysis, 262
Perception, 17
    of physical world vs. self, 153–158
Perception-behavior model, 35
Perceptive learning, 17
Perceptron, 9
Period-doubling process, 91
Periodic motion, 90
Pervasiveness
    of bell membership function, 145–148
    of normal cloud model, 144
    of normal distribution, 144–145
PField_Clustering algorithm, 220–221
    comparison with other clustering algorithms,
        226
    Iris data set clustering result, 226
Philosophy, challenges to cognitive physics by,
        340
Physical Symbol System (PSS) hypothesis,
        23, 24
PLA University of Science and Technology, xiii
Plant variation, simulating with extended cloud
        model, 322–324
Poincare, Henri, 89
Poisson distribution, 331
Poisson's law of large numbers, 70
Polynomial equations, 5
Position vector, 233
Possibility distribution, 81
Possibility measure, 81, 111
Postcondition, 273
    probability density functions in, 285
Postcondition cloud generator, 273–276, 274,
        275–276

Potential energy functions, in dynamic data fields,
        327
Potential entropy, 173
    time complexity of computing, 177
Potential fields, 158
    of data, 160–172
    equipotential surfaces for, 168–169
    from five data objects, 174
    hierarchical clustering based on, 215–226
    hierarchical clustering based on topology of,
        220–221
    and object interactions, 160
    optimization with influence coefficient, 176
    topology of, 221
Potential functions, 166
    effects on distribution of data potential fields,
        163–164
    of gravitational-like fields, 163
    nuclear-like, 163
    of nuclear-like data fields, 161, 163
Power law distribution, 73–74, 331, 332
    in scale-free networks, 329
Precise granularities, 87
Precise thresholding, dissimilarity to human
        thinking, 246
Precision
    in science, 149
    of sets, 85
Precondition, perception as, 273
Precondition cloud generator, 273–274
    one-dimensional, 274–275
Predetermination, 44
Predicate calculus, 24–26
Predicates, expression of relationships between
        concepts by, 52
Prediction. See also Time series data mining
        (TSDM)
    in data mining, 204
Price fluctuating index (PFI), in stock market
        analysis, 257
Principal component analysis (PCA), 100
    dimensional reduction via, 197
Principal curve, 102–103
Principle curves, 94, 100–104, 143
    in cloud models, 142
Principle of economy, 53
Probability, axiomization definition, 63
Probability control method, 284–286
Probability density function, 66, 69, 140, 141, 166
    in cloud drops' distribution, 138
    joint, 142
    of qualitative concepts in postcondition, 286
    of qualitative concepts in precondition, 285
Probability distribution function, 65–67
Probability theory, 61–62, 103, 111

Bayes' theorem, 62–65
central limit theorem, 71–72
entropy, 74–76
laws of large numbers, 70–71
normal distribution, 67–70
power law distribution, 73–74
probability distribution function, 65–67
and shooting competition, 135
Production rule, 28
Professional knowledge, *vs.* commonsense
    knowledge, 55–56
Programmable robots, 11–12
PROLOG, 27
Proportional control, of triple-link inverted
    pendulum, 297
Proportional-Integral Derivative (PID) control,
    291
Purchasing point, cloud-based prediction of, 265

Q

Qianlong stock analysis software, 256
Qualitative concepts
    in association rule mining, 247
    cloud graph in precondition, 287
    contributions by cloud drops, 124
    contributions to, 123
    in data mining, 203
    extracting from raw continuous data, 183
    in human thinking, 249
    membership function in precondition, 281
    obscure boundaries in, 249
    positively/negatively large, 301
    probability density function in postcondition,
        286
    probability density function in precondition,
        285
    representing by quantitative expressions, 113
    in rule generators for triple-link inverted
        pendulum, 299
    soft and, 278, 279
    in stock market analysis, 257, 268
    uncertainty in, 203, 316
Qualitative control mechanism
    fuzzy, probability, and cloud control methods,
        280–289
    virtual cloud, 288
Qualitative knowledge, reasoning and control of,
    273
Qualitative-quantitative transform model, 107,
    144. *See also* Cloud model
Qualitative rule construction
    from cases to rule generation, 279–280
    by cloud method, 273
    double-condition-single-rule generator, 278

joint distribution of cloud drops for, 275
precondition/postcondition cloud generator,
    273–276
and quantitative transformation of "soft and"
    concept, 279
rule generator, 276–278
single-condition-single-rule generator,
    276–277
Quantitative data
    transforming from qualitative concepts via
        uncertainty, 316
    transforming to qualitative concepts in data
        mining, 204
Quantum computer, 315
Quantum mechanics, 45
Quantum physics, 56
    of weak field, 155
Quasi-period process, 91, 254
Quasiperiodic motion, 90

R

R-dimensional normal distribution, 69
Random events
    failure to obey normal distributions, 145
    independence of, 64
Random graph model, 329, 330
Randomness, 43
    beauty of, 46–47
    objectivity of, 53–56
    orderliness in, 339
    as physics concept, 45
    and probability theory, 61
    relationship to fuzziness in concepts, 110–112,
        144
    in self-similarity of complex events, 323
    in shooting competition, 137
Ratio of convergence, 89
Raw images, facial expressions generated from,
    180
Raw state space, 196
Reasoning
    and control of qualitative knowledge, 273
    use of language in, 316
Recursive functions, 21, 143, 233
    in classification, 214
    in cloud models, 142
Redundance, 58
Reflexivity, 80
Regression analysis, 101
Relative fluctuating index (RFI), in stock market
    analysis, 260
Relative fluctuating relation (RFR), in stock
    market analysis, 260
Relativity, in concept tress, 182

Repeatability, in science, 149
Representative data
    dynamic clustering of, 232–233
    equipotential lines generated by, 231
    initial cluster partition based on, 232
Resolution principle, 24–26
Right continuous, 66
Road net density, 250
    association rules on, 252
Robot control
    and behaviorism, 36–37
    similarity to double-link inverted pendulum
        system, 291
    soccer match example, 273
    standing and walking challenges, 291–292
Robot World Cup, 12
RobotÇup, 36
Robotics, historical achievements, 11–12
Rochester, Nathaniel, 1
Rotational potentiometers, in inverted pendulum
        systems, 302
Rough granularities, 87
Rough membership function, 85
Rough relations, 86–88
Rough set theory, 81–82
    characteristics of rough sets, 84–85
    and granularity, 87
    imprecise category and rough set, 82–84
    related parameters under different knowledge
        granularities, 88
    rough relations, 86–88
Roughly equality, 86
Roughly inclusion, 86
Rule activation
    with fuzzy control, 283
    in Mamdani fuzzy control method, 290
Rule choice/execution, 28
Rule control, expert system-based, 37
Rule database, with probability control method,
        284
Rule generator, 276–278
Rule sets
    in extended cloud model, 321
    simulating plant variation with extended cloud
        effect on, 323
    for triple-link inverted pendulum, 298, 300–301
Russell, Bertrand, 149
Rutherford model, 153

S

Saddle points, in hierarchical clustering, 218
SARS prevention focus, 325
    geographical and temporal variation, 326–327
    simulating, 339

Scalar fields, 158, 159
Scalar potential, 160, 170
Scale-free models
    of complex networks, 328–329, 331
    generation of networks, 332–338
Scale-free network generator algorithm, 333, 334,
        335, 337
Scale-free network topology, 336
Scale-free networks, 329
Science
    and art, 341–342
    relationship to art, 50
Search-based recursive relocation approach, to
        classification, 214
Second-order fuzziness, in cloud models, 133
Second-order randomness, in cloud models, 133
Security measures, uses of AI for, 9
Self-adaptation, 7, 37
    of behaviorist systems, 36
    in intelligent control, 38
    in neural networks, 33
Self-adaptive robots, 12
Self-learning, 7, 37
    in intelligent control, 38
Self-organization, 37
    of force lines for data force fields, 172
    in intelligent control, 38
    in neural networks, 33
Self-similarity, 91, 321
    randomness in, 323
Self-spin entropy, 75
Semantic learning, 17
Sensation words, conceptual fuzziness in, 53
Sequential minimal optimization (SMO) method,
        230
Shadow line classification algorithm, 259
Shadow lines, in stock forecasting, 258
Shangshu, 9
Shannon, Claude, 1
Shannon's entropy, 173
Shooting competition, cloud model of, 134–138
Short-range field, and high-order gravity formula,
        227
Signature recognition, 9
Simon, Herbert, 2, 23, 341
Single-condition-single-rule generator, 276–277
Single-input/single-output problems, 36
Single-link inverted pendulum, 292
    balancing pattern 1, 306
    balancing pattern 2, 307
Singular value decomposition (SVD), 197
Small-world generator algorithm, 333
Small world model, 329
Small-world models, of complex networks,
        328–329, 331

SOFT AND, 278, 279, 320
Soft computing, 150
Soft division
  attribute table after, 195
  in classification, 210
SOFT OR, 320
Soft production, 12
Soft zero, 258, 301, 302
Softened mood operations, 320
Software, independence from programming,
  315
Solar terms, represented by cloud model, 125
Spatial cost, in data mining, 203
Speech recognition, 9
Spherical clusters, bias toward, 227
Spring and Autumn Period, 124
SQL database system, use of PROLOG in, 28
Square-well potential, 159
Stability
  in dynamic systems, 44
  of Hopfield neural networks, 33
Stabilization
  in double-link inverted pendulum, 293
  in single-link inverted pendulum, 292
  of triple-link inverted pendulum, 295–297
Stabilized balance points, 33
State space
  for knowledge discovery, 196
  major operations in transformation, 199–200
  three kinds of, 196–197
  transformation of, 197–198, 198
Statistical analysis
  of cloud drops' certainty degree, 140–143
  of cloud drops' distribution, 138–139
  and data mining, 203
Statistical database tables, 185
Statistical mechanics, 45
STING clustering algorithm, 214
Stochastic processes, 62
Stock data forecasting, 256–257
  bottom control strategy to exclude false
    purchasing signal, 266
  classes of shadow lines, 258
  cloud-based description on K line data,
    257–261
  examples of K line prediction, 264–269
  match amount/match price in, 267
  opening and closing prices, 257
  PFI in, 257
  prediction mechanism based on cloud K line,
    261–263
  prediction of consecutive yang patterns by
    Analyzer, 267
  prediction of consecutive yang patterns by
    cloud model, 268

prediction of consecutive yang patterns with
    amount-price relation, 269
  recognition of morning star by Analyzer, 264
  recognition of morning star by cloud method,
    266
  RFR and RFI, 260
Strength of interaction, 161
Strengthened mood operations, 320
Strong association rules, 244. *See also*
  Association rules
Strong force, 155
Subjective determination approach, 62
Subjective world, randomness in, 46
Subsystems, 157
Subtraction, natural language operations, 317
Super-systems, 157
Supervised learning
  classification as, 205
  with Iris test data set, 222
Support set, 77
Support threshold, 253
  in association rule mining, 246
Support vector machine, 97–100, 100
Syllogism, 25
Symbolic approach, to AI research, 109
Symbolic logic, concealment in expert systems, 29
Symbolic mathematics, 24
Symbolism methodology, 21, 39
  birth and development, 21–24
  expert systems, 28–29
  logic programming languages and, 26–28
  predicate calculus and resolution principle,
    24–26
Symmetric cloud model, 115, 116
Symmetry, 80
Synapses, 31
System stabilization, by feedback, 291

T

Temporal cost
  of clustering analysis, 215
  in data mining, 203
Thermo-entropy, 75
Thinking machines, 6–7
Tilting angle, of triple-link inverted pendulum,
  295, 298
Time
  and changes in SARS preventive focus,
    325–327
  in human cognitive process, 325
  visual fading relative to, 179
Time complexity
  of outlier detection, 239
  of potential entropy computations, 177

Time series data mining (TSDM), 253–269
  based on cloud models, 255–256
  cloud-based expression on predicted
    knowledge, 255
  knowledge expression with semiperiodic
    regulation, 255
  stock data forecasting, 256–269
Time series prediction, 253
  cloud-based, 255–256
Training data set
  absence in clustering tasks, 205
  for decision tree induction, 206
Transitivity laws, 77, 80
Transmission Control Protocol/Internet Protocol
    (TCP/IP), 13
Traveling salesman problem (TSP), 30
Triple-link inverted pendulum
  balancing patterns, 309–310
  car position, 295
  car velocity, 295
  cloud controller of, 297–302
  control flowchart, 302
  dynamically switching curve between
    balancing patterns, 311
  eight signals of, 303–305
  experimental block graph, 294
  illustration graph, 296
  parameter set of qualitative concepts in rule
    generators, 299
  periodic variation in fourth balancing pattern,
    310
  qualitative analysis, 295–297
  robust experiment, 306
  rule sets, 298, 300–301
  tilting angles, 295
Turing, Alan, 4
Turing Awards, 2
Turing machine, 21, 315
Turing Test, 4–5
  lack of breakthroughs, 7
Two-dimensional cloud model, 118
  and 2D membership function, 136
Two-dimensional membership function, and 2D
    cloud model, 136
Two-dimensional normal distribution, 69, 70
Two-dimensional principal component, 101
Two-point distribution, in complex networks, 332

U

Uncertainty
  certainty in, 339
  and chaos, 89
  classification and clustering with, 205–244
  in classification problems, 87
  in clustering, 205
  in commonsense knowledge, 54–56
  in concept hierarchy, 182–196
  in data mining, 201–205, 202–204
  data mining for knowledge discovery with, 201
  discovering association rules with, 244–253
  and discretization of continuous data, 183–186
  in financial/stock market analysis, 340
  and fuzziness, 47–50
  in human thinking, 247
  impermanence of knowledge, 58–60
  incompleteness of knowledge, 57–58
  incoordination of knowledge, 58
  of knowledge, 43, 57–60
  in knowledge discovery, 204–205
  in languages, 52–54
  in linguistic values vs. mathematical symbols,
    110
  mathematical foundation of, 60, 61
  in natural languages, 51–54
  new directions for AI with, 315–316
  principle of, 45
  in qualitative concepts, 203
  and randomness, 53–57
  regularity in complex networks, 329–332
Union, 77, 80
Universality, 91
Unsupervised learning
  clustering as, 205
  with Iris test data set, 222

V

Vagueness, 48, 50, 149
Variance, 139
  in cloud drops' distribution, 138
  of influence coefficient, 174
VC++
  backward normal CG with certainty degree in,
    129–130
  backward normal CG without certainty degree
    in, 131
  1D normal CG in, 120–122
Vector intensity function, 170
  and scalar potential, 160
Velocity vector, 233
ViaVoice® software, 9
Vibration entropy, 75
Virtual artificial lives, 8
Virtual cloud, 288
Virtual pan concept tree, 186–188
Virtual point sources, 172
Virtual production, 12
Visual fading, relative to time, 179
Visual memory, 179

Visual perception, 17
   climbing-up strategy and algorithms, 188–196
   simulation with data fields, 178–181
   and virtual pan concept tree, 186–188
Visual thinking, 178
   importance in Go gaming, 178
   stimulating via data fields, 179
Voice mining, 11
Von Neumann architecture, xi, 7, 315

W

Warring States Period, 124
WaveCluster algorithm, 214
Weak force, 155
Weak interactions, 155
Weakened normal distribution, 149
Web mining, 11
World Wide Web, 13–14

Wright clustering, 235
   convergence using, 227
   experimental results, 236
Written language, 51
   knowledge accumulation through, 52

Y

Yang line patterns
   prediction using cloud model, 268
   prediction via Analyzer, 267
   prediction with amount-price relation, 269

Z

Zadeh, L.A., 316
Zipf cloud generators, 337
Zipf law, 74, 337